FINANCE

William H. Jean

The Dryden Press

Library of Congress Catalog Card Number 72-12248
ISBN: 0-03-089034-9
Printed in the United States of America
3345-071-987654321

CONTENTS

Part Three
The Investment Decision in Risk Situations
page 121

7
Decision Theory Under Risk and Uncertainty
page 123

8
Capital Budgeting Under Risk
page 147

1

INTRODUCTION TO FINANCIAL MANAGEMENT

A corporation's activities are typically summarized in financial terms: "investment in plant and equipment reached \$2.1 billion by the end of 1971"; "total bank debt is \$45.3 million"; "earnings per share were \$6.86"; "return on equity was 15.3 percent and return on sales 4.8 percent"; and so forth, rather than in social terms, such as "we stopped polluting three more rivers this year" or "the corporation trained 75 handicapped veterans to perform useful tasks." While social goals may be the overriding concern of some corporations' stockholders, in a capitalistic society most people buy stock for financial motives, to receive a dividend income or realize a capital gain. Because the stockholders are collectively the employers of management, the management of the corporation must be responsive to the financial desires of stockholders.

Financial management is therefore concerned with the activities of the corporation that affect the well-being of stockholders. That well-being can be partially measured by the dividends received, but a more accurate measure is the market value of the stock. For example, dividend payment could be boosted by lowering earnings retention, but the market value of the stock might suffer due to investors' reclassification of the stock from "moderate growth" to "no growth." To plan financial actions properly, therefore, the financial management group must be aware of the determinants of the market price of stocks. Perfect knowledge of financial markets is not possible (otherwise the possessor could shortly be a billionaire), but the basic determinants of prices are worthy of serious study.

Maximizing the market price of the corporation's common stock is the ultimate goal, and many activities in financial management must be performed en route to that goal. For example, a corporation that cannot meet its current bills will likely have its operations disrupted by legal proceedings.

The first task of the financial manager is to plan and control the corporation's cash balance so that obligations can be met in full on time. After that is accomplished the investment and fund raising activities can be planned for optimum results.

The key to the cash management problem is an accurate system of forecasting and budgeting of funds. If the normal operations produce a surplus of cash, the excess can be used to purchase additional assets, reduce liabilities, or pay added dividends. When normal operations will result in deficient cash balances, the financial manager can recommend the sale of some assets, the incurring of added liabilities, or in extreme cases the reduction of dividends or the issue of additional stock or other securities.

The acquisition of assets, borrowing, and changes in equity capital are not just the residual of the operating cash balance fluctuation however. The financial manager must be able to determine when it is desirable to borrow funds to acquire operating assets, for example. The expansion of the corporation's activities is not automatically desirable—the earnings from the asset expansion must be greater than the cost of the funds used. Much of this book is concerned with this comparison.

A Simple Model of the Corporation's Financial Results

One approach to analyzing the corporation's activities is to divide fund uses and fund sources, as in the conventional balance sheet presentation. The corporation's use of funds is to purchase assets that are expected to earn some return. The corporation's sources of funds are debt incurred and equity contributed by the owners. Suppose a simple example is used of a corporation with $1,000,000 of assets:

Balance Sheet

Assets	$1,000,000	Liabilities	$ 400,000
		Owners' equity	600,000
	$1,000,000		$1,000,000

The objective in the selection of assets is to maximize the rate of return on assets. Suppose the capital budgeting problem, the selection of assets for investment, has been solved and the overall rate of return on assets is 10 percent a year. The total return from assets in the example would be $100,000.

The selection of funds sources, the capital structure problem, is based on the minimization of the payments necessary to fund suppliers. The rate of payment on the original contribution is the corporation's overall cost of capital. Suppose in the example that the corporation's minimum overall cost of capital is also 10 percent. The total payments to fund suppliers would therefore also be $100,000.

The overall cost of capital can be divided into the cost of capital for debt, the interest rate required by the liability holders, and the cost of capital for equity, the rate of return expected by buyers of the corporation's stock. For the example, the debt cost of capital is 7 percent, so the total payments to liability holders is $28,000 a year. The equity cost of capital is 12 percent, making total payment to stockholders of $72,000 a year.

So far in the example everything balances, and the liability holders and stockholders are exactly satisfied. The numbers now are to be changed so that stockholders get more than they originally expected.

First, suppose that the corporation's officers found more profitable assets than expected, so the rate of return on assets turned out to be 12 percent. The total return would therefore be $120,000 a year. If liability holders are still satisfied with a 7 percent return, $28,000 in total, $92,000 will be left for distribution to stockholders, $20,000 more than anticipated, and obviously the stockholders are better off as a result.

The $20,000 of added income is likely to have an effect on the market value of the corpora ion's stock. If the market capitalization rate for the corporation's stock is 12 percent, in the original example the market value of the stock would be

$$\frac{\$72{,}000}{12\%} = \$600{,}000$$

exactly the book value of owners' equity. If the market capitalization rate for the corporation's stock remains unchanged the new value of the stock after the increase in return on assets is

$$\frac{\$92{,}000}{12\%} = \$766{,}667$$

If the stockholders originally paid $600,000 for their stock they have realized a $166,667 capital gain. This capital gain is the reward for the "excess earning power" of the corporation.

The higher the return on assets, given a fixed debt cost of capital and equity cost of capital, the greater will be the market value of the stock and the capital gain of the original stockholders.

Now suppose the original example with $1,000,000 assets returning 10 percent a year is modified to show the optimization of capital structure and the resulting gain to stockholders. First the overall cost of capital is reduced simply by persuading fund suppliers to charge less. If the interest rate on debt is reduced to 6 percent and the required return of the original stockholders to 11 percent, then the total required payments to capital sources is

$$6\%\ (\$400{,}000) + 11\%\ (\$600{,}000) = \$90{,}000$$

and the overall cost of capital is

$$\frac{\$90{,}000}{\$1{,}000{,}000} = 9\%$$

Since the amount earned on assets is $100,000, after paying $24,000 to liability holders the remaining $76,000 is distributed to stockholders. Using the market capitalization rate of 11 percent for equity the total market value of stock is now

$$\frac{\$76{,}000}{11\%} = \$690{,}909$$

The capital gain for the original stockholders is $90,909. They are better off because the overall cost of capital has been reduced.

A more likely step to reduce the overall cost of capital is a change in the debt-equity ratio, a change in the capital structure. Suppose the original example is changed to a structure where the amount of debt is $700,000 and the equity total is $300,000. Because more risk is perceived by liability holders the interest rate charged increases from 7 percent to 8 percent. For the same reason the required yield by purchasers of the stock increases to 13 percent. The initial overall cost of capital is therefore

$$\frac{8\%\ (\$700{,}000) + 13\%\ (\$300{,}000)}{\$1{,}000{,}000} = 9.5\%$$

To demonstrate that stockholders benefit from this reduction in the overall cost of capital consider the distribution of residual income to stockholders. From the \$100,000 earnings from assets is subtracted the \$56,000 payment to liability holders, leaving \$44,000 for stockholders. Stockholders only required \$39,000 (13% × \$300,000), so the market value of their stock goes from \$300,000 to

$$\frac{\$44{,}000}{13\%} = \$338{,}462$$

They have realized a capital gain of \$38,462.

The simple example has demonstrated two ways in which the well-being of the corporation's stockholders can be raised through financial management. Measures can be taken to increase the return on assets and/or to reduce the cost of funds to the corporation.

Asset Turnover and Margin on Sales

One approach to disaggregating the return on assets figure is to consider that number as a product of "asset turnover" and "margin on sales." In the original example of the preceding section the \$100,000 total earning on asset could have been the result of \$500,000 annual sales. Asset turnover is total sales divided by total assets,

$$\frac{\$500{,}000}{\$1{,}000{,}000} = 0.5$$

and the margin on sales is total earnings divided by sales,

$$\frac{\$100{,}000}{\$500{,}000} = 20\%$$

The return on assets, 10 percent, is the product of asset turnover and margin on sales,

$$0.5(20\%) = 10\%$$

When the return on assets was increased to 12 percent in the first revision of the example that increase could have come from an increase in the asset turnover ratio to 0.6,

$$0.6(20\%) = 12\%$$

or from an increase in the margin on sales to 24 percent,

$$0.5(24\%) = 12\%$$

Separation of the return on assets into the two components is sometimes helpful in isolating the activities that can be improved in the corporation. Increasing sales without increasing the investment in assets, thereby increasing the asset turnover ratio, may be a marketing function, for example. Increasing the margin on sales could come about through more economical production methods, a production management function. Of course the financial manager is always interested in increasing the well-being of stockholders, and that may be accomplished through many routes.

Breakeven Points and Financial Leverage

The selection of a capital structure establishes a class of fixed costs, the interest expense on debt. The capital structure can therefore be studied through the use of breakeven analysis. When $400,000 of liabilities were incurred at an interest rate of 7 percent the corporation increased its fixed expenses by $28,000. Any earnings on assets above $28,000 then belonged to stockholders. When the example was later changed to $700,000 debt at 8 percent, the fixed expenses increased to $56,000.

The earnings of stockholders as a proportion of the original purchase price of stock, their yield, can be expressed as a simple linear function of earnings on assets:

$$\text{stockholder yield} = \frac{\text{earnings on assets} - \text{interest on debt}}{\text{original purchase price of stock}}$$

For the first capital structure

$$\text{stockholder yield} = \frac{\text{earnings on assets} - \$28{,}000}{\$600{,}000}$$

The yield with the later capital structure is

$$\text{stockholder yield} = \frac{\text{earnings on assets} - \$56{,}000}{\$300{,}000}$$

The breakeven point with the first capital structure is $28,000 of earnings on assets, and with the later structure the breakeven value is $56,000.

The breakeven value can also be expressed as a return on assets percentage. Stockholder yield will be zero if

$$\begin{array}{c}\text{return on assets}\\ \text{(percentage)}\end{array} = \text{(debt/assets)(interest rate on debt)}$$

For the first structure the debt-assets ratio is 40 percent and the interest rate on debt 7 percent, so the breakeven percentage return on assets is 2.8 percent. With the later structure, the debt-assets ratio is 70 percent and the interest rate 8 percent, so the corporation must realize a yield of 5.6 percent on assets to achieve a zero stockholder yield.

To get an increase in stockholder yield of 1 percent with the first structure, total earnings on assets must increase by $6,000, or the percentage return on assets must increase by 0.6 percent. An increase of only $3,000 in total earnings on assets (0.3 percent in the percentage return) will increase stockholder yield by 1 percent for the later structure. This response in stockholder yield to changes in earnings on assets can be used as a measure of the degree of financial leverage in the capital structure. Leverage refers to the relationship between operating income, earnings on assets in this context, and residual income, stockholders yield. Financial leverage could also be measured by the size of the debt in proportion to assets or equity, or by the amount of fixed charges in proportion to assets or equity. However measured, the later capital structure of the example is more highly leveraged than the first structure.

Leverage and the income characteristics of the corporation's residual owners will be reviewed and extended in Chapter 13. The effect of taxes and the variation in earnings on assets that were ignored in the example of this chapter will alter the leverage results somewhat.

The Organization and Approach of the Book

To aid in the understanding of managerial finance the textbook has been organized in six parts, ranging from the management of current assets to capital structure and dividend policy. The stress of the exposition is on theory so that the student will be better able to understand financial practices when he has graduated and been employed by a corporation. Rather than listing rules-of-thumb and financial formulas, the approach is aimed at helping the individual reason out solutions to the problems he will be facing. Facts are important, but tax rules, government regulations, and even the form of financial institutions are likely to change between the time this text was written and the time when the reader is actively involved in the financial environment.

The assumption for most of the presentation is that the corporation involved is engaged in a manufacturing or a merchandising operation rather than in providing financial services to other businesses. The specialized regulations and environment facing a life insurance company are only cursorily described, for example, since the description is from the aspect of a customer (a borrower) of the financial institution. The special problems of nonprofit and governmental corporations are not covered.

The prerequisite background for full appreciation of the book's content includes basic accounting, statistics, and microeconomics. A knowledge of where the accounting figures used for analysis come from, and the estimates and conventions followed in their derivations is necessary for nearly every subject covered. The statistical formulas used come mostly in the section on investment analysis under risk, although the concept of expected value appears in most parts of the book. The microeconomic background will be useful in the sections on security market theories and on the market value criterion for the optimum capital structure.

This book is not intended to be a mathematics text with financial applications. The formulas used are basically simple and comprehensible and do not require an advanced standing in mathematics. Occasionally an advanced mathematical theorem is used to speed the attaining of a result, but the application of the result is not dependent on being able to prove the theorem.

Part I, "The Management of Current Assets," treats a class of investment decisions that come from the current manufacturing or merchandising operations of the firm. In the typical operating cycle the corporation acquires inventory, sells it on open account, and then collects its accounts receivable sometime later. If the inventory is purchased from outside sources rather than being manufactured, an account payable is created that will be paid after some time lag. The balances of accounts receivable and of inventories are related to sales, but can be optimized to some extent independently. The residual of the operating cycle is the corporation's liquid balance that can be divided between cash and marketable securities. The models for optimization presented in Part I do not require very sophisticated capital budgeting tools.

Before analyzing the acquisition of other assets, though, part of the tools of analysis are developed in Part II, "Capital Budgeting Under Certainty." The techniques of summarizing variable cash flows over time into a single number for decision are demonstrated at length in this section. Ultimately the best measure to use as the appraisal value of an investment project is shown to be the present value.

Because the cash flows from investment projects are estimates that are subject to some uncertainty as to their realization, a further set of tools for handling uncertainty are covered in Part III, "The Investment Decision in Risk Situations." Two measures, the expected present value and the variance of present value, are used to analyze risky investments. The variance is normally suggested as a measure of risk, and the expected value as a measure of return. Because two measures are used, a unique preference ordering may not be possible among all alternatives without specific investment rules being expressed by the corporate board or the investor.

In Parts II and III several examples of investment projects are used to illustrate the tools. In Part IV, "Loan and Security Forms," the capital sources side of financial management is begun. The various alternatives for types of loan and security issues are described in this part.

After the description of the alternatives that may exist for the corporation's capital raising activities, the market environment in which those activities must be conducted is explored in Part V, "The Debt and Capital Markets." When the corporation seeks to borrow from a financial institution it is engaging in a financial market for loans where many lenders and borrowers are continuously transacting business. The availability and cost of those funds will vary over time and by the lender's assessment of the borrower's credit-worthiness. The operation in a financial market is more evident when the corporation sells debt or equity securities. The responsibility of the corporation to the buyer does not end when the securities are sold, however, since those securities have a continuing market as long as they are outstanding. The corporation's operating results, projections, and information releases may have an effect on that market value. To realize the full inferences of the capital market environment, much study beyond the basics presented in this part will be necessary.

Once the background is covered the last section, Part VI, "Capital

Structure and Dividend Policy," contains the models to determine the mix of capital sources and the dividend payment policy that will be optimum for common stockholders.

Chapter 1 References

Anderson, Leslie P., Miller, Vergil V., and Thompson, Donald L. *The Finance Function.* Scranton, Penn.: International Textbook, 1971.

Van Arsdell, Paul M. *Corporation Finance.* New York: Ronald, 1968.

Weston, J. Fred *The Scope and Methodology of Finance.* Englewood Cliffs, N.J.: Prentice-Hall, 1966.

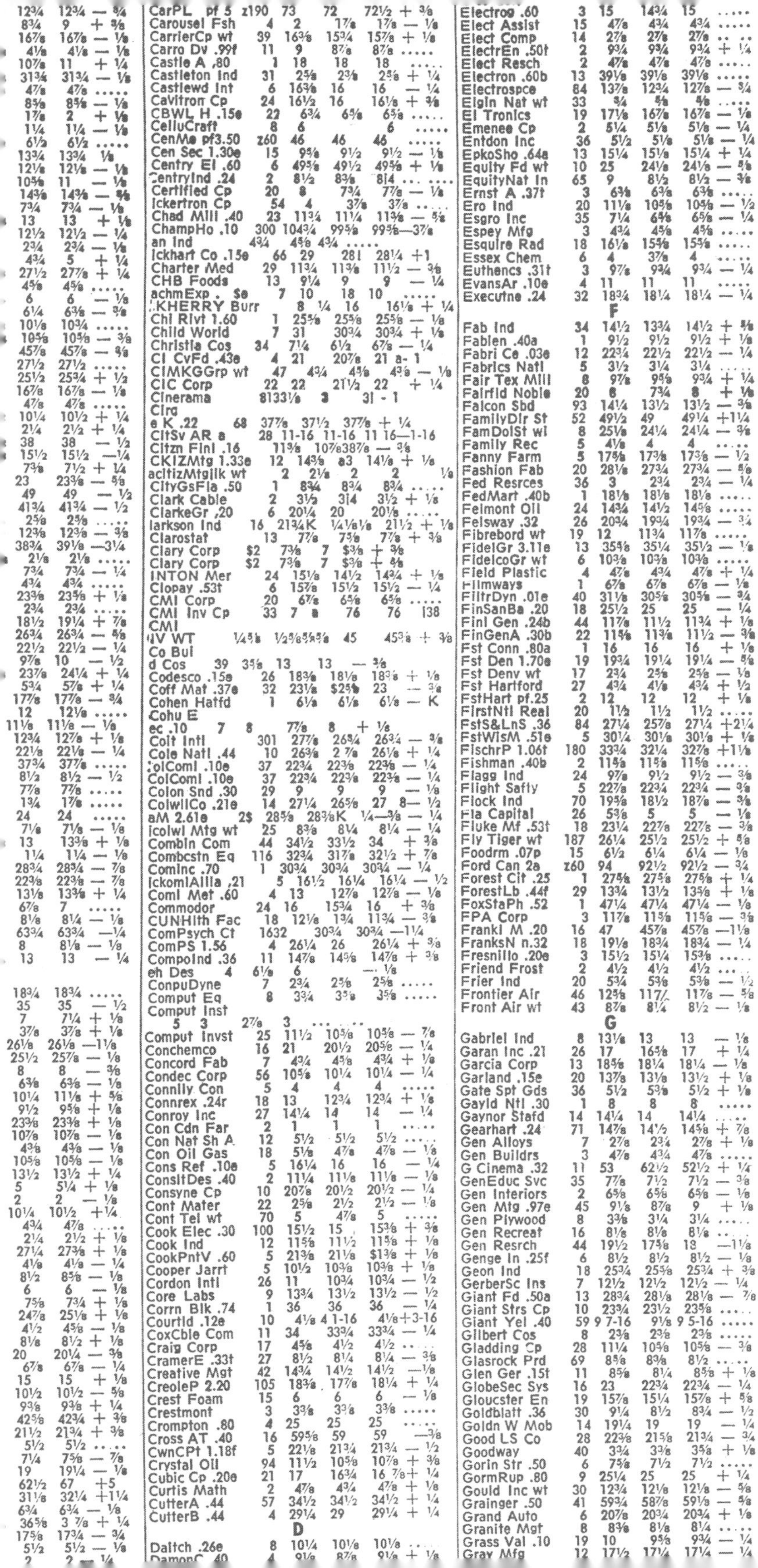

PART ONE

THE MANAGEMENT OF CURRENT ASSETS

Current asset management involves a common set of problems concerned with the size of investment required in those assets. The selection of an optimum size is based on the idea of maximizing profits, with the additional concept of considering the amount of cash invested. When the annual profit is divided by the size of investment, a simple summary measure of the projected investment's benefits, the return on investment, is derived.

Two basic analytical concepts are introduced in these chapters: the use of a return on investment measure for decision on a projected course of action, and the use of expected costs or expected profits as an aid to decision in cases where outcomes are the result of random processes.

The first chapter of this part is concerned with the management of cash balances and the division of liquid assets between cash and marketable securities. Although cash is necessary for the corporation to pay its bills, excessive cash balances result in an opportunity cost in the form of foregone earnings. The excessive cash could have been invested in some asset that would yield a return. For the purposes of Chapter 2 the alternative asset is a portfolio of marketable securities that could be easily sold to meet unexpected cash needs. The assumed costs in the cash-marketable securities model are foregone interest earnings if the cash balances were too large, and transactions costs of selling securities if too much of the liquid balance was held in marketable securities form. Cash requirements during a time period are the random variable, and a particular cash-marketable securities split of the liquid asset balance results in an expected total cost figure. An efficient search procedure for the optimum split, expressed as the optimum precautionary cash balance, is developed in the chapter.

Chapter 3 treats the credit policy of the corporation as a determinant of the sales volume. If credit standards are loosened sales should increase. To trace the entire results of the loosening, the increase in gross profits must be netted against increased collection and bad debt expense, and the increased investment in accounts receivable and other assets measured. The results are expressed as a return on investment.

In Chapter 4 two models for inventory management are developed, the economic order quantity model and the safety stock model. The economic order quantity establishes the optimum frequency of inventory procurement when acquisition is in discrete lots. The optimum safety stock allows some amount of extra inventory to be used to meet unexpected requirements during an order cycle. The size of the safety stock is based on consideration of overstock costs and out-of-stock costs, along with the statistical distribution of requirements. The model and the expected total cost criterion are mathematically identical to a model used in Chapter 2.

2

CASH AND MARKETABLE SECURITIES MANAGEMENT

The overriding consideration in the management of the corporation's financial activities is to insure that enough cash is available to meet every payment in full and on time. Within this overall constraint it is possible to manage cash balances in an efficient manner, investing surplus cash in short-term marketable securities on a temporary basis. Idle cash balances earn no return, so excess cash balances cause an opportunity cost in the form of foregone interest earnings.

Certain practices in cash management are obvious, and need little mention in this chapter. Payments should normally be scheduled on the due date of the obligation, not before, and control must be maintained over collections to insure that customers pay their accounts promptly. Some other techniques are less obvious, so some space is devoted to matters such as the lock-box collection system to resolve geographical difficulties that lead to time lags between payment by customers and spendable balances for the corporation.

Because investment in other current assets and the current liabilities of the corporation may vary seasonally, the cash balances of the corporation may have a pronounced seasonal variation. Rather than depend on providing for the seasonal variation in fund requirements through short-term borrowing, it may be desirable for the corporation to accommodate the seasonal requirements by drawing the cash from a pool of short-term marketable securities. For example, if money is needed for a seasonal expansion of inventory running from October through January, enough securities might be liquidated at the end of September to pay for the inventory expansion. Then when the seasonal needs end on the first of February, additional securities could be purchased with the excess cash.

Planning for seasonal holdings of marketable securities involves the forecasting of cash balances for some period in advance. A simple sales forecast-based cash budgeting system will be presented to serve as a basis for determining approximate cash needs.

Besides seasonal patterns of cash requirements provision must be made for random requirements. The final model of this chapter is designed to determine the optimum allocation of funds between precautionary cash balances and the stock of marketable securities. In this model a period is defined where replenishing cash from marketable securities cannot be accomplished without incurring transactions costs. If too large a precautionary balance is maintained a foregone interest opportunity cost is incurred, and if the balance is too small extra transactions costs of selling securities are incurred. The optimum precautionary balance is the level that minimizes the expected total of these costs.

Economizing on Cash by Speeding Collections

Cash is an idle asset that contributes nothing directly to the earnings of the corporation. Therefore the financial managers of the corporation should try to minimize the corporation's holdings of cash while still maintaining enough to insure payment of obligations. One method of optimum cash management is to speed collections of usable cash from customers' payments of receivables.

For the corporation selling to customers over a wide distribution of territory, the time lag in processing checks and the transmittal of cash balances over the country may be significant in reducing *usable* cash balances. A corporation with a central office in New York receiving checks from a customer in California has two time lags due to geography to contend with before the cash involved becomes spendable. The first time lag is the amount of time it takes for the check mailed in California to get to New York, and the second time lag is the amount of time it takes a check written on the California bank and deposited in a New York bank to clear through the Federal Reserve's check clearing system. The constructive date of payment is the time the check is mailed, so the receiving corporation bears the full amount of the mail delivery time lag. The corporation normally[1] cannot spend the deposited funds until the Federal Reserve credits the corporation's bank for the check. The Federal Reserve allows a maximum of two days for the check clearing process, therefore this part of the lag will have a maximum length of two days.

The total time lag due to geography may be as much as five days, three days for the mail delivery time and two days for the check clearing. If the corporation had an average daily collection of $100,000 from that distant location this would mean that on average $500,000 is tied up in unusable form. It might be worthwhile for a financial manager to see if the time lag and the unusable balance could be reduced some way.

One method that has gained increasing popularity over the last few years is the "lock-box collection" system. In the lock-box collection system a series of regional mailing addresses for receipt of accounts is established. The mailing address is usually a post office box, hence the "lock-box" term. An agent, usually a local bank, is commissioned to empty the post office box two or three times a day and deposit the funds in a local bank account. Because the lock box location is close to the invoice payer the time lag is reduced in both its components. The mail time lag may be reduced to one day and the check clearing lag to one day. The funds in the local bank may then be used for check writing or the funds transferred by wire to the central office bank account in New York.

Maintaining the regional lock-boxes will involve some additional expenses. If a bank performs the box-servicing, the bank's compensation may be in the form of the maintenance of a certain size deposit balance rather than an explicit fee. If the bank requires a $100,000 balance, for example, part of the cost of the lock-box is the foregone interest earnings on that idle, unusable balance. A separate fee would probably also be charged for the wire transfer of funds. Usually some duplicate records must be kept, and the mailing of microfilm copies of the checks received to the central office will add to the expenses of the lock-box collection system.

The decision to install a lock-box should therefore be based on the comparative costs with and without the arrangement. In the example above the unusable balances due to geography would be reduced from five days' collections, $500,000 to two days' collections, $200,000. If the servicing bank required a compensatory balance of $100,000, the net increase in usable cash balances would be $200,000. If those funds could be invested at an annual interest rate of 6 percent, the imputed annual interest earnings due to the lock-box would be $12,000. The additional explicit annual expenses of the lock-box could then be compared to the $12,000 to determine the economic feasibility of the arrangement. If those expenses were less than $12,000, install the lock-box system; if the expenses were greater than $12,000, stay with the centralized collection system.

For a corporation having nationwide sales activities it may be worthwhile to decentralize the collection system as well. Rather than having regional lock-boxes, the local sales office could also handle the collection of customer accounts, and make disbursements or transfer the collections to the corporation's central office. Such a system of decentralized collection is likely to be more expensive than the lock-box collection system, however, because of the addition of personnel to those sales offices, the increased costs of internal control measures, and similar duplication-of-activities expenses. Regional collection under either arrangement will reduce the unusable cash balances, but the gains must be balanced against the increased expenses required.

Cash Forecasting

One of the more important items of interest to a corporation's management is the amount of cash that will be available at points in the future. If the cash balance is deficient either the corporation must borrow funds or it must sell some assets, preferably some of its supply of marketable securities that has been held as a liquid reserve.

Forecasting of cash balances may be accomplished by some crude method whereby rough projections of sales, operating expenses, and other cash transactions are combined to give a first approximation to the corporation's needs for cash, or it may be performed on a very exacting basis whereby rigid operating budgets are followed by every operating division with daily reports prepared to show over- and under-budget performance, with the objectives of achieving both a highly accurate short-term forecast of cash and internal, centralized control over expenditures.

Generally the longer the period forecast, the less accurate the projections are expected to be. Therefore a corporation's financial employees may be involved simultaneously in a six-month forecast, a one-month forecast, and a one-week forecast. The six-month projection would serve as a rough guide to financing requirements, the one-month forecast as an aid to decision about the purchase of short-term marketable securities, and the one-week projection for arranging transfers of funds from bank account to bank account.

The forecast for longer periods should be based upon a sales forecast with the resulting operating cycle of (1) purchases of inventory to meet the sales requirements, (2) payment for the purchases, (3) sales on an open account basis, (4) payment of cash operating expenses, and (5) the collection of accounts receivable.

In the operating cycle some time lags exist that are important in determining cash balances. For example, purchases (or other acquisition) of merchandise for inventory precede the expected sales. The purchase of merchandise is normally on open account, and the payment of the resulting accounts payable will occur after some time lag. When sales are made cash receipts are usually delayed because part of the sales are on a credit basis, and there is a time lag before collection of accounts receivable.

To illustrate the preparation of a cash forecast based upon a sales forecast with a fixed operating cycle, a simple retail merchandising operation where a seasonal pattern in sales exists will be used. The forecast of sales by months for a nine-month period shown in Table 2.1 forms the basis for the projection.

TABLE 2.1
Example Sales Forecasts

September	$1,000
October	1,100
November	1,600
December	2,000
January	900
February	1,000
March	1,400
April	1,100
May	1,200

For the construction of the forecast of cash flows it is assumed that purchase of merchandise for inventory precedes sale by exactly one month. The corporation has a uniform markup policy on all merchandise so that its cost is 70 percent of the retail price. Therefore, to meet $1,600 of sales in November $1,120 must be purchased in October, for December sales of $2,000, $1,400 must be purchased in November, and so forth.

All merchandise is purchased on an open account basis, and payment is made one month after the date of purchase. The October purchases of $1,120 are therefore paid in November. The purchase time lag and the payment of payables time lag are of the same length, exactly offsetting each other in this example.

This corporation's sales are 20 percent for cash, and 80 percent on credit. Accounts receivable are collected in full two months after the credit sale. The November sales of $1,600 result in $320 cash receipts in November and $1,280 cash receipts in January.

The other cash operating expenses of the corporation are divided into a fixed component, $100 a month, and a variable component that is 15 percent of sales. November's cash payments for other operating expenses are $100 (fixed) and $240 (variable), 15 percent of $1,600.

The conversion of the sales forecast of Table 2.1 into a cash forecast is summarized in Table 2.2. For each month, November through May, the two cash receipts, cash sales and collections of accounts receivable, are added. From that total is subtracted the total of the three payments, payment of accounts payable, fixed other cash expenses, and variable other cash expenses, to give the net increase or decrease in the cash balance for that month. The increases and decreases are then cumulated over the seven months of the forecast.

TABLE 2.2
Cash Forecast from Operating Cycle

Total Sales	September 1,000	October 1,100	November 1,600	December 2,000	January 900	February 1,100	March 1,400	April 1,100	May 1,200
Cash sales	200	220	320	400	180	200	280	220	240
Collection of accounts receivable	?	?	800	880	1,280	1,600	720	800	1,120
Total receipts			1,120	1,280	1,460	1,800	1,000	1,020	1,360
Payment of accounts payable			1,120	1,400	630	700	980	770	840
Fixed other cash expenses			100	100	100	100	100	100	100
Variable other cash expenses			240	300	135	150	210	165	180
Total payments			1,460	1,800	865	950	1,290	1,035	1,120
Net increase (decrease) in cash balance			(340)	(400)	595	850	(290)	(15)	240
Cumulative change in cash balance due to operating cycle			(340)	(740)	(145)	705	415	400	640

The cash balance falls in November and December, rises in January and February, falls again in March and April, and then rises again in May. The largest cumulative amount of cash needed to continue the operating cycle is $740 in December.

Although the example chosen is very simple, it does demonstrate what may happen to cash balances as a result of fluctuating sales levels. The company enjoys a Thanksgiving-Christmas sales expansion that results in an immediate pressure on cash balances. The cash benefits come later, in January and February. The smaller Easter expansion in March results in a smaller decrease in cash balance in March than occurred in December, and the upsurge in cash receipts for that seasonal fluctuation occurs in May.

Besides the results of the projected operating cycle other transactions of the corporation will result in changes of the cash balance. Other sources of cash would include proceeds from the sale of assets other than inventory, and proceeds from new loans or the sale of securities. Other payments of cash include interest and dividend payments, tax payments, the repayment of loans, and the purchase of additional assets other than inventories. Fortunately most of these other items are easily forecastable since most result from contractual arrangements that are independent of the sales results of the corporation.

In constructing the numerical example some other accruals were ignored that could make the results of cash more easily determinable. Many expenses are commonly accrued before being paid, so the "other operating expenses" of the example may involve other time lags, increasing the amount of planning time possible for meeting cash deficiencies.

Even in the operating cycle results as summarized in Table 2.2, some "early warning" on cash balance changes is possible if sales do not meet the projected levels. Suppose in the numerical example that sales for

December only reached $1,800 instead of the $2,000 projected in Table 1. The immediate (December) drop in cash receipts is only $40, the change in receipts from cash sales. The collections from accounts receivable during December are for credit sales in October. The fall in December sales would not change the payment of accounts payable or the fixed other cash expenses. Since variable other cash expenses are 15 percent of current sales this cash payment would fall by $30. The net change in December cash receipts due to the $200 deficiency in sales would therefore be $10.

The major effects in cash balances would occur in January and February. The January effect would be caused by a reduction in purchases of merchandise in December (if the reduction in sales was realized soon enough to reduce the purchases for the following month's requirements), which reduces the amount of payment of accounts payable in January by 70 percent of $200–$140. The cash balance in January would therefore be $140 *higher* as a result of the December sales deficiency.

Of course collections of accounts receivable in February would be reduced by $160 because February's collections are for December's credit sales. The net changes in the cash balance for the three months affected by the failure to meet sales forecasts in December are

December	– $ 10
January	+ $140
February	– $160

Because the bulk of the effect is lagged in time through the time lag in collection for credit sales, the corporation's financial managers may have time to arrange for additional financing through short-term borrowing or disposal of marketable securities in an orderly manner.

There are many other possible causes for variation in actual cash balances from forecasted quantities. Each of the quantities used in the construction of the numerical example may vary from the estimate used, either in terms of the percentages, or the length of the time lag. Variable other cash expenses may not be exactly 15 percent of sales, the percentage of cash sales could be 21 percent, the collection lag for receivables can vary, and so forth. To allow for variations from forecast cash balances, some precautionary liquid balances should be kept, either in cash or in the form of marketable securities.

Marketable Securities as a Temporary Investment of Extra Cash Balances

Rather than replenishing cash balances by short-term loans from banks or other financial institutions, a corporation may maintain a liquid reserve in the form of highly marketable short-term securities. If the corporation does maintain some quantity of marketable securities, replenishing cash balances involves selling some of those securities (or letting them mature), and if the corporation has excess cash balances these can be used to acquire additional securities.

Besides serving as a temporary investment the stock of marketable securities may be used as a liquid reserve for precautionary reasons. Some of all of the securities may have to be sold on very short notice.

Because the securities must have a high degree of liquidity only certain types would ordinarily qualify for holding under normal circumstances. Three-month Treasury bills and prime commercial paper form the bulk of corporations' marketable securities holdings.

The three-month Treasury bills are issued by the U.S. Treasury and are repaid after three months. If the investor corporation wishes to hold the securities for less than three months purchases or sales of outstanding bills can be readily made in the New York money markets. Of course if a holding period less than three months is contemplated a purchase transaction cost or sales transaction cost must be deducted from the interest earned on the bill. That transaction cost could be high enough so that it would not be worthwhile for the corporation to try investing cash for very short periods of time.

For example suppose the corporation has projected extra cash of $10,000 for one week. If the annual yield on Treasury bills is 6 percent, $10,000 invested for one week will earn approximately $12 interest before transactions costs are subtracted. If the one-week holding period would require transactions costs of more than $12, 0.12 percent, it would not be worthwhile to invest the $10,000 under these circumstances.

Commercial paper is a form of unsecured promissory note issued by private corporations. If the purchaser of commercial paper buys a large enough quantity the issuer will tailor the maturity schedule to fit the buyer's requirements. A corporation with $3,000,000 to invest in commercial paper for 18 days can usually find an issuer who will accommodate the term requirements, but a corporation with $10,000 to invest probably cannot. For the large corporation commercial paper is a desirable short-term investment for excess cash because transactions costs, the cost of buying or selling outstanding securities, can be avoided. The smaller corporation may still be subject to transactions costs, however. Some care must be taken in the selection of the issuer in either case, however, since not all commercial paper issuers have the same credit-worthiness. Normally reliance is placed on independent ratings made by financial reporting services such as Dun & Bradstreet, Inc., and only prime-rated paper purchased.

In an effort to increase the interest yield corporate treasurers sometimes invest temporary funds in other security forms than Treasury bills and commercial paper. Short-term securities are sometimes issued by U.S. government agencies such as the Export-Import Bank, and such agency issues are usually considered equal in investment quality to the direct issues of the government. The major agencies issuing debt securities for public sale are the Federal Land Banks, Federal Intermediate Credit Banks, Banks for Cooperatives, Federal Home Loan Banks, Federal Home Loan Mortgage Corporation, Government National Mortgage Association, Farmers Home Administration, Export-Import Bank, and the Tennessee Valley Authority. Although the Federal National Mortgage Association is technically a privately owned corporation, the federal government's sponsorship of the corporation's activities lead to the usual classification of its debt securities as "government agency."

The yields of government agency securities are typically higher than direct issues of the government in spite of the certainty of interest and principal payment. Probably this disparity in yields can be explained by the smaller volume of issues outstanding and the resulting limitation in secondary market size for these issues. A holder of a Tennessee Valley Authority note who must liquidate it prior to maturity might be forced to do so at some sacrifice in price for immediate sale, or might be forced to wait a few days for a buyer to come along who is willing to pay the seller's price. The lower degree of marketability increases the holding risk of these agency securities resulting in the higher yield being required on average for the holders.

Other maturity length securities than three-month Treasury bills are sometimes used in the corporation's marketable securities program. When longer-term securities are held for short-term periods, however, an additional type of risk, interest-rate risk, is incurred by the corporation. Suppose for example that a corporation purchased an original issue of 6-month Treasury bills with an expected yield of 6 percent (expressed, as always, as an annual interest rate). Since the security is issued on a discount basis the corporation would pay 97.087 percent of the maturity value for the bill. Now suppose that the corporation sells the bill three months later on the open market, where in the meantime yields on three-month bills have risen to 8 percent. The corporation would receive 98.039 percent of the maturity value for the bill. Its actual yield for the three month holding period is less than 4 percent.

Interest-rate risk works the other way as well—if interest rates fall during the corporation's holding period, its realized yield on the longer-term security will be greater than the original stated yield. Sometimes corporate treasurers use the strategy of investing in longer-term securities to attempt to gain from falls in interest rates.

Another form of security that has come into existence in the last decade is the negotiable certificate of deposit (NCD) issued by commercial banks. The original holder of the NCD gets it by depositing a certain sum of money in a commercial bank. The difference from an ordinary time deposit is that the amount cannot be withdrawn without penalty before the term of the certificate is up. The holder of the NCD can liquidate it before the term is up by selling on the open market. Of course the price received will depend on market rates of interest at the time. Although the typical size of the NCD is well beyond the $20,000 limitation of the Federal Deposit Insurance Corporation the investment quality of NCD's is not often questioned by analysts. Possibly this is because of the low rate of failure of commercial banks in the period since banks were authorized to issue NCD's.

Other forms of marketable securities will be discussed more extensively in later chapters. For now attention is confined to those securities where a relatively low interest rate will be earned for a short period of time, the issue can be readily sold or purchased in a securities market at some fixed cost, and no appreciable risk of default by the issuer of the security exists.

Precautionary Cash Balances Model

So far cash balances have been treated as if they can be forecast exactly, and the resulting implication has been that cash balances can be reduced almost to zero by investing the "extra" cash in marketable securities. However, requirements for cash cannot always be predicted exactly, and therefore some precautionary balance of cash must be maintained.

The problem is how large the precautionary balance should be. In analyzing the size of the precautionary balance the alternative to cash will be assumed to be marketable securities, so one of the consequences of a certain size balance will be foregone interest earnings on the marketable securities that could have been held.

A simple model will be constructed to demonstrate a method of determining the optimum precautionary balance at the beginning of a time period. The time period is chosen so that no transactions costs are incurred if securities are purchased at the beginning of the period and held to the end of the period. If securities have to be sold in the middle of the period to meet cash requirements a transaction cost is incurred. The solution of the model will be that precautionary cash balance that minimizes the expected total costs due to the balance.

In the model a fixed time period, one month, is assumed for analysis. Cash requirements during that time period are a random variable with a known statistical distribution. If the total cash requirements during the time period are less than the beginning balance of cash, those requirements can be met entirely from that balance. If requirements are greater than that balance, then the deficiency must be met by selling some of the corporation's stock of marketable securities. It is therefore assumed that all cash requirements can be met, either from the beginning balance of cash or from the proceeds of marketable securities sales.

A symbolic notation will simplify some of the model's development. Let X be the total cash requirements for the one-month model time period, and Q be the beginning balance of cash. X is a random variable with a known statistical distribution, and $P(X)$ will be used for the probability of a particular value of X. Q is the decision variable whose optimum size will be determined by the solution of the model.

If requirements, X, are greater than the beginning balance, Q, then marketable securities equal to the deficiency, $X - Q$, must be sold. It is assumed that a transactions cost is incurred that is a percentage of the amount of securities sold. That transactions cost is assigned the symbol c, so the total transactions costs for a period when X is greater than Q is

$$c\,(X - Q)$$

If the beginning balance, Q, is greater than the requirements, X, then an excess amount of cash equal to $Q - X$ is carried for the one-month period. That excess could have been invested in marketable securities, so the consequence of the excess is foregone interest earnings. If the *monthly* interest rate earned on marketable securities is r, the total foregone interest earnings on the excess amount of cash is

$$r\,(Q - X)$$

The corporation in this model either incurs transaction costs or foregoes interest earnings, an opportunity cost. The amount of cost incurred depends on X, an amount determined outside the solution of the model and therefore called an "exogenous" variable, and on the quantity Q, which is the decision variable. The listing of possible total costs can be summarized by the mathematical statement

$$\text{Total costs} = c\,(X - Q)\ ;\ \text{if } Q < X$$
$$\text{Total costs} = r\,(Q - X)\ ;\ \text{if } Q \geqslant X$$

The criterion for selection of Q is the minimization of expected total costs, where the word "expected" is used in the statistical sense. The computation of the expected total cost for a certain Q value can best be illustrated with a numerical example, and later a symbolic formula for the optimum Q level will be developed.

Suppose the requirements of cash follow the discrete probability distribution listed in Table 2.3.

TABLE 2.3
Distribution of X (in $000)

X	$P(X)$
10	0.1
20	0.2
30	0.4
40	0.2
50	0.1

The probability that requirements will equal $10,000 is 0.1, that requirements will equal $20,000 is 0.2, and so forth.

The transaction cost per dollar, c, is 2 percent, so if $30,000 of marketable securities must be sold the total transactions costs are $600. The monthly interest rate, r, is 0.5 percent.

The beginning cash balance Q can be any quantity, but only a few values of Q will be used to compute expected total costs. The computation of expected total costs for a Q of 10, 20, 30, 40, and 50 ($000) is summarized in Table 2.4.

In each section of Table 2.4 the possible cash requirements X are listed with the corresponding amounts available from the beginning balance Q. If Q is less than X a transactions cost is incurred equal to

$$c\,(X - Q) \text{ or } 2\%\,(X - Q)$$

If Q is greater than X an interest opportunity cost of

$$r\,(Q - X) \text{ or } 0.5\%\,(Q - X)$$

is realized. If Q is equal to X neither cost is incurred. The third and fourth columns of the table are listings of the total transactions cost and total interest opportunity cost. In the fifth column the probabilities of the X values, and therefore of the particular costs, are listed.

TABLE 2.4
Expected Total Costs for Various Q Levels

	X	Q	$c(X-Q)$	$r(Q-X)$	$P(X)$	Product of cost and probability
$Q = 10$	10	10	0	0	0.1	0
	20	10	200	0	0.2	40
	30	10	400	0	0.4	160
	40	10	600	0	0.2	120
	50	10	800	0	0.1	80
						400 = expected total cost
$Q = 20$	10	20	0	50	0.1	5
	20	20	0	0	0.2	0
	30	20	200	0	0.4	80
	40	20	400	0	0.2	80
	50	20	600	0	0.1	60
						225 = expected total cost
$Q = 30$	10	30	0	100	0.1	10
	20	30	0	50	0.2	10
	30	30	0	0	0.4	0
	40	30	200	0	0.2	40
	50	30	400	0	0.1	40
						100 = expected total cost
$Q = 40$	10	40	0	150	0.1	15
	20	40	0	100	0.2	20
	30	40	0	50	0.4	20
	40	40	0	0	0.2	0
	50	40	200	0	0.1	20
						75 = expected total cost
$Q = 50$	10	50	0	200	0.1	20
	20	50	0	150	0.2	30
	30	50	0	100	0.4	40
	40	50	0	50	0.2	10
	50	50	0	0	0.1	0
						100 = expected total cost

Column six contains the product of the probability and the cost, so the sum of column six is the expected total cost for that value of Q.[2]

The expected total costs for the various levels of Q calculated in Table 2.4 are

Q	Expected total cost
10	400
20	225
30	100
40	75
50	100

Since the lowest expected total cost is 75, a beginning balance of 40 is the optimum Q size.

Only a few discrete values of Q were investigated in Table 2.4, and the conclusion that 40 units is the optimum Q is possibly premature, since values such as 38, 42, and so forth are possible for Q. Before the demonstration that Q of 40 is optimum is shown, though, the procedure for finding an optimum must be shortened since the iteration of expected total costs for every possible value of Q is not an efficient means of seeking an optimum.

Instead an incremental analysis can be performed to determine the effect on expected total costs of adding one more unit to Q. If expected total costs are lowered by the incremental unit it should be added, or if expected total costs are increased by the incremental unit it should not be added.

In the numerical example of Tables 2.3 and 2.4, suppose a unit is added to Q starting at a base quantity of $Q = 30$. That unit if added would make $Q = 31$. From the probabilities of Table 2.3 it can be determined that the probability that the incremental unit will be unneeded to meet cash requirements and therefore increase the interest opportunity cost is 70 percent (the sum of the probabilities at $X = 10$; $X = 20$; and $X = 30$). The probability that the incremental unit will be used to meet cash requirements and therefore reduce the transactions cost (since sales of marketable securities would be lowered by one unit) is 30 percent. The change in expected total costs due to the incremental unit (the 31st) can be calculated as

$$70\% \,(0.5\%) - 30\% \,(2\%) = -\,0.25\%$$

Because the units of Q are expressed in thousand dollars the change in expected total costs is –\$2.50. It is worthwhile to add that unit to the beginning balance of cash.

The same result of the change in expected total costs will apply to the next 9 units increase in Q, the 32nd through the 40th units, because the probabilities do not vary. The change in expected total cost will change sizes only when another point in the probability distribution is reached.

For an increment of one unit added to a base of $Q = 40$, for the 41st unit, the change in expected total cost will be

$$90\% \,(0.5\%) - 10\% \,(2\%) = 0.25\%$$

The probability that the unit of Q will be unneeded increases to 90 percent, and the probability that transactions costs will be saved falls to 10 percent. Adding the 41st unit to Q will increase expected total costs by \$2.50.

These changes in expected total costs can be used to verify the results in Table 2.4. For the change in Q from 30 to 40 the increment in Q is 10 units. Multiplying 10 by the change per unit, –0.25 percent, yields –2.5 percent which is the change in thousand dollars, –\$25, shown in Table 2.4.

For the move from 40 to 50 the increment of 10 units is multiplied by the change per unit, 0.25 percent, to yield

$$10\,(0.25\%) = 2.5\%$$

This agrees exactly with the results of Table 2.4 again where an increase in expected total costs of \$25 is shown.

The numerical results above can be generalized to symbolic form by the statement that a unit increment to a base quantity $Q - 1$ is desirable if

$$P(X<Q)r - [1 - P(X<Q)]c < 0$$

The unit is undesirable, will increase the expected total costs, if

$$P(X<Q)r - [1 - P(X<Q)]c > 0$$

These inequalities can be rearranged slightly to solve for the probability separately. A unit increment to the base quantity $Q - 1$ is desirable if

$$P(X<Q) < \frac{c}{r+c}$$

It is undesirable if

$$P(X<Q) > \frac{c}{r+c}$$

The point sought for the optimum Q is where the inequality changes from $<$ to $>$. If Q were continuously variable the optimum Q would be where

$$P(X<Q) = \frac{c}{r+c}$$

To demonstrate a continuously variable Q a different probability distribution for X must be defined. Now X is a continuous random variable with a probability density function $f(X)$. To derive the probability $P(X<Q)$ the probability density function must be integrated over the range of X values less than Q:

$$P(X<Q) = \int_{-\infty}^{Q} f(X)\,dX$$

Therefore the general solution for the optimum beginning balance of cash is the Q value that satisfies

$$\int_{-\infty}^{Q} f(X)\,dX = \frac{c}{r+c}$$

Figure 2.1
Rectangular Distribution of Cash Requirements

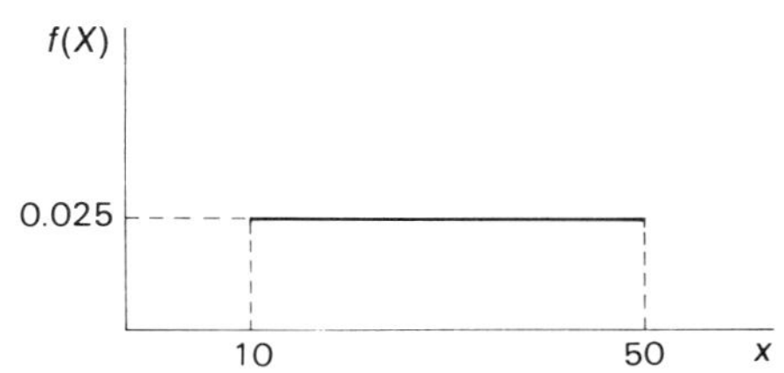

To avoid the difficulty of integration two simple continuous distributions will be used to illustrate the calculation of the optimum beginning balance. The first distribution is a rectangular (or uniform) distribution defined for X between the limits of 10 to 50. The probability density function is graphed in Figure 2.1.

The problem is to solve for a value Q between 10 and 50 that will satisfy

$$P(X<Q) = \frac{c}{r+c}$$

The value of c is still 2% and the value of r is 0.5%. Therefore the point Q should be such that

$$P(X < Q) = \frac{2\%}{0.5\% + 2\%} = 0.8$$

Since the probabilities in Figure 2.1 are represented by areas under the curve the point Q should be 42 so that the area under the curve between 10 and Q will equal 0.8. 42 is the optimum Q for this revised example.[3]

It is interesting to note the significance of this value of 42. It will pay the corporation to maintain idle balances most of the time (80 percent to be specific) so that the frequency of replenishing cash balances by selling marketable securities can be low (20 percent). The result is based on the fact that it costs less in terms of the foregone interest on excess cash balances than the cost of selling the securities to replenish cash balances.

One more continuous distribution that is easy to solve is where the distribution of X is the Normal distribution. To use the Normal distribution, the mean and the standard deviation of X must be known. If the mean is 30 and the standard deviation is 10, the distribution of X will look like that shown in Figure 2.2. Using tables for the Normal distribution that can be found in any statistics textbook, the optimum value of Q, the value so that the probability of an X value less than Q will be 0.8, is 38.42.

Figure 2.2
Normal Distribution of Cash Requirements

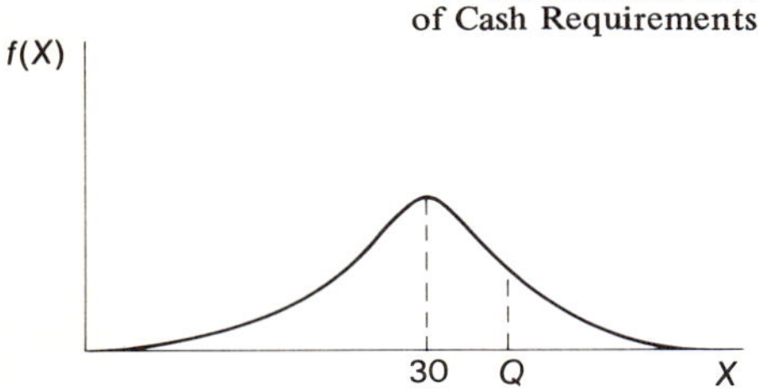

The major problem with the practical application of this precautionary cash balances model is the determination of the statistical distribution of cash requirements during the planning period. Although three different distributions were used for examples here, no claim is made that any one of them will adequately approximate reality for a given corporation. To use this model the corporation's financial managers must spend some time deriving the statistical distribution as well as the applicable costs used in the model.

Cash Management Without a Marketable Securities Balance

The assumption has been that the corporation maintains a pool of marketable securities that can be liquidated to meet any unusual cash requirements. That is, the alternative to cash has been the marketable securities portfolio. Some corporations do not have sufficient funds to hold such a large marketable securities balance. For these corporations the alternative to cash is other assets such as inventories or equipment. Since those other assets cannot be readily liquidated such corporations may depend on short-term loans to meet unexpected cash requirements.

Rather than negotiate a separate loan each time funds are needed the corporation may have a standby arrangement with a bank or other lender so that funds up to a certain limit may be drawn with little or no notice. Such an arrangement, a "line of credit," will be discussed more extensively in Chapter 9, but usually involves a fixed fee based on the limit size with interest on the credit actually used.

In some cases the use of temporary loans can be considered as a negative holding of marketable securities with the interest payments being similar to foregone interest earnings. However, interest rates charged by the bank or other lender are typically above what the corporation could earn on marketable securities. For example, when the prevailing yield on marketable securities is 4 percent the interest rate charged by a lender might be 6 percent, the extra 2 percent being a compensation to the lender for the financial risk incurred through lending to the corporation rather than investing in the "risk-free" marketable securities.

A given corporation may both hold marketable securities and have short-term debts outstanding at the same time in spite of the interest rate differential. The justification for this behavior is the possible uncertainty regarding further loans if more funds are needed—the marketable securities can always be liquidated without going before the bank's loan officer or committee, but a loan application might be turned down. Rather than incur the risk of being unable to pay obligations on their due dates the corporation may accept the interest differential between marketable securities and loans.

Summary

Cash is necessary to pay bills, but excess cash can be invested in interest-earning securities. After a financial manager institutes all the steps appropriate to maximize usable cash balances, such as adopting a lock-box collection procedure, then forecasting techniques are necessary to give an advance estimate of cash balances.

The corporation is likely to have seasonal patterns in cash balances where excess balances can be invested temporarily in interest-earning securities. The appropriate securities for most corporations are very short-term government securities, three-month Treasury bills, or prime-grade commercial paper. If possible the maturity of the securities chosen should be matched to the investment period required so that transactions costs can be avoided.

Because cash flows cannot be forecast exactly most corporations must maintain some precautionary cash balances. An alternative to those balances is a liquid reserve of marketable securities. A model for determining the proper size of precautionary cash balances was used where foregone interest earnings were the consequence of maintaining excessive precautionary balances, and transactions costs from liquidating marketable securities were the consequence of deficient precautionary balances. For a statistical distribution of cash requirements the solution to the optimum precautionary balance is that level that minimizes the expected total of those costs. The planning period of the model was chosen so that investment in marketable securities for the entire period required no transactions cost. Therefore the length of the planning period is equal to the term of the securities chosen for short-term investment. The cash requirements in the model presumably represented the excess of cash outlays over cash inflows from operations that must be met from the liquid reserves, cash or marketable securities, of the corporation. Obviously more complicated models than the one presented could be built, but the one used serves to demonstrate the basic principles of selecting a procedure to minimize expected total costs.

[1]In some cases a bank will allow the corporation to count deposited but uncleared amounts toward minimum balances required under a loan agreement, therefore in this situation the effect is that the corporation has the use of the funds at the time the checks are deposited.
[2]The computation follows the well-known formula for the expected value of a random variable Z. If Z follows a discrete probability distribution with probability $P(Z)$, then the expected value of Z is

$$E(Z) = \int_Z Z f(Z)\,dZ$$

Here Z is the cost associated with the outcome of the random process. If Z were a continuous random variable with probability density function $f(Z)$, the expected value would be

$$E(Z) = \sum_Z Z P(Z)$$

[3]Q could be solved directly from the integral expression defining Q. For this distribution the probability density function is a constant

$$f(X) = 0.025$$

The lower limit of X is 10, so the integral equation is

$$\int_{10}^{Q} 0.025\,dX = 0.8$$

$$0.025\,(Q - 10) = 0.8$$

$$Q = 42$$

Chapter 2 Questions

1. If cash is not an earning asset why do corporations hold cash?
2. What is the cost of not being able to meet bills as they come due?
3. Why might it be better to maintain a "buffer stock" of marketable securities that can be sold to meet unexpected cash requirements rather than depend on short-term borrowing from banks?
4. Is it really necessary to have cash in a checking account before checks are written, or could a corporation depend on a "float," some time lag before checks clear, and only deposit funds some time after the checks are issued?
5. In preparing a cash forecast only the merchandising cycle (from the acquisition of merchandise through the collection of cash from receivables) was considered. Are all the other cash transactions of the corporation easily and exactly forecastable?
6. What effect on the forecast methodology would result from the collection of accounts receivable having a variable time lag instead of a fixed lag?
7. Is the tailoring of maturities possibility a strong enough reason to

choose commercial paper over Treasury bills for the corporation's marketable security portfolio?

8. What are the transactions costs for buying and selling marketable securities?

9. Determine the current yields on commercial paper, Treasury bills, and other short-term debt securities that might be appropriate for the marketable security portfolio.

10. Instead of buying securities a corporation might simply deposit funds in a savings account with a bank or other financial institution. What are the possible advantages and disadvantages of that arrangement?

11. Corporations will frequently have a portfolio of marketable securities at the same time as they carry a net short-term debt to banks. Is there a discrepancy in this behavior since the yield on the securities is usually less than the interest rate on their debt?

12. In the precautionary balance model the assumption was made that the random cash requirements would be met only from the precautionary cash balance or the sale of securities. How does the model reconcile with the cash generated from operations during the time period?

13. For internal control reasons the lock-box agent is usually a bank rather than an individual or other institution. Apparently it is thought that separate bonding or auditing of transactions will be unnecessary with such an agent, reducing the costs of this regional collection system. Comment.

Chapter 2 Problems

1. ABR Corporation sells widgets in Seattle even though its main offices are in Chapaqua, North Carolina. So far it has been asking all its customers to forward their payments to the main office, even though that results in a mail time lag of three days and a check clearing time lag of two days, for a total time lag before the collections become usable of five days. Sales (and collections) in the Seattle area average $60,000 a day.

The cash manager of ABR is considering a lock-box collection system for the Seattle area. A Seattle bank would act as agent for opening the lock-box, depositing the checks, and transferring the funds to Chapaqua by wire. That bank does not require a compensating balance for its services, but will charge an explicit fee for its actions that is still the subject of negotiation.

The lock-box arrangement will reduce the total time lag for spendability from five days to two days. ABR currently pays an interest rate of 10 percent a year for borrowed funds. What is the maximum annual fee that ABR can afford to pay the Seattle bank for servicing the lock-box?

2. It may not pay a corporation to invest funds in marketable securities for very short periods of time because of transactions costs. If the cost of selling, or buying, a $10,000 Treasury bill is $40, and the annual yield on the Treasury bill is 5.0 percent, how many days must the bill be held before the transaction cost is made up by interest accruals (assume 360 days in a year)?

3. ZAB Corporation has a one-month planning period for managing the cash-marketable securities during one month will be 1 percent if the security is held the full period, and the cost of selling a security during the period to meet cash outflow requirements is ½ percent. The (discrete) distribution of cash requirements is:

Requirements (in $000)	Probability
40	0.2
50	0.3
60	0.3
70	0.2

What should be the level of precautionary cash balances at the first of the one-month period?

4. BZZ Corporation uses a two-month period for the cash-marketable securities decision model, so its interest earnings on securities will be 1.6 percent for the period. The sales cost for premature liquidation of securities during the period is 0.6 percent. The distribution of cash requirements during the two-month period is a Normal distribution with a mean of $60,000 and a standard deviation of $20,000. What should BZZ's precautionary cash balance at the first of the period be to minimize expected total costs?

5. ABC has an inventory procurement policy whereby merchandise is acquired two months in advance of estimated sales, at a price equal to 60 percent of its retail selling price. All merchandise is purchased on open account, and the average payment terms are one-half month in length. ABC's sales are one-third cash and two-thirds on open account with an average payment period of one month. Estimated total sales for May are $1.0 million, June $1.2 million, July $1.4 million, August $1.1 million, and September $0.9 million. If the forecasted sales are accurate what should be the end of July balances of

a. Accounts receivable.
b. Inventory.
c. Accounts payable.

6. Referring to problem 5, suppose ABC's actual sales in June were $1.0 million instead of the forecasted $1.2 million. If it takes one month for the information lag to adjust purchases of merchandise (that is, in July) how will the cash receipts from cash sales and collection of receivables, and the cash payments for accounts payable for the months of June, July, and August be changes from the original forecast?

7. Referring to problem 5, suppose that the collection time lag for receivables becomes 1½ months as of May because of a local recession. What will be the change (from problem 5's results) in cash collections for July, August, and September?

8. XYZ, a manufacturing corporation, produces all its merchandise *after* firm orders are received from customers. Because the time lag of manufacturing is one month the average investment in work-in-process inventories is ½ month's sales at cost. The cost of merchandise is 65 percent of the selling price, and no accruals are taken on this cost—the manufacturing expenses are cash outlays. All of XYZ's customers are allowed one month's credit, so the average accounts receivable balance is one month's sales. The other cash expenses do not vary with sales, but are fixed at $100,000 per month. Given the four-month sales forecast:

January	$ 1,300,000
February	1,100,000
March	1,200,000
April	1,400,000

what should be the change in cash balances for February and March?

Chapter 2 References

Archer, Stephen H. "A Model for the Determination of a Firm's Cash Balances." *Journal of Financial and Quantitative Analysis,* March 1966.

Baumol, William J. "The Transactions Demand for Cash: An Inventory Theoretic Approach." *Quarterly Journal of Economics,* November 1952.

Beranek, William. *Working Capital Management.* Belmont, California: Wadsworth, 1966.

Blake, W. H., Jr. "Cash Flow Forecasting." *Best's Review,* February 1969.

Eppen, Gary D., and Fama, Eugene F. "Solutions for Cash Balance and Simple Dynamic-Portfolio Problems." *Journal of Business,* January 1968.

Girgis, N. M. "Optimal Cash Balance Levels." *Management Science,* November 1968.

Hewitt, Leroy H. "Inventory Techniques Applied to Cash Management." *Management Services,* July 1970.

Horn, Frederick E. "Managing Cash." *Journal of Accounting,* April 1964.

Lerner, E. M. "Simulating a Cash Budget." *California Management Review,* Winter 1968.

Mason, Clyde D. "Cash Planning." *Price-Waterhouse Review,* Autumn 1968.

Miller, Merton H., and Orr, Daniel. "A Model of the Demand for Money by Firms." *Quarterly Journal of Economics,* August 1966.

Neave, Edwin H. "The Stochastic Cash-Balance Problem with Fixed Costs for Increases and Decreases." *Management Science,* March 1970.

Orgler, Yair E. *Cash Management.* Belmont, California: Wadsworth, 1970.

Sethi, Suresh P. "A Note on a Planning Horizon Model of Cash Management." *Journal of Financial and Quantitative Analysis,* January 1971.

Stancill, James McN. *The Management of Working Capital.* Scranton, Pennsylvania: International Textbook, 1971.

White, D. J., and Norman, J. M. "Control of Cash Reserves." *Operational Research Quarterly,* September 1965.

3

THE MANAGEMENT OF ACCOUNTS RECEIVABLE

Accounts receivable, representing the unsecured short-term claims of the corporation on its credit customers, require a considerable investment in assets by some corporations. For the usual short-term accounts receivable resulting from open account sales no explicit interest is charged, and therefore accounts receivable is sometimes classified as a non-earning asset whose size is to be minimized.

However, accounts receivable result from sales of merchandise or services, and the credit policies of the corporation may have a significant relation to sales. One technique that may work to increase sales is to offer more liberal credit terms. Therefore accounts receivable management cannot be separated from sales management, and to classify accounts receivable as a non-earning asset is misleading.

The techniques of accounts receivable management are quite different for retail sales to individuals and wholesale sales to other business firms. Usually retail accounts receivable do not have a prompt payment or cash discount, but are simply due in full on a specified date. For open account sales to other business firms frequently a cash discount is specified on the invoice form through terms such as 2/10, n/30. The notation 2/10, n/30 means that the customer can take a 2 percent discount on the invoice amount if the invoice is paid within 10 days of the invoice date, but the invoice amount is due in full by 30 days from the invoice date. Other common abbreviations used in invoices are COD, collection on delivery of the merchandise, and EOM, end of the month, used in specifying a due date.

In the past few years the growth of bank credit cards and general-purpose credit cards has meant that a feasible alternative to open account credit for small-sized retail sales has developed. A retailer who accepts the necessity of selling on credit may find it economical to pay the fixed percentage fee charged by the credit card company rather than go to the expense and investment involved in open account charge accounts. Probably because of the average size of credit purchases no equivalent alternative to open account credit is available to the business firm selling to other business firms. In a few cases the wholesaler can arrange outside financing for the purchasing firm, but such an arrangement is not usual.

The credit policy of a corporation includes the acceptance standards for new credit customers, the size of allowable charges (a maximum balance), the size and period of eligibility of cash discounts, and the final term of payment of charges. Each of these aspects of credit policy will have some influence on sales revenue, expenses, and the corporation's investment in assets. In some cases a decision as to a credit policy can be based on a comparison of the change in profits to the change in asset investment. For a "loosening" of a credit policy the two changes should be positive, and the ratio of the changes, a return on investment measure, can be used to indicate the desirability of the policy change.

Administration of Credit Policy

When terms are established for the credit sales of the corporation some efforts must be devoted to "enforcement" of those terms. If a cash discount is allowed for prompt payment of invoices, some internal control is desirable to assure that a customer does not take a discount when he is not entitled to it because he has exceeded the discount period. For the normal due date of invoices or of accounts a prompt reporting and reconciliation procedure is desirable to keep tabs on slow payers.

If a customer is only a few days late in payment or if a cash discount taker pays on the eleventh day instead of the tenth day some discretion is necessary in challenging the customer's actions. If the corporation is too aggressive, future sales may be lost. On the other hand if the corporation is too permissive, the customer may be even later with his payment the next time. Some fine balance in this aspect of credit policy administration must be achieved between driving good customers away and letting slow payers "lean on" the corporation.

In cases where strict due dates are not specified on credit sales some additional analysis may be necessary to keep the accounts current. An aging report by individual account, indicating what amount is 0-30 days old, 30-60 days old, or over 60 days old, will aid in identifying where specific collection efforts should be directed.

Besides timing payments, the credit manager must perform the screening for acceptance of new credit accounts and must establish and enforce credit limits for individual accounts. The credit manager also has the task of evolving a collection procedure for those accounts that do not turn out well. To collect a series of reminder letters and then threatening letters may be sufficient, but eventually legal action may be necessary.

The credit manager's performance of these administrative functions is one case where human talents and judgment are particularly necessary. Some of the operating procedures may be mechanized, but increasing complaints of customers trying to straighten out errors in their accounts by writing letters to the computer may indicate a brewing customer revolt.

Information for Judging Credit-Worthiness of Customers

Trying to gauge the credit-worthiness of new credit customers can be a very expensive process if outside aid from professional information-gathering organizations is not obtained. Fortunately two organizations make information available at relatively low fees.

For information about retail customers, individuals and very small business firms, local credit bureaus maintain files that can be used to estimate credit-worthiness. The information is available to businesses for a fee, usually as part of a continuing subscription to the credit bureau's services. Local credit bureaus maintain exchanges of information, so even if the credit customer has recently moved into the community it may be possible to get enough information through the bureau to make a judgment.

If information from a credit bureau is unavailable, about the only practical alternative is to request the customer to fill out a credit application form listing relevant information. This information would probably include as a minimum age, sex, marital status, number of children, type of employment, income, home ownership, listing of checking and savings accounts, and a listing of other charge accounts and credit cards. Independent verification of at least parts of the information provided by the prospective customer would be desirable, but very extensive verification is prohibitively expensive.

To obtain information and a credit assessment of business firms the corporation should be a subscriber to the credit reporting services of Dun & Bradstreet, Inc. Subscribers are provided with the *Reference Book,* containing information about *millions* of business firms. The information is updated by Dun & Bradstreet frequently, and new summaries provided every two months. If more extensive information than is provided in the *Reference Book* is desired, special reports are available for an extra fee from Dun & Bradstreet.

In the absence of sufficient information from the credit services of Dun & Bradstreet or other specialized organizations it may be possible to solicit information from the business firm itself. If the requested credit is important enough to the customer, such information as recent financial statements, bank references, and the like may be provided. Of course, requests for such information may be viewed as an invasion of the applicant firm's privacy, so discretion must be exercised in the requests for information. The anonymity of the source is one powerful reason for relying on external sources such as credit bureaus and Dun & Bradstreet's credit service for information about new credit customers.

Available Alternatives in Retail Credit

For companies dealing with retail customers (individuals and very small businesses) several alternatives to open account credit—charge accounts—are available. With the expansion of general purpose credit cards such as the American Express Card, Diners Club Card, Bankamerica Card, Master Charge Card, and others, a reasonable alternative exists for retailers dealing in small sales amounts. Rather than maintain charge accounts one or more of these general purpose cards may be accepted in payment for credit sales.

Naturally the use of these cards involves a cost to the retailer that must be weighed against the cost of maintaining charge accounts. The usual terms with the cards provide for immediate payment to the retailer, with no recourse of the card company to the retailer on uncollectible amounts. The fee is a fixed amount of the charges, varying sometimes by the type of sale, but usually in the range of 3 to 5 percent of the charge. The retailer's cost is therefore the total of the card company's fee and the bookkeeping costs involved.

Such costs can be compared to what it would cost the retailer to maintain normal charge accounts. For charge accounts the bookkeeping costs would be greater, some collection costs and bad debt expenses would be incurred, some costs would be incurred for initial credit investigation of new accounts, and the retailer would have an investment in accounts receivable. The comparison of credit cards and charge accounts must take all these costs into account.

An example will demonstrate the comparison. Friendly Corner Pharmacy, Inc. (FCP) is considering the expansion of business that would result from allowing credit on prescriptions. If credit is allowed, an extra 1,000 sales per month with an average size of $20 would be generated whether general purpose credit cards or ordinary charge accounts are used.

If credit cards are used the card company will charge FCP 4 percent of the amount of the charge, \$800 per month, but payment will be made immediately so that FCP will have no investment in receivables. Because charge slips must be made out, filed, totaled, and forms for submission to the card company filled out, it is estimated that the bookkeeping costs of the credit card system will average \$.25 per charge slip, \$250 a month. The total monthly cost of credit cards will therefore be \$1,050.

If charge accounts are used for the credit expansion, the bookkeeping requirements will be somewhat greater since summary account records must be maintained. The bookkeeping costs are estimated at \$.40 per charge, \$400 a month. Some collection costs, including mailing statements, processing receipts, and hounding slow payers will be incurred, and these are estimated to be 1 percent of credit sales, \$200 a month. Because not all customers are able or willing to pay bills, an allowance for bad debts of 1 percent of credit sales, \$200 a month, must be made. To establish new credit accounts it will be necessary to perform some minimal credit investigation, costing \$1 per new account. There will be some start-up costs, and some continuing costs of credit investigation since new accounts will continue to be opened in the future. If the number of new accounts is assumed to be at a rate of 100 per month, the monthly credit investigation costs will be \$100.

The total monthly costs of the charge account system exclusive of the carrying costs of the accounts receivable will be \$900, which is a savings of \$150 over the monthly costs of the credit card system. Under the charge account arrangement FCP must carry some accounts receivable, however. If the accounts receivable balance averages one month's sales, FCP must maintain an investment of \$20,000 in accounts receivable.

To get the monthly savings of \$150, an annual savings of \$1,800, the investment of \$20,000 must be made. FCP's return on this investment can be calculated as

$$\frac{\$1{,}800}{\$20{,}000} = 9\%$$

The return of 9 percent should be compared to FCP's cost of funds to make the final determination as to which credit system would be best. If FCP must pay more than 9 percent for funds or if it has other investments available that will yield more than 9 percent, the credit card system is preferred over the charge account system.[1]

The example demonstrates a basic procedure for analysis of business problems where an act will require an investment in assets, but will reduce costs or increase profits. The summary measure of the act's benefits can be expressed in terms of a return on investment. That return must then be further compared to other alternatives, including the situation where the business must raise additional funds by borrowing or increasing owners' equity. The size of the required investment in proportion to the other assets may also be a crucial figure, as shown in the next example.

For retailers selling durable goods such as furniture or appliances, and automobiles, other alternatives to open account charges exist. Normally the customer requires a much longer time period, one to three years, for payment, so installment financing arrangements with explicit payment of interest are necessary. Typically these installment sales contracts call for the customer to make a down payment of between 20 and 40 percent of the sales price, with the remainder to be paid over a 12 month or longer time period. The interest rate charged ranges from 10 to 20 percent per year.

If the retailer does not wish to carry his installment paper, an arrangement can usually be made to sell (discount) the installment contract to a local bank or finance company. The sale may be made on a non-recourse basis, where the paper purchaser cannot come back to the retailer for uncollectible amounts, or on a recourse basis where the retailer has a contingent liability for the contract balance. Repossession of the merchandise if the customer does not conform to the contract provisions is usually the responsibility of the retailer in furniture and appliance sales, but the installment finance company or bank bears this responsibility in automobile sales.

The decision to sell the installment contracts can be based upon the size of investment in the receivables and the foregone interest revenues associated with the sale. A high-volume appliance dealer may find it difficult to carry his own installment paper because of the size of the investment. The retailer may have a total investment (equity) in his business of $100,000 and generate annual sales of $1,000,000, for example. If those sales are all installment with an average length of payment of 18 months, the average balance of installment receivables would be about $750,000. The retailer in this case would probably have to sell his installment contracts because of the sheer size of investment required.

If the retailer sells the contracts it might be at a price in excess of the principal amount, so his foregone interest earnings would be less than the contract interest rate. If the contract rate were 18 percent, the price paid the retailer might be such that the bank or finance company expects to gross 14 percent if the payments are made in full on time. The retailer then would be foregoing an interest return of 14 percent by selling the contracts. If the sale is made and the buyer assumes the record-keeping function, the retailer can save some bookkeeping and collection costs. When the sale is on a non-recourse basis the retailer will save some bad debt expense as well. These cost savings must be netted against the foregone interest earnings in deriving the net effects of the contract sale.

Available Alternatives in Credit to Business Customers

Some alternatives to open account credit for business customers are available to the selling corporation. The corporation can arrange for the factoring of receivables, the sale of the receivables, to a specialist financial institution. The sale of receivables would probably only be feasible if the collection period is long enough, and the average size of receivables is large. The buying financial institution will charge a fee to the seller which is established to include some amount for the costs of servicing (bookkeeping) the accounts, and an amount that is an imputed interest charge for the time for which the institution has its funds tied up in the receivables. The sale may be on a non-recourse basis where the institution bears the risk of bad debts, or on a recourse basis. The fee charged by the institution is adjusted to cover all the expenses involved plus a profit for the institution, so the cost of eliminating receivables by factoring is likely to be quite high.

Another alternative is to pledge receivables for short-term loans. The corporation still holds the receivables but its investment is offset to some extent by the loan obtained. Again the cost is likely to be relatively high compared to the cost of other financing sources. Both factoring and pledging of receivables are considered as sources of short-term financing, and are discussed in more detail in a later chapter on financing sources.

In some equipment sales transactions, the selling corporation has the alternative of "carrying the customers' paper" or arranging outside financing for the purchase. The arranging of financing is intended to facilitate the sales effort, but may develop into a source of income to the corporation.

Because the equipment financing is not strictly short-term, but extends over a one- to five-year period, for example, the financing contract will include an explicit interest payment. Rather than engage directly in the financing business, many equipment manufacturers have found it feasible to organize sales financing subsidiary corporations or leasing subsidiaries. In this fashion the activities of the parent corporation can be kept directed at the manufacturing and selling activities. It is also sometimes easier to arrange financing through a specialist subsidiary.

The Payment Period as a Credit Policy

One result of a carefully planned credit policy is the establishment of a payment period. In dealing with wholesale customers, other business firms, it may be assumed that invoices will be paid on the last possible date, the due date of the invoice.

If a cash discount is given for prompt payment, such as in terms like 2/10, n/30, customers should choose to pay the invoice on the tenth day to obtain the 2 percent discount rather than wait until the thirtieth day and pay the net (stated) amount of the invoice. The implied interest charge in these terms is so high—2 percent for an additional 20 days of credit is approximately a 36 percent annual rate—that any rational, or nonbankrupt company should be unwilling to pay so much for the additional credit.

Some other cash discount terms may not result in so clear-cut a decision for these business customers. If the terms were 1/15, n/45, for example, the 1 percent discount for the additional 30 days is approximately a 12 percent annual rate. At this level probably some customers would pay at 15 days but others would wait the full 45 days.

When a cash discount is to be offered, therefore, both the size of the discount and the net due date periods are important in predicting customer response to those terms.

Even if no cash discount is offered the due date of invoices, the expected payment period, will have some effect on the sales level, the payment time lag, and the resulting accounts receivable balance—therefore on the corporation's investment in assets and net income. To illustrate the results consider the following numerical example.

Suppose ABC Corporation has had an established credit policy of n/30 on invoices, and sales have been running at a level of $1,000,000 a month. Assuming that all customers are credit customers and each pays on the last possible date, ABC's accounts receivable balance would also average $1,000,000.

Now in an effort to increase sales the invoice terms are changed to n/45 for all customers. If sales increase to $1,100,000 a month, the average accounts receivable will go to $1,650,000. The n/45 terms are applied not only to the increase in sales of $100,000 a month, but to the base sales of $1,000,000 as well. To gain the $100,000 per month increase in sales an additional investment of $550,000 is necessary for accounts receivable.

To support the higher sales level added investments in other assets may be necessary. If ABC's inventory levels are proportional to sales levels, the 10 percent increase in sales will require a 10 percent increase in inventories. To the extent that inventories are financed by accounts payable this net increase in asset investment may be less than the increase in inventories. Suppose ABC has a policy of maintaining inventories equal to 60 percent (at cost) of one month's sales, and ABC's accounts payable balance equals two-thirds of the inventory. The sales increase of $100,000 a month will require an increase in inventories of $60,000, but this is offset by an increase in accounts payable of $40,000, so the net investment increase is $20,000.

Besides the changes in accounts receivable, inventories, and accounts payable other asset investments may be necessary to support the higher sales level. If the product sold is manufactured by ABC and it was operating at full capacity before, additional manufacturing capacity would be necessary. For the numerical example of ABC Corporation no additional investments beyond the $550,000 increase in accounts receivable and the $20,000 inventory-accounts payable net increase will be assumed. The net investment required as a result of the liberalization of credit terms is therefore $570,000.

Presumably the $100,000 per month increase in sales will increase the net income of ABC. If variable costs due to sales (cost of goods sold, wages and commissions, and other operating costs) are 85 percent of sales, for example, the change in net income will be $15,000 a month, or $180,000 a year. The return on the $570,000 investment is

$$\frac{\$180,000}{\$570,000} = 31.6\%$$

To determine that the change in terms is desirable, the 31.6 percent return should be compared to the cost to ABC of the funds that will be required for the added $570,000. If ABC pays less than 31.6 percent (before taxes) for capital, the liberalization of invoice terms is desirable.

The example demonstrates some of the difficulty in evaluation of the payment period problem of credit policy. As a minimum the planner must know when the payment period is modified:

1. The change in sales.
2. The change in accounts receivable average balances.
3. The change in inventories and accounts payable.
4. The change in investment in other assets.
5. The variable costs due to sales.
6. The cost of funds for the corporation's investment in assets.

The Acceptance Standard for Accounts as a Credit Policy

Another facet of the credit policy of the corporation is the standards used in determining which customers should be granted credit. Those standards might be loosened in an effort to increase sales, but the ramifications of the loosening should be explored thoroughly before such a step is taken.

The loosening of account acceptance standards is likely to result in an increase in bad debt losses and an increase in collection costs for slow payers. The amounts of these two costs will have to be estimated to make a systematic determination of a credit policy possible.

If customers with less than perfect credit-worthiness are added through the loosening of standards, some of their payments will take longer than the stated invoice period. Of those accounts that go beyond the stated period a portion will be paid late, another portion may require specific collection efforts, and still another portion may be written off as uncollectible.

Suppose ABC Corporation is considering adding a group of credit customers that would add sales of $100,000 a month if they are allowed credit. Based on ABC's credit manager's past experiences the collection record to be based on n/30 invoice terms with this group is:

80% ($80,000) collected in full at end of 30-day period;
10% ($10,000) collected in full at end of 45-day period with no additional collection costs;
8% ($8,000) collected in full at end of 60-day period by incurring $2,000 additional collection costs; and
2% ($2,000) uncollectible (bad debt expense) at end of 60-day period even after incurring $1,000 additional collection costs.

This estimate of collections assumes an optimum collection procedure, including reminder and warning letters for the 31st through the 46th days, and then either the services of a collection agency or legal fees for the accounts over 46 days old.

The collections estimate can be used to judge the credit standards proposal in a similar fashion to that used in the preceding section for the payment period. To begin with the increase in average accounts receivable would be

$$\$80{,}000 + 1.5\,(\$10{,}000) + 2\,(\$10{,}000) = \$115{,}000$$

The $80,000 is outstanding for one month, the $10,000 for one and a half months, and the final $10,000 for two months before being collected or deemed uncollectible. The collection period for the base $1,000,000 of sales is unchanged with the addition of these new customers, so the net increase in accounts receivable is $115,000.

To support the higher level of sales, inventories are increased by $60,000, offset by an increase in accounts payable of $40,000. The net increase is therefore $20,000, making a total increase in asset investment by ABC of $135,000.

Using the figures previously estimated for ABC's variable costs due to sales of 85 percent, the increase in profits before the collection and bad debt expenses would be $15,000 a month. From the $15,000 must be subtracted the $3,000 collection expense and the $2,000 bad debt expense to derive a net increase in profits of $10,000 a month—$120,000 a year.

The return on investment is therefore

$$\frac{\$120{,}000}{\$135{,}000} = 88.8\%$$

before taxes. If ABC's cost of funds is less than 88.8 percent the credit standards should be lowered.

The example demonstrates the minimum amount of information necessary to evaluate a change in acceptance standards for new credit accounts. For a fixed change in those standards the analyst must know:

1. The change in sales.
2. The collection schedule of the new accounts including a time distribution and the percentage of bad debts.
3. The collection costs for slow payers.
4. The change in inventories and accounts payable.
5. The change in investment in other assets.
6. The variable costs due to sales.
7. The cost of funds for the corporation's investment in assets.

Besides the credit period and the acceptance standards for new accounts the other aspects of credit policy could be reviewed in a similar fashion. Those other aspects include the determination of the size and period of cash discounts, the administration of individual accounts, and the procedures followed for collection of late and delinquent accounts. The estimation of data, such as the collection experience for the new accounts of ABC above, is likely to be the hardest part of the analyst's task.

Summary

Accounts receivable management can be facilitated by the use of planning in establishing credit policies. If credit terms are changed the result will be both a change in the profits of the corporation and a change in the required investment in assets. The liberalization of credit terms can therefore be analyzed as an investment alternative where some rate of return is expected on the investment in assets.

The amount of investment required for the liberalization will be the sum of the increase in accounts receivable average balances, the increase in inventories necessary to support the higher sales level offset to some extent by an increase in accounts payable and other accrued liabilities, and the increase in plant and equipment that may be necessary. The change in profits results from netting additional costs against the increase in sales revenue. Those additional costs include the cost of merchandise sold, collection costs for receivables, and bad debt expenses.

The rate of return computed can then be compared to the other alternatives open to the corporation. If the liberalization of credit terms will result in a return on investment of 12 percent, and the corporation has other investments available that yield 15 percent, the liberalization should probably be rejected.[2] The cost of funds to the corporation will establish a floor for the acceptance of an investment project. If the corporation's cost of funds (in later chapters called its "cost of capital") is 10 percent, then no proposal with return less than 10 percent should be accepted.

The management of an existing credit policy was only briefly discussed in this chapter. The techniques are usually presented under the general topic title of "Credits and Collections," and the reader interested in this specialized area should pursue his research in textbooks, pamphlets, and periodicals catalogued under this general category.

Notes

[1] The return on investment measure will be further refined in Chapter 5, where the "internal rate of return" measure will be substituted. Under certain assumptions the internal rate of return will be identical to return on investment as used in the current chapter.

[2] Differing degrees of risk must also be taken into account in the comparison. A systematic method of measuring and comparing risk characteristics is explored in Chapter 7.

Chapter 3 Questions

1. When the general purpose credit card was considered as an alternative to open account credit for a retailer, the implicit assumption was made that credit standards would be the same for the credit customer so that no change in the volume of credit sales would result. Do credit card companies have the same standards for card issuance as granters of open account retail credit?

2. A related question to number 1 in the assumption of equal sales volume is the universality of credit card ownership. Are all the customers of a given retail establishment likely to possess an acceptable credit card?
3. Since credit policy is a part of the selling function, can breakeven analysis be used to derive the optimum policy—one that maximizes profits or return on investment?
4. What legal recourse is available to the retailer when credit customers are slow in paying their accounts?
5. What legal recourse is available to a wholesaler when business customers are delinquent in payment of accounts?
6. Does the dissemination of information through credit reporting services constitute an invasion of privacy or do business firms have the right to know a new credit customer's previous bill payment record?
7. In the numerical examples a collection cost for slow paying accounts was assumed. A common arrangement for very late accounts is the use of a specialized collection agency whose services may be obtained on a contingent basis. What are the goodwill implications of the corporation allowing the collection agency complete control over the methods of collection used?
8. In any credit system one of the costs most likely to be ignored is the record-keeping cost. How much does it cost to record a credit sale from the initial sale through the collection of payment? Is this figure likely to be a fixed amount per sale, not varying by the size of the sale? If so does this provide a partial explanation of why retail credit is more expensive than credit to business customers?
9. Is the cost to the seller of providing credit facilities likely to be included in the price of the merchandise? If it is, would it be worthwhile for a cash customer to bargain for a discount on the usual price?

Chapter 3 Problems

1. The terms 1/10, n/30 implicitly define a rate of interest for the extra 20 days of credit. What is that rate expressed as an annual percentage rate (assume 360 days in the year)?
2. If ACB Corp.'s standards for acceptance of new credit accounts are lowered an additional $100,000 per month sales will come from the new customers. For the new customers the collection experience is expected to be:

80% collected at end of one month
15% collected at end of two months
5% uncollectible

No special collection expenses are anticipated, and the corporation's gross margin on sales is 10 percent. If no additional investment in inventories or other assets other than the added accounts receivable are necessary, what is the anticipated return on investment from the loosening of account acceptance standards?
3. ACB (refer to problem 2) has another option to increase sales by $100,000 per month. Instead of adding new accounts, the terms on the old accounts can be lengthened, allowing all credit customers two

old accounts can be lengthened, allowing all credit customers two month's credit instead of one month. If this change is made monthly sales will go to $600,000 from $500,000. Since this increase comes entirely from existing customers there should be no "slow payers," and no bad debt expense. Assuming no increase in expenses other than cost of goods sold, 90 percent of sales, and no increase in inventory or other asset investment other than accounts receivable, what is ACB's return on investment for this credit policy loosening?

4. (Refer to problem 3.) Suppose the extension of the payment period by ACB results in some customers' getting into financial difficulties so that 6 percent of all customers' accounts go delinquent. Of those delinquent accounts two-thirds are collected at the end of the third month, and one-third are uncollectible. In addition extra collection activities in the credit department add $1,000 a month to expenses. Now what is ACB's return on investment?

5. A retailer has a choice between open account credit and use of a bank-issued credit card. If open account credit is used the average payment period will be one month, and bookkeeping, bad debt, and collection expenses will total 3 percent of credit sales. If the bank credit card is used there will be no investment in accounts receivable, the bookkeeping costs will be ½ percent of credit sales, and the credit card issuer will charge the retailer a 4 percent fee.

   a. Express the open account–credit card choice as a return on investment.
   b. If the retailer must borrow funds to carry the accounts receivable at an annual interest rate of 10 percent, should the retailer choose open account credit or the credit card arrangement?

6. Suppose a wholesaler offers his customers a choice among:

   1. A 1 percent discount for paying for merchandise 20 days *in advance* of delivery;
   2. Paying list price on C.O.D. payment terms;
   3. 40 days credit with a surcharge of 2 percent on list price.

   What are the implied interest rates from a comparison of

   a. (1) and (2).
   b. (2) and (3).
   c. (1) and (3).

Chapter 3 References

Bartels, Robert. *Credit Management,* New York: Ronald Press, 1967.

Benishay, Haskel. "Managerial Control of Accounts Receivable–A Deterministic Approach." *Journal of Accounting Research*, Spring 1965.

Bierman, Harold, Jr. *Financial Policy Decisions.* New York: Macmillan, 1970.

Chatterjee, Samprit, and Barcun, Seymour. "A Non-Parametric Approach to Credit Screening." *Journal of the American Statistical Association,* March 1970.

D'Agostino, R. S. "Accounts Receivable Loans–Worthless Collateral." *Journal of Commercial Bank Lending,* March 1970.

Greer, Carl C. "A Benefit-Cost Model for Credit Decisions." *Journal of Finance,* March 1967.

Johnson, Robert W. "More Scope for Credit Managers." *Harvard Business Review,* November-December 1961.

Levy, Ferdinand K. "An Application of Heuristic Problem Solving to Accounts Receivable Management." *Management Science,* February 1966.

Manger, Charles C. "Yardstick for Cost of Investment in Accounts Receivable." *Credit and Financial Management,* June 1967.

Mao, James C. T. *Quantitative Analysis of Financial Decisions.* New York: Macmillan, 1969.

Myers, James H., and Forgy, Edward W. "The Development of Numerical Credit Evaluation Systems." *Journal of the American Statistical Association,* September 1963.

Smith, Paul F. "Measuring Risk on Consumer Installment Credit." *Management Science,* November 1964.

Soldofsky, Robert M. "A Model for Accounts Receivable Management." *N. A. A. Bulletin,* January 1966.

Wrightsman, Dwayne. "Optimal Credit Terms for Accounts Receivable." *Quarterly Review of Economics and Business,* Summer 1969.

4 INVENTORY MANAGEMENT

The third major component of current assets for the typical corporation is inventory. Inventories may include raw materials, work in process, and finished goods for the manufacturing concern, and would consist mainly of merchandise held for resale for a merchandising concern. Stocks of office supplies, parts for repair of machines, and the like are not usually included within the definition of inventories. Inventories here are physical goods held for the purpose of eventual sale.

Total inventories make up about one-third of total current assets for the typical nonfinancial corporation in the United States according to statistics collected by the federal government. At the end of the third quarter of 1969, for example, the total current assets of nonfinancial corporations were \$536.8 billion and total inventories were \$178.7 billion.[1] Because these figures are totals for all nonfinancial corporations there should be no implication that

$$\text{inventories} = 1/3 \text{ current assets}$$

is a "norm," or goal that the managers of an individual corporation should strive for.

Instead it is the purpose of this chapter to develop techniques to determine an optimum inventory policy for a corporation. The inventory policy should include an average order size and frequency of inventory acquisition, and a safety stock or buffer stock size.

To determine the inventory policy systematically the problem is broken into two stages. In the first stage the optimum order size for a batch acquisition-continuous requirements inventory flow-through will be calculated on the assumption that requirements per unit of time are certain. In the second stage the requirements per unit of time are allowed to be a random variable, and the optimum safety stock is computed.

In the first stage the total costs attributable to the inventory ordering policy are minimized, and since the variables used are continuous and certain, the technique of optimization uses simple differential calculus. In the second stage the criterion used is based upon minimizing the expected total cost due to the safety stock level. In this second stage inventory requirements will be assumed to follow a fairly simple statistical distribution so that the computations of the expected total costs will be relatively easy. In the appendix to this chapter a special statistical distribution applicable for some retail inventories will be demonstrated.

The General Characteristics of Inventories

It is desirable to study the models for inventory management because certain costs are incurred through holding (or not holding) inventories. If a manufacturing corporation does not maintain an inventory of raw materials, inputs to its production process, but depended on shipments from a supplier, any time delay in receipt of the raw materials could prove very expensive because a production process would have to be slowed up or shut down. If excessive amounts of raw material inventories are held, the carrying costs would be higher than necessary. Carrying costs include allowances for storage, obsolescence or deterioration, and some cost allocated on the basis that the corporation has funds invested in the inventory.

There are two main reasons that a raw material inventory may be held by a manufacturing corporation. First it may be physically impossible to match the rate of acquisition of the raw materials to the rate of use. Normally materials are acquired in batches, quantities received at discrete points in time, but the utilization may be continuous in the manufacturing process. In this case an inventory will naturally result. Second, the rate of receipt and the rate of use of raw materials may not be forecast exactly, so some inventory may be maintained as a precautionary balance to guard against shortages.

The manufacturing corporation will have some work in process inventory because the manufacturing process is not instantaneous. The size of the work in process inventory will vary as the amount produced in a unit of time changes, and according to the type of manufacturing operations. No attempt will be made here to develop an optimum production design, so the work in process inventory will be accepted as a fixed quantity.

The manufacturing corporation will presumably maintain a finished goods inventory for much the same reasons as the raw material inventory. It may not be economical for the manufacturer to attempt to match exactly the production rate with the sales rate of the finished good. If the manufacturing operation is by "job lots" rather than a continuous production process, the output is in batches, the lots are finished at discrete points in time. Unless the production is strictly to order, where the goods are not started until the customer's order is received, some discrepancy will exist between the production line output and sale to customers.

In the pure merchandising corporation no manufacturing of goods is performed, but the corporation buys finished goods from a supplier and sells those goods to a customer. The usual pattern will be batch acquisition with a continuous outflow of the merchandise. If inventory must be obtained in discrete lots it is unlikely that the acquisition time pattern can be matched exactly to the requirements time pattern of customers. Some inventory will necessarily result.

Inflow-Outflow Patterns and the Resulting Inventory Balance

Four simple cases can be distinguished for the inflow-outflow time patterns:

1. Inflow batched, outflow batched.
2. Inflow continuous, outflow continuous.
3. Inflow continuous, outflow batched.
4. Inflow batched, outflow continuous.

In each case where the flow is continuous a constant rate of flow per unit of time will be assumed.

For the first case where inventory is acquired in batches and disposed of (used) in batches, if the timing of the batches are different but the size of batches the same, the inventory balance over time can be shown

Figure 4.1
Batch Inflow–Batch Outflow, Unmatched Times

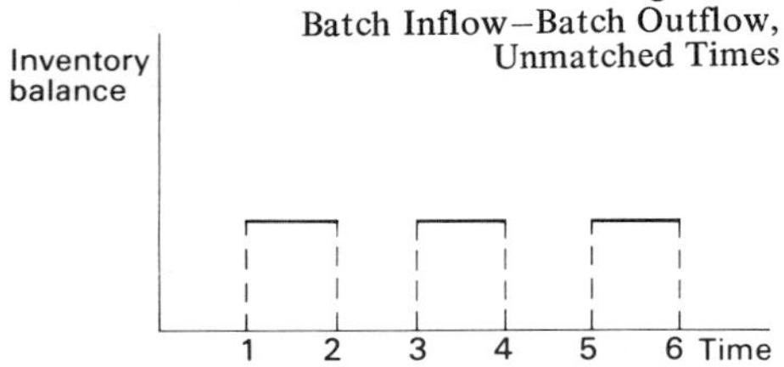

Figure 4.2
Batch Inflow–Batch Outflow, Matched Times

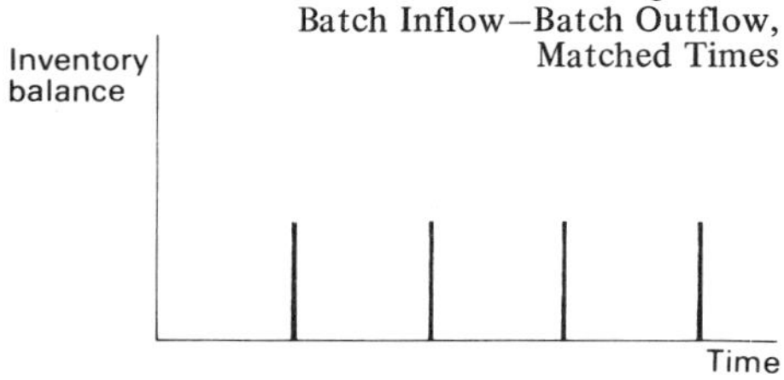

Figure 4.3
Continuous Inflow–Continuous Outflow, Matched Rates

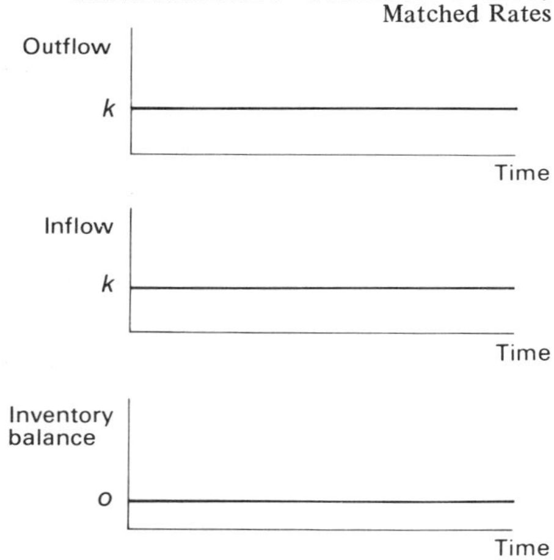

Figure 4.4
Continuous Inflow, Batch Outflow

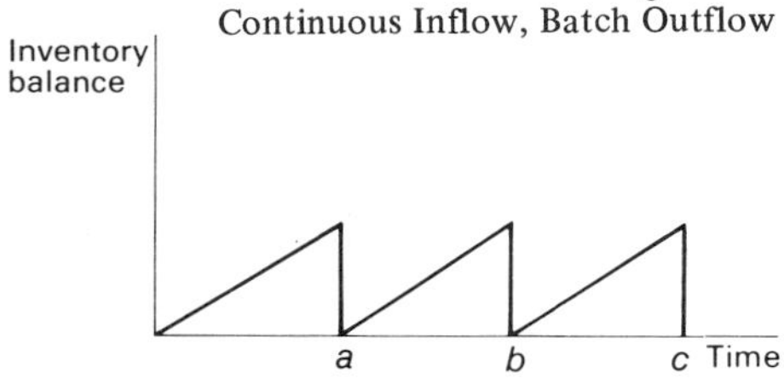

graphically as in Figure 4.1. At time 1 a batch is received, at time 2 a batch is disposed of, at time 3 a batch is received, and so forth. Between the disposal of a batch and the receipt of a new batch, for example between time points 2 and 3, the inventory balance is zero because the size of the batches in and out is the same.

The inventory balance shown in Figure 4.1 is not optimized, however, because a shift of the timing of batches can be made to reduce the average inventory. If the batches are received at the same time point that the batches go out, as in Figure 4.2, the average inventory balance can be reduced to zero. The optimal design for the first inflow-outflow pattern is therefore to match the batches, and reduce the average inventory to zero. This result can be attained without any further analysis, so this pattern will not be carried forward to the following section where the inventory order size and timing under certainty is optimized.

In the second case where inflow and outflow are both continuous over time the assumption of a constant rate of flow per unit of time makes optimization easy again. If the rate of outflow is k units per day, for example, the inventory acquisition policy can be adjusted so that the rate of inflow is also k units per day, and the corporation will maintain a zero inventory balance again. This matching of rates is shown in Figure 4.3. Since the inventory balance at any time is the cumulative inflow minus the cumulative outflow the balance is zero for every time point.

The third pattern, inflow continuous and outflow batched, shows a time pattern of inventory balance that is shown in Figure 4.4. In this case the batch outflows are assumed to be the same size each time, and equally spaced over time. The outflows occur at times a, b, c, and so forth in the diagram, and the inflows at a continuous rate over the entire time span. If the rate of inflow is set at the correct level the buildup of inventory during the time segments such as a to b is just sufficient to meet the batch outflow at time b.

The corporation's managers have control in an inventory framework only over the procurement of inventory, not over its disposal. Therefore in the pattern shown in Figure 4.4 the size and timing of the batch outflows must be taken as a given environment. As a result the only inventory policy practicable is to choose a rate of inflow of inventory sufficient to meet the required outflows. Unless the management is willing to suffer an out-of-stock event or schedule an excess of inventory no other course of action is possible.

Only in the fourth case, batched inflow and continuous outflow, will inventory policy be challenging enough to investigate through a cost minimization optimization. If the continuous outflow is at a constant rate, and equal sized and time-spaced inflow batches are used, the time pattern of inventory balances will look like that of Figure 4.5.

In Figure 4.5 the outflow of inventory is at the rate of 500 units per unit of time. The inventory policy here is to acquire 100 units in each batch, so it is necessary to acquire inventory 5 times per unit of time. The first batch is acquired at time 0, and inventory at time 0 is therefore 100 units. The inventory flows out at a constant rate, 500 units per unit of time, so the inventory is just exhausted when the next batch arrives at time 0.2.

One of the results of this inventory policy will be to establish an average inventory balance. That average for Figure 4.5 is one-half the order size, or 50 units.

A different inventory policy could have been chosen to meet the requirements of 500 units per unit of time. In Figure 4.6 inventory is acquired 10 times per unit of time with a batch size of 50 units. The revision drops the average inventory level to 25 units. The more frequent the inventory orders, the smaller the average inventory will be. At some point of frequency of orders, or of order size, there may be an optimum. The determination of the optimum ordering policy will involve balancing the cost of ordering against the carrying cost of the average inventory.

Figure 4.5
Batch Inflow–Continuous Outflow, First Policy

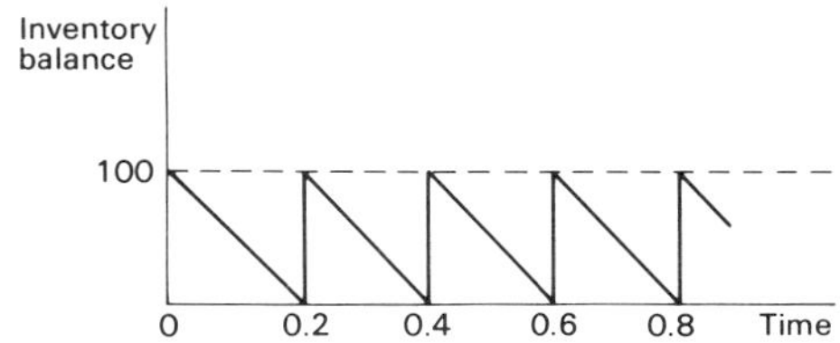

The Economic Order Quantity Model

The procedures for establishing an inventory policy in the case of batch inflow-continuous outflow where requirements are at a fixed rate over time are standard enough to have acquired a name, the "economic order quantity" (EOQ) model. In the EOQ model two costs are defined as functions of the order (batch) quantity, and then the order quantity is found that minimizes the sum of those two costs.

Figure 4.6
Batch Inflow–Continuous Outflow, Second Policy

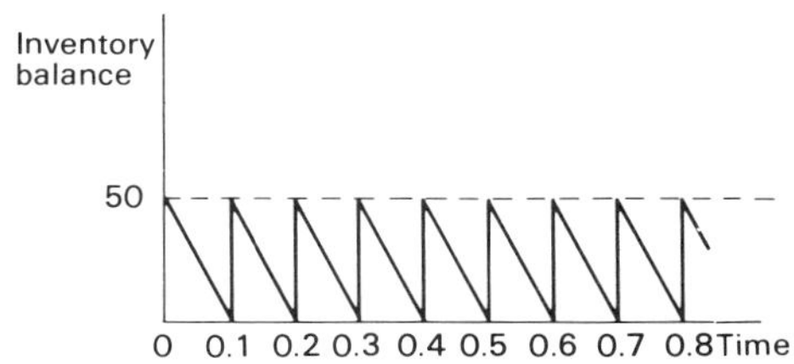

The first cost here is the carrying cost of inventory. That cost will vary directly (by assumption) with the average inventory level. One of the carrying cost components will necessarily be the cost of storing that inventory quantity. For example, storage might cost \$1 per unit of inventory per unit of time.

Another type of carrying cost is an obsolescence or deterioration charge if the goods in question have physical characteristics such that age will reduce the goods' value. To construct a numerical example suppose the obsolescence charge is \$.50 per unit of inventory per unit of time.

The third component of carrying costs is an imputed interest cost to allow for the corporation's investment of funds in the inventory. This interest cost may be significant in size. Suppose, for example, that the unit of time is a year, the value of a unit of inventory is \$10, and the corporation must pay 9 percent interest on borrowed money. To carry a unit in inventory for a year would therefore cost the corporation \$.90 in interest (before adjustment for corporate income taxes).

If the three components, storage, obsolescence, and imputed interest, are added together, the carrying cost of a unit of inventory for a unit of time is \$2.40 in the example. The \$2.40 can be multiplied by the average inventory balance to yield a total inventory carrying cost for a particular inventory policy. If the average inventory were 50 units, as in Figure 4.5's policy, then the total inventory carrying costs for a unit of time would be \$120.

The second cost defined in the EOQ model is the order cost. Presumably each time an order for new inventory is placed some cost is incurred which varies only by number of orders placed, not by size of order. For a manufacturing corporation's raw material inventory or the merchandising corporation's merchandise inventory, the order cost would be something like the estimated costs of processing the paperwork for a purchase order, receipt-of-merchandise verification, and the paperwork for payment of the invoice costs. For the manufacturing corporation's finished goods inventory the order cost could be interpreted as the set-up cost of a production batch. In the numerical example a cost of $6 per order is assumed.

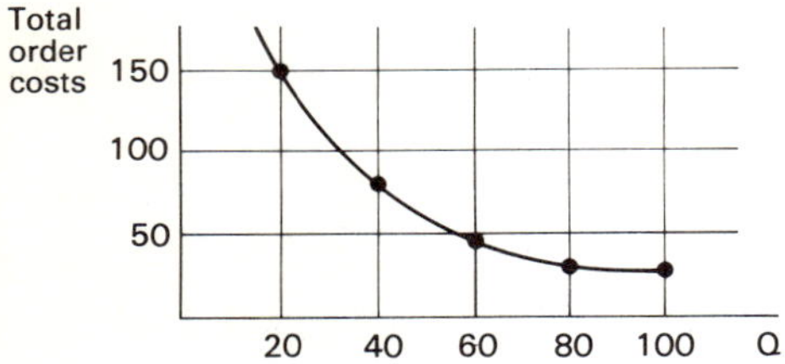

Figure 4.7
Total Order Costs as a Function of Order Quantity

Both costs will vary as the inventory order size and frequency vary. If Q is the order quantity, and the outflow (requirements) per unit of time are 500, then the number of orders per unit of time is $500/Q$. The total order costs per unit of time then are

$$\$6 \left[\frac{500}{Q}\right]$$

This cost is plotted against Q in Figure 4.7.

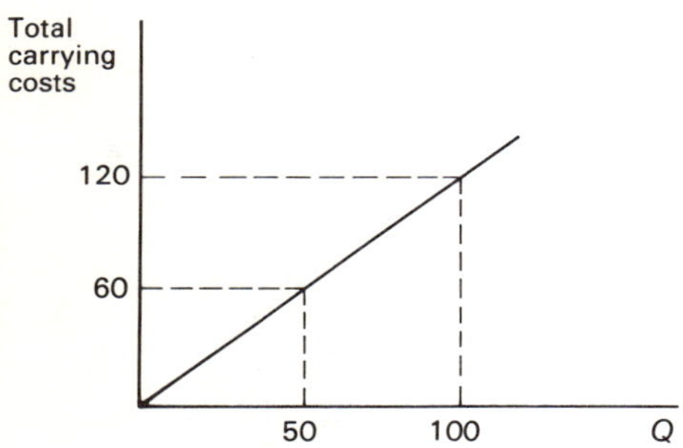

Figure 4.8
Total Carrying Costs as a Function of Order Quantity

The average inventory quantity will be $Q/2$, as was developed in connection with Figures 4.5 and 4.6. Because the carrying costs per unit of inventory per unit of time are $2.40, the total carrying costs as a function of the order quantity are

$$\$2.40 \left[\frac{Q}{2}\right]$$

This cost function is plotted in Figure 4.8.

Total inventory cost is the sum of the order cost and the carrying cost

$$\$6 \left[\frac{500}{Q}\right] + \$2.40 \left[\frac{Q}{2}\right]$$

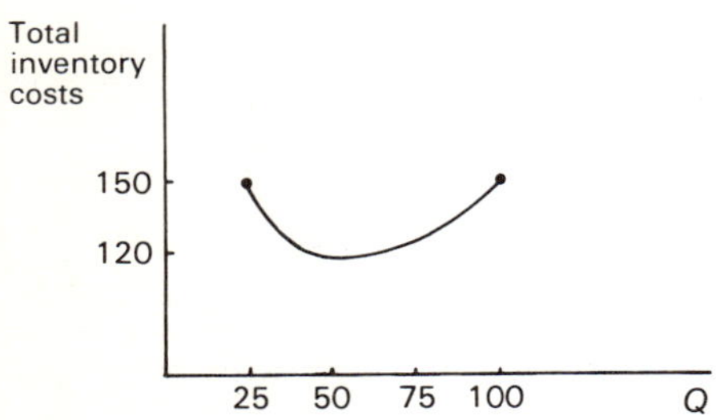

Figure 4.9
Total Inventory Costs as a Function of Order Quantity

The total inventory costs are plotted against the order quantity in Figure 4.9.

The optimum order size, the "economic order quantity," can be determined from Figure 4.9 to be 50 units. A Q of 50 results in the lowest total inventory cost of $120.

To generalize the results of the example a symbolic notation should now be defined for each of the quantities in the model. Suppose R is used for the total requirements per unit of time, b for the order cost per order, and c for the carrying cost of a unit of inventory per unit of time. Then the total inventory cost, T, can be expressed in general form as

$$T = b \left[\frac{R}{Q}\right] + c \left[\frac{Q}{2}\right]$$

For the numerical example

$$T = \$6\ [\frac{500}{Q}] + \$2.40\ [\frac{Q}{2}]$$

To minimize T with respect to Q, to derive a formula for the optimum value of Q, Q^*, the total cost function is (1) differentiated with respect to Q, (2) the derivative is set equal to zero, and (3) that equation is solved for Q:[2]

(1) $$\frac{dT}{dQ} = -b\ [\frac{R}{Q^2}] + \frac{c}{2}$$

(2) $$0 = -b\ [\frac{R}{Q^2}] + \frac{c}{2}$$

(3) $$Q^* = \sqrt{\frac{2\,b\,R}{c}}$$

The optimum order quantity can be solved directly from the results of the third step by substituting the appropriate values in the right side of the equation:

$$Q^* = \sqrt{\frac{2\,(\$6)\,(500)}{\$2.40}} = 50$$

The optimum inventory policy at this stage can be expressed in terms of the order size Q (=50), or in terms of the number of orders per unit of time, R/Q (=10).

The Assumptions of the EOQ Model and Possible Modifications

The assumptions built into the EOQ model may not fit reality, and therefore a more complicated model may be required before practical application is made. The complications may come from the elimination of the use of a constant rate of inventory outflow, or from a modification of the simple cost function forms derived.

Because the outflow of goods is at a constant rate the average inventory balance was the simple expression $Q/2$. The constant rate of outflow also allowed the equal spacing over time of order points without a further demonstration that equal spacing and equal-sized orders are optimum. If the rate of outflow is made a function of time, as for example could be done if inventory utilization had a known seasonal pattern, the average inventory balance over an inventory cycle (the time from receipt of one order until the receipt of the next order) is no longer $Q/2$, but a more complicated mathematical expression. It also may be true that equal order sizes are not optimum.

The function describing the total carrying costs of inventory was a constant, c, times the average inventory level, $Q/2$. A constant carrying cost per unit (per unit of time) may be reasonable as a first approximation, but cost functions in reality may be more complicated.

The order cost may not be a fixed amount per order, b, so the total order cost would be more complicated than $b(R/Q)$. Particularly when the inventory is a finished goods inventory for a manufacturing corporation, the order cost, here the set-up costs of the job-lot production run, will not always be constant for each order.

Rather than pursue these types of modifications any further here,[3] the modification that will be made to the model in the next section is to consider the requirements (outflow) during an inventory cycle as a random variable, and therefore introduce the safety stock as an additional problem in inventory management.

Determination of the Optimum Safety Stock

The inventory cycle length is determined by the results of an EOQ computation, and it must be decided if it is worthwhile to keep a safety stock, and if so, how large the safety stock should be. The problem of a safety stock arises because it is not possible to assume always that the rate of outflow will be constant during the inventory cycle, that the total outflow will be equal to the economic order quantity.

Figure 4.10
Random Outflow During an Inventory Cycle

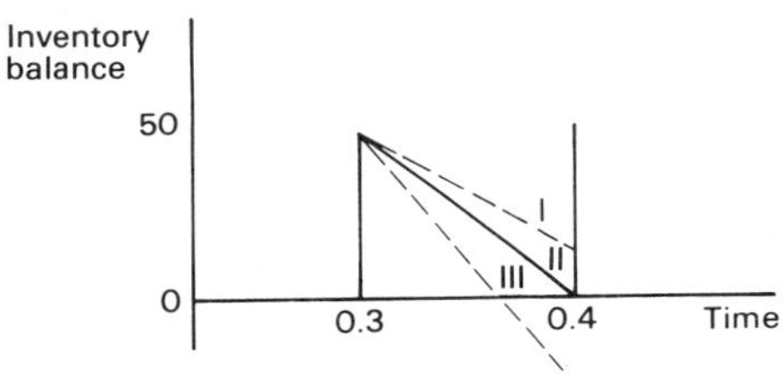

Some possible outflows during an inventory cycle for the example used above are shown graphically in Figure 4.10. During the inventory cycle from time point 0.3 to time point 0.4 the outflow could amount to 40 units, represented by the dashed line I; to 50 units, represented by the solid line II; or to 60 units, represented by the dashed line III. Since the inventory cycle length here is 0.1 of a unit of time, line I corresponds to a *rate of outflow* of 400 units per unit of time, line II to a rate of 500, and line III to a rate of 600. Line II represents the outcome of the inventory balance if the outflow occurs exactly at the rate used in establishing the EOQ of 50. Lines I and III represent two other possible requirement outcomes.

If requirements are less than the amount stocked, line I, some cost of carrying the excess inventory is incurred. The costs when requirements are greater than the amount stocked, line III, are harder to define. For finished goods inventories it is obvious that if the corporation has stocked only 50 units but 60 could have been sold some customers are going to be disappointed. Those customers may not defer their purchases until following periods, and their degrees of dissatisfaction may be such that they would shift their business to other corporations permanently. If the inventory is a raw material inventory, being out-of-stock will interrupt the production process, causing additional expenses and other ramifications. The proper safety stock inventory policy will minimize costs due to being overstocked or out of stock.

In building a model to determine the optimum safety stock level, it will be assumed that the corporation can replenish the safety stock at the next order point. In the example of Figure 4.10 a safety stock of 10 units might be used. At time point 0.3 the inventory balance would start at 60 units, the sum of the regular order size of 50 units and the safety stock of 10 units. Then if requirements during the period were 40 units, an overstock condition would result during the period, and an order of 40 units at time point 0.4 would be sufficient to bring the beginning inventory balance for the following period up to 60 units. If requirements were 50 units during the 0.3-0.4 time period, the order at time point 0.4 would be 50 units. If requirements during the period were 60 units, the regular inventory and the safety stock quantity would be depleted, so the order size at time point 0.4 would have to be 60 units to reestablish the safety stock and the regular inventory quantities.

The safety stock level to be determined can be defined in terms of the inventory cycle period, then, instead of any longer period of time. The proper level of safety stock will minimize the expected total of overstock costs and out-of-stock costs.

The term "expected total" is used in the statistical sense of expected value, the mean or average value. To derive an expected value it will be necessary to know the probability distribution of the random variable. The probability distribution here is the distribution of inventory requirements during the inventory cycle, and from this distribution it will be possible to derive the distribution of specific costs due to a certain safety stock level.

Suppose the distribution of inventory requirements during the cycle consists of the discrete points listed in Table 4.1. (This distribution is artificially constructed so that the expected requirement is 50 units. At a later point this coincidence of the expected value of 50 and the order size of 50 units will be investigated.)

TABLE 4.1
Distribution of Inventory Requirements, First Example

Requirements	Probability
40	0.3
50	0.5
60	0.1
70	0.1

To this distribution must be added some assumed cost values to construct the numerical example. Suppose that excessive inventory costs $.24 per inventory cycle for the carrying costs of storage, obsolescence, and imputed interest. The cost of being out of stock, the "badwill" from dissatisfied customers and the foregone gross profits if this is a finished goods inventory, or the cost of delaying production if the inventory is raw materials, is $1 per unit.

For a safety stock of 10 units, which means a total beginning inventory balance for the inventory cycle of 60 units, the conditional costs of Table 4.2 would be derived.

TABLE 4.2
Costs for a Safety Stock of 10 Units

Requirements	Inventory available	Excess inventory	Deficient inventory	Overstock cost	Out-of-stock cost
40	60	20	0	$4.80	0
50	60	10	0	2.40	0
60	60	0	0	0	0
70	60	0	10	0	10.00

The expected total costs for the safety stock of 10 units using the probabilities of Table 4.1 is

$$0.3\ (\$4.80) + 0.5\ (\$2.40) + 0.1\ (0) + 0.1\ (\$10.00) = \$3.64$$

For a safety stock of 20 units the conditional costs of Table 4.3 would be derived.

TABLE 4.3
Costs for a Safety Stock of 20 Units

Requirements	Inventory available	Excess inventory	Deficient inventory	Overstock cost	Out-of-stock cost
40	70	30	0	$7.20	0
50	70	20	0	4.80	0
60	70	10	0	2.40	0
70	70	0	0	0	0

The expected total cost for this safety stock is

$$0.3\ (\$7.20) + 0.5\ (\$4.80) + 0.1\ (\$2.40) + 0.1\ (0) = \$4.80$$

The safety stock could be 0 units, giving the conditional costs of Table 4.4.

TABLE 4.4
Costs for a Safety Stock of 0 Units

Requirements	Inventory available	Excess inventory	Deficient inventory	Overstock cost	Out-of-stock cost
40	50	10	0	$2.40	0
50	50	0	0	0	0
60	50	0	10	0	10.00
70	50	0	20	0	20.00

The expected total cost for the safety stock of 0 units is

$$0.3\ (\$2.40) + 0.5\ (0) + 0.1\ (\$10.00) + 0.1\ (\$20.00) = \$3.72$$

For the three safety stock levels tried, the safety stock level of 10 units is best because it yields the lowest expected total cost.

Calculating the expected total cost for every possible safety stock will prove too cumbersome a method of solution, especially when more complicated problems with a continuous distribution of requirements are attempted. Instead, a marginal approach to investigate the effect of "adding one more unit" to the safety stock on expected total costs will facilitate determination of the optimum safety stock. (The reader will no doubt by now have noticed that this inventory model is very similar to the precautionary cash balances model of Chapter 2. Mathematically they are identical; they differ only in the definition of the costs. Rather than skip the steps to the solution formula, though, those steps are repeated again in this chapter in a slightly different format.)

In the example, a reasonable starting point is to consider adding one more unit to the safety stock, starting at a level of 0. If one unit is added (making the safety stock equal to one unit), according to the probability distribution 80 percent of the time that unit will remain unsold, causing \$.24 of overstock costs. The probability that unit will remain unsold is the probability that requirements will be less than 51 units, the sum of the probability of 40 units and the probability of 50 units. So whatever the expected total cost before that unit is added, the increase in expected total cost *due to added overstock costs* will be

$$0.8\ (\$.24) = \$.192$$

The addition of that marginal unit to the safety stock will reduce the out-of-stock cost by \$1 20 percent of the time because the probability of requirements being equal to or greater than 51 units is equal to the sum of the probability of 60 units and the probability of 70 units. The reduction in expected total costs *due to the reduction in out-of-stock costs* is therefore

$$0.2\ (\$1) = \$.20$$

Netting the overstock cost and out-of-stock costs together, taking care about the signs of the change, gives the net change in expected total costs due to the one unit change in the safety stock

$$0.8\ (\$.24) - 0.2\ (\$1) = \$.192 - \$.20 = -\$.008$$

This change of $-\$.008$ will hold for every unit added to the safety stock through the tenth unit, where total available inventory reaches 60 units. At that point the change in expected total costs changes values because the probabilities of overstocking and being out-of-stock change. For the 11th unit of the safety stock, the 61st unit in beginning inventory, the probability of that unit remaining unrequired, overstocked, is 90 percent (the sum of the probabilities of 40 units, 50 units, and 60 units). The probability of reducing the out-of-stock costs by \$1 becomes 10 percent. Therefore for the 11th unit added to the safety stock the change in expected total costs is

$$0.9\ (\$.24) - 0.1\ (\$1) = \$.116$$

Because that amount is positive the 11th unit should not be added to the safety stock. The optimum level of the safety stock is where the last unit added reduced the expected total costs and the next unit to be added would increase the expected total costs. For the numerical example that optimum level is 10 units for a total beginning inventory of 60 units.

It is time to develop a general symbolic notation to summarize what has been learned from the numerical example. Therefore let Y be the requirements in units for the inventory cycle, and X be the (total) beginning inventory. Y is a random variable with a known probability distribution. Here it will be assumed that Y assumes only integer values, so Y has a discrete distribution. The probability of a particular value of Y is $P(Y)$.

Because the carrying costs defined in an earlier section were for a different period of time it would not be appropriate to use the same notation (c) for the overstock cost per unit. Instead let the overstock cost per unit for the inventory cycle be the quantity a. The out-of-stock costs per unit are m.

Using the symbolic notation then, the change in expected total costs due to adding the xth unit to the total beginning inventory is

$$P(Y < X)a - P(Y \geqslant X)m$$

The expression $P(Y < X)$ can be stated verbally as "the probability that requirements are less than the beginning inventory," which is the probability that the Xth unit will remain in inventory and cause an overstock cost. The expression $P(Y \geqslant X)$ is "the probability that requirements will be greater than or equal to the beginning inventory," the probability that the Xth unit will reduce the out-of-stock costs.

The expression for the change in expected total costs can be used to state the optimum total beginning inventory, X^*. For requirements that assume only integer values the optimum total beginning inventory is defined as the value X^* that satisfies the two inequalities:

$$P(Y < X^*)a - P(Y \geqslant X^*)m < 0$$

and

$$P(Y < X^* + 1)a - P(Y \geqslant X^* + 1)m > 0$$

In the numerical example X^* is 60 units, which can be verified from the inequalities:

$$0.8\ (\$.24) - 0.2\ (\$1) < 0$$

and

$$0.9\ (\$.24) - 0.1\ (\$1) > 0$$

If Y is assumed to be a continuous random variable rather than being confined to integer values the definition of X^* can be expressed more succinctly. X^* is the value of X where the change in expected total costs is zero;

$$P(Y < X^*)a - P(Y \geqslant X^*)m = 0$$

For X less than X^* the expression is negative, meaning that expected total costs can be reduced by increasing X. For X greater than X^* the expression is positive, meaning that expected total costs are increased by increasing X.

Since

$$P(Y < X) + P(Y \geqslant X) = 1$$

the value $[1 - P(Y < X)]$ can be substituted for $P(Y \geq X)$ to derive a shorter expression for X^*:

$$P(Y < X^*)a - [1 - P(Y < X^*)]\, m = 0$$

or finally

$$P(Y < X^*) = \frac{m}{a + m}$$

Figure 4.11
Continuous Distribution of Requirements

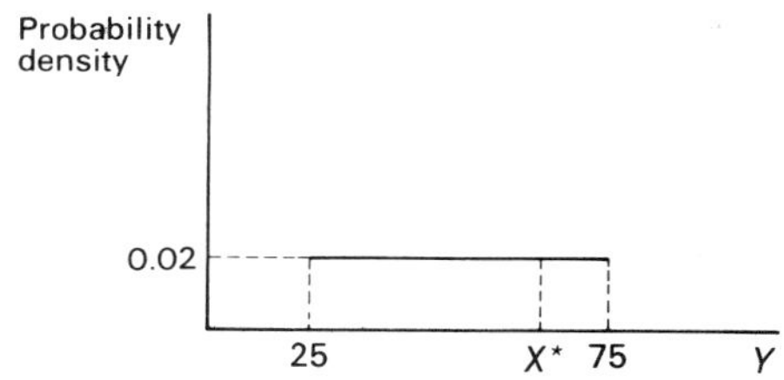

A change in the numerical example will be necessary to demonstrate a continuous Y Suppose the rectangular distribution of Y shown in Figure 4.11 is the actual distribution of requirements during the inventory cycle instead of the discrete values in Table 4.1. The probability must now be expressed in terms of ranges of values for Y. For example the probability of Y between 50 and 75 is 50 percent. In this distribution the lowest possible value of Y is 25 units, the highest possible value is 75 units, and the mean of Y is 50 units.

The costs do not need to be changed. The overstock cost per unit, a, is still \$.24, and the out-of-stock cost per unit, m, is \$1. X^* is chosen so that

$$P(Y < X^*) = \frac{\$1}{\$.24 + \$1} = 0.81$$

From Figure 4.11 it may be seen that X^* must be located so that the area under the curve to the left of X^* is 81 percent. An X^* of 66 will yield such a result. Therefore the optimum beginning inventory for the revised example is 66 units, a safety stock of 16 units.

Further examples of continuous distributions will not be presented in the chapter. Instead a special distribution, the Poisson distribution, is used for retail inventories in the appendix to the chapter. Under relatively simple assumptions that distribution seems to be appropriate where there is no theoretical limit to the amount required during an inventory cycle.

The Combination of EOQ and Safety Stock Models

The suggested sequence of planning inventories when inflow is instantaneous (in discrete batches) and outflow continuous, and that outflow is a random variable, is first to determine the EOQ, and then determine the safety stock for each inventory cycle. The formula for the EOQ is modified slightly to account for the fact that requirements for a unit of time, R, is a random variable. Now the expected requirements for a unit of time, $\bar{R}$, is used in the total order and carrying cost formula (making it an expected total cost formula):

$$T = b\frac{\bar{R}}{Q} + c\frac{Q}{2}$$

and the resulting equation for Q^*:

$$Q^* = \sqrt{\frac{2b\overline{R}}{c}}$$

Solution for the order size Q^* must now be interpreted as solving for the *average* order size. Sometimes more must be ordered to replenish the safety stock and sometimes less. What the solution for Q^* accomplishes is to establish the frequency of ordering, R/Q^* times per unit of time, and therefore the length of the inventory cycle, Q^*/R units of time.

In the second stage of the solution some amount of safety stock must be added to the average order size Q^* to get X^*, the total inventory available at the beginning of the inventory cycle. The amount X^* is chosen to minimize the expected total overstock cost and out-of-stock cost for the inventory cycle. If the requirements for the inventory cycle, Y, are expressed in terms of integer values, X^* is defined by the two inequalities

$$P(Y < X^*)a - P(Y \geqslant X^*)m < 0$$

$$P(Y < X^* + 1)a - P(Y \geqslant X^* + 1)m > 0$$

If Y is a continuous variable X^* is defined by the equation

$$P(Y < X^*) = \frac{m}{a + m}$$

Y is a random variable that is derived from R, the total requirements per unit of time. Y is the inventory requirement in the inventory cycle, while R is the requirement in the unit of time.

Some further stages could be added to the inventory management problem if it proved desirable to become increasingly realistic. For example the time from ordering of inventory to receipt of inventory is not always exact in real life situations. The receipt-order time lag could be used for a further modification of the models to choose the optimum order point in the time sequence of the inventory cycle. Fortunately there is a practical limit to the number of models to be considered in this chapter. That limit was reached after the safety stock model.

Notes

[1] *Economic Report of the President* (Washington, D.C.: U.S. Government Printing Office, 1970).

[2] The first derivative test is a necessary condition for a minimum. For a sufficient condition the second derivative must be positive, as is

$$\frac{d^2T}{dQ^2} = 2b\left[\frac{R}{Q^3}\right]$$

3. A survey of possible inventory management models, a review of the state of

the theoretical art at the date of its writing, can be found in Arthur F. Vienott, Jr., "The Status of Mathematical Inventory Theory," *Management Science*, July 1966.

APPENDIX TO CHAPTER 4

The Use of Exact Probability Distributions to Determine the Safety Stock

In certain cases it may be possible to derive exact probability distributions for use in determining the optimum inventory cycle beginning inventory. For the numerical example in Chapter 4 the distribution of requirements during the cycle was assumed to be a rectangular distribution as shown in Figure 4.11. Instead of that distribution a Poisson distribution can be used if the inventory requirements follow some simple assumptions.

In the usual description of the Poisson distribution the variable in question is the number of arrivals (as at the end of a waiting line) during a segment of time. Instead of the number of arrivals, here the variable will be the number of units of inventory required during a period of time. The assumptions that the Poisson distribution requires are: (1) arrivals connot be simultaneous; (2) the probability of an arrival is proportional to the length of the time segment; and (3) the probabilities of different items arriving are independent. For the inventory requirements application, the corresponding assumptions are: (1) two or more units cannot be required at the same instant of time; (2) the probability of requirements are proportional to the length of the time segment; and (3) the event that one unit is required is independent of another unit being required.

The third assumption will limit the application of the Poisson distribution to finished goods inventories where it can be assumed that the company's customers form an infinite population. The requirements for a raw materials inventory come from the production process, and obviously the nature of those requirements do not fit the third Poisson population definition.

The probability of Y arrivals in a period of time with length T is given by the formula

$$P(Y) = \frac{e^{-\alpha T} (\alpha T)^{Y}}{Y!}$$

(Fortunately this formula does not have to be evaluated by hand since tables for the Poisson distribution are available in statistics textbooks as well as other reference sources.) In the Poisson distribution the parameter aT (or λ) is the only quantity that needs to be known. T is of course the length of time, and α is the average number of occurrences in a unit of time.

For the inventory safety stock application, Y is the number of units required from inventory. Remember that "required" here means that the unit is requested, and if the unit is not available the requirement cannot be met. One of the corollaries of the third assumption above would therefore be that if an order for one unit is not filled that will not discourage other customers from ordering other units.

The quantity α is the expected requirements per unit of time, 500 in the numerical example of the chapter. The time segment T is the length of the inventory cycle, 0.1. Therefore for the example

$$\alpha T = 50$$

The probability used to determine the optimum level of beginning inventory, X^*, was defined by

$$P(Y < X^*) = \frac{m}{a + m}$$

In the numerical example m is \$1 and a is \$.24 so the probability is

$$P(Y < X^*) = 0.81$$

In using the Poisson distribution it is necessary to search the cumulative distribution table to find a number of occurrences, a value X^*, such that the probability of achieving an actual number of occurrences less than that is equal to 0.81.

Because the parameter αT for the example is so large, 50, it is possible to use the Normal distribution to approximate the Poisson distribution for the example solution. To use the Normal distribution it is necessary to know the mean of the distribution, $\overline{Y}$, and the standard deviation, σ_Y. In the Poisson distribution the mean of the distribution is αT and the standard deviation is $\sqrt{\alpha T}$. For the numerical example then,

$$\overline{Y} = 50$$

$$\sigma_Y \sqrt{50} = 7.1$$

Normal distribution tables are laid out in various ways, but one common way is to express values of the random variable in terms of a standardized variable Z where Z is given by the formula

$$Z = \frac{Y - \overline{Y}}{\sigma_Y}$$

The probabilities in the table may be expressed either as the probability of a value between $-\infty$ and Z, or as the probability of a value between 0 and Z. Assuming the first convention is followed for the table used the desired probability of 0.81 corresponds to a Z value of 0.865. In words, then, the solution to the optimum beginning inventory is a number of units 0.865 standard deviations above the mean requirements for the inventory cycle. A value of 56.145 units will be the optimum X^*. Of course this value of X^* should be rounded off to 56 units.

Using the Poisson distribution method therefore yields a safety stock of 6 units to be added to the average order quantity of 50 units so that

56 units will be available at the beginning of each inventory cycle. To attain this result it was not necessary to assume anything about the distribution of requirements during the inventory cycle other than that the expected requirements, αT, were 50, and that the requirements followed the three assumptions listed above.

Chapter 4 Questions

1. Identify all the components of the carrying costs of inventories.
2. How can the "bad-will" cost of disappointed customers when the corporation runs out of merchandise be estimated?
3. How realistic is the assumption of a fixed order cost per order in the EOQ model? What other costs that vary as the order size could be added to the order cost to make a more meaningful model?
4. To determine how sensitive the total costs in an EOQ model are to small variations in the order size compute the total costs for a Q 10 percent below the optimum size, for a Q 10 percent above the optimum, and compare those cost figures to the total cost with the optimum order size.
5. Besides the four combinations of batch-continuous flow inventory receipts and disbursements what other time paths of inventory balances are possible?
6. Some inventory is subject to physical spoilage, such as garden produce in a grocery store. If that sort of inventory is unusable after the end of an inventory cycle, an addition of spoilage costs must be made to the safety stock model. Will the mathematical form of the model be changed by this modification?
7. What forms of the statistical distribution of inventory requirements can be assumed for raw materials inventories where the requirement is dependent on the production line characteristics?
8. Can any of the models of this chapter be modified for use with a work-in-process inventory?
9. Justify the use of the criterion of minimizing expected total costs for the optimum safety stock model.

Chapter 4 Problems

1. Order costs are \$30 per order, carrying costs of inventory are \$.50 per unit per unit of time, and total requirements for a unit of time are 600 units.
   a. What should the average order size be?
   b. How frequently should orders be placed?
2. Suppose order costs vary with the size of the order, Q, as in this cost function:

$$\text{Order costs per order} = \$10 + \$0.2\,Q$$

and carrying cost per unit per unit of time are \$1. Total requirements for a unit of time are 400 units. What should the average order size be to minimize the total of order costs and carrying costs?
3. Suppose the corporation can get quantity discounts on merchandise

by varying the order size. The price of merchandise is expressed as a function of the order size Q:

$$\text{Price per unit} = \$4 + \frac{\$3}{Q}$$

Order costs are \$10 per order, carrying costs of inventory are \$1.50 per unit per unit of time, and requirements are 100 units per unit of time. Taking the variation in price of inventory into account as well as the order costs and carrying costs, determine the optimum order size Q^*.

4. Instead of a continuously variable price of merchandise, the supplier offers just two prices, \$5 a unit for orders of less than 12 units, or \$4 a unit for orders of 12 or more units. If order costs are still \$10 per order, carrying costs of inventory are \$1.50 per unit per unit of time, and requirements per unit of time are 100 units, what is the optimum order size?

5. Requirements for inventory during an inventory cycle follow this statistical distribution:

Requirements	**Probability**
30	0.3
50	0.5
70	0.2

a. Calculate expected requirements.

b. Suppose 55 units are stocked at the first of every inventory cycle, what percentage of the time will the corporation be able to meet requirements, and what percentage of the time will an overstock condition result?

c. Suppose out-of-stock costs are \$3 a unit, overstock costs are \$1.20 a unit, and the corporation stocks 50 units at the first of the inventory cycle. What is the expected total cost of this inventory policy?

d. Assume the same costs as in part c, but the beginning inventory balance is 30 units. Calculate the expected total cost of this inventory policy, and determine whether 30 units or 50 units is better for the corporation.

6. Requirements for inventory during an inventory cycle follow a uniform or rectangular distribution defined between the limits of 40 units and 100 units. The cost of being out-of-stock is \$5 per unit, and the carrying cost of excessive inventory is \$2 per unit per inventory cycle. How large should the inventory at the first of the cycle be to minimize expected total costs?

7. The distribution of requirements for inventory during a cycle follow a Poisson distribution with parameter $\alpha T = 12$. (α is the average requirement per unit of time, 240, and the length of the inventory cycle, T, is 0.05 units of time.) Out-of-stock costs are \$4 per unit, and the overstock cost is \$1 per unit. Find the optimum beginning inventory.

Chapter 4 References

Beranek, William. "Financial Implications of Lot-Size Inventory Models." *Management Science,* April 1967.

Buchan, Joseph, and Koenigsberg, Ernest. *Scientific Inventory Management.* Englewood Cliffs, N. J.: Prentice-Hall, 1963.

Buffa, Elwood S. *Production-Inventory Systems: Planning and Control.* Homewood, Ill.: Irwin, 1969.

Falkner, Charles A. "Optimal Ordering Policies for a Continuous Time, Deterministic Inventory Model." *Management Science,* July 1969.

Hadley, G., and Whitin, T. M. *Analysis of Inventory Systems.* Englewood Cliffs, N. J.: Prentice-Hall, 1963.

Herron, D. P. "Inventory Management for Minimum Cost." *Management Science,* December 1967.

Hillier, Frederick S., and Lieberman, Gerald J. *Introduction to Operations Research.* San Francisco, Calif.: Holden-Day, 1967.

Kaplan, Robert S. "Dynamic Inventory Model with Stochastic Lead Times." *Management Science,* March 1970.

Sargent, Robert, and Bradley, Hugh E. "Variable *S* Inventory Model." *Management Science,* July 1969.

Snyder, Arthur. "Principles of Inventory Management." *Financial Executive,* April 1964.

Stancill, James McN. *The Management of Working Capital.* Scranton, Penn.: International Textbook, 1971.

Vienott, Arthur F., Jr. "The Status of Mathematical Inventory Theory." *Management Science,* July 1966.

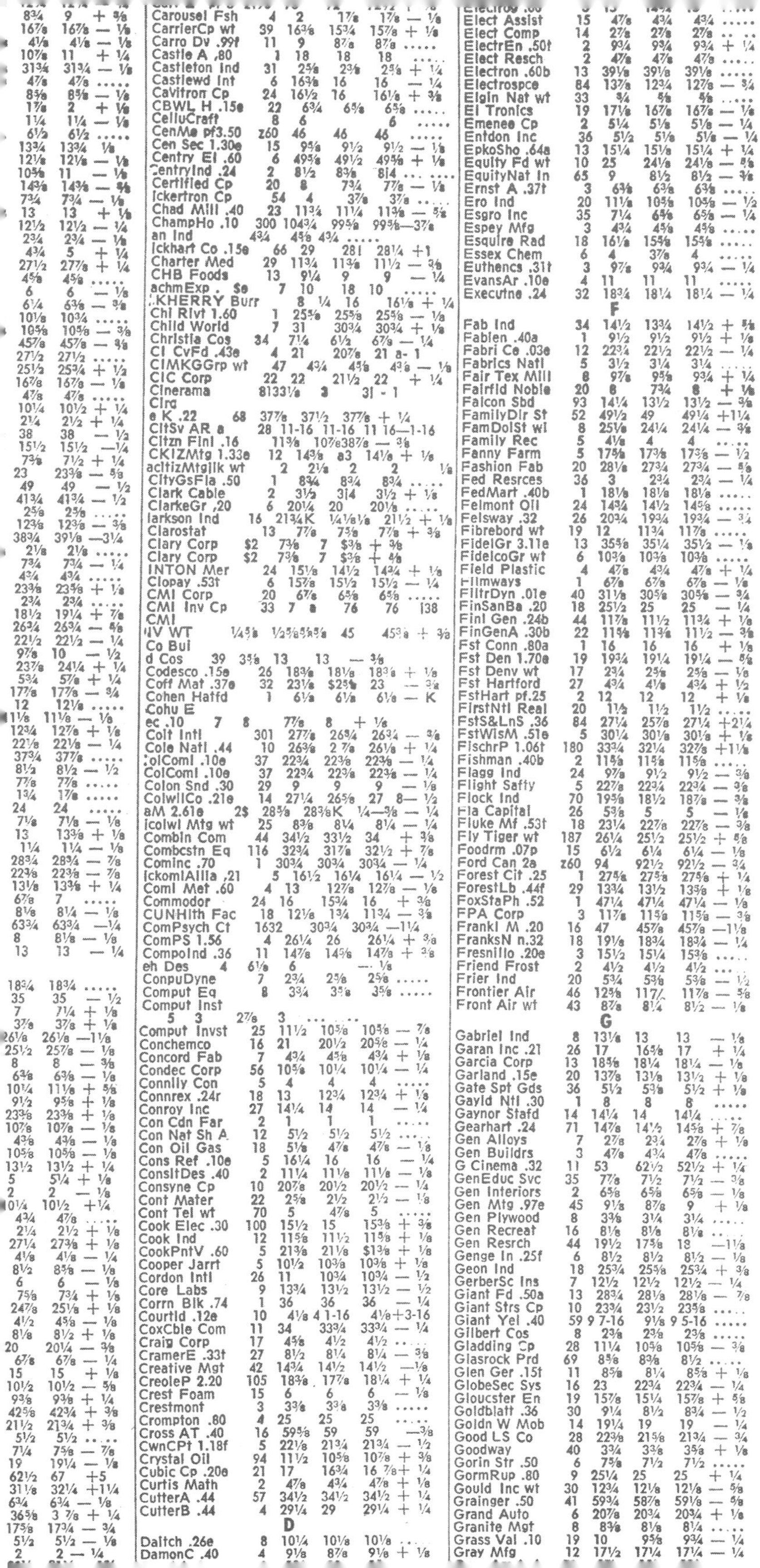

PART TWO

CAPITAL BUDGETING UNDER CERTAINTY

Capital budgeting is the process of selecting the corporation's investment projects. The available projects are likely to have a series of cash flows that are irregular over time so that the simple return on investment measures used in Part I are inadequate for general use. Instead, two new interrelated measures, the present value and the internal rate of return, are defined and used in the investment criteria of Part II.

Three basic decisions are described, the accept-reject decision for a single project, the ranking of two mutually exclusive investment projects, and the selection of an optimum set of investment projects to meet a fixed budget. To facilitate the choice in the third stage, an additive measure of a project's worth is desirable, leading to the adoption of the present value as the best measure to use in capital budgeting situations. The present value of the net cash flows of a project serves as the appraisal value for that project.

The capital budgeting procedures developed in Part II are based on the assumption of certainty regarding the cash flows of projects. These procedures will be modified in Part III to account for the uncertainty and possible statistical variation in cash flows.

Present values can be used for investment decisions other than the selection of new plant and equipment. The introduction of new products, the acquisitions of operating businesses, and the selection of a portfolio of securities are examples in which present values are used for decision. The common characteristics of these investments are that an initial cash outlay is made, to be followed by a series of cash inflows. If those cash flows can be estimated, a present value can be computed and used as the appraisal value of the investment.

Chapter 5 is primarily concerned with the interest compounding process and the definitions of terminal value, present value, and the internal rate of return. The capital budgeting criteria are analyzed in Chapter 6.

5

TERMINAL VALUE, PRESENT VALUE, AND APPRAISAL VALUE

In this chapter the computations of the commonly accepted measures used in evaluating investment projects are developed. Up to this point relatively simple investment decisions have been treated, in which the pattern of cash returns was regular and not subject to significant period-to-period fluctuation. Now the regularity assumption is dropped and a new set of techniques to account for such fluctuation must be developed.

First to be considered is the process of interest compounding. An amount of money subject to a compounding process grows to a larger amount due to the passage of time. A mathematical relationship, the compound interest formula, relates the amount entering the compounding process to the later amount, the terminal value, by using the per-period interest rate with a measure of time.

A reversal of the computation of terminal values leads to the computation of present values. The present value of a later amount is the amount which must be entered into the interest compounding process in order to yield the later sum of money. Terminal values and present values are therefore inverses of each other with respect to the interest compounding process.

Once the present value of a single amount is defined and illustrated, the computation is made of the total present value of a series of future cash amounts. The series of cash amounts received from an investment project are the benefits from the project, and the present value of the series is used as the appraisal value of the project.

A considerable portion of this chapter is devoted to analyzing the mathematical behavior of the present value as a function of the rate of interest chosen for its computation. Usually the present value is a decreasing function of the interest rate. One interest rate, the one that makes the present value of the cash inflows equal to the price of the project, is the "internal rate of return," or yield of the project. This measure is frequently used as the summary of an investment project's characteristics in a capital budgeting process, even though certain mathematical and theoretical difficulties are encountered with that use. The discussion of most of the difficulties with the internal rate of return as an investment criterion are postponed to Chapter 6, and this chapter will focus on the mechanics of the interest rate formulas, and the derivation of appraisal values for investment projects.

Compound Interest

The simplest example of interest compounding is encountered in bank savings accounts where automatic reinvestment of earned interest is assumed. An amount of money is deposited at the beginning of the process (time zero), and interest is computed and added to the account at the end of a period.

Suppose $100 is deposited at an annual interest rate of 5 percent. At the end of the first year the amount of interest earned is $5 which is added to the account balance to yield a total of $105. The second year interest is earned on the $105, amounting to $5.25. Therefore the balance of the account after interest is compounded at the end of the second year is \$110.25. The computation of the two later amounts can be summarized by these equations:

$$
\begin{aligned}
\$105 \quad &= \$100(1+0.05)\\
\$110.25 &= \$105(1+0.05)\\
&= \$100(1+0.05)\,(1+0.05) = \$100(1+0.05)^2
\end{aligned}
$$

The quantity (1+0.05) is called "the compound interest factor," and is the multiplier of the account balance at the beginning of a period to yield the account balance at the end of the period. The balance at the end of the second year can be computed directly from the initial deposit by applying the compound interest factor twice. The balance at the end of still later periods can be found in the same manner—multiply the initial deposit by the compound interest factor as many times as periods elapse. For example the account balance at the end of five years would be

$$\$100(1+0.05)^5 = \$127.60$$

The compound interest formula should be generalized by adopting a symbolic notation at this point. Suppose A_0 is used for the amount entered into the compounding process at the beginning (time zero), and A_n is the balance n periods later, at time n. If r is the symbol used for the per-period interest rate the compound interest formula can be expressed as:

$$A_n = A_0(1+r)^n \tag{5-1}$$

In the example above \$100 was used as A_0, 0.05 was the interest rate r, and the two account balances were \$105 as A_1, and \$110.25 as A_2.

To facilitate compound interest computations Table 1 at the end of the book can be used. In this table are presented the amount that \$1 would compound to by the end of a certain number of periods. To use the table look up the value of r to determine the column of the table, and the number of periods n determines the row. For example to find the value to which \$1 would compound at a rate of 10 percent for 5 periods, the entry in the tenth column and fifth row of Table 1 is 1.61051. This entry is

$$(1+r)^n = (1+0.10)^5$$

which is part of equation (5-1) above. To find the compound amount of \$20 multiply \$20 by 1.61051 to get \$32.21.

Interest compounding is a type of growth process where the growth or increase comes instantaneously at the end of the period. This type of compounding is called discrete compounding, as contrasted to continuous compounding. Continuous compounding where the growth in the amount of money occurs continually will be treated in the appendix to this chapter. Discrete compounding is used for nearly all financial transactions, so this form rather than continuous compounding will be used throughout this book. Continuous compounding applications are sometimes shown in theoretical financial models, but most applications are in the physical sciences.

The Present Value

In equation (5-1) two amounts of money are involved, A_0, an amount at time zero, and A_n, an amount dated n periods in the future at time n. A_0 is also called the "present value," and A_n, the "future value." It is desirable to be able to compute the present value from a known future value (with known time passage and interest rate as well). To compute the present value equation (5-1) is solved for A_0, deriving equation (5-2):

$$A_0 = \frac{A_n}{(1+r)^n} = A_n(1+r)^{-n} \tag{5-2}$$

The present value has several interpretations depending on the circumstances in which it is computed. To return to the bank account example above the \$100 present value is the amount that must be deposited at time zero to enable an account balance of \$110.25 at time two. Suppose an account balance of \$950 at the end of the fourth period is desired. If the interest rate earned is still 5 percent per period, the required deposit, the present value, can be computed using equation (5-2):

$$A_0 = \frac{\$950}{(1+0.05)^4} = \$781.54$$

If \$781.54 is deposited and left compounding at 5 percent for four periods, the amount available in the account at the end will be \$950.

Because the computation of present values by the direct evaluation of equation (5-2) is tedious, Table 2 at the back of the book is provided to shorten such calculations. Table 2 gives the present value of \$1 when calculated for different interest rates and different numbers of periods. The entry in the table is of the quantity $\frac{1}{(1+r)^n}$, where the value of r determines the column used and the value of n determines the row. These "present value factors" of Table 2 can be multiplied by the future value to yield the present value desired. For the example the present value factor $\frac{1}{(1+0.05)^4}$ is found by looking in the fifth column and the fourth row to find the factor's value, 0.82270. This factor is then multiplied by the future amount, \$950, to yield

$$\$950(0.82270) = \$781.54$$

The computation of a present value is thereby reduced to a single multiplication.

Sums of Present Values

The next step in the procedure is to consider sums of present values. In a typical investment project a series of future cash receipts rather than a single receipt is anticipated. The series of net cash flows received at various times in the future must first be estimated, a problem which will be deferred to Chapter 6. This set of cash inflows can be converted into a total present value to serve as an appraisal of the investment project's worth. The present value computation is a method of adjustment of the cash flows to a common base point in time—the present.

The common base point is necessary for meaningful addition of cash amounts. A dollar to be received two years from now does not have the same real value as a dollar to be received one year from now. It is always possible to invest money in some interest-bearing form, and if money is to be borrowed to buy an investment project, the interest rate on the loan must be taken into account. The choice of an appropriate interest rate for the present value computation will be discussed at a later point.

If a series of cash inflows

$$A_1, A_2, \ldots, A_n$$

is to be received from an investment project, each cash inflow can be converted into a present value by application of equation (5-2). The set of present values can then be added meaningfully to derive a total present value for the cash flow series. The formula for the sum of present values is

$$\sum_{j=1}^{j=n} \frac{A_j}{(1+r)^j} \qquad (5\text{-}3)$$

Suppose for example a project is evaluated that promises a cash inflow of $100 at the end of the first year, $60 at the end of the second year, and $120 at the end of the third year. This series of cash inflows can be summarized as

$$(100, 60, 120)$$

If an annual interest rate of 6 percent is appropriate for computing present values in this context the present value of this series can be calculated with equation (5-3):

$$\frac{100}{(1+0.06)^1} + \frac{60}{(1+0.06)^2} + \frac{120}{(1+0.06)^3} =$$

$$100(0.94340) + 60(0.89000) + 120(0.83962) =$$

$$94.34 + 53.40 + 100.75 = 248.49$$

The total present value of $248.49 has an interpretation as an equivalent amount which is worth exploring at this point. $248.49 is the amount that would have to be deposited in a 6 percent savings account to enable withdrawals to be made from the account of \$100 at the end of the first year, \$60 at the end of the second year, and \$120 at the end of the third year, leaving a zero balance in the account after the last withdrawal. Suppose the \$248.49 is considered as being split into its three parts, \$94.34, \$53.40, and \$100.75. The deposit of \$94.34 at time zero will grow to \$100 at the end of the first year—which is then withdrawn from the account. The deposit of \$53.40 at time zero will grow to \$60 by the end of the second year, allowing that withdrawal. The deposit of \$100.75 at time zero will increase to \$120 by time three, meeting the withdrawal requirement of that time. The present value of this investment project is then the equivalent amount that would have to be deposited in the savings account to match the cash inflows to be received from the project.

The Annuity Formula

In one case a short-cut formula may be substituted for equation (5-3). If the cash inflows are all the same amount, an annuity, then a shorter computation form may be used. When the symbol A is used for the constant amount that is received at the end of the period for n periods, the present value of the annuity is

$$A\left[\frac{(1+r)^n-1}{r(1+r)^n}\right] \tag{5-4}$$

Table 3 at the back of the book contains values of the factor

$$\frac{(1+r)^n-1}{r(1+r)^n}$$

The usual format is followed in this table, the value of r determines the column, and the value of n the row of the table.

For example suppose there is a project that yields a net cash inflow of \$100 at the end of each of four years, and the appropriate interest rate is 8 percent. The present value factor from Table 3, the entry in the eighth column and fourth row, is 3.31213. \$100 is multiplied by 3.31213 to derive the present value of this annuity of \$331.21.

The annuity formula, equation (5-4), is useful in several practical situations. The level payment for a series of years is typical of a variety of contractual arrangements. Installment loans, for example, call for a level payment to the lender, each payment including some interest and some repayment of principal. When evaluating corporate or government bonds the annual or quarterly interest payments comprise an annuity which is received by the holder until maturity of the security. Insurance companies frequently sell annuity contracts, where for paying a fixed sum at time zero an individual will be assured a per-period payment for the rest of his life. The length of life used in the computations is determined from longevity tables maintained by the company.

To illustrate the use of equation (5-4) and Table 3 in the case of an installment contract, take the example of an automobile purchase loan where $2,000 is to be repaid over an 18-month period by the borrower, with interest compounded monthly at a *per-month* interest rate of 1 percent. From Table 3 an annuity of $1 per month for 18 months at 1 percent per month has a present value of $16.39827. The question here is how many $1 amounts must be paid each month to amortize the $2,000 loan? If $2,000 is divided by the present value factor of 16.39827, the result $122.07 is the amount of monthly payment necessary (the size of the annuity) to exhaust the loan of $2,000 by the end of the 18th month. Actually specialized tables are used by sales finance companies to determine the monthly payments, saving some arithmetic.

Another special case of present value computation is found where the per-period payment (annuity) is not limited as to term, but continues forever. The payment of dividends on preferred stock is an example of such a case, barring any provisions for redemption or recall of the preferred stock. Suppose for example a company sells a preferred stock to an investor with a stated annual dividend of $5. The holder of that preferred stock expects to receive that annual dividend forever.

For a constant amount per period, A, received forever and evaluated at an interest rate r, the present value is

$$\frac{A}{r} \tag{5-5}$$

If the holder of the preferred stock paying $5 per year requires an interest rate or yield of 8 percent, the present value of that dividend stream would be

$$\frac{\$5}{0.08} = \$62.50$$

The preferred stock example is a case where the present value might be interpreted as an appropriate price to pay for a stream of income to be received by the purchaser. If the purchaser of the preferred stock requires a return of 8 percent he will achieve that return by paying $62.50 for that stock.

Present Value as a Function of the Rate of Interest

At this point it is desirable to consider the behavior of present values as the interest rate used in their computation is changed. As the rate of interest is increased the present value factors' values are reduced. This conclusion can be anticipated by perusal of the rows of Table 2. This can also be shown by considering the present value formula for a single sum, equation (5-2):

$$A_0 = \frac{A_n}{(1+r)^n}$$

Assuming A_n is a positive number and n is positive, if r is increased A_0, the present value, must decrease.

Suppose the present value of a series of cash inflows for varying interest rates is plotted to get an idea of the behavior of the present value. The cash inflows are 50 at the end of the first period, 80 at the end of the second period, and 100 at the end of the third period. The series of cash inflows is written in summary fashion as (50, 80, 100). The table below summarizes the present value of the series for the interest rates shown:

r	Present value
0	230.00
0.05	206.56
0.10	188.70
0.20	155.10
1.00	57.50

Figure 5.1
Present Value as a Function of the Interest Rate

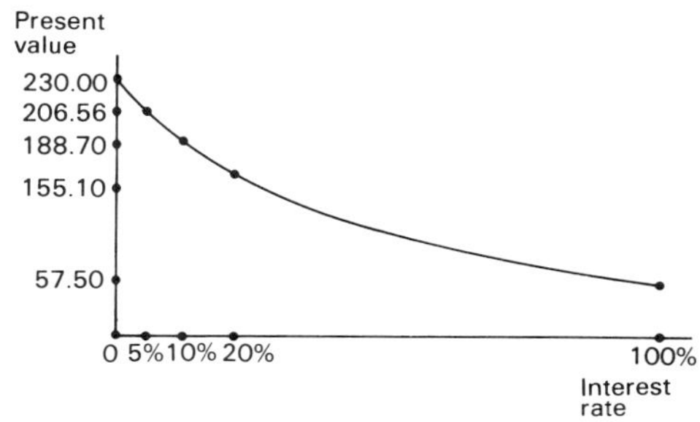

It can now be seen graphically that the present value of the series decreases as the interest rate is increased. The present value tends toward zero as the interest rate goes to infinity. At an interest rate of zero the present value is simply the sum of the cash flows.

The Internal Rate of Return

The present value of the series of cash inflows from investment projects has been computed so far for specified interest rates. For some interest rate the present value of those inflows will be equal to the price of the project. That rate of interest is the "internal rate of return" of the project.

The internal rate of return, or yield, of a project can be computed by adjusting the interest rate used in the present value computation until the equality is found. If the symbol P_0 is used for the price of the project at time zero the internal rate of return is the value of r that satisfies equation (5-6):

$$P_0 = \sum_{j=1}^{j=n} \frac{A_j}{(1+r)^j} \qquad (5\text{-}6)$$

The internal rate of return concept can be illustrated by an example with a predetermined internal rate of return. A project costing \$100 is expected to generate a net cash inflow of \$20 at the end of the first period, \$39 at the end of the second period, and \$66 at the end of the third period. The internal rate of return of this project is 10 percent. (Try evaluating equation (5-6) with these numbers to show that the equality is achieved.)

This project is equivalent to a savings account where interest is compounded at a rate of 10 percent. The account balances can be stepped through the periods, computing balances at each time point to illustrate this equivalency. The \$100 beginning balance grows to \$110 after interest is compounded at the end of the first period. A withdrawal of \$20 is made immediately after compounding, leaving a balance of \$90 to earn interest for the second period. After interest is compounded at the end of the second period, the account balance is \$99, from which \$39 is withdrawn. The balance after the second withdrawal is \$60, so after interest is compounded at the end of the third period the account balance is $66, which is then withdrawn leaving a zero balance in the account. The compounding-withdrawal procedure is summarized as:

End of period	1	2	3
Beginning balance	100	→ 90	→ 60
Interest earned	+10	+9	+6
Total	110	99	66
Withdrawal	−20	−39	−66
New balance	90	60	0

Notice that one of the essential characteristics that distinguishes an investment project from a savings account is that the withdrawals from the project are fixed and unalterable by the investor. This fixed size of the withdrawals will become very important when captial budgeting criteria are discussed.

To compute internal rates of return there is a choice of approximation methods. There is no direct solution for the rate in the general case, but the approximations can be made as exact as desired. The degree of exactness desirable will of course vary according to the use to which the internal rate of return is to be put, but for textbook examples the nearest tenth of a percent will be adequate.

To illustrate the approximation of the internal rate of return use the example of a project that costs $80 at time zero and has the net cash inflows (30, 20, 90). The first approximation method is called "the table method." In this method an arbitrary interest rate is chosen to start, the present value of the cash inflows for that rate is computed, the present value is compared with the price of the project, and then a new rate is tried based on the relative size of the present value and the price.

Suppose the first interest rate tried is 10 percent. Using the present value factors of Table 2 the present value is derived:

$$30(0.90909) + 20(0.82645) + 90(0.75131) = 111.42$$

This value is above the price of $80, so a higher interest rate should be used for the next approximation. The present value at an interest rate of 20 percent is

$$30(0.83333) + 20(0.69444) + 90(0.57870) = 90.97$$

This number is still larger than 80, so an interest rate of 30 percent is tried:

$$30(0.76923) + 20(0.59172) + 90(0.45517) = 75.88$$

This value is less than 80, so the internal rate of return is between 20 percent and 30 percent. For 25 percent:

$$30(0.80000) + 20(0.64000) + 90(0.51200) = 82.88$$

Since this is above 80 the next interest rate chosen should be higher than 25 percent. Suppose an increase of 1 percent is used, a rate of 26 percent:

$$30(0.79365) + 20(0.62988) + 90(0.49991) = 81.40$$

The rate is increased again to 27 percent:

$$30(0.78740) + 20(0.62000) + 90(0.48819) = 79.96$$

This present value is very close to 80, so the internal rate of return is slightly below 27 percent. Because the table only gives present values to whole percentages the next step must be to interpolate between the two values 26 percent and 27 percent. Even though the present value function is not linear in the interest rate a linear approximation should give sufficient accuracy for this small range.

The difference between the two present values is

$$81.40 - 79.96 = 1.44$$

The "true" present value is 80, which is 0.04 above 79.96. Therefore the internal rate of return is

$$27\% - \frac{0.04}{1.44}(1\%) = 26.97$$

Since internal rates of return are rounded to the nearest tenth of a percent the result is 27.0 percent.

The present value table method is not hard to use for simple problems with only a few cash flows given a desk calculator for the arithmetic. It does involve operator decision as to which interest rate to try next, so the method would be a little more difficult to adapt to computer solution.

A diagram will help to illustrate the steps used above in isolating the internal rate of return. If the values of the present value calculated for the various interest rates are plotted the convergence to the value of 80 can be seen in Figure 5.2. Unfortunately the diagram could not be drawn before the computation of the present values, but the location of the points illustrate the rule of progression to the next interest rate. So long as the present value was above 80 the interest rate was too low. When the present value was below 80 the interest rate was too high. The closer the present value was to 80 the closer was the interest rate to the internal rate of return.

Figure 5.2
Steps in Approximating the Internal Rate of Return

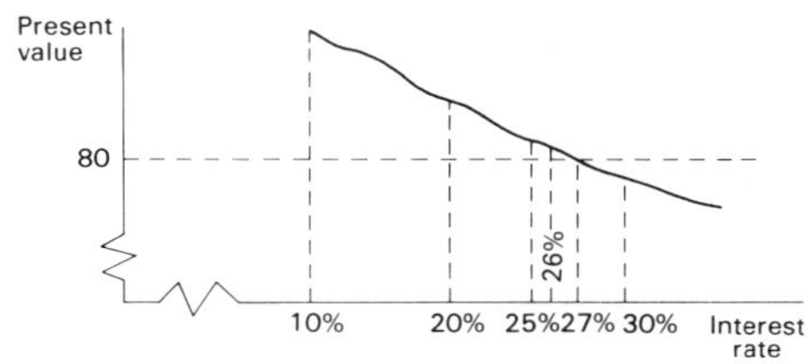

There are a variety of computer methods for approximation of the internal rate of return, one of which will be reviewed at this point. The procedure of finding the internal rate of return for a given series of cash flows is based on solution methods for a polynomial in a single variable.

Suppose equation (5-6) is rewritten as

$$0 = -P_0 + \sum_{j=1}^{j=n} A_j [\frac{1}{1+r}]^j \tag{5-7}$$

All the cash flows, the price P_0 and the cash inflows A_j, are known numbers. The expression is actually a polynomial in the present value $[1/1+r]$. If equation (5-7) is evaluated with the numbers from the last example the polynomial form is

$$0 = -80 + 30[\frac{1}{1+r}] + 20[\frac{1}{1+r}]^2 + 90[\frac{1}{1+r}]^3$$

If the symbolic substitution

$$X = [\frac{1}{1+r}]$$

is made the polynomial will be even more obvious:

$$0 = -80 + 30X + 20X^2 + 90X^3$$

In this example the degree of the polynomial is only three (the highest power of X is the third), but generally the polynomial is of the n-th degree. For second degree polynomials (the quadratic), third degree polynomials (the cubic), and fourth degree polynomials (the quartic) direct solution methods for the value of X and therefore of the internal rate of return exist. But for higher degree polynomials, investment projects that last longer than four periods, no direct method of solution exists. Instead an approximation method such as Newton's Method must be used to derive a numerical answer.

In Newton's Method a chain of successive approximations to the value of X is developed for the polynomial of the form

$$0 = f(X)$$

The rule to find the next approximation is

$$X_{i+1} = X_i - \frac{f(X_i)}{f'(X_i)}$$

An arbitrary approximation, X_1, is used for the first calculation, but the following approximation will involve the subtraction of the ratio of the polynomial to its derivative from the prior approximation.

The method will be more easily understood if the numerical example is used. The polynomial is

$$f(X) = -80 + 30X + 20X^2 + 90X^3$$

The derivative of the polynomial is

$$f'(X) = 30 + 40X + 270X^2$$

The formula for the next approximation will therefore be

$$X_{i+1} = X_i - \frac{-80 + 30X_i + 20X_i^2 + 90X_i^3}{30 + 40X_i + 270X_i^2}$$

Now all that is needed is a beginning approximation of X, X_1.

There is a special limitation of the permissible range of X in present values. If only positive internal rates of return are allowed the value of X must be between zero and one. For very low interest rates, for example r of zero, the value of X will be close to one. For very high interest rates the value of X will be close to zero. Therefore an X value outside the zero to one range corresponds to an inadmissible interest rate.

A beginning value of X to use in most circumstances is 0.8. For this value the interest rate is 25 percent:

$$0.8 = \frac{1}{1 + 0.25}$$

If that value is used as X^1 the second approximation using Newton's Method is

$$X_2 = 0.8 - \frac{-80 + 30(0.8) + 20(0.8)^2 + 90(0.8)^3}{30 + 40(0.8) + 270(0.8)^2} = 0.7873$$

For this value of X the value of r is 0.2702.

A third approximation should be made:

$$X_3 = 0.7873 - \frac{-80 + 30(0.7873) + 20(0.7873)^2 + 90(0.7873)}{30 + 40(0.7873) + 270(0.7873)^2} = 0.7876$$

For this value of X the value of r is 0.2697.

The series of approximations is terminated at this point because the internal rate of return to the nearest tenth of a percent is desired. The computations are limited by rounding operations as well.

In this simple example the Newton formula only had to be evaluated twice. The beginning approximation of 25 percent was close to the true value of 27.0 percent, but the method has a relatively rapid convergence anyway.

Newton's Method is more readily adaptable to computer usage than the present value table method because the steps to successive approximations are mechanical and do not depend on the calculator's intuitions. The Newton's Method is also practical for desk calculator solution if the number of time periods is not excessive. Several other methods of approximation of the internal rate of return have been successfully used, and may be available as library programs from a computer center.

Mathematical Problems With the Internal Rate of Return

A student of algebra may wonder why only one solution value is obtained for the internal rate of return. After all, there may be as many roots (solution values of X) as the degree of a polynomial. The answer to this lies partially in the restriction of the meaningful values of X defined in finance and partially in the signs of the cash flows that appear in equation (5-7).

First the range of X that is meaningful is limited to the zero to one interval. If r can assume only positive values, since

$$X = \frac{1}{1 + r}$$

then X's lowest possible value is zero, and X's highest possible value is one. If a value of X outside this interval is encountered in the solution process it is discarded.

If the cash inflows from the project are all positive then an application of Descartes' Rule of Signs to the polynomial of equation (5-7) will limit the number of positive solution values of X to one. The coefficients of the polynomial in equation (5-7) have only one sign change.

If one of the cash inflows from the project is negative, multiple internal rates of return may be encountered. The most commonly encountered case of negative cash inflows (a net cash outlay) is where major renovation expenditures must be made to an asset in the middle of its life. The period during which that renovation is made may not generate enough cash inflow to offset that expenditure. Whether multiple solutions for the internal rate of return are possible depends on the relative size of the periods' cash flows.[1] The possibility of multiple solutions in some cases does limit the use of the internal rate of return as a capital budgeting criterion.

Net Present Value

In putting the polynomial in the discount factor into the standard form for the Newton approximation above the price of the project was subtracted from the present value of the cash inflows in equation (5-7). This difference is called the "net present value," and is sometimes used as the summary measure of benefits from the project.

The net present value of a project can be looked on as a surplus or excess, or as some sort of "profit." Suppose for example an investment project is considered that requires an outlay of \$100 and will return a net cash inflow of \$50 at the end of the first period and \$120 at the end of the second period. If an interest rate of 10 percent is used in evaluating the cash inflows the present value is

$$50(0.90909) + 120(0.82645) = 144.63$$

If the price, \$100, is subtracted the net present value is \$44.63.

The use of the interest rate of 10 percent in a capital budgeting context infers that the required rate of return on investment projects is that rate of 10 percent. The example project has a higher internal rate of return than 10 percent since the net present value is positive at that rate. The value of $44.63 is a dollar measure of the excess over requirements.

If the project had cost $144.63 instead of $100 the internal rate of return would have been 10 percent, as can be seen by evaluating equation (5-6). The net present value can then be seen as an amount "saved" at time zero, which could be used to invest in other projects.

Net Terminal Value

A related amount to the net present value is the net terminal value of a project. The net terminal value is found by compounding all the dollar amounts to time n, the end of the project's life. The formula for the computation of the net terminal value of a project is

$$-P_0(1+r)^n + \sum_{j=1}^{j=n} A_j(1+r)^{n-j} \tag{5-8}$$

For the last example above the net terminal value is

$$-100(1+0.10)^2 + 50(1+0.10) + 120 = 54$$

This amount can sometimes be considered a "profit" in the usual sense of the word. Suppose the firm could invest in another project, say a bank account, that would pay a 10 percent per-period interest rate. If the firm invests in the example project instead it will be ahead by $54 by the end of time period two. Consider the two alternatives. If the firm simply puts its $100 into the bank account it will compound to a value of $121 by time two. However if it buys the example project it will have $50 at time one to put into the bank account, which will compound to $55 by time two. If the $55 is added to the $120 cash inflow at time two there is a total of $175 cash by time two. That amount of cash is $54 greater than if the firm had not bought the example project.

The net terminal value is a multiple of the net present value. If the net present value is multiplied by the factor $(1+r)^n$, the result will be the net terminal value. For the example

$$44.63(1+0.10)^2 = 54.00$$

The net present value of a project is the present value of the net terminal value.

The net terminal value could be used for the computation of the internal rate of return of an investment project, just as the net present value or present value of cash inflows was used. The interest rate that makes the net terminal value zero is the internal rate of return. The present value approach is preferred, however, because the degree of the computations is slightly less.

The net terminal value can be used interchangeably with the net present value as an appraisal value for an investment project in capital budgeting criteria. The usual convention in investment analysis is to use present values, however.

Before present value is defined as the appraisal value for an investment some time should be spent considering the choice of an interest rate to use in computations. The following three sections describe approaches to the selection of a value of r to use in the present value and terminal value computations.

r as the Cost of Borrowed Funds

One approach to the selection of an interest rate to use in computing the present value of a series of cash inflows is to identify the interest rate as the cost of borrowed funds to the investor. If the investor can borrow money in varying amounts for varying periods of time at a fixed interest rate of 5 percent, then 5 percent can be used as the rate for evaluation of investment projects.

When an investment project with a price of \$100 and projected net cash inflows of \$60 at the end of the first period and of \$55 at the end of the second period is analyzed using the interest rate of 5 percent, the present value of the cash inflows is

$$60(0.95238) + 55(0.90703) = 107.03$$

The price can be subtracted to yield a net present value of \$7.03. The interpretation of this \$7.03 is as a type of surplus.

If the investor borrowed \$107.03 instead of \$100 from the bank the cash inflows from the project would be sufficient to pay off the bank loan in full. That is, the payment of \$60 at time one and \$55 at time two would fully amortize a \$107.03 loan at a 5 percent interest rate. Thus if the investor actually borrowed \$107.03 there would be \$7.03 in excess of the price of the project which could be used for other purposes—such as the purchase of other projects.

A slightly different interpretation of the amount borrowed from the bank will yield the same type of surplus interpretation of the net present value \$7.03. Suppose the investor has previously borrowed from the bank at this interest rate for some other purposes, and now borrows an additional \$100 for this investment project. The cash inflows of \$60 and \$55 will pay off the \$100 loan, and \$7.03 principal amount of other loans. Obviously the higher the net present value of a project the more other loans can be repaid from the project, and the better off the investor will be.

When the investor is a corporation the interpretation of borrowing can be broadened somewhat from the bank loan example to include other sources of funds. A corporation raises funds not only from direct loans by financial institutions, but by selling securities such as bonds, preferred stock, common stock, and others. In every case the supplier of funds to the corporation expects some rate of return on his investment. Those rates of return to the supplier are the "costs of capital" to the issuing firm after appropriate adjustments are made for the tax-deductibility of interest payments. If the corporation selects investment projects that more than meet the required rates of return for capital suppliers there will be a surplus left over for the residual owners of the corporation, as shown in Chapter 1.

The net terminal value computed with a "borrowing" interest rate has an exact interpretation of profit, where profit is used in the ordinary meaning of the word. The net terminal value for the example project is

$$-100(1.10250) + 60(1.05000) + 55 = 7.75$$

The investor has $7.75 left over at the end of the second period after the loan and accumulated interest charges are repaid from the cash inflows of the project. The present value of the $7.75 profit is

$$7.75(0.90703) = 7.03$$

the net present value of the project.

r as the Internal Rate of Return on Alternate Investments

Another means of defining the appropriate interest rate to use in present value computations is to consider the opportunity costs of investing in this project as opposed to other available projects. If the investor's supplies of cash are limited the purchase of one project may mean that other projects must be rejected. The opportunity cost of accepting the project would then be the internal rate of return of the project foregone.

Some problems with considering alternate projects are the indivisibility of projects and the lack of control over the timing of the cash flows from a project. To avoid those problems a theoretical investment project alternate will be assumed where full control over amounts invested and withdrawn is held by the investor, and the internal rate of return will be the same. That is, any amount can be invested in the theoretical project where it will earn a fixed rate of return, and withdrawals can be made at any time as well. Suppose an example theoretical alternate with internal rate of return of 6 percent is used. If an actual investment project that requires a price of $100 and returns a net cash inflow of $70 at the end of the first period and of $60 at the end of the second period is evaluated, the present value of the cash inflows computed at the interest rate of 6 percent is

$$70(0.94340) + 60(0.89000) = 119.44$$

The net present value is $19.44.

If $119.44 were invested in the theoretical alternate, sufficient amounts would be generated within the alternate to allow withdrawals of $70 at the end of the first period and $60 at the end of the second period, leaving a zero balance in the alternate at the end of the process. The actual project requires a price of only $100 to allow the same withdrawals, therefore saving an outlay at time zero of the difference, $19.44. Again the net present value can be interpreted as a surplus.

Now as to the validity of assuming the theoretical alternate investment for a corporation, there are such alternates for a corporation that have freedom of investment and withdrawal of funds in every case—savings accounts and high grade short-term securities are examples. Unfortunately the price paid for such flexibility of investment and withdrawal is a lower rate of return. While interest rates do vary on those investment forms from time to time, the general average after-tax return has ranged from about 2 percent to 4 percent per year.

If the large firm with many investment projects starting every period is posited such a freedom of investment and withdrawal can be approached even with ordinary investment projects. If a corporation could buy 100 machines, each of which will earn an internal rate of return of 10 percent, then the firm could buy 71 if some funds could be diverted to another investment project. Divisibility of initial investment would be achieved in that situation. Freedom of withdrawal could be achieved in much the same way—in later years if more funds become available the purchase of machines could be increased.

When the net terminal value for the project is computed:

$$-100(1.12360) + 70(1.06000) + 60 = 21.84$$

the \$21.84 can be interpreted again as the profit from investing in the actual project rather than the theoretical alternate project. The \$100 outlay is diverted from the alternate where it would have compounded to \$112.36 by the end of the second period. The \$70 inflow at the end of the first period is invested in the theoretical alternate where it compounds to \$74.20 by the terminal time point. The net of these amounts defined at the terminal point is \$21.84.

The present value of \$21.84 is

$$21.84(0.89000) = 19.44$$

so the present value of the (later) profit from the actual project is \$19.44.

r Based on Time Preference for Money

A more theoretical approach to determination of an appropriate interest rate for present value calculation is to base that rate on an arbitrary measure that will approximate the investor's preference for money receipt over time. It is a generally accepted proposition in economic theory that an individual will be happier with a dollar the sooner it is received. This internal valuation mechanism of the individual may be simulated by appropriate present value computations.

Suppose the present value factors for an interest rate of 25 percent are considered as a sequence:

$$\left[\frac{1}{1 + 0.25}\right]^1 = 0.800$$

$$\left[\frac{1}{1+0.25}\right]^2 = 0.640$$

$$\left[\frac{1}{1+0.25}\right]^3 = 0.512$$

The present value of a dollar received one year from now is \$.80—only 80 percent as much as a dollar received at the present. The dollar received two years from now has a present value of \$.64, implying it is "worth" less than two-thirds of a present dollar.

The present value computation is a method of reducing the equivalent value of cash as its time date becomes more distant. The present value factor, a multiplier, becomes smaller as it is taken to a higher power, the time index.

An interest rate may be chosen that will reduce future cash flows in proportion to their value in the opinion of the investor. If the investor determines that a time period's passage will reduce the value of an incremental dollar to him by 20 percent, then the appropriate present value factor is 0.8, which is achieved with an interest rate of 25 percent. If the appropriate reduction is 10 percent the present value factor must have the value 0.9, and the required interest rate is 11.1 percent. The interest rate r can be chosen to value the time distribution of cash flows in accordance with the investor's acutal preferences, if those preferences can be measured.

A note of caution should be mentioned at this point. The use of present value factors in a present value equation treats all amounts of money received at a particular time point the same way. That is, using an interest rate of 25 percent will result in multiplying all amounts received at time one by the factor 0.8 no matter the size of the cash amount. It is probable that a cash inflow of \$1,000,000 is not one hundred times as valuable as an inflow of \$10,000 to an average investor. The present value computation does not take account of the diminishing marginal utility of money, just the time preference aspect of the cash flows. In Chapter 7 more attention will be paid to the concept of marginal utility of money.

A Single Value for Investment Decisions

To facilitate the investment decision it is desirable to summarize the projected cash inflows of a project into a single number. That number could be the project's internal rate of return, computed by the formula that uses all the cash inflows, time dated, and the price of the project—all the available information about the project. Another number that utilizes all the cash flows and their timing as well as an externally provided interest rate is the net present value or its relative, the net terminal value.

Present values have some advantages over internal rates of return as should have become obvious by now. First, computation of a present value is simpler than solution for an internal rate of return. A present value is unique for a project with a given rate of interest, but in some cases multiple solutions for the internal rate of return may exist. Other disadvantages to the internal rate of return, among those the "reinvestment rate problem," will be demonstrated in Chapter 6.

The present value of a project's cash inflows can be interpreted as an appraisal value. When the interest rate used in the calculation is the investor's minimum required rate of return, the present value is the maximum price the investor should be willing to pay for the project. If the actual price is less than the present value, the net present value is positive, the investor should buy the project. Another way of expressing the desirability in this situation is to say that the project's yield, its internal rate of return, is greater than the investor's minimum required yield.

Summary

This chapter has been concerned with the development of the basic compound interest and present value formulas to be used in later chapters of the book. Several equations were defined and illustrated for the treatment of various situations. To facilitate numerical calculations the three tables at the back of the book, (1) compound interest factors, (2) present value factors, and (3) present value of annuities were explained and used in working examples.

The internal rate of return of an investment project was defined as the rate of interest that makes the present value of the series of cash inflows equal to the price of the project. An alternative way of expressing that definition is to say that the internal rate of return is the interest rate that makes the net present value of the project zero. Although direct solution for the internal rate of return is not usually possible, the two approximation methods presented can be used to obtain numerical results.

While the present value method will form the basis for capital budgeting evaluations in the next chapter, it will be necessary to use the net terminal value concept as well. Accordingly the definition and illustrations were presented in this chapter.

An appraisal value is a single value that measures the theoretical worth of an investment project's cash flows. There were three choices for an appraisal value described in this chapter, the (net) present value, the net terminal value, and the internal rate of return. Although the internal rate of return can be considered as more objective than the other two since no external interest rate is necessary for its computation, it is a less preferred measure for use in investment project evaluation because of possible multiple solutions and because of the reinvestment rate problem to be discussed in the following chapter.

The terminal value is an amount compounded to a future point in time, presumably the terminal point of the investment project or projects in question. In most cases the terminal value is an artificial value like the present value since compounding of cash flows at an arbitrary rate of interest is assumed for computation. The adjective "net" is used when the initial outlay is included in the compounding.

The present value is the most commonly used for an appraisal value of an investment project. Rather than use values computed at some time point in the future the cash flows of future time points are all converted into an equivalent present value before being summed. Without further adjustment the present values of projects with different length lives can then be compared.

Note

1 A further description and limitation of the cases of multiple internal rates of return can be found in W. H. Jean, "On Multiple Rates of Return," *Journal of Finance,* March 1968, and W. H. Jean, "Reply," *Journal of Finance,* March 1969.

APPENDIX TO CHAPTER 5

Continuous Compounding and Discounting

The continuous compounding of interest is seldom used in finance because common business practice has been to compound interest discretely, at the end of some natural time division such as a year or a quarter. Recently a few financial institutions have adopted continuous compounding on savings accounts in an attempt to exceed slightly government agency-imposed maximum interest rates on those accounts. Continuous compounding has more natural use in theoretical financial models where a continuous stream of income is analyzed. The continuous compounding formulas developed here will bear a striking similarity to growth and diffusion models used in some physical sciences and certain social sciences.

The development of the continuous formulas proceeds from consideration of increasing indefinitely the number of times interest is compounded. If interest is compounded m times per period and the interest rate r is still defined as per-period, equation (5-1) is converted into

$$A_n = A_0 \left(1 + \frac{r}{m}\right)^{mn} \tag{5A-1}$$

As an example suppose interest is quoted as 10 percent per year, but interest is to be compounded twice a year. \$100 compounded for three years would amount to

$$\$100\left(1 + \frac{0.10}{2}\right)^{2(3)} = \$134.00$$

Now consider what happens to this compound interest factor $(1+r/m)^{mn}$ as m is increased indefinitely. To show the derivation of e^{rn} a substitution of

$$b = \frac{m}{r}$$

is made so the compound interest factor can be written as:

$$[(1+\frac{1}{b})^b]^{rn}$$

Now as m goes to infinity, b goes to infinity. So as the value of m is increased indefinitely, the compound interest factor becomes

$$\lim_{b\to\infty} [(1+\frac{1}{b})^b]^{rn} = e^{rn}$$

It is traditional to use the letter t in situations of continuous time rather than n which is used for discrete time. The continuous formula for compound interest is therefore written:

$$A_t = A_0 e^{rt} \qquad (5A\text{-}2)$$

The interest rate r is still quoted as a rate per unit of time, and the time variable t is the number of units of time that elapse. As an example the value of \$100 by the end of three years is computed with a rate of 20% per year:

$$\$100e^{(0.20)3} = \$182.21$$

(The answer is not the same as would be obtained by compounding discretely using equation (5-1).)

The continuous compounding formula can be converted to solution of present values:

$$A_0 = A_t e^{-rt} \qquad (5A\text{-}3)$$

In this form the present value of a single amount received at time t can be calculated. That is, suppose \$100 is to be received at the end of two periods, and an appropriate interest rate to use is 12 percent per period. The present value of this receipt is:

$$\$100e^{-(0.12)2} = \$78.66$$

Instead of computing the present value of a series of future payments it may be desirable to find the present value of a *stream* of payments. In this case the cash movement is a flow of cash, rather than discrete receipts. The flow or stream of cash must be represented as a function of time, $f(t)$. The present value of the stream received up to time T is:

$$\int_0^T f(t)e^{-rt}\,dt \qquad (5A\text{-}4)$$

Because of the difficulty of specifying a function, $f(t)$, to describe the stream of receipts equation (5A-4) is applied to only a few theoretical cases. Two such cases are described below.

Suppose a constant stream of income of $20 per period is received for four periods. For this problem $f(t)$ is a constant,

$$f(t) = 20$$

If an interest rate of 10 percent per period is used, the present value of this stream is:

$$\int_0^4 20e^{-(0.10)t}\,dt = \$65.94$$

The other case is that of a growth stock. A simple growth stock is one where dividends grow at a constant rate, g. Dividends are paid continuously to the holder of the stock, and the rate of payment is the product of a base rate, D, and a continuous compound interest factor, e^{gt}. D is the rate of payment at time zero, and the rate of receipt of dividends at any time t is:

$$f(t) = De^{gt}$$

Because the holder of stock receives dividends forever the upper integration limit in equation (5A-4) is infinity. The present value of this income stream to the stockholder is computed as:

$$\int_0^\infty De^{gt}e^{-rt}\,dt = \frac{D}{r-g}$$

Suppose the base dividend rate, D, is $1 per period, the growth rate, g, is 4 percent, and the appropriate interest rate, r, is 10 percent. The present value of this stream of dividends would be

$$\frac{\$1}{0.10-0.04} = \$16.67$$

In later chapters where growth stocks are evaluated discrete compounding formulas will be used to derive similar results.

Chapter 5 Questions

1. How does the concept of net present value as a surplus or profit differ from the usual accounting concept of profit?
2. When analyzing contracts involving cash receipts and payments over a number of years is it reasonable to assume that the rate of interest the corporation pays for borrowed funds will remain constant over the entire period?
3. How can the present value function be modified to allow for different interest rates over time?
4. Explain how the computation of present values with a fixed interest rate implies that the corporation can both obtain (borrow) funds and invest (lend) funds at that interest rate.

5. What is the relationship between the return on investment measure used in earlier chapters and the internal rate of return defined in this chapter?
6. Suppose interest is compounded at an interest rate of 1 percent every quarter instead of being compounded at a rate of 4 percent once a year. What would be the difference in a bank account balance at the end of two years under the two systems?
7. A present value can be interpreted as an appraisal value of a stream of cash flows. Explain this interpretation under the circumstances where the rate of interest used in the computations is a minimum required rate of return of a prospective purchaser of an investment project.
8. Extend the explanation in question 7 to the concept of net present value as a margin of safety over appraisal value.
9. Why isn't the net terminal value method used for the computation of the internal rate of return instead of the net present value method?
10. Under what circumstances would the net terminal value of an investment project equal the "accounting" net profit?
11. If two positive solutions for the internal rate of return of an investment project were obtained, which should be used for a decision on an investment project?
12. In the internal rate of return examples of the chapter, the set of cash flows started with an outlay at time zero, followed by a series of inflows. In a typical borrowing contract a set of cash flows is defined that starts with an inflow, the proceeds of the loan, and is followed by a series of outlays, the payment of interest and repayment of the loan principal. If this set of cash flows is analyzed by the techniques of this chapter what is the interpretation of (a) the internal rate of return, (b) the present value, and (c) the net terminal value?

Chapter 5 Problems

1. How much cash must be deposited in a bank account to enable withdrawals of $100 at the end of the first year, $75 at the end of the second year, and $150 at the end of the third year (reducing the balance to zero) to be made if interest is compounded annually at a rate of 5 percent?
2. Suppose a sharp operator offers you the proposition, "Pay me $80 now and I'll give you back $30 at the end of each of the next five years." What is the implied interest rate that the operator is paying and you will be earning in this proposition?
3. Suppose in problem 2 you can borrow the $80 from a bank with an interest rate of 10 percent. What is the net present value of the proposition to you?
4. In problems 2 and 3 what is the net terminal value at the end of the fifth year?
5. Plot the net present value as a function of the rate of interest for the set of cash flows:

Time	0	1	2	3	4
Cash flow	−100	40	10	90	50

6. Determine the internal rate of return for the cash flows in problem 5.
7. Plot the net terminal value at time 4 as a function of the rate of interest for the cash flows of problem 5.
8. For the project with cash flows

Time	0	1	2	3
Cash flow	−100	60	15	44

the internal rate of return is 10 percent. Compute the net present value at 10 percent and the net terminal value at the 10 percent interest rate.
9. Verify that the internal rate of return of this project is 10 percent:

Time	0	1	2
Cash flow	−60	35	50

The cash flows of the project in problem 8 are multiples of the cash flows of this project. Is the net present value of the problem 8 project at an interest rate of 6 percent a multiple of the net present value of this project?
10. The cash flows of an investment project are:

Time	0	1	2	3
Cash flow	−20	12	3	8.8

a. Compute the internal rate of return of this project.
b. Approximate the internal rate of return by linear interpolation from the interest rates of 10 percent and 40 percent.
c. Refine the approximation of the internal rate of return by a linear interpolation from the interest rates of 20 percent and 30 percent.
11. A borrowing contract calls for this set of cash flows:

Time	0	1	2	3
Cash flows	100	−10	0	−130

Use the definition of the internal rate of return (the interest rate that makes the net present value zero) to compute the "true" rate of interest on this borrowing contract.

Chapter 5 References

Bierman, H., Jr., and Smidt, S. *The Capital Budgeting Decision.* 3rd ed. New York: Macmillan, 1971.
Fleischer, Gerald A. *Capital Allocation Theory.* New York: Appleton-Century-Crofts, 1969.
Grant, Eugene, and Ireson, W. Grant. *Principles of Engineering Economy.* New York: Ronald, 1964.
Hubbard, Charles L., and Hawkins, Clark A. *Theory of Valuation.* Scranton, Penn.: International Textbook, 1969.
Jean, William H. *Capital Budgeting.* Scranton, Penn.: International Textbook, 1969.

—— *The Analytical Theory of Finance.* New York: Holt, Rinehart and Winston, 1970.

Johnson, Robert W. *Capital Budgeting.* Belmont, Calif.: Wadsworth, 1970.

Merritt, A. J., and Sykes, Allen. *The Finance and Analysis of Capital Projects.* New York: Wiley, 1963.

Porterfield, James T. S. *Investment Decisions and Capital Costs.* Englewood Cliffs, N. J.: Prentice-Hall, 1965.

Quirin, G. David. *The Capital Expenditure Decision.* Homewood, Ill.: Irwin, 1967.

Solomon, Ezra. *The Management of Corporate Capital.* New York: Free Press, 1959.

—— *The Theory of Financial Management.* New York: Columbia University Press, 1963.

Taylor, George A. *Managerial and Engineering Economy.* Princeton, N. J.: D. Van Nostrand, 1964.

Van Horne, James C. ed. *Foundations for Financial Management.* Homewood, Ill.: Irwin, 1966.

6 CAPITAL BUDGETING DECISIONS UNDER CERTAINTY

To decide among a set of possible investment projects requires the use of the appraisal values developed in Chapter 5. For the decision criteria demonstrated in this chapter the cash flows projected for projects and the applicable interest rates are assumed to be certain quantities, so the capital budgeting decision models must be classified as those applicable under conditions of certainty.

There are two commonly used criteria for capital budgeting, the internal rate of return and the net present value, that explicitly use the concept of the time value of money through an interest compounding process. Another variation, net terminal values, can be used instead of net present values with complete consistency. Two other criteria, the pay-back period and the average return on investment, suffer from the lack of time value of money consideration, and therefore could lead to an incorrect investment decision.

The form of the investment decision that must be made is used for the sequence of presentation of this chapter. First is the single project accept-reject decision. Then the ranking of investment projects is described where the implication is that the corporation only has the funds to buy one out of a set of available projects. Finally the procedures for selecting an optimum set of projects from the available set are described at some length. The combinatorial problem of this last stage is complex enough to have inspired a new area of mathematical programming, integer programming. Rather than present a rigorous computer algorithm search for the optimum combination expressed in formal mathematical terms, a simple procedure for solution is described that involves a minimum of arithmetic.

Before the decision criteria are described some additional definitions are necessary. First is the definition of cash flows and interest rates on an after-tax basis.

The Measurement of Cash Flows and Interest Rates on an After-Tax Basis

An investment project should be defined thoroughly at this point. An investment project is a contract entered into by the corporation that requires an initial cash outlay (the price), and results in later cash inflows. In later chapters financing arrangements will be considered where a cash inflow is received initially, and is followed later by cash outlays.

One basic principle is used in constructing the set of cash flows for an investment project: the cash flows are defined as after-tax cash amounts. A great deal of difficulty is avoided in the capital budgeting criteria by assuming that every possible means of avoiding, minimizing, or delaying corporate or individual income taxes are taken. For example if the purchase of a depreciable machine on which accelerated depreciation can be taken for tax purposes is considered, it would normally be desirable to take the accelerated depreciation rather than straight-line depreciation since the payment of taxes on the stream of income from the machine would be delayed. If a dollar of income taxes can be deferred to a later period the dollar can be invested in some interest-bearing form in the interval. The choice of depreciation method does alter the after-tax inflows because the amount of taxes paid in the period does change.

Correspondingly the interest rates used in the evaluation should also be adjusted to an after-tax basis. If a corporation subject to a 40 percent income tax rate borrows funds at a stated interest rate of 10 percent the after-tax interest rate is 6 percent. When funds are acquired where the payment is not tax-deductible, as for example when preferred stock is sold by the corporation, then no tax adjustment is necessary for the interest rate. If the interest rate used in the evaluation is an opportunity cost rate from other available projects, that rate should be after-tax as well.

If the cash flows are after-tax the internal rate of return will be an after-tax rate. A present value calculated from after-tax cash flows and interest rates will be an after-tax present value.

The Estimation of Cash Flows for an Investment Project

The derivation of future cash flows can be an extremely difficult task, in some cases causing the executive in charge to make a personal investment in a dart board. A new product line, for example, has a set of cash flows that may last forever if the product is successful. In any event projection of the cash flows involves not only setup and production costs, but a variable sales revenue as well.

In a few cases the cash flows from a project can be estimated with a high degree of accuracy. For example if the project is a new machine to produce an existing item, the cash inflows are expense savings from the machine. If an automatic machine costing $60,000 will replace an existing machine and two workers, and produce the same product, then estimation of the cash flows becomes relatively easy.

Suppose that the annual wages of the two workers total $20,000 a year, that the old machine was fully depreciated and had no scrap value, that repairs will amount to the same for the new machine as the old machine, and that the expected life of the new machine is five years. The before-tax cash flows due to the new machine would therefore be:

Time	0	1	2	3	4	5
	−60,000	20,000	20,000	20,000	20,000	20,000

To derive the after-tax cash flows two additional pieces of information are needed—the depreciation method used and the corporate income tax rate. Suppose the sum-of-the-years-digits method is to be used with no scrap value, and the corporation's tax rate is 48 percent. The depreciation charges for the five years will be:

1	2	3	4	5
20,000	16,000	12,000	8,000	4,000

The changes in taxable income due to the new machine will therefore be:

1	2	3	4	5
0	4,000	8,000	12,000	16,000

The increases in corporate taxes, cash outlays, are:

1	2	3	4	5
0	1,920	3,840	5,760	7,680

The net after-tax cash flows due to the investment project are:

0	1	2	3	4	5
−60,000	20,000	18,080	16,160	14,240	12,320

In this example the cash flows were easy to estimate because there was no change in revenues. Had the new machine resulted in a greater output, the value of that output would have to be entered into the computations.

Because the cash flow estimates are subject to error, a complete capital budgeting procedure should take into account the uncertainty of the estimates. The subject of decisions under risk and uncertainty is covered in Chapter 7, and applications to capital budgeting under risk and uncertainty form the content of Chapter 8. For now the estimated cash flows for an investment project will be treated as certain quantities, and therefore the present value, terminal value, or internal rate of return computed from those cash flows are exact amounts to be used for an investment decision.

The Present Value Criterion for a Single Project

Present values can be used for the decision to accept (purchase) an investment project or reject the investment project. Here the decision result takes only two forms—accept or reject; there is no consideration of buying a fraction of a project. The criterion involves a comparison of the appraisal value of the project, its present value, with the price of the project.

The criterion can be expressed in three different ways depending on how the present value computations are expressed:

1. Accept the project if the present value of the cash inflows is greater than the price of the project.

2. Accept the project if the net present value of the project is positive.

3. Accept the project if the ratio of the present value of the cash inflows to the price of the project is greater than one. Each of these three ways of expressing the criterion will lead to the same result.

Suppose an investment project with price of \$100 and cash inflows of \$20 at time one and \$120 at time two is evaluated. The present value of the cash inflows at an interest rate of 10 percent is

$$20(0.90909) + 120(0.82645) = 117.36$$

Using the rule as expressed by the first criterion, this project should be accepted since \$117.36 is greater than \$100. The net present value of this project is

$$\$117.36 - \$100 = \$17.36$$

which is positive, so it is accepted by form (2). The ratio of the present value of the cash inflows to the price of the project, sometimes called the "profitability index," is

$$\frac{\$117.36}{\$100} = 1.1736$$

which is greater than one. Therefore using form (3) of the accept-reject criterion the decision is also accept.

The accept-reject criterion can be shown graphically in Figure 6.1 below. The present value of the cash inflows and the price of the project are plotted in this diagram. The interest rate of 10 percent used for the example results in present values that make the project acceptable. If the interest rate used in the computations was higher than 20 percent the project would be rejected. The interest rate of 20 percent is the internal rate of return for this project.

Figure 6.1
Present Value of a Project

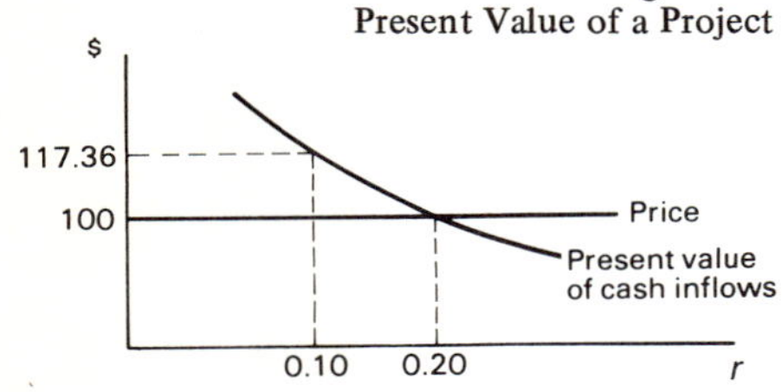

The Internal Rate of Return Criterion for a Single Project

The results for the numerical example above suggest that the internal rate of return criterion would involve comparing the internal rate of return with an external interest rate. This external interest rate would be the one chosen for present value computations, and might be the rate which is the corporation's cost of borrowed funds, the internal rate of return on alternate investments, or a rate based on an absolute time preference for money, as described in Chapter 5. That external rate will be called the "hurdle rate."

The internal rate of return criterion is expressed as:

Accept the investment project if its internal rate of return is greater than the hurdle rate.

This criterion is consistent and easily applied if the investment project is simple in nature with all the cash inflows being positive as in the last example. The diagram of present value and price for that type of example is reproduced again in Figure 6.2 below. In Figure 6.2 the interest rate where the present value of cash inflows is equal to the price of the project is labelled IRR, standing for the internal rate of return of the project. If the hurdle rate is to the left of IRR (is less than the internal rate of return) the project is accepted. If the hurdle rate is to the right of IRR (is greater than the internal rate of return) the project is rejected. The internal rate of return criterion will yield exactly the same results as the present value criterion for this sort of project.

Figure 6.2
Internal Rate of Return of a Project

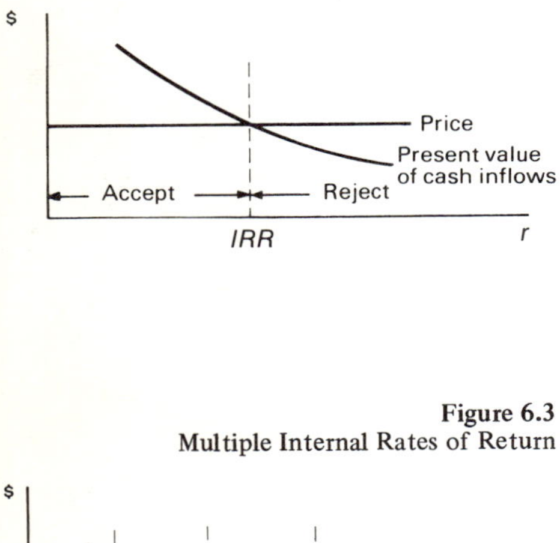

Unfortunately there may possibly be multiple solutions for the internal rate of return if the cash inflows of the project are not all positive, as indicated in Chapter 5. If a negative cash inflow (a net cash outlay) occurs in the middle of the project's life the present value of the cash inflows may behave as shown in Figure 6.3. In this case there are three solutions for the internal rate of return, IRR_1, IRR_2, and IRR_3. Each is a legitimate solution, and no way exists of making a choice among them. Therefore the internal rate of return criterion cannot be used for this type of project.

Figure 6.3
Multiple Internal Rates of Return

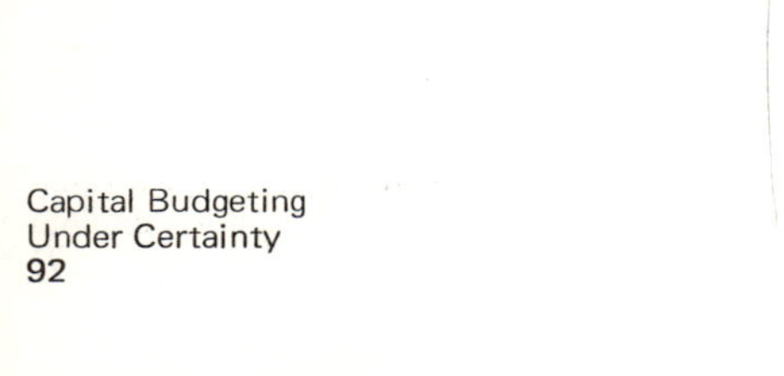

An example project that has the sort of present value behavior shown in Figure 6.3 is the project with cash flows:

0	1	2	3
−100	396.6	−517.8	222.8

This project has a large negative flow (an outlay) that occurs at time two. This outlay could represent extensive repairs or renovation that extend a machine's life, or the outlay could result from a contractual deferment of part of the purchase price. Such a later outlay may be a relatively common thing in investment projects therefore.

Solution of the example cash flows for the internal rate of return yields three answers, 11.1 percent, 25.0 percent, and 42.9 percent. The *net* present value is positive for interest rates below 11.1 percent and rates between 25.0 percent and 42.9 percent, and is negative for interest rates between 11.1 percent and 25.0 percent and for rates above 42.9 percent.

The possibility of an investment project that exhibits the behavior of present value shown in Figure 6.3 leads to the conclusion that the internal rate of return criterion should be rejected or at least used with extreme caution. The present value in Figure 6.3 is uniquely determined by the interest rate used in its computation, so the present value criterion can still be used consistently even when negative cash flows occur. Other reasons will be developed later for preferring the present value method over the internal rate of return method when ranking two or more investment projects, or when selecting the optimum combination of projects.

The Present Value Criterion for Ranking Projects

Frequently a choice must be made between two investment projects. The firm may have insufficient funds to buy both, or the projects may be mutually exclusive in nature. The choice can be based on a comparison of present values to find the better project.

To avoid difficulties, assume the two projects to be compared have the same size—the same price. (Choosing among projects of differing sizes will be analyzed later.) The preference criterion can again be expressed in three differing ways, depending on how the present values of cash flows and the price are used:

1. The project with the larger present value of cash inflows is preferred.
2. The project with the larger net present value is preferred.
3. The project with the larger ratio of the present value of cash inflows to the price of the project (the larger profitability index) is preferred.

Because the projects are assumed to have the same price the three statements of the criterion will yield identical results.

The same interest rate r is used in evaluating the present values of the two projects. The choice of an appropriate interest rate is crucial to the ranking, as demonstrated by the examples graphed in Figure 6.4. If interest rate r_1 is used in the calculations Project 2 would be preferred. If the higher rate, r_2, is used Project 1 is better.

Figure 6.4
Two Projects' Present Values

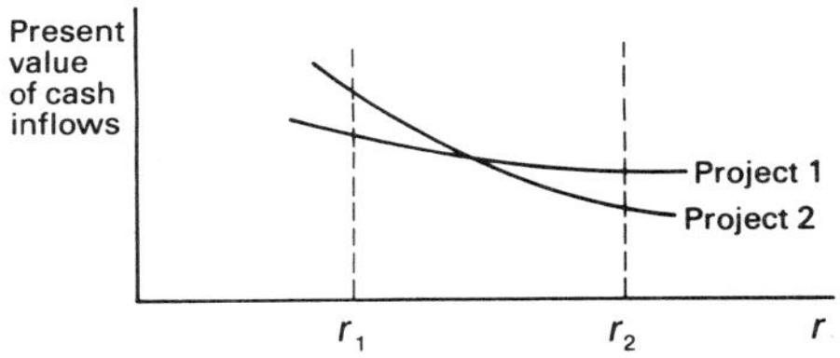

An intersection of the present values such as is shown in Figure 6.4 will not necessarily occur, but there is also the possibility of multiple intersections. An example with one intersection as in Figure 6.4 are the two investment projects:

Project	Cash inflow at time one	Cash inflow at time two
1	60	80
2	20	124

At an interest rate of 10 percent the present values of cash inflows are the same:

$$60\,(0.90909) + 80\,(0.82645) = 120.66$$
$$20\,(0.90909) + 124\,(0.82645) = 120.66$$

At an interest rate of 5 percent (r_1 in Figure 6.4), Project 2 has a higher present value:

$$60\,(0.95238) + 80\,(0.90703) = 129.71$$
$$20\,(0.95238) + 124\,(0.90703) = 131.52$$

At an interest rate of 15 percent (r_2) Project 1's present value is higher:

$$60\,(0.86957) + 80\,(0.75614) = 112.67$$
$$20\,(0.86957) + 124\,(0.75614) = 111.15$$

The Internal Rate of Return Criterion for Ranking Projects

The internal rate of return is sometimes used for ranking investment projects, although there are some conceptual problems with that use. The criterion itself would be stated as:

The project with the higher internal rate of return is preferred.

To use the criterion the internal rate of return is first calculated and then compared.

An obvious problem with use of this criterion is the possibility of multiple solutions for the rate for a project. If a project has three internal rates of return which should be used for comparison? But even if projects have a single unique solution there are questions about whether the project with the higher rate is really better for the corporation.

Suppose two example projects are used that have the same internal rate of return, 20 percent:

Project	Price	Cash inflow at time one	Cash inflow at time two
1	100	20	120
2	100	80	48

Because the internal rates of return are equal the criterion would lead to the conclusion that the corporation should be indifferent between the two. However, the corporation's other uses of cash should be explored as in present value or terminal value computations.

Suppose the corporation's alternative is investing in short-term securities with an after-tax yield of 4 percent per period. The cash inflow at time one from the investment project selected will be invested in these short-term securities for at least the following period, until time two. If Project 1 is selected $20 is put into the 4 percent form and compounds to $20.80 by time two. To that figure is added the $120 inflow at time two for the project, making a total cash on hand by the end of the planning period of $140.80. Now suppose Project 2 is taken instead. The cash inflow at time one is $80, which compounds to $83.20 by time two from the earnings on the short-term securities. Add to this the time two cash inflow of $48, and the total cash on hand at the end is $131.20. Obviously the corporation will be better off in terminal value (and present value) if Project 1 is chosen over Project 2.

The root of the discrepancy lies in the length of time funds are invested at the internal rate of 20 percent as compared to the time when the funds must be invested at the lower rate of 4 percent. To illustrate more fully the tabular representation of Project 1 is:

	Time one	Time two
Beginning balance	100	100
Interest earned during period	20	20
Total	120	120
Withdrawal	−20	−120
	100	0

For Project 1, $100 is earning at the rate of 20 percent during time period two. Now for Project 2:

	Time one	Time two
Beginning balance	100	40
Interest earned during period	20	8
Total	120	48
Withdrawal	−80	−48
New balance	40	0

For Project 2 there is only $40 earning at the rate of 20 percent during time period two.

This difficulty with the internal rate of return is called the "reinvestment rate problem." The internal rate of return does not take account of the rate at which cash generated by an investment project can be reinvested. The internal rate of return criterion may therefore be misleading for investment decisions.

The Use of Differential Interest Rates in Present Values

Occasionally it may be desirable to change from the usual practice of applying a single interest rate over time to a project's cash flows to a computation with a changing interest rate. For example a small growing corporation's management may anticipate that its borrowing costs will become lower as the corporation becomes more stable, larger, and better known in the financial community. To evaluate investment projects, therefore, high interest rates are used for near time periods with lower rates for later time periods. The opposite progression, increasing interest rates with respect to time, are sometimes used by corporations as an informal adjustment for risk and uncertainty. The reasoning is that the later cash flows come in the life of a project, the less certain they are, and therefore the less should be their contribution to the appraisal value of the project. Of course the normal single-rate present value computation weights later cash flows less than earlier flows, but the variable rate method can be used to accentuate the weighting.

Using the notation r_1 for the interest rate applicable to the first time period, r_2 for the second time period, and so on, the present value computation with time differential interest rates follows the formula:

$$A_1\left[\frac{1}{1+r_1}\right] + A_2\left[\frac{1}{1+r_1}\right]\left[\frac{1}{1+r_2}\right] + \ldots$$

$$= \sum_{i=1}^{i=n} A_1 \prod_{j=1}^{j=i} \left[\frac{1}{1+r_j}\right]$$

The Pay-Back Period and the Average Return on Investment Criteria

Two other methods are sometimes used for evaluation of projects in capital budgeting, neither of which take explicit account of the time value of money. The pay-back period is the length of time it takes the firm to recover the price of the project. For example Project 1:

Price	Cash inflow at time one	Cash inflow at time two	Cash inflow at time three	Cash inflow at time four
100	30	40	40	80

has a pay-back period of three. By the end of three periods the cash inflows received total \$110, which is greater than the price of \$100. Note that the last cash inflow, \$80, is not counted on the pay-back period.

The cash flows of Project 2 are:

Price	Cash inflow at time one	Cash inflow at time two	Cash inflow at time three	Cash inflow at time four
100	30	30	50	10

This project's pay-back period is also three, so if the pay-back criterion is applied Projects 1 and 2 are equally desirable. However there are obvious differences between the two projects. The cash inflow at time four for Project 1 is much greater than that of Project 2. Even within the pay-back period (the first three periods) the time distribution of the cash inflows is different.

The pay-back period may be usable as a crude measure for discriminating among projects—it does have the advantage of simplicity of computation. In comparing projects of the same time pattern of cash flows, such as in producing oil wells, the pay-back period may serve as an accurate comparison device. Finally, in cases of high risk projects where there is increasing uncertainty of outcomes for later periods there may be a case for selecting the project with the faster pay-back.

An average return on investment may be computed where the time distribution of cash inflows can be ignored. Suppose Project 1 above is used to compute the average return on investment. The sum of the cash inflows is $190, and the price $100 is subtracted to derive a profit of $90. Because the profit is received over four years $90 is divided by 4, yielding an average profit per period of $22.50. The average investment in the project is $100/2 = $50, and when $22.50 is divided by $50 the average return on investment is 45 percent.

For Project 2 the computations are performed the same way:

30 + 30 + 50 + 10 − 100 = 20 (profit)
$20/4 = $5 (average profit per period)
$100/2 = $50 (average investment)
$5/$50 = 10% (average return on investment)

Since 45 percent is greater than 10 percent Project 1 would be preferred under this criterion.

The average return on investment criterion is less desirable than a present value criterion because no distinction is made of the time at which cash inflows occur.

The Net Terminal Value Criteria

The net terminal value can be used for the accept-reject decision instead of the net present value criterion. If the net terminal value is positive so will the net present value be positive. Therefore exactly consistent results will be attained in the accept-reject decision.

When net terminal values are used for ranking projects care must be taken to use the same terminal date in both projects. This does not infer that the two projects must have the same length of life, however. The project that lasts three periods can be compared by net terminal value to a project that lasts four periods by computing both terminal values as of time four, for example.

The ranking by net terminal value will be the same as that achieved by a net present value ranking (assuming that the net present values are positive in the first place.) If

$$NPV_1 > NPV_2$$

then

$$NTV_1 > NTV_2$$

since

$$NTV_1 = (1 + r)^n NPV_1$$

and

$$NTV_2 = (1 + r)^n NPV_2$$

An Example Where Time Comparison Is Critical

One case where obtaining appropriate present values for comparison of alternatives involves some manipulation of time periods is the equipment replacement policy decision. Determination of the optimum time to replace delivery trucks, for example, can be treated as a capital budgeting ranking problem. The capital budgeting techniques should enable a "scientific" comparison of repair and renovation costs with economic depreciation to arrive at an optimal replacement time.

Suppose for example that trucks can be replaced at the end of the first year, second, third, fourth, or fifth year. As a truck ages the annual operating expenses, mainly repairs, rise. The truck's tradein or scrap value falls with age. Assuming a constant price of a new truck of $5,000, the costs of various age trucks can be summarized as:

Age of truck	Variable operating expenses per year	Scrap (tradein) value end of year	Cash required for a new truck
1	400	4,000	1,000
2	600	3,000	2,000
3	900	2,000	3,000
4	1,300	1,000	4,000
5	1,800	0	5,000

If a truck is kept for three years, operating expenses of $400 are incurred (at the end of) the first year, $600 the second year, and $900 the third year; the tradein value is $2,000, so $3,000 cash plus the old truck is necessary to get a new truck at the end of the third year.

Assuming that expenses are defined on an after-tax basis the cash outlay patterns for the possible replacement times can be derived from the information above:

Replacement point	time 1	time 2	time 3	time 4	time 5
1	1,400				
2	400	2,600			
3	400	600	3,900		
4	400	600	900	5,300	
5	400	600	900	1,300	6,800

Now the problem is to get a common basis for comparison of two replacement policies. As presented above the cash flow sequences cover differing time periods. One way to approach the problem is to define the same total length of time period, as for example defining a two-year time length for comparing the one-year replacement with the two-year replacement policy. Over two years the one-year replacement will require the truck to be replaced twice, resulting in this sequence of cash outlays:

1,400; 1,400

That sequence is to be compared to the two-year replacement's sequence of cash outlays:

400; 2,600

The present value of each time sequence can be computed and the results compared, but a slightly shorter procedure would be to take the difference of the cash outlays and compute the present value of the differences. The difference in cash outlays (two-year replacement minus one-year replacement) is

400	2,600
−1,400	−1,400
−1,000	1,200

Assuming an applicable interest rate of 10 percent the present value of the -1,000, 1,200 sequence is

$$-1{,}000(0.90909) + 1{,}200\,(0.82645) = \$82.65$$

Because this present value is positive a two-year replacement policy "costs" more than a one-year replacement, so the one-year replacement is better than the two-year.

The results of the comparison can also be expressed in terms of an internal rate of return. If a one-year replacement is selected over the two-year replacement an additional outlay of $1,000 is required at time one of the two-period sequence. Due to the $1,000 outlay at time one $1,200 of outlay is saved (an inflow at time two. That amount is the equivalent of a 20 percent rate of return. Since 20 percent is greater than the hurdle rate of 10 percent the arrangement (a one-year replacement policy) that yields the 20 percent should be accepted.

To continue the comparisons a three-year replacement policy can be compared to the two-year replacement. To achieve equal starting and finishing times a six-year cycle must be analyzed. The six-year cycle results and the differences in cash flows are:

Time	1	2	3	4	5	6
Three-year replacement	400	600	3,900	400	600	3,900
Two-year replacement	400	2,600	400	2,600	400	2,600
Three minus two	0	−2,000	3,500	−2,200	200	1,300

The present value of the sequence of differences in cash outlays is:

$$0(0.90909) - 2{,}000(0.82645) + 3{,}500(0.75131) - 2{,}200(0.68301) + 200(0.62092) + 1{,}300(0.56447) = \$1{,}819.67$$

Because this present value is positive a three-year replacement is worse than a two-year replacement.

The two-year replacement's advantage can also be expressed in terms of an internal rate of return. Treating the sequence −2,000, 3,500, −2,200, 200, 1,300 as the schedule of cash flows due to an investment project, an internal rate of return of 26.42 percent is derived. Use of the internal rate of return for a set of irregular cash flows such as these, however, involves many conceptual difficulties as described earlier.

The next comparison, of the four-year replacement with the three-year replacement, will involve a cycle of 12 years, and to compare the five-year and four-year a cycle of 20 years. There is a shorter method of comparison, however, that will serve for the selection of an optimum replacement policy.

The new method of comparison involves the computation of an "equivalent annual payment" for each replacement. In the computation a level annual payment is sought that will have the same present value as the original sequence of varying payments. Because the level annual payments will be constant for every time period those amounts can be compared for the various replacement policies.

The present values for the original sequences of cash flows are first computed:

Replacement point		Present value
1	1,400 (0.90909)	= 1,272.73
2	400 (0.90909) + 2,600 (0.82645)	= 2,512.41
3	400 (0.90909) + 600 (0.82645) + 3,900 (0.75131)	= 3,789.62
4	400 (0.90909) + 600 (0.82645) + 900 (0.75131) + 5,300 (0.68301)	= 5,155.64
5	400 (0.90909) + 600 (0.82645) + 900 (0.75131) + 1,300 (0.68301) + 6,800 (0.62092)	= 6,645.86

To convert these present values into a comparable basis an equivalent annual payment for each is derived. This equivalent annual payment will be the figure that has the present value equal to that of the original cash flow sequence. Each of the present values above is divided by a present value factor for an annuity of the corresponding length of time from Table 3:

Replacement point		Equivalent annual payment
1	1,272.73/0.90909	= 1,400.00
2	2,512.41/1.73554	= 1,447.66
3	3,789.62/2.48685	= 1,523.89
4	5,155.64/3.16987	= 1,626.44
5	6,645.86/3.79079	= 1,753.16

The equivalent annual payment of $1,753.16 for the five-year replacement, for example, is an amount if paid as an annuity for five years that has a present value of $6,645.86. The cash flow sequence 1,753.16, 1,753.16, 1,753.16, 1,753.16, 1,753.16 has the same present value, $6,645.86, as the cash flow sequence 400, 600, 900, 1,300, 6,800. Because the present values are equal the sequences are equivalent.

The single cash amount $1,753.16 can be compared to the equivalent annual payment for the four-year replacement of $1,626.44. Adopting a four-year replacement is equivalent to incurring an annual outlay of $1,626.44 forever. Since the five-year replacement is equivalent to incurring an annual outlay of $1,753.16 forever, the five-year replacement is more expensive than a four-year replacement.

The selection of the optimum is now the choice of the replacement period that has the lowest equivalent annual payment. The one-year replacement has the lowest figure, $1,400.00, so it is optimum.

A Pragmatic Approach to a Criterion for the Optimum Combination of Projects

When considering the determination of an optimum combination of investment projects to buy with a fixed budget, many mechanical difficulties are encountered in discriminating among the possible combinations that can be made of the available projects. One thing that will minimize the difficulties is to choose an appraisal or benefit value that is additive for projects. Present values (or terminal values) of projects can be added together meaningfully so long as the same interest rate is used in the computations.

Suppose a combination consists of two projects. There is a choice of method for computing the present value for the set; (1) first add the cash flows together for each time period, and then compute the present value of these totals, or (2) compute the present value for each project, and then add these present values together. Either method will yield the same result. Let A_i be the cash inflow for the ith time period for the first project and B_i be the cash inflow for the ith time period for the second project. The first computation method would be:

$$(A_1 + B_1)\left[\frac{1}{1+r}\right] + (A_2 + B_2)\left[\frac{1}{1+r}\right]^2 + \ldots + (A_n + B_n)\left[\frac{1}{1+r}\right]^n$$

This result is equal to that obtained under the second method:

$$A_1\left[\frac{1}{1+r}\right] + A_2\left[\frac{1}{1+r}\right]^2 + \ldots + A_n\left[\frac{1}{1+r}\right]^n$$

$$+ B_1\left[\frac{1}{1+r}\right] + B_2\left[\frac{1}{1+r}\right]^2 + \ldots + B_n\left[\frac{1}{1+r}\right]^n$$

It will normally be more convenient to compute the total present value of combinations by the second method since the number of present value computations is limited to the number of projects, not the number of combinations.

The internal rate of return criterion will not be used to select the optimum combination of investment projects. Besides the two problems discussed earlier, the possibility of multiple solutions for the internal rate of return and the reinvestment rate problem, an additional mechanical problem would be encountered when dealing with sets of projects.

The internal rate of return criterion would be to select the combination of investment projects that gives the highest internal rate of return of the possible combinations, where the budget provided serves as the price and the total cash inflow from the combination of projects serves as the cash inflow for each period. The internal rate of return could only be calculated for the combination of projects—the internal rate of return of the combination cannot be computed from the internal rates of return of the individual projects.

To illustrate this difficulty suppose there are two projects with prices, P_A and P_B, and net cash inflows, A_i and B_i. The internal rate of return of the first project would be the interest rate r_i that is the solution of:

$$0 = -P_A + A_1 \left[\frac{1}{1+r_1}\right] + A_2 \left[\frac{1}{1+r_1}\right]^2 + \ldots + A_n \left[\frac{1}{1+r_1}\right]^n$$

The internal rate of return of the second project is the value of r_2 that solves:

$$0 = -P_B + B_1 \left[\frac{1}{1+r_2}\right] + B_2 \left[\frac{1}{1+r_2}\right]^2 + \ldots + B_n \left[\frac{1}{1+r_2}\right]^n$$

If both projects are to be accepted, the internal rate of return of the combination is the value of r_3 that satisfies:

$$0 = -(P_A + P_B) + (A_1 + B_1) \left[\frac{1}{1+r_3}\right] + (A_2 + B_2) \left[\frac{1}{1+r_3}\right]^2$$

$$+ \ldots + (A_n + B_n) \left[\frac{1}{1+r_3}\right]^n$$

The value of r_3 cannot be obtained from the values r_1 and r_2.

Suppose six projects are under consideration—there are 64 possible combinations that can be made of those projects. There would be 64 internal rates of return that might have to be calculated in seeking the optimum combination.

The number of calculations does not grow so dramatically in the case of present values. With six projects only six present values must be calculated, since the present values for the 64 combinations can be obtained by adding part of the six present values together. It is much easier to make 64 additions than to solve for the internal rate of return 64 times.

The Solution Method

To demonstrate the selection process assume the example set of investment projects whose characteristics are summarized in Table 6.1.

There is a budget of $200 that can be spent for a set of projects. The

TABLE 6.1

Project	Price	Net present value of cash inflows
1	50	80
2	100	150
3	80	104
4	40	50
5	120	160

problem is to select the set that does not exceed the budget and maximizes the total of net present values.

The solution method should be one that does not require enumerating all the possible combinations of projects. There are $2^5 = 32$ possible combinations of projects in this example, a manageable number here even if every combination is investigated. However to make a selection from 30 projects the number of combinations would be 2^{30}, which is not. Therefore it is worthwhile to develop some techniques to set an upper bound and a lower bound on the number of projects to be included in the combinations that must be enumerated.

An upper bound can be set on the number of projects that can be accepted by a ranking of projects by price and a comparison with the budget total. If the projects are ordered in ascending order by price the ordering can be summarized as (4, 1, 3, 2, 5). That is, Project 4 has the lowest price, Project 1 the next higher, and so forth. Now projects are accepted in that order until the budget of \$200 would be exceeded. Projects 4, 1, and 3 can be accepted, but Project 2's inclusion would go over the budget. The number of projects that can be accepted is counted, three, and this is the upper bound to the number of projects. All the four-project combinations and the five-project combination can be discarded from further consideration since all those combinations would exceed the allowable budget. Some of the three-project combinations may exceed the budget as well, but these will be detected at a later step.

A lower bound on the number of projects accepted can be established by using an ordering by net present values. The projects are arranged in *descending* order by net present value, (5, 2, 3, 1, 4). Projects are accepted in this order, stopping just before the budget is exceeded. Only one project, number 5, can be accepted—the combination of Project 5 and Project 2 would require a total outlay of \$220. The other one-project combinations can be eliminated from consideration because the net present value of each is less than that of Project 5. Those combinations with fewer than one project—the zero-project combination in this case—have been eliminated from further consideration in this lower bound procedure.

By the upper bound-lower bound procedures, 11 combinations of the original 32 have been eliminated from further consideration. This is a small gain in the case of the simple example, but larger gains would be seen with larger examples.

The next step is to enumerate the remaining combinations, first to check for feasibility, and then to select the combination with the highest net present value. The three-project combinations and the total outlay (total of prices) for each are listed in Table 6.2:

TABLE 6.2

Projects	Total of prices
1, 2, 3	230*
1, 2, 4	190
1, 2, 5	270*
1, 3, 4	170
1, 3, 5	250*
1, 4, 5	210*
2, 3, 4	220*
2, 3, 5	300*
2, 4, 5	260*
3, 4, 5	240*

The asterisks (*) indicate the combinations that exceed the budget of $200 and are therefore eliminated from further consideration.

The total outlay for the two-project combinations is shown in Table 6.3:

TABLE 6.3

Projects	Total of prices
1, 2	150
1, 3	130
1, 4	90
1, 5	170
2, 3	180
2, 4	140
2, 5	220*
3, 4	120
3, 5	200
4, 5	160

Again the asterisk (*) indicates that a combination is infeasible, exceeds the alloted budget.

There are 12 feasible combinations to select from. At this stage the total net present value for these combinations is computed and the results shown in Table 6.4:

TABLE 6.4

Projects	Total net present value
1, 2, 4	280 ←
1, 3, 4	234
1, 2	230
1, 3	184
1, 4	130
1, 5	240
2, 3	254
2, 4	200
3, 4	154
3, 5	264
4, 5	210
5	160

The arrow indicates the combination with the highest total net present value, Projects 1, 2, and 4. This combination is the solution to the problem.

The selection procedure can be summarized by four steps:

1. Determine upper bound to the number of projects that can be purchased.
2. Determine lower bound to the number of projects that need to be considered.
3. Evaluate budget utilization (total of prices) for the remaining projects, and eliminate those combinations that are infeasible.
4. Evaluate total net present value of those combinations not eliminated by steps 1, 2, or 3, and select the combination with the highest total present value.

Incorrect Ranking Methods

To avoid excessive arithmetic and enumeration of combinations some ranking techniques are sometimes suggested that unfortunately lead to incorrect results. One of these erroneous methods is to rank by profitability index and accept projects sequentially until the budget is exhausted. The profitability index (present value divided by price) is added to the information of Table 6.1 to give Table 6.5:

TABLE 6.5

Project	Price	Present value of cash inflows	Profitability index
1	50	130	2.6
2	100	250	2.5
3	80	184	2.3
4	40	90	2.25
5	120	280	2.33

The ranking by profitability index in descending order is (1, 2, 5, 3, 4). According to a strict interpretation of the method, only Projects 1 and 2 could be selected, since the inclusion of Project 5 would exceed the budget of $200.

The only time the profitability index ranking method can be relied upon to yield the correct result is when the projects all have the same price. (Remember that earlier in the chapter the ranking of projects by present value was performed only for projects of the same size–price.) Suppose the example is changed to such a situation:

TABLE 6.6

Project	Price	Net present value of cash inflows	Profitability index
1	100	160	1.6
2	100	150	1.5
3	100	130	1.3
4	100	125	1.25
5	100	133	1.33

With a budget of $300 the optimum combination of projects is Projects

1, 2, and 5. This combination can be found by ordering by the profitability index, (1, 2, 5, 3, 4), and selecting sequentially until the budget is exhausted. The projects are perfectly interchangeable with respect to budget utilization because they have the same price. This interchangeability was not achieved in the earlier example.

The ranking method might yield a result that is close to the optimum as in the example summarized in Table 6.5 where Project 4 could be added to the ranking results of Projects 1 and 2. The ranking method may yield results that are farther away from the true optimum, as illustrated by the following example:

TABLE 6.7

Project	Price	Net present value of cash inflows	Profitability index
1	60	78	2.3
2	80	112	2.4
3	100	150	2.5
4	150	300	3.0
5	200	320	2.6

The budget allowed for this example is \$400.

The ranking by profitability index is (4, 5, 3, 2, 1). The ranking method would result in Projects 4 and 5 being selected for a total budget usage of \$350 and total net present value of \$620. No additional project could be added by skipping down the list of projects because the outlays of the other three projects are all over \$50. However, Project 5 could be deleted and Projects 1, 2, and 3 added, resulting in the acceptance set of (1, 2, 3, 4). For this set the total net present value is \$640—better than \$620—and the total outlay is within the budget. From the set (4, 5) to the set (1, 2, 3, 4) involves quite a modification of the ranking method.

A Formal Mathematical Statement of the Problem

The problem of the selection of a set of investment projects to meet a limited budget and maximize total present value can be stated as a 0-1 integer programming problem. There will be no further solution methods for this problem because integer programming solution methods are beyond the scope of this book.

First a variable X_i is defined for each investment project. Those variables must have the value 0 or the value 1. The value of X_i will be 0 if the ith project is rejected, or the value of X_i will be 1 if the project is accepted.

The net present value of the cash flows of the ith project is given the symbol a_i. The price of the ith project is expressed as b_i, and the total budget allowed is B.

For a problem with n investment projects the solution will be that set of X_i values that will

$$\text{Maximize} \quad \sum_{i=1}^{i=n} a_i X_i$$

subject to $\sum_{i=1}^{i=n} b_i X_i \leqslant B$

and $X_i = 0, 1$

The five-project example used above would translate into the integer programming framework as:

Maximize $80X_1 + 150X_2 + 104X_3 + 50X_4 + 160X_5$

subject to $50X_1 + 100X_2 + 80X_3 + 40X_4 + 120X_5 \leqslant 200$

and $X_1 = 0, 1$

The solution values of the X_i are:

$X_1 = 1$ (accept)
$X_2 = 1$ (accept)
$X_3 = 0$ (reject)
$X_4 = 1$ (accept)
$X_5 = 0$ (reject)

For these values of the decision variables the objective function value, the total net present value is:

$$80(1) + 150(1) + 104(0) + 50(1) + 160(0) = 280$$

The budget constraint is satisfied:

$$50(1) + 100(1) + 80(0) + 40(1) + 120(0) \leqslant 200$$

The solution was obtained above by the four-step procedure rather than by an integer programming algorithm. Computer routines may be available for the pure integer programming problem.

Summary

Five methods of computing a measure of an investment project's "worth" for use in a capital budgeting decision were described in this chapter. Two of these methods, the payback period and the average return on investment, were discarded because of the lack of consideration of the time value of money in their computation.

The internal rate of return has four disadvantages that may make it a less preferred measure to the net present or net terminal value. Those disadvantages are (1) difficulty of calculation, (2) the possibility of multiple solutions, (3) the reinvestment rate problem, and (4) the lack of additivity of projects' internal rates of return.

The final two measures, the net present value and the net terminal value, can be used interchangeably in capital budgeting criteria since they are multiples of each other. The net present value is used more often in practice than the net terminal value because of the natural selection of a time point for evaluation, the present.

Three decision situations were demonstrated in the chapter, the accept-reject decision for a single project, the ranking of equal-sized projects, and the determination of the optimum combination of projects to meet a fixed budget. In the latter the mechanical difficulties of combinatorial analysis can be met by use of an integer programming algorithm or by following the four-step procedure described in the text.

APPENDIX TO CHAPTER 6

Capital Budgeting Programs over Multiple Time Periods and Mathematical Programming Models

The model presented in the chapter to select a set of investment projects to meet a fixed budget can be extended to consider several budgets spaced over time. The expansion to a series of budgets will add a number of additional constraints to determine the feasibility of a particular combination of projects, but the basic solution technique will remain unchanged. The situation of multiple budgets is sometimes called a "capital budgeting program."

If budgets are to be provided for different time points presumably some investment projects will start (require an outlay) at those time points. The relevant cash flows, including outlays, for an example are shown in Table A.6.1:

TABLE A.6.1

Project	Time zero	Time one	Time two	......	Net present value
1	−100	20	30	......	150
2	− 50	20	10	......	80
3	− 40	30	10	......	80
4	0	−60	30	......	100
5	0	−80	20	......	120

The negative value in the table indicates a net cash outlay at that time, a zero value indicates no activity from that project, and a positive number indicates a net cash inflow. It can be seen from the numbers in the array that Projects 1, 2, and 3 start at time zero, and Projects 4 and 5 start at the end of the first period.

Budgets of \$100 at time zero and \$100 at time one are provided. It is assumed that net cash inflows from one project can be used in the investment program to purchase other projects. That is, if Project 3 is accepted its \$30 cash inflow at time one could be used to partially meet the \$60 outlay for Project 4 at that time. Another assumption used is that unused budgets cannot be carried over to the following period. For example if only Projects 2 and 3 are purchased at time zero \$10 would be left over from the budget of \$100. That \$10 is not added to the budget for time one, but is lost from the investment program.

The four-step solution method presented in the chapter must be adjusted for the inclusion of a second budget. The basic procedure remains the same.

Step one, the determination of an upper bound to the number of projects that can be accepted, will involve two orderings, one for each budget period. The ordering for time zero by ascending size of net outlay would be (5-4, 3, 2, 1). A zero is the lowest outlay of course. The projects are accepted in this order until the budget is gone. Four projects can be purchased before the budget of $100 is exhausted.

Next the time one budget is tested. The ordering by outlay at time one is (3, 2-1, 4, 5). Accepting in order, all five projects could be accepted. The negative outlays (net inflows) of Projects 3, 2, and 1 are actually added to the budget of $100 to allow purchase of Projects 4 and 5.

The time zero test resulted in an upper bound of four projects, and the time one test in an upper bound of five projects. The lower number is chosen and the results of step one are an upper bound of four projects.

Step two is a test for a lower bound to the number of projects. The ordering by descending net present value is (1, 5, 4, 2-3). This ordering will be the same for testing against the two budgets. The time zero budget is exhausted after one project, Project 1, is accepted. The time one budget would allow two projects to be accepted, Projects 1 and 5, before it would be exceeded by the addition of another project (Project 4). The lowest lower bound of the two budgets is one project.

Step three must therefore be performed for all the four-project combinations, all the three-project combinations, and all the two-project combinations. The test must be performed against each budget, therefore two total outlays are computed for each combination. For the four-project combinations the results are presented in Table A.6.2.

TABLE A.6.2

Projects	Total outlay at time zero	Total outlay at time one
1, 2, 3, 4	190*	− 10
1, 2, 3, 5	190*	10
1, 2, 4, 5	150*	100
1, 3, 4, 5	140*	90
2, 3, 4, 5	90	90

Again the asterisks (*) indicate the combinations that exceed the budget. The time zero budget eliminates four combinations from further consideration. The time one budget eliminated no combinations, but there is only one four-project combination that meets both budget constraints.

The same tests are performed for the three-project combinations in Table A.6.3.

There are two three-project combinations that meet both budget constraints.

TABLE A.6.3

Projects	Total outlay at time zero	Total outlay at time one
1, 2, 3	190*	– 70
1, 2, 4	150*	20
1, 2, 5	150*	40
1, 3, 4	140*	10
1, 3, 5	140*	30
1, 4, 5	100	120*
2, 3, 4	90	10
2, 3, 5	90	30
2, 4, 5	50	120*
2, 3, 4	40	110*

Now for the two-project combinations:

TABLE A.6.4

Projects	Total outlay at time zero	Total outlay at time one
1, 2	150*	–40
1, 3	140*	–50
1, 4	100	40
1, 5	100	60
2, 3	90	–50
2, 4	50	40
2, 5	50	60
3, 4	40	30
3, 5	40	50
4, 5	0	140*

There are seven two-project combinations that meet both budget constraints.

Step four is to evaluate the total net present values of the feasible combinations. The results are presented in Table A.6.5:

TABLE A.6.5

Projects	Total net present value
2, 3, 4, 5	380 ←
2, 3, 4	260
2, 3, 5	280
1, 4	250
1, 5	270
2, 3	160
2, 4	180
2, 5	200
3, 4	180
3, 5	200
1	150

The solution is to buy Projects 2, 3, 4, and 5. The cash inflows from Projects 2 and 3 at time one are added to the time one budget to enable the purchase of Projects 4 and 5 at that time.

More budgets can be added for successive periods as desired. The application of the four-step procedure for solution will be more complex, but the basic steps are unchanged. An upper bound and lower bound are established by a ranking procedure, the remaining combinations are checked for feasibility, and then the feasible combinations' present values are enumerated and the highest one chosen for the solution to the problem.

As the number of projects and the number of budgets are expanded it may become more worthwhile to explore the solution by a formal integer programming algorithm. The addition of projects adds decision variables, X_i, and the addition of budgets expands the number of constraints. The integer programming formulation of the example above would be:

$$\text{Maximize} \quad 150X_1 + 80X_2 + 80X_3 + 100X_4 + 120X_5$$

$$\text{subject to} \quad 100X_1 + 50X_2 + 40X_3 + 0X_4 + 0X_5 \leqslant 100$$

$$-20X_1 - 20X_2 - 30X_3 + 60X_4 + 80X_5 \leqslant 100$$

$$\text{and} \quad X_1 = 0, 1$$

In the general case if a_i is the net present value of the ith project, b_{it} is the net cash outlay at time t for the ith project, and an external budget of B_t is provided at time t, then the integer programming problem statement for a capital budgeting program covering T periods is:

$$\text{Maximize} \quad \sum_{i=1}^{i=n} a_i X_i$$

$$\text{subject to} \quad \sum_{i=1}^{i=n} b_{i1} X_i \leqslant B_1$$

$$\sum_{i=1}^{i=n} b_{iT-1} X_i \leqslant B_{T-1}$$

$$X_i = 0, 1$$

If the investment projects were strictly divisible, the a_i redefined to be the net present value *per unit* of the ith project, and the b_{it} redefined to be the net outlay at time t per unit of the ith project, then a simple linear programming problem is defined to solve the capital budgeting program:

$$\text{Maximize} \quad \sum_{i=1}^{i=n} a_i X_i$$

$$\text{subject to} \quad \sum_{i=1}^{i=n} b_{i1} X_i \leqslant B_1$$

$$\sum_{i=1}^{i=n} b_{iT-1} \leqslant B_{T-1}$$

$$X_i \geqslant 0$$

In this formulation the X_i are constrained only to positive values, and the value X_i in the solution is the number of units of the ith project to be purchased.

For example suppose the corporation has the choice of various amounts of three investment projects distributed over two budget periods. As a linear programming problem the situation involves three decision variables with two constraints, a particularly easy problem to solve.

The relevant cash flows and net present values *per unit* of the projects are summarized as:

Project	Time 0	Time 1	Net present value
1	−10	5	20
2	0	−8	10
3	− 4	−2	12

The first project requires an outlay at time 0 and produces an inflow at time 1; the second project does not start until time 1; and the third project requires outlays at both time 0 and time 1. The other periods' cash flows were used to compute the net present values shown here.

External budgets of 50 at time 0 and 30 at time 1 are provided. Cash inflows (from project 1 in this example) at time 1 can be used to meet outlays on other projects—the reinvestment assumption is retained.

Using the criterion of maximizing total net present value while staying within the budget constraint the capital budgeting problem for the example is:

Maximize $20X_1 + 10X_2 + 12X_3$

subject to $10X_1 + 0X_2 + 4X_3 \leqslant 50$

$-5X_1 + 8X_2 + 2X_3 \leqslant 30$

$X_1, X_2, X_3 \geqslant 0$

The solution, found by the simplex method in this case, is

$X_1 = 5; X_2 = 6.875; X_3 = 0$

Both budgets are used to the limit, and the 25 cash inflow from project 1 is spent on the outlay required for project 2 at time 1. The value of the objective function, the total net present value, for this optimum solution is 168.75.

One additional piece of information is obtained from the linear programming solution that was not available when the integer programming model was used, the shadow prices of the budget constraints. The shadow price is the ratio of the change in value of the objective function to the change in the constraint quantity (the external budget). For the example the shadow price of the first constraint, the time 0 budget, is 2.625, and the shadow price for the time 1 budget is 1.25. The interpretation of these prices is that if the budget at time 0 is increased by 1 dollar the total net present value for the new optimum mix of investment projects will be increased by 2.625 dollars. If the time 1 budget were increased by 1 dollar the total net present value would increase by 1.25 dollars.

The set of shadow prices can serve as a valuable guide for the reallocation of budgets over time. In the example some of time 1's budget might be reallocated to time 0. Such a switch would increase the net present value of the investment program by 1.375, the net of 2.625 gained through the time 0 budget and the 1.25 lost through the time 1 budget.

The shadow prices could serve as guides for the corporation's fund raising activities as well. If a period's shadow price is greater than zero (assuming the interest rate used for present value computation is equal to the corporation's interest rate on incremental borrowings), it is worthwhile for the corporation to borrow more money to increase that period's budget.

The set of shadow prices may be used in a costing procedure for the corporation's dividend policy as well. If dividends are paid this reduces the amount of money available for the investment program. Expressed positively, the shadow price of 2.625 indicates that a dollar reduction in dividends paid at time 0 would result in a net present value increase in the corporation's investment program of 2.625—which might be reflected in a greater market value for the common stock of the corporation.

Shadow prices can be obtained for other continuous mathematical programming models' solutions as well, so long as the decision variables are not constrained to integer values. The mathematical programming models can serve as a basis for a theoretical model of a firm's investment activity.

Chapter 6 Questions

1. When will the present value, net present value, and profitability index criteria give the same results in an accept-reject decision about a single investment project?
2. The profitability index is sometimes called a benefit-cost ratio. Why?
3. Explain why the payback period and the average return on investment measures are considered inadequate for investment project evaluations.
4. Will the internal rate of return and net present value criteria ever give conflicting results in a single project decision?
5. Can the net terminal value and net present value be used interchangeably in all single project accept-reject decisions and in all two-project rankings?
6. Is it correct to say that when changing the interest rate in the net present value computations changes the ranking of two projects, this demonstrates the inconsistency of the net present value criterion?
7. Demonstrate graphically the case where the internal rate of return criterion will give a different ranking of two projects from the net present value criterion.
8. The internal rate of return criteria ignore the reinvestment rate, and the present value criteria are based on the reinvestment rate. Comment.
9. Is it possible that an interest rate (for use in present values) based on the corporation's cost of funds, a rate based on the internal rates of return on alternative projects, and a rate based on the corporation's stockholders' rates of time preference for dividend income would lead to three different rates being applied to every investment project?
10. Show that it is meaningful to add together present values of different projects so long as the same interest rate was used in the calculations, but that adding together the internal rates of return of different projects would give nonsense results.
11. Explain the equivalent annual outlay used in the equipment replacement policy example.
12. If the capital budget is fixed, where does the interest rate for present value computation come from?
13. In considering the combinations of investment projects that can be made from the available set each combination could be considered as a new project. For those combinations that meet the budget constraint then does the selection of an optimum resemble the ranking problems of the preceding chapter?
14. Is it possible to adapt the internal rate of return criterion for the problem of selecting a set of investment projects?

15. Is it reasonable to assume that most of the investment projects a corporation has available will be fixed in size?
16. Suppose an optimum combination of projects does not entirely exhaust the available budget. What happens to the unused cash?
17. Would it be better to use the sum of net present values or the sum of net terminal values as a criterion in selecting the optimum set of investment projects?
18. Is there any simpler technique for solving the capital rationing problem than the algorithm described in the chapter?
19. Is it reasonable to assume a fixed capital budget or was that assumption made to simplify the long-term financial optimization by separating the investment selection problem from the capital-raising problem?
20. If all investment projects were the same size or if all were variable in size, what kind of ranking procedure could be used to select the optimum set?
21. Suppose some investment projects are fixed in size but others can vary in size. Outline a procedure to find the optimum combination of projects.
22. Because of the possibility of an optimum combination not resulting in complete expenditure of the budget is it possible that the use of present values of inflows as a criterion would result in a different combination of projects than using the net present value of all cash flows as a criterion?
23. Is it meaningful to add together the present values of two projects when the lives of the two projects are different?

Chapter 6 Problems

1. A single investment project is under consideration for purchase by a corporation with a hurdle rate, a required rate of return on investments, of 10 percent. The estimated net cash flows of the project are

Time	0	1	2	3
Cash flow	−80	40	30	20

Is the project acceptable using:
- a. The internal rate of return criterion.
- b. The net present value criterion.
- c. The net terminal value criterion.

2. The corporation has many investment projects available to it with internal rates of return of 12 percent so the corporation's opportunity cost for cash is 12 percent. A special project with net cash flows of:

Time	0	1	2	3	4
Cash flow	−150	70	50	80	30

has become available. Evaluate that project using:

a. The net present value of cash flows.
b. The present value of cash inflows.
c. The profitability index.

3. A person says to you "I'm indifferent between a dollar of income a year from now and 75 cents of income now." What interest rate is implied by this statement?

4. The corporate income tax rate on ordinary income is 48 percent and on long-term capital gains it is 30 percent. Calculate the (after-tax) internal rates of return on these two investment projects:

a. A piece of land is purchased for $10,000 and sold two years later for $15,000.
b. A piece of land is purchased for $10,000, is then leased to a parking lot operator for a net rental of $2,500 a year, and is sold at the end of two years for $10,000.

5. Two investment projects are available, and the corporation only has sufficient funds to buy one of them. The two investment projects are:

Time	0	1	2	3	4
Cash flows of #1	−1,000	700	400	200	100
Cash flows of #2	−1,000	500	500	100	500

Rank the two projects by:

a. The pay-back period.
b. The average return on investment.
c. Net present value at an interest rate of 11 percent.

6. The two investment projects with cash flows:

Time	0	1	2	3
Cash flows of #1	−100	40	70	90
Cash flows of #2	−200	40	90	100

are available, and the hurdle rate for the corporation is 10 percent. Rank the projects using:

a. The present value of cash inflows.
b. The net present value.
c. The profitability index.

7. The two projects with cash flows:

Time	0	1	2	3
Cash flows of #1	−100	30	50	70
Cash flows of #2	−100	40	60	40

are available, and the hurdle rate for the corporation is 10 percent. Rank the projects using:

a. The present value of cash inflows.
b. The net present value.
c. The profitability index.

8. Two projects' cash flows are:

Time	0	1	2	3
Cash flows of #1	−100	20	80	60
Cash flows of #2	−100	70	15	60

The two projects are to be ranked by net present value, using interest rates of:

a. 10 percent.
b. 15 percent.
c. 20 percent.

9. Rank the two projects in problem 8 by net terminal value, using interest rates of:

a. 10 percent.
b. 15 percent.
c. 20 percent.
d. 30 percent.

10. The cash flows of two projects are:

Time	0	1	2	3
Cash flows of #1	−100	90	16	24
Cash flows of #2	−100	15	35	92

a. Rank the projects by internal rate of return.
b. Rank the projects by net present value using an interest rate of 6 percent.

11. An investment project is available with originally estimated cash flows of:

Time	0	1	2	3	4
Cash flow	−100	30	40	40	50

if the project runs its full term. The corporation does have the option of abandoning this project early and realizing these scrap values:

Time abandoned	1	2	3	4
Scrap value	80	60	30	0

The corporation's cost of capital is 12 percent, and all the cash flows defined above are net after taxes. Find the optimum life of the project, the life that yields the highest net present value.

12. The corporation has $200 available for the purchase of investment projects this period. Four indivisible projects are available:

Project	Outlay at time zero (price)	Present value of cash inflows
1	100	150
2	50	70
3	180	288
4	50	72

Select the optimum combination of investment projects using the following selection methods:

a. Rank by profitability index, accepting projects in descending order until the budget is exhausted.

b. Select the combination that gives the highest present value of cash inflows.

c. Select the combination that gives the highest net present value of all cash flows.

13. The corporation has $320 available for the purchase of investment projects this period. Four indivisible projects are available:

Project	Outlay at time zero (price)	Present value of cash inflows
1	100	120
2	100	140
3	100	130
4	100	145

Select the optimum combination of investment projects using the following selection methods:

a. Rank by profitability index, accepting projects in descending order until the budget is exhausted.

b. Select the combination that gives the highest present value of cash inflows.

c. Select the combination that gives the highest net present value of all cash flows.

14. An investor has $2,000 to spend on a portfolio of common stocks that will be sold at the end of one year. Disregarding risk considerations and transactions costs, select the investor's portfolio from the following list of securities to maximize his payoff at the end of the year:

Common stock	Price per share now	Price per share at end of year
1	10	14
2	20	27
3	10	13
4	25	36

15. The corporation's capital budget is $500. Select the best combination of investment projects from this list:

Project	Outlay at time zero (price)	Present value of cash inflows
1	150	200
2	200	310
3	180	200
4	60	70
5	240	290

16. The corporation's capital budget is $800. Select the best combination of investment projects from this list:

Project	Outlay at time zero (price)	Present value of cash inflows
1	200	240
2	300	400
3	400	500
4	250	300
5	500	700
6	100	150

17. The corporation can replace its stamping machines at the end of four years or at the end of seven years. The stamping machines will have an original cost of $10,000 each, straight-line depreciation is used for tax purposes, and the corporation is subject to a 48 percent income tax rate. If the machines are replaced at the end of four years the scrap value will be $3,000, and if they are replaced at the end of seven years the scrap value will be zero. The cash operating expenses in each year of the machines' lives are:

Time	1	2	3	4	5	6	7
Cash operating expenses	400	500	700	900	1,000	1,000	1,000

Which machine replacement policy is better assuming a cost of capital of 8 percent, four years or seven years?

Chapter 6 References

Bailey, Martin. "Formal Criteria for Investment Decisions." *Journal of Political Economy*, October 1959.

Baumol, W. J., and Quandt, R. E. "Mathematical Programming and the Discount Rate under Capital Rationing." *Economic Journal*, June 1965.

Bernhard, Richard H. "Mathematical Programming Models for Capital Budgeting." *Journal of Financial and Quantitative Analysis*, June 1969.

Bodenhorn, Diran. "A Cash-Flow Concept of Profit." *Journal of Finance*, March 1964.

Edwards, James W. *Effects of Federal Income Taxes on Capital Budgeting*. Research Monograph #5, National Association of Accountants, 1969.

Fisher, Lawrence. "An Algorithm for Finding the Exact Rates of Return." *Journal of Business*, January 1966.

Hirschleifer, Jack. "On the Theory of the Optimal Investment Decision." *Journal of Political Economy*, August 1958.

Jean, William H. "On Multiple Rates of Return." *Journal of Finance*, March 1968.

—— "Reply." *Journal of Finance*, March 1969.

—— "Terminal Value or Present Value in Capital Budgeting Programs." *Journal of Financial and Quantitative Analysis*, January 1971.

Kaplan, Seymour. "Computer Algorithms for Finding Exact Rates of Return." *Journal of Business*, October 1967.

Lusztig, Peter, and Schwab, Bernhard. "A Note on the Application of Linear Programming to Capital Budgeting." *Journal of Financial and Quantitative Analysis*, December 1968.

Mao, James C. T. "The Internal Rate of Return as a Ranking Criterion." *Engineering Economist*, Winter 1966.

—— "Survey of Capital Budgeting: Theory and Practice." *Journal of Finance*, May 1970.

—— *Quantitative Analysis of Financial Decisions*. New York: Macmillan, 1969.

Petri, E. "Use of Capitalized Cost in Repeated Replacement Problems." *Management Accounting*, September 1969.

Teichroew, Daniel, Robichek, Alexander A., and Montalbano, Michael. "An Analysis of Criteria for Investment and Financing Decisions under Certainty." *Management Science*, November 1965.

Weingartner, H. Martin. "The Excess Present Value Index–A Theoretical Basis and Critique." *Journal of Accounting Research*, Autumn 1963.

—— *Mathematical Programming and the Analysis of Capital Budgeting Problems*. Englewood Cliffs, N. J.: Prentice-Hall, 1963.

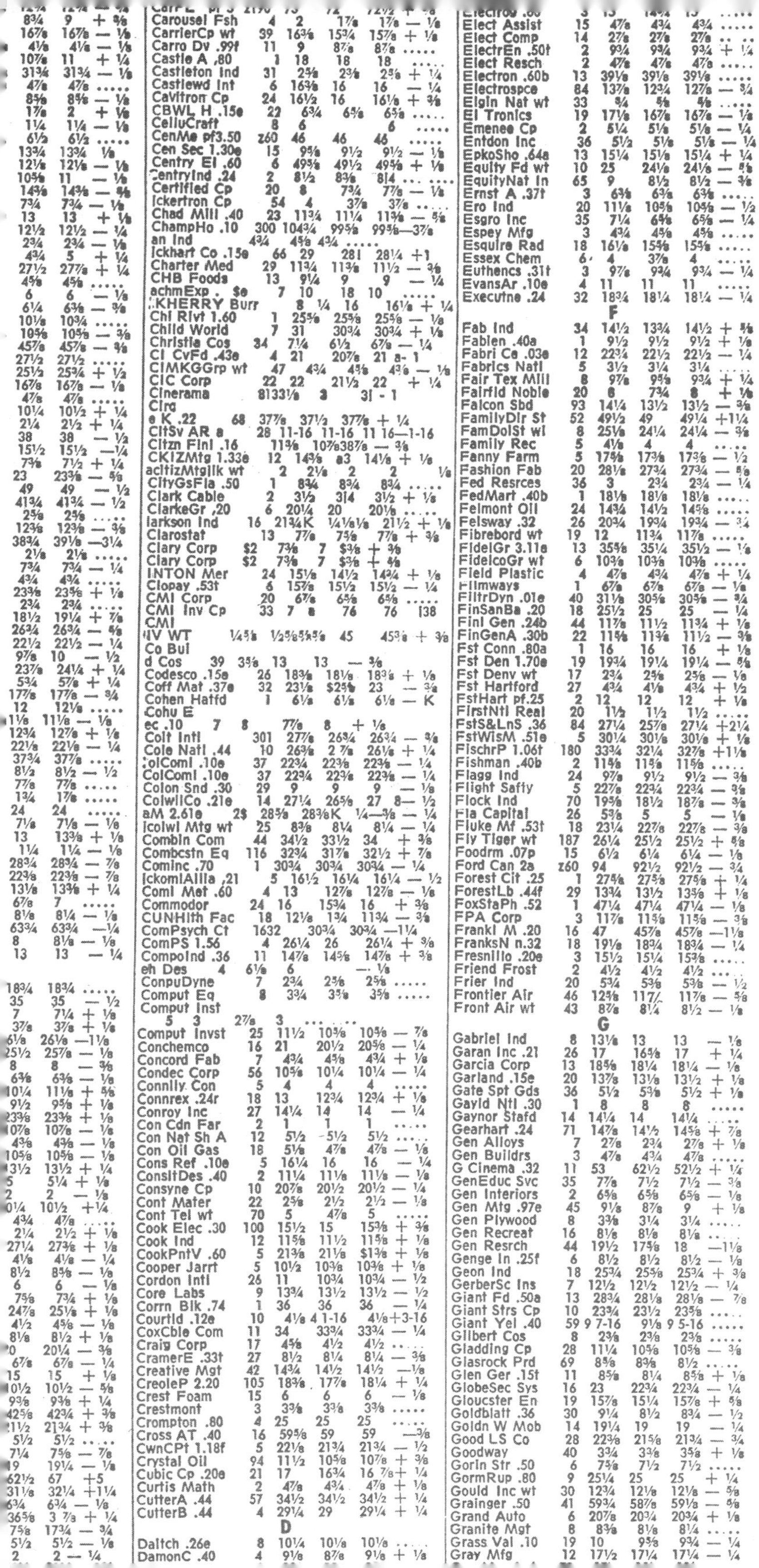

PART THREE

THE INVESTMENT DECISION IN RISK SITUATIONS

The use of net present value for an investment criterion may prove inadequate when the cash flows from the projects are uncertain or subject to risk. In risk situations either the statistical distributions of the cash flows or estimates of the means and variances of those distributions are assumed to be available for use. A consistent procedure for using the two measures, the mean and variance of present value, in a decision model is developed in this section of the book.

To separate as far as possible the decision criterion itself from the computational problems of deriving the statistical measures of present values, Part III is divided into two chapters. In Chapter 7 only one-period investment projects are considered where present value computation is unnecessary for ranking measures. In that chapter the decision criterion for risk situations is developed and demonstrated. Chapter 8 contains the extension to multi-period projects, and therefore the capital budgeting procedures under risk are only fully developed there.

The device of an investor's utility function for money income is used to demonstrate the possible inaccuracy of basing investment decisions exclusively on mean values. The addition of a measure of the dispersion of outcomes, the variance or its square root, the standard deviation, improves the accuracy of the decision criterion. Through the use of some relatively weak assumptions that an investor will be a return-seeker and a risk-averter, efficiency conditions are derived that allow choice to be made among investments under certain circumstances without specific knowledge of the investor's utility function. When those efficiency conditions are not met, the mean and variance measures are used for a decision that depends on the exact form of utility function.

The problem of a linear combination of random variables arises frequently in these two chapters. In Chapter 7 the linear combination is a set of investment projects, and in Chapter 8 the linear combination is the present value of cash flows. If Z is the linear combination of the two random variables X and Y such that

$$Z = aX + bY$$

then the mean of Z, $\bar{Z}$, is found by

$$\bar{Z} = a\bar{X} + b\bar{Y}$$

and the variance of Z, σZ^2, by

$$\sigma_Z^2 = a^2\sigma_X^2 + b^2\sigma_Y^2 + 2ab\text{Cov}(XY)$$

[Cov (XY) is the covariance of X and Y, as defined and illustrated in Chapter 7.] A complete knowledge of these two formulas will facilitate the reader's understanding of Chapters 7 and 8.

7

DECISION THEORY UNDER RISK AND UNCERTAINTY

The framework for handling investment decisions under risk is rather complex, particularly when the time dimension is considered. Accordingly in this chapter the decision situations are limited to those where the time distribution of cash flows can be ignored—where the outcome of an investment is a single cash receipt. In Chapter 8 the risk-handling procedures will be modified to allow for cash inflows from investment projects distributed over time.

The chapter begins with a consideration of the amount of information available to the decision-maker. The progression of techniques follows the elaboration of information available, going from game theory models to probabilistic models, finally modifying the techniques to account for the individual investor's preferences regarding amounts of money receipts. The utility-based decision model is then modified to a decision based on the mean and variance of a probability distribution. Using the risk-aversion assumption, dominance conditions that result in efficient combinations are shown to make some choices independent of specific utility functions.

Classes of Information Available to the Decision-maker

The situation an investor faces can be classified with respect to the degree of uncertainty regarding the outcome of an investment. The worst possible situation occurs (1) when the possible outcomes cannot be identified—no information is available upon which to make a decision. A somewhat better situation is (2) when the possible outcomes can be listed, but no estimate of the likelihood of those outcomes is available. The still better situation is (3) when the possible outcomes and their likelihood of occurrence are known. The best possible circumstance is (4) when there is no uncertainty about the outcome of the investment—it is certain.

In the first case, in which there is no information about possible outcomes, there is no basis for a rational decision. Even though this circumstance is a common event, the only thing to do is to seek more information.

The second case describes the typical "game theory" situation. The decision that results from the application of game theory methods would not necessarily be optimum if the additional information of the likelihood of the outcomes were available. It may be worthwhile therefore to spend additional effort (and money) to obtain that information.

When both the possible outcomes and their likelihoods are available, the approach to the optimum decision among investments is not necessarily obvious. The outcomes and likelihoods must be combined into a summary number or numbers. The bulk of this chapter will be concerned with that summary.

The situation of certainty will not be treated again in this chapter. Decisions under certainty were analyzed in Chapters 5 and 6 for multiperiod investment projects.

Decisions Based Upon Possible Outcomes-Game Theory

A game theory framework to deal with two-person conflict situations arrays the possible outcomes of the situation in accordance with the strategies adopted by the participants. For example the array for a game may be represented as:

		A	
		1	2
B	1.	20	−10
	2.	− 5	15

The entries in the table are payments made by one player to the other, in this case from B to A. For example if A selects his strategy 2 and B selects his strategy 2, then B must pay A $15. From the aspect of A the best possible combination of moves—strategies—would be A-1 and B-1, where A would receive $20. For B the best possible outcome would result with A-2 and B-1, where the entry −10 indicates a payment of $10 from A to B.

Rather than two active participants in investment situations the players are limited to one decision-maker and an opponent called "Nature." Nature is a term used to indicate the outcome of a random process, where the likelihood of those outcomes are not known to the active player. The game against Nature array using the outcomes above would be:

		Decision-maker	
		1	2
Nature	1.	20	−10
	2.	− 5	15

The decision-maker must choose between his courses of action, #1 and #2. His choice is now conditioned on the fact that Nature's choices are randomly selected rather than being selected deliberately by an active player to minimize the payment to the decision-maker. If the decision-maker chooses #1, he will receive a payment of $20 or must make a payment of $5, depending on Nature's choice, the outcome of a random process. If he chooses #2 he will pay $10 or receive $15. His choice is assumed still to be in complete ignorance of any of the probabilities associated with the random outcomes.

There are three approaches to solution of the decision-maker's problem. The first is based on the maximin principle, a "conservative" approach. The term maximin is a contraction of the phrase "maximum of minimums." In this approach the decision-maker first identifies the minimum receipt for each strategy, and then selects that strategy that gives the highest (maximum) minimum receipt. For the example above the minimum receipts are −5 for #1 and −10 for #2. The higher number is −5, so the decision-maker should choose #1.

The maximin principle is a conservative approach to decision-making, since it amounts to selecting an alternative that will minimize losses or assure a minimum gain. A more daring decision-maker may prefer to gamble, and aim for the maximum of maximums. That is, he might look at the array of possible receipts and choose that strategy that has the highest possible receipt listed as a possible outcome. For the example the highest receipt is 20, so the daring decision-maker would choose #1 on the "maximax" basis.

For this example both the maximin criterion and the maximax criterion lead to the choice of #1. For a different example the maximin and maximax methods might lead to different choices.

A third approach to choice is possible when repetitions of the game can be considered possible. The approach is the choice of a "mixed strategy" where the decision-maker elects strategy #1 part of the time and strategy #2 the rest of the time. Each play is chosen on a random basis, but with a probability of selection of #1 or #2 determined in advance. This frequency of choice is that frequency that will make the average outcome the same no matter what Nature's choice is.

The symbol p is used to stand for the frequency with which the decision-maker uses strategy #1. Strategy #2 will be used with frequency $(1 - p)$ therefore. The average outcome when Nature's choice is 1 will be:

$$p(20) + (1 - p)(-10)$$

With Nature 2 the average outcome will be

$$p(-5) + (1 - p)(15)$$

If p is to be chosen to make these average outcomes equal, p can be found by solving:

$$p(20) + (1 - p)(-10) = p(-5) + (1 - p)(15)$$

The solution is

$$p = 0.50$$

The decision-maker should use #1 half the time and #2 half the time. He could accomplish this frequency in a random choice by flipping a coin—use #1 if heads come up, #2 if tails.

The average outcome when Nature's choice is 1 is:

$$0.50(20) + (1 - 0.50)(-10) = 5$$

The same value is computed for the second possible state of Nature:

$$0.50(-5) + (1 - 0.50)(15) = 5$$

In a sense Nature's choice no longer matters to the decision-maker—he expects an average outcome of \$5 regardless of Nature.

To be able to compute p, the frequency of use of strategy #1, two characteristics of the example must be present in the game situation. First, the outcomes must be grouped by state of Nature. For example if there were three possible outcomes listed under strategy #1 and two outcomes listed under #2 the five outcomes could not be classified by state of Nature. The array of outcomes must at least be "rectangular," with the same number of outcomes for each strategy.

The second condition for computation of p is that there be the same number of states of Nature as choices for the decision-maker. The array of outcomes must be "square," otherwise the frequency of use of the strategies may not be determinable.

The mixed strategy approach therefore requires some mathematical conditions before it can be applied. In addition the *rationale* of the mixed strategy with respect to its applicability in situations where the exact game cannot be repeated should be explored.

When the game cannot be repeated, the terminology is changed from "average outcome" to "expected outcome." The value p is not the actual frequency of use of strategy #1, but the probability of use of strategy #1. The decision-maker may use a random selection method for his *one* choice of strategy, choosing strategy #1 if the coin comes up heads, for example.

The expected outcome is therefore an expected value in the statistical sense of expectation. It is determined mathematically by multiplying each possible outcome by the respective probability, and summing those products. The expected outcome of \$5 in the original example would never actually be attained in any play of the game—the outcome must be \$20, –\$5, –\$10, or \$15. However, the decision is based on this expected value, a measure of the central tendency of outcomes.

Three decision criteria, the maximin, maximax, and mixed strategy, can be used to make choices where no likelihood of the state of nature can be expressed. In the maximin method the decision is based upon the worst possible outcomes, and in effect the other outcomes are ignored. In the maximax the decision is based only on the best possible outcomes. The mixed strategy is based upon consideration of all outcomes. From the aspect of utilization of information it would seem that the mixed strategy might be the best of the three techniques.

The mixed strategy technique is an example of a decision based on expected money values. The decision approaches considered so far have treated every dollar of game outcome as the same, even though some of those dollars may be more important than others. The outcome –\$15, for example, may mean disaster for the game player, and therefore be more than three times as important as the –\$5 outcome. Another player may think there is little difference between the –\$15 outcome and the –\$5 outcome. The device that utilizes individual preferences toward money receipts and payments is the "utility function."

The Utility of Money and Expected Utility

Utility is an index of satisfaction for the individual. The index is expressed as a cardinal number whose size indicates "real value" to the individual. If one object has utility of 30 it is twice as valuable to the person as an object with utility of 15.

Utility, as used here, is the measure of satisfaction that is derived from money receipts. It is assumed that a mathematical function can be used that relates money receipts to the corresponding utility levels attained by the individual. That function is the "utility function."

The utility function may be represented graphically as in Figure 7.1. In this case $200 does not yield twice as much satisfaction to the individual as $100. Reading off the coordinates of the utility axis, $200 yields 140 percent of the satisfaction that $100 yields.

Figure 7.1
Example Utility Function

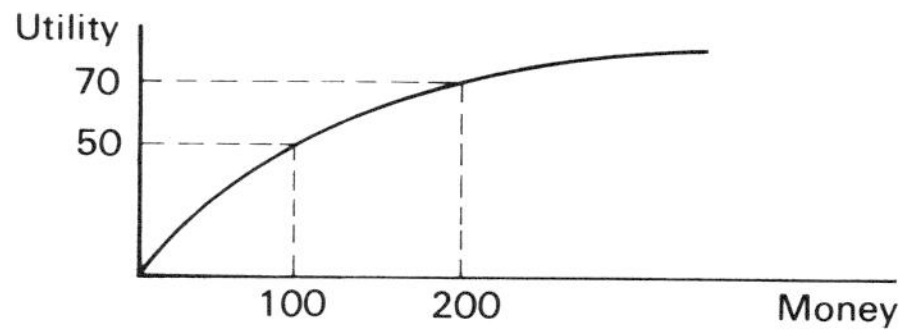

The utility function is also known by the term "preference function" in some areas of business administration. The function does express the preferences of an individual.

Each individual is assumed to have a utility (or preference) function, but different persons may have different attitudes toward money receipts, and therefore different utility functions. A utility function for groups of people will not be defined here.

The experimental measurement of an actual person's utility function is described in the appendix to the chapter.

The function shown in Figure 7.1 demonstrates the characteristics normally assumed for a utility function. Utility always increases as money receipts increases, but at a diminishing rate. The curve in Figure 7.1 has a positive slope, but the slope decreases as money increases. The curve is concave downward.

Using the symbol U for utility, and X for money, the utility function can be expressed in the general form:

$$U = f(X)$$

Then the two characteristics of the utility function can be expressed mathematically as:

1. $\dfrac{dU}{dX} > 0$

2. $\dfrac{d^2U}{dX^2} < 0$

Verbally: the first derivative (the slope) is always positive; and the second derivative (the rate of change of the slope) is always negative.

The slope of the utility function is the "marginal utility," the ratio of changes in utility to changes in money. Marginal utility is always positive, but becomes smaller as money increases. The concavity of the function therefore expresses the condition of "diminishing marginal utility."

The condition of diminishing marginal utility demonstrates the concept mentioned in the preceding section. "Some dollars may be more important than others"—the increment to utility of another dollar depends upon how much money the person has already received. An additional dollar may add 1.3 units of satisfaction if it is added to a base of ten dollars, but it would add only 0.5 units of satisfaction if it is added to a base of 100 dollars.

The shape of the assumed utility curve is crucial to the following analysis of the decision process. The concavity of the curve will result in the determination that expected monetary payoffs are inadequate as a basis for decision.

Instead of basing decisions on expected money income, decisions will be based on expected utility. Money income is the random variable, utility is a function of money income, so expected utility is computed from the values of a function of a random variable.

Figure 7.2
Expected Utility

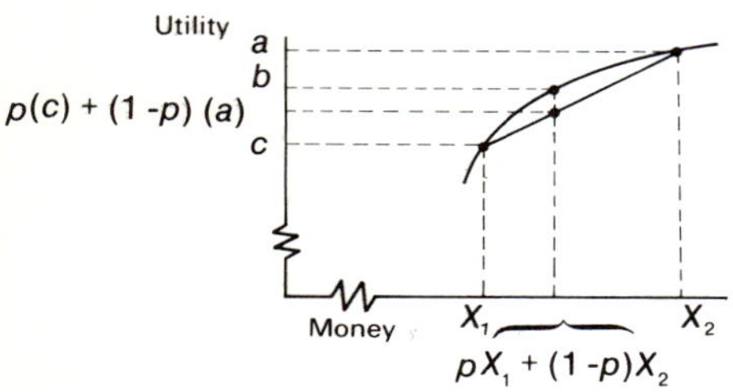

A part of a concave utility function is reproduced in Figure 7.2. Two amounts of money, X_1 and X_2, are to be combined in an expected value computation. The value p is the probability of X_1 and $(1-p)$ is the probability of X_2. The expected monetary payoff is therefore

$$pX_1 + (1-p)X_2$$

If this amount were substituted in the utility function the resulting utility would be b in the diagram. However, the expected value of utility is

$$p(c) + (1-p)a$$

a linear combination of the utility of X_1, c, and the utility of X_2, a. The result is that the utility of the expected monetary payoff is not equal to expected utility. The use of expected money values alone may seriouslydistort the decision process if the decision-maker has a concave utility function, since expected money income overstates the satisfaction level attained from the risk situation.

The concave utility function gives rise to another term to describe the decision-maker. If his utility function is concave he is said to be "risk-averse." The combination of the possibility of X_1 and the possibility of X_2 makes this situation one of risk. The expected utility from this risk situation is the quantity

$$p(c) + (1-p)a$$

If the decision-maker could get a *certain* receipt of

$$pX_1 + (1-p)X_2$$

his utility level would be b, a higher level. He therefore is averse to the risk situation.

Not all individuals will necessarily be risk-averse. Three different utility curves are presented in Figure 7.3.

Figure 7.3
Possible Risk Responses

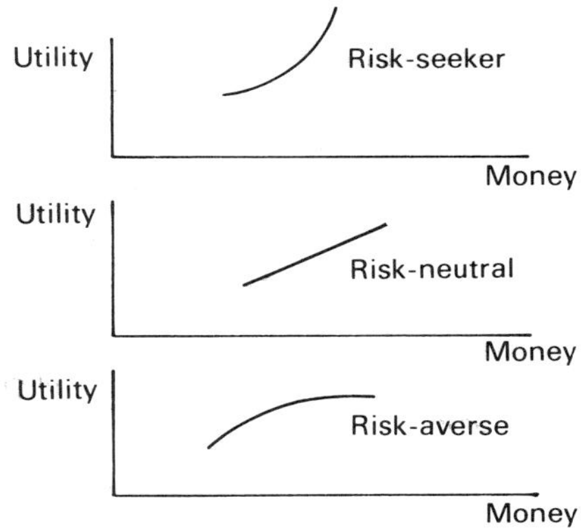

The risk-seeker, a person with a convex utility function, would prefer a risk situation with an expected money return to one in which that amount of money is certain. The risk-neutral individual, with a linear utility function, is indifferent between risk and certainty. The risk-averse individual would prefer certainty.

The risk-seeker is an unusual case that will be noted only as a possibility, and given no further attention. The risk-neutral case, though, should be explored a little further.

In the risk-neutral case the utility function is linear, which means that the expected utility for a risk situation is the same as the utility of the expected monetary outcome for that situation. The expected value of money can therefore be used alone in the decision process, with no modification for risk.

The utility function as represented in Figure 7.1 may be approximately linear for the higher levels of money income. When studying the decision process for a wealthy individual, the approximation may be used that *small* increments of income due to a decision may be treated as movements along a linear utility function, therefore that use of expected money values alone will not materially distort the choice among alternatives. The size aspect of this conclusion should be emphasized and it should be stressed that making decisions on expected money values alone will not be sufficient in the general case of the risk-averse individual.

Decisions Using Expected Utility

To demonstrate the use of expected utility for decision assume the following two investments with equal prices for an example:

#1		#2	
Outcome	**Probability**	**Outcome**	**Probability**
20	0.10	0	0.10
30	0.20	30	0.40
40	0.50	40	0.30
50	0.20	80	0.20

It is assumed that the exact form of the utility function of the decision-maker is known. The utility function is

$$U = \ln (1 + 0.10X)$$

where U is utility, X is the cash outcome (return), and ln stands for the natural logarithm, the logarithm with the base e.

This utility function exhibits the characteristics indicated in the preceding section for the risk-averse individual. The function is increasing with respect to X, and is concave.

Now that the utility function is known and the exact distribution of the outcomes is known, the expected utility of investment #1 can be calculated directly:

X	*U*	*P(X)*	*U·P(X)*
20	1.09861	0.10	0.109861
30	1.38629	0.20	0.277258
40	1.60944	0.50	0.804720
50	1.79176	0.20	0.358352
		Expected utility =	1.550191

The utility values are multiplied by the probabilities of their realizations and the products summed to derive the expected utility. For investment #1 the expected utility is 1.550191.

For investment #2 the calculation of expected utility in tabular form is:

X	*U*	*P(X)*	*U·P(X)*
0	0	0.10	0
30	1.38629	0.40	0.554516
40	1.60944	0.30	0.482832
80	2.19722	0.20	0.439444
		Expected Utility =	1.476792

The expected utility of #2 is 1.476792.

These expected utility values are compared and the conclusion is that #1 is more desirable than #2. The result is not just an ordinal ranking of the two investments, but a cardinal ranking as well. The difference in expected utilities is

$$1.550191 - 1.476792 = 0.073399$$

so #1 is 0.073399 units of expected utility better than #2.

The results from expected utilities can be compared to those using only expected money outcomes. For the first investment the expected money outcome calculated in tabular form is:

X	*P(X)*	*X·P(X)*
20	0.10	2
30	0.20	6
40	0.50	20
50	0.20	10
	Expected Money Outcome =	38

For the second investment the expected money outcome is:

X	$P(X)$	$X \cdot P(X)$
0	0.10	0
30	0.40	12
40	0.30	12
80	0.20	16
Expected Money Outcome =		40

According to the expected money outcomes #2 is better than #1, the opposite results from the utility analysis.

The example investments serve to demonstrate the point made in the preceding section with regard to the risk-averse investor. Even though investment #2 has a higher expected return, it must be perceived by the investor as a riskier investment than #1. By inspecting the listing of possible outcomes it can be seen that #2 has a wider dispersion of cash returns—the extreme values possible (the range) are wider than #1, and a measure of variability would probably be higher for #2 as well.

A standard measure of variability for a statistical distribution is the variance, or its square root, the standard deviation. The variance for a discrete distribution is defined as:[1]

$$\sigma_X^2 = \sum_X [X - \overline{X}]^2 P(X) = \sum_X X^2 P(X) - (\overline{X})^2$$

where the summation is over all possible values of X, and the symbol $\overline{X}$ is the expected value of X (the mean). Normally the second form of the formula will be easier to use for calculations.

The variances for the two example investments can be calculated to check the relative variability. For investment #1:

X	X^2	$P(X)$	$X^2P(X)$
20	400	0.10	40
30	900	0.20	180
40	1600	0.50	800
50	2500	0.20	500

$$\sum_X X^2 P(X) = 1520$$

$$\sigma_X^2 = 1520 - (38)^2 = 76$$

For investment #2:

X	X^2	$P(X)$	$X^2P(X)$
0	0	0.10	0
30	900	0.40	360
40	1600	0.30	480
80	6400	0.20	1280

$$\sum_X X^2 P(X) = 2120$$

$$\sigma_X^2 = 2120 - (40)^2 = 520$$

The variance of money outcomes for #2 is much higher than the variance for #1. This measure of variability can be used as support for the statement that investment #2 is riskier.

It is sometimes considered desirable to have a measure of risk defined which can be computed and used individually in a decision process. The variance of money outcomes is a measure that is commonly used, although it is not necessarily a completely accurate summary of the risk characteristics of the investment. The adequacy of the variance as a summary of risk is further explored in the appendix to this chapter.

If the variance is adopted as a measure of risk the two parameters of the distribution, the expected outcome (the mean) and the variance of outcomes, can be abstracted and used in a decision model instead of using the complete probability distribution of money outcomes.[2]

Decisions Based on the Mean and Variance

To use the mean and the variance in a utility-based decision model the expected utility function must be redefined. Instead of utility as a function of X, the actual money outcome, expected utility must be expressed as a function of the mean, $\bar{X}$, and the variance, σ_X^2:

$$U = f(\bar{X}, \sigma_X^2)$$

Figure 7.4
Typical Mean–Variance Indifference Curves

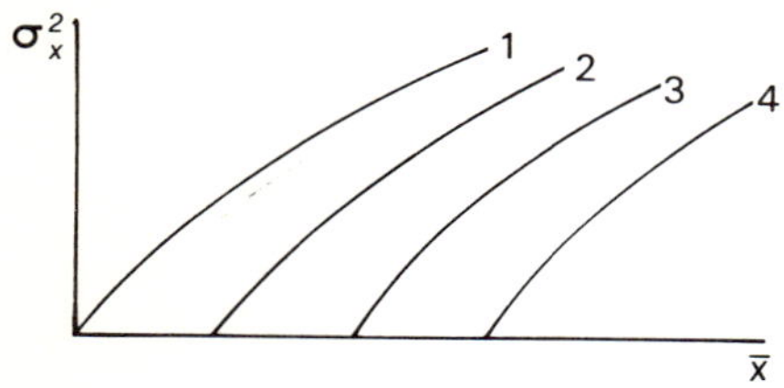

(From this point on U is expected utility, a small change in notation.) A specific form is not assumed for this function. Instead some generalizations about the response characteristics expected from variations in the mean and variance will be used.

The investor is assumed to be a return-seeker and a risk-averter. The return sought is the expected money outcome, $\bar{X}$ in the utility function above. Therefore U will increase as $\bar{X}$ increases:

$$\frac{\delta U}{\delta \bar{X}} > 0$$

Figure 7.5
Choice Among Investments

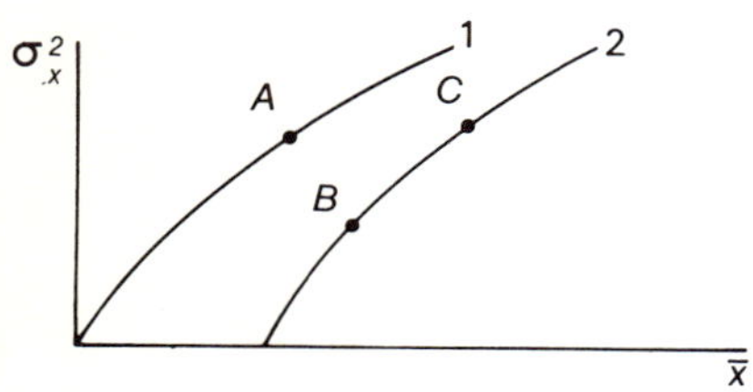

If the investor is risk-averse his utility will decrease as the variance of money outcomes increases.

$$\frac{\delta U}{\delta \sigma_X^2} < 0$$

The device of indifference curves is adopted to allow representation of the utility function graphically in two dimensions. A family of indifference curves, which are in effect contours of the utility function, are shown in Figure 7.4.

Each curve is the collection of $\bar{X}$ and σ_X^2 values that yield equal values of U. Therefore the points on curve 1 in Figure 7.4 represent combinations of return and risk that are equally satisfactory to the investor. He is indifferent between the combinations.

As a point is moved to the right from one indifference curve to a higher-numbered curve, utility increases. Curve 2 represents a higher utility level than curve 1 for example.

The indifference curve diagram can be used to demonstrate choices between investments. In Figure 7.5 three investments are presented by the three points on the diagram.

Investment B is preferred to A; it lies on a higher indifference curve. The investor is indifferent between investments B and C because they are on the same curve. If the investor has determined he can buy one of the three he will choose B or C.

Some other possible indifference curves are shown in Figure 7.6.

In Figure 7.6 the indifference curves with negative slope belong to the risk-seeker, one who likes both mean and variance, and will be satisfied (indifferent) to trade a higher mean for lower variance or a higher variance for a lower mean. The indifference curves that are vertical lines belong to the risk-neutral individual. His satisfaction is not affected by changing the variance, only by changes in the mean. Once again, only the risk-averse or risk-neutral investor will be assumed.

Figure 7.6
Risk Attitudes of Investors

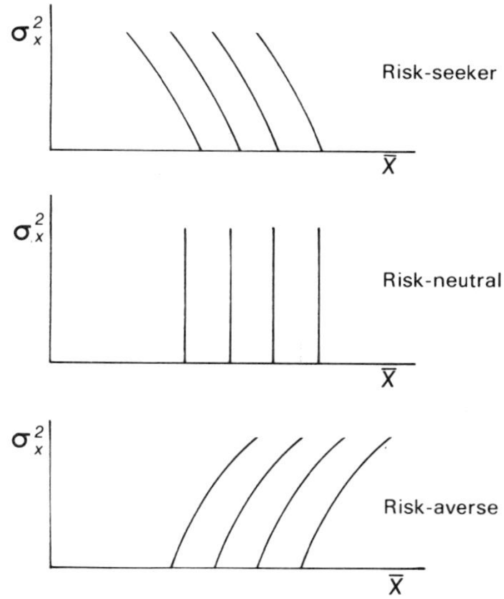

Clear Dominance and the Efficient Set

Some results in discriminating among risky investments can be achieved even when the exact form of the utility function is unknown. If the investor is risk-averse and a return seeker an investment combination will dominate some other combinations, as shown in Figure 7.7.

The point *A* would clearly be preferred to any point in the shaded region of Figure 7.7. Those points in the shaded region either (a) have the same mean but a higher variance, (b) have a smaller mean and a higher variance, or (c) have a smaller mean and the same variance when compared to point *A*. When a point such as *A* is clearly dominant over some other points, *A* is "efficient" with respect to those points.

Figure 7.7
Dominance Region of an Investment

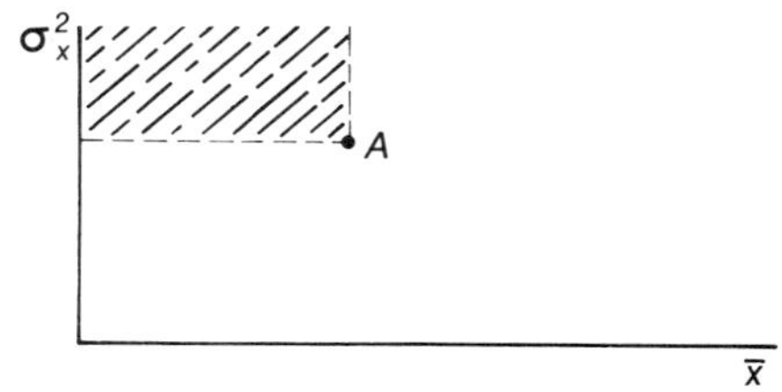

The "north-west region" procedure demonstrated in Figure 7.7 can be used to reduce a feasible (with respect to a budget) set of investment possibilities to a smaller set, the efficient set. Consider the five feasible investments in Figure 7.8.

Each of the five points represents an attainable combination with the available budget. The investor must choose one of the five. When the dominance conditions are checked *C* dominates *B* but *D* dominates *C*. *D* therefore dominates (eliminates from further consideration) *A*, *B*, and *C*. When points *D* and *E* are compared neither can be eliminated on the grounds of dominance. *E* has a higher variance than *D*, but it also has a higher mean. The original feasible set is reduced to the efficient set, *D* and *E*.

Figure 7.8
Efficient Set Example

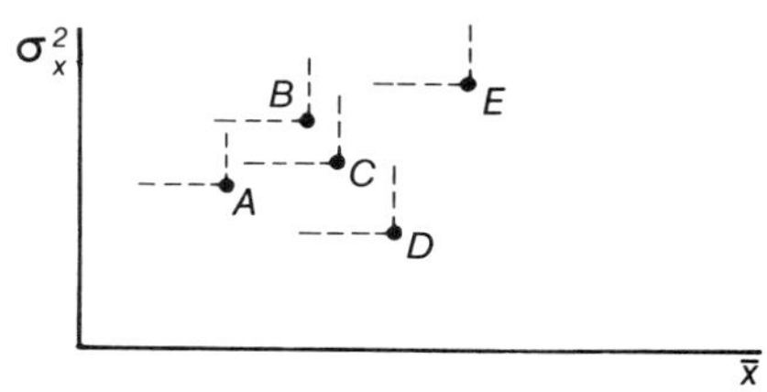

The investor must still make the decision between *D* and *E* in Figure 7.8 based upon his exact trade-off between risk and return. The efficient set derivation has reduced his necessary choice from one selected out of five to one selected out of two.

When continuous combinations of investment projects are used, the feasible set can be represented as a region in the diagram, as shown in Figure 7.9.

When the efficiency rules are applied to this continuous case the resulting efficient set is the collection of points on the southeast border of the feasible set, shown as the bold curve in Figure 7.9. Each of the points in this efficient set dominates some of the points in the feasible set, but no point in the efficient set dominates another point in the efficient set.

The Certainty Equivalent

Corresponding to the set of possible outcomes of a risky investment there is a certain amount that is equally satisfactory to the investor. The certain amount that is equivalent to the risky set is called "the certainty equivalent." The certainty equivalent derivation can be shown with the aid of the indifference diagram in Figure 7.10.

Figure 7.9
Continuous Investment Combinations

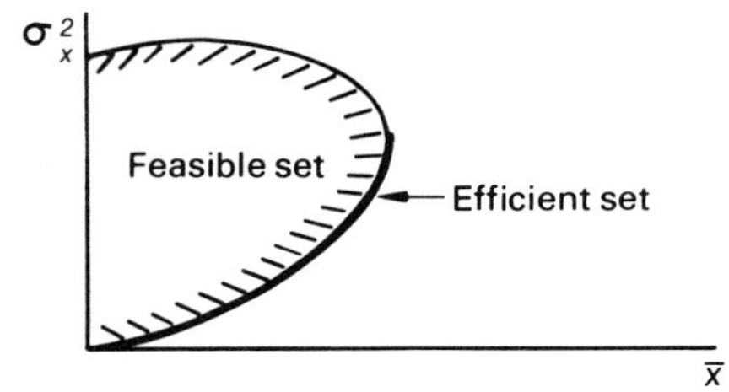

The combination B is equivalent to the mean-variance combination A because the investor is indifferent between the two—A and B are on the same indifference curve. B is a certain outcome because its variance is zero. B is therefore the certainty equivalent for A, as well as for any other combination on that indifference curve.

The certainty equivalent can serve as a summary of the characteristics of an investment. The certainty equivalents of two investments can be compared, and the higher certainty equivalent would be preferred. Since the certainty equivalent is a single number the investment choice may be easier to express in terms of certainty equivalents instead of means and variances. However, the exact derivation of the certainty equivalent requires specific knowledge of the investor's utility function (shown here in indifference curve form).

Figure 7.10
The Certainty Equivalent

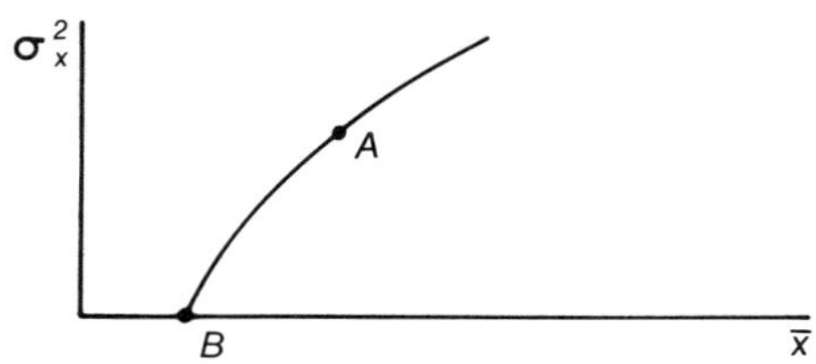

The certainty equivalent might in practice be obtained by less formal means. The investor could be questioned to ascertain his preferences: given a particular risky set of outcomes, what certain amount would be exactly equivalent in your mind? The estimation of certainty equivalents can be made by similar techniques to the derivation of utility functions described in this chapter appendix.

No further use of the certainty equivalent will be made in this chapter, but it will be used in the next chapter in a present value computation to summarize the cash flows of a risky investment project.

Combinations of Investments and the Portfolio Effect

Up to this point the decision under risk has been expressed in terms of single investments, each with a mean and variance of money outcomes. Now combinations of investments, and the resulting means and variances of those combinations must be considered.

First consider the linear combination of two random variables X and Y. If $Z = aX + bY$ the mean of Z and the variance of Z can be expressed in terms of X's and Y's parameters. The mean of Z, $\bar{Z}$, is found by

$$\bar{Z} = a\bar{X} + b\bar{Y}$$

The variance of Z, σ_Z^2 is slightly more complicated:

$$\sigma_Z^2 = a^2\sigma_X^2 + b^2\sigma_Y^2 + 2ab\sigma_{XY}$$

The term σ_{XY} is the covariance between X and Y, which is a measure of the linear relation of the two variables.

The covariance between two random variables can be computed by the formula:

$$\sigma_{XY} = \sum_{X,Y} (X - \overline{X})(Y - \overline{Y}) P(X,Y)$$

The summation is over all pairs of X and Y values, and the probability, $P(X,Y)$, is the probability of that pair of X and Y values.

The covariance is related to the linear correlation coefficient ρ_{XY}; actually the correlation coefficient is

$$-\sigma_X\sigma_Y \leq \sigma_{XY} \leq \sigma_X\sigma_Y$$

The covariance can therefore be expressed as the product of the correlation coefficient and the two standard deviations

$$\sigma_{XY} = \rho_{XY}\sigma_X\sigma_Y$$

The covariance is limited in its range of values:

$$\rho_{XY} = \frac{\sigma XY}{\sigma_X \sigma_Y}$$

The highest possible value of the covariance is the product of the two random variables' standard deviations. This value is attained only when the two random variables are perfectly positively correlated.

The lowest possible value of the covariance is the negative of the product of the two random variables' standard deviations. This value would be attained when the two random variables are perfectly negatively correlated.

It is easy to see that since the covariance term can be negative it is possible to combine investments and thereby reduce the risk by this diversification. It is not necessary that the covariance be negative to reduce the risk of a diversified combination from that of a concentrated combination, however.

A simple example will demonstrate the combination of two investments. The two investments consist of the purchase of shares of stock of two companies. Each company's stock is priced at \$1 per share, and pays no dividend. The stock is to be sold at the end of one year, and the proceeds of that sale are the money outcome of the investment.

The money outcome *per hundred shares* of the first stock is X, and the money outcome *per hundred shares* of the second stock is Y. The means, variances, and covariance are estimated as:

$\overline{X} = 200$ $\qquad \sigma_Y^2 = 144$

$\sigma_X^2 = 160$ $\qquad \sigma_{XY} = 50$

$\overline{Y} = 180$

If the investor has \$100 to spend on the stock he can buy any combination of 100 shares. The mean outcome is expressed as

$$\bar{Z} = a(200) + b(180)$$

and the variance as

$$\sigma_Z^2 = a^2\ (160) + b^2\ (144) + 2ab(50)$$

First the results of an entirely concentrated portfolio are computed, where the investor buys only stock of the first company. In this case

$$a = 1.0 \text{ and } b = 0$$

so the mean of the combination is

$$\begin{aligned} Z &= 1.0(200) + 0(180) \\ &= 200 \end{aligned}$$

The variance is

$$\sigma_Z^2 = (1.0)^2\ (160) + (0)^2\ (144) + 2\ (1.0)\ (0)\ (50) = 160$$

The other concentrated portfolio is where the investor buys only stock of the second company. Since

$$\begin{aligned} a &= 0 \text{ and } b = 1.0 \\ Z &= 0(200) + 1.0(180) \\ &= 180 \end{aligned}$$

and

$$\sigma_Z^2 = (0)^2\ (160) + (1.0)^2\ (144) + 2\ (0)\ (1.0)\ (50) = 144$$

Now consider one of the possible diversified portfolios. Suppose the investor buys 40 shares of the first company and 60 shares of the second. In this case

$$a = 0.4 \text{ and } b = 0.6$$

The mean for this combination is

$$\begin{aligned} \bar{Z} &= 0.4(200) + 0.6(180) \\ &= 188 \end{aligned}$$

The variance for this combination is

$$\sigma_Z^2 = (0.4)^2\ (160) + (0.6)^2\ (144) + 2\ (0.4)\ (0.6)\ (50) = 101.42$$

The mean for the diversified combination came out between the means for the concentrated cases, but the variance in the diversified case is lower than either of the variances for the concentrated cases.

The results for the diversification by buying 40 shares of the first company and 60 shares of the second are superior by the efficiency conditions to the results when 100 shares of the second company are purchased. Efficiency cannot be used to conclude that the purchase of 100 shares of the first company is dominated by the 40-60 combination since the mean, 200, is higher than 188.

The gains from diversification, the portfolio effect, can clearly be seen from the reduction in variance (in risk) in this numerical example. The example could be extended by computing the means and variances of all the other combinations that could be made of the two securities, and some of these combinations would be efficient and others inefficient. The resulting combinations available to the investor with $100 to spend on the two stocks are represented by the curve in Figure 7.11. In Figure 7.11 the point 1 indicates the results when the entire $100 is spent on the first stock (X), point 3 where only the second stock (Y) is purchased, and the points in between various combinations of the two stocks. Point 2 is the combination that yields the lowest variance, 46 shares of the first stock and 54 shares of the second. The efficient set in this example is the set of combinations between points 1 and 2.

Figure 7.11
Combinations of Two Investments

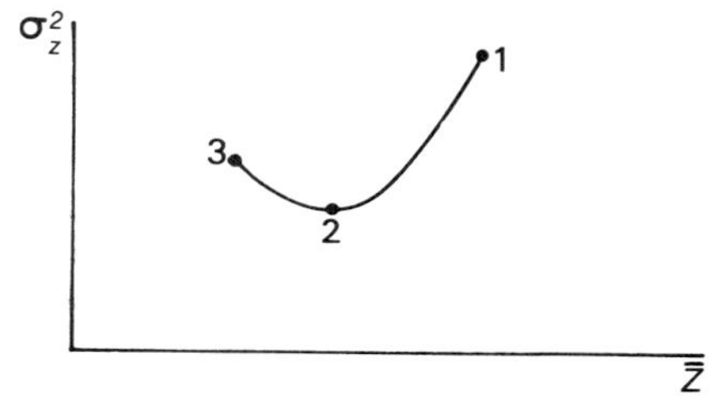

Summary

To build a general theory of decision under risk the device of utility functions is used. To each money income there is a corresponding cardinal measure of the individual's satisfaction level, a utility value. Although specific mathematical forms for a utility function are difficult to derive, a considerable amount of insight is gained from the assumption of qualitative characteristics of utility, that marginal utility is positive but decreasing. Those qualitative characteristics can be expressed in terms of derivatives, a positive first derivative and negative second derivative, or by saying that the utility function is monotonically increasing and concave.

From those qualitative assumptions the result is that the investor is a return-seeker and is risk-averse. Expected utility is then expressed as a function of the mean and variance of money outcomes. Expected utility for the risk-averse investor is an increasing function of the mean and a decreasing function of the variance.

When the mean and variance parameters are determined for feasible investments the feasible set can be reduced to a smaller set, the efficient set, by application of the qualitative characteristics of expected utility. While ultimate investment decisions must be made by reference to the investor's exact mean-variance trade-off, the concept of efficiency does reduce the range of choice for the investor.

The chapter was concluded by an analysis of the diversification or portfolio effect. The formulas for a sum of random variables are used to derive the mean and the variance of a combination of investments from the individual means and the individual variances. In the following chapter some techniques of estimation of means, variances, and correlation coefficients will be discussed.

Notes

[1]For a continuous distribution of X with probability density function $f(X)$ the variance is

$$\sigma_X^2 = \int (X - \overline{X})^2 f(X) dX$$

[2]There is a practical reason for using the mean and variance instead of the complete distribution. Well-known techniques exist for estimating those measures statistically, where corresponding techniques for estimating the whole probability distribution do not.

APPENDIX TO CHAPTER 7

Estimating Utility Functions

A considerable amount of work has been done in the field of empirically estimating utility functions for use in investment decisions in recent years. Most of the techniques use some variation of the "von Neumann-Morgenstern" cardinal index construction method.[1] In this method the utility index is constructed from a series of probabilities in a reference lottery where the subject is given a choice between a sure amount and a chance in the lottery.

An example will serve to illustrate the utility index construction. Suppose the investor's utility levels for money income between $1,000 and $10,000 are to be derived. A reference lottery with two possible outcomes is defined, with the first outcome below the lowest money income level and the second outcome above the highest money income level. In this case it will be convenient to define the reference lottery to have outcomes of 0 and $20,000. The outcome $20,000 can be called "winning," and the lower outcome, 0, can be called "losing."

To determine the utility level for one amount of certain money income, say $1,000, the subject is given a choice between the $1,000 and a ticket in the reference lottery with a known probability of winning. Suppose the first choice offered the subject is a ticket with a probability of winning of 0.20. If the subject chooses the lottery ticket the next choice is a lottery ticket with a lowered probability of winning.

Suppose the next choice is the $1,000 or the lottery ticket with a winning probability of 0.10. If the subject chooses the certain $1,000 the next choice offered has a higher probability of winning. The series of choice continues until a probability of winning is found where the subject is indifferent between the $1,000 and the lottery ticket. Suppose that probability is 0.14. The probability, 0.14, where the subject is indifferent (cannot choose) is the utility index for the $1,000 money income level.

Each certain money income level is compared to the same reference lottery, 0-$20,000. Suppose the utility index constructed for the discrete points is:

Money income	Utility index	Money income	Utility index
1,000	0.14	6,000	0.45
2,000	0.24	7,000	0.47
3,000	0.32	8,000	0.49
4,000	0.38	9,000	0.51
5,000	0.42	10,000	0.52

The final stage is to fit a mathematical function to the observed points. The form of the function, a polynomial, exponential, or logarithmic function, for examples, should be chosen to fit the data as closely as possible. Once the mathematical form is established, possibly by intuition, the numerical values of the function should be established by curve fitting procedures, most likely the least squares regression method.

The von Neumann-Morgenstern cardinal utility index is theoretically correct for an individual's utility function, but methods of constructing utility functions for groups of individuals are still in the preliminary stages with unresolved theoretical difficulties. Therefore construction of a utility function for a corporation (for the stockholders of the corporation) is probably not possible yet.

If it can be assumed that stockholders of the corporation are risk-averse the efficiency conditions developed in the chapter can be used to make some choice among risky investments. Those conditions did not depend on an exact knowledge of the stockholders' preferences.

A More Formal Justification of Utility as a Function of the Mean and Variance

When the original utility function

$$U = f(X)$$

was defined in the chapter a specific form was assumed for working a numerical example. It is desirable to derive decisions models with general functions as much as possible to avoid theoretical conclusions that are dependent on specific numerical characteristics of an assumed function.

In addition to sticking with general utility functions, the analysis deals with general probability distributions rather than specific numerical examples. The following presentation will accordingly be based upon such general functions and distributions.

A function that cannot be evaluated directly can usually be approximated by a Taylor's series expansion about a fixed value of X. If the utility function is expanded around a fixed value, $\bar{X}$, the Taylor series would be:

$$U = f(\bar{X}) + f'(\bar{X})\,[X-\bar{X}] + \frac{f''(\bar{X})}{2!}\,[X-\bar{X}]^2 + \frac{f'''(\bar{X})}{3!}\,[X-\bar{X}]^3 + \ldots\ldots$$

The terms in the series are partly constants and the rest simple expressions involving the variable X. Since $\bar{X}$ is a fixed value the function evaluated at $\bar{X}$, $f(\bar{X})$, is fixed (a constant), the first derivative $f'(\bar{X})$ is fixed, and the higher order derivatives have fixed values. The expressions involving the variable X have the form

$$[X-\bar{X}]^k$$

The next step in the operation is to take the expected value of each side of the Taylor series expression. The notation $E(Y)$ is used to indicate the expected value of Y. The result of taking expected values when X is the random variable is:

$$E(U) = f(\bar{X}) + f'(\bar{X})E[X-\bar{X}] + \frac{f''(\bar{X})}{2!}E[X-\bar{X}]^2$$
$$+ \frac{f'''(\bar{X})}{3!}E[X-\bar{X}]^3 + \ldots\ldots$$

The terms on the right side of the equality must now be interpreted.

$f(X)$ is the original utility function evaluated at the mean money outcome. $E(X-\bar{X})$ is zero, so the second term is zero. In the third term $E(X-\bar{X})^2$ is the variance of X, $\sigma_X{}^2$, which is multiplied by a constant. In the fourth term $E(X-X)^3$ is the third moment around the mean, a measure of the skewness of the probability distribution. A shorter notation, M_3, can be used for the third moment which is multiplied by a constant,

$$\frac{f'''(\bar{X})}{3!}.$$

The results so far can be summarized by saying that expected utility can be expressed as a function of the mean, the variance, and the third moment of the probability distribution:

$$E(U) = g(\bar{X}, \sigma_X^2, M_3, \ldots)$$

Only the first four terms of the Taylor series expansion have been shown, but the further terms would involve higher degree moments of the distribution of X.

Some conclusions can be drawn regarding the response of expected utility to changes in the parameters of the distribution of X. Expected utility is an increasing function with respect to increases in the mean. This conclusion comes from the assumption that the original utility function increases as X increases.

Expected utility should be a decreasing function with respect to the variance. The assumption is that the investor is risk-averse, has a concave utility function as represented in Figure 7.2. If that curve is concave, then $f''(X)$ is negative for all values of X, and therefore

$$\frac{f''(\bar{X})}{2!}$$

in the Taylor series expression will be negative. If the investor is risk-averse then he must be "variance-averse" as well.

The response of expected utility to changes in the third moment are not as clear-cut. It is likely that expected utility is an increasing function of the third moment, as would be found in the logarithmic utility function example in the chapter. The third moment is a measure of skewness of the distribution, and the more positive skewness (tail to the right) probably the happier the investor would be.

The analysis in decision theory is usually terminated after consideration of the second moment, the variance, and no attention paid to the third moment and higher degree moments. There are three ways to justify this termination.

The first has to do with the mathematical form of the utility function,

$$U = f(X)$$

A common assumption made in theoretical literature is that the utility function is a quadratic (second-degree polynomial) in money, X, and therefore the third and higher degree derivatives of the function are zero. In the Taylor series expansion

$$\frac{f'''(\bar{X})}{3!}$$

would be zero, so the term involving the third moment would be zero.

The second justification is based on the form of the probability distribution. If the distribution is symmetric about the mean the third moment would be zero, and of course the corresponding term in the Taylor series would be zero.

The third way to justify the termination is based upon the idea of "sufficient approximation." To apply the Taylor series expansion successfully it is necessary that the successive terms in the expansion tend to zero. Because the term involving the third moment is supposed to be smaller than the term involving the variance, it may not contribute sufficient information to justify inclusion. Using the mean and the variance may yield an adequate approximation to the value of expected utility.

The decision under risk is usually based on consideration of the mean and variance of money outcomes. The variance is *a* measure of risk, although not necessarily an exact measure. As financial theory develops, a more refined concept of risk will evolve, possibly being measured by the series of moments of the statistical distribution.

Investment Choice Through Stochastic Dominance

There is another alternative to the mean-variance method for choices among risky investments, the stochastic dominance method. In the stochastic dominance approach the entire probability distribution of outcomes for an investment is compared with the probability distribution for the other investment. A preference ordering can be derived from the cumulative probability functions, first-degree stochastic dominance, or from the integral of the cumulative probability functions, second-degree stochastic dominance, without reference to the investor's utility function except a check for some weak conditions on marginal utility.

To demonstrate stochastic dominance two investment projects are defined with probability density functions $f_1(X)$ for the first project and $f_2(X)$ for the second project. The variable X is money returns from the project, and the projects are assumed to be mutually exclusive and equally-priced so that the decision situation can be resolved by a ranking of the projects.

First degree stochastic dominance exists whenever one project's cumulative probability density function, $F(X)$, has a lower value than the other project's cumulative probability density function for all values of X. That is, project 2 dominates project 1 if

$$F_1(X) \geqslant F_2(X) \text{ for all } X.$$

The cumulative probability density function for the continuously distributed random variable X is defined as

$$F_1(X) = \int^{X} f_1(X)\,dX$$

Figure A.7.1
First Degree Stochastic
Dominance Examples

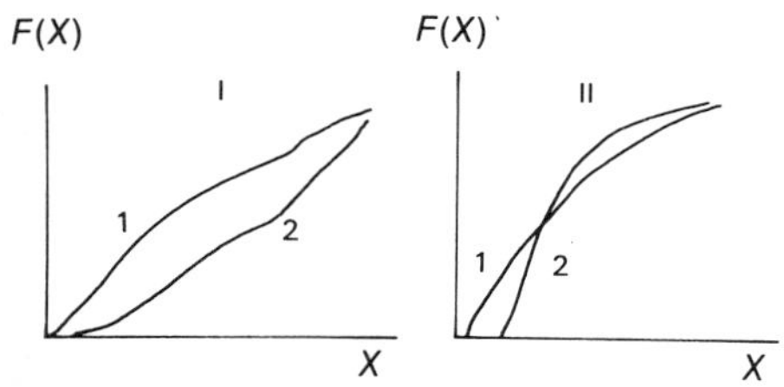

where the integral is over all values of the random variable less than or equal to X. $F_1(X)$ is therefore the probability of a value less than or equal to X occurring. [In the case of a discretely distributed random variable with probability $P(X)$ the cumulative probability function is

$$F_1(X) = \sum_{i=1}^{i=X} P(X)\,.]$$

First degree stochastic dominance is demonstrated visually in Figure A.7.1.

In Quadrant I of Figure A.7.1 project 2 dominates project 1 because $F_1(X) > F_2(X)$ for every X value. In Quadrant II neither project is dominant because the cumulative probability density functions cross.

Figure A.7.2
Second Degree Stochastic
Dominance Example

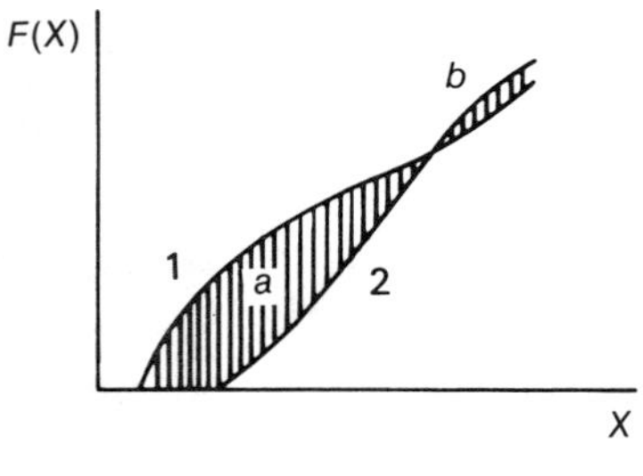

Second degree stochastic dominance is defined in terms of the integrals of the cumulative probability density frunction. Project 2 dominates project 1 if

$$\int^{X} F_1(X)\,dX \geq \int^{X} F_2(X)\,dX$$

for all X values. This integral can be interpreted graphically as the area under the $F(X)$ curve between the lower limit of X and the particular X that is the upper limit of the integral. A situation where project 2 dominates project 1 is shown in Figure A.7.2.

In Figure A.7.2 the area under curve 1 is greater than the area under curve 2. That the areas differ can also be determined by comparing the shaded areas a and b in the diagram.

Comparison of Figures A.7.1 and A.7.2 shows that second degree stochastic dominance exists sometimes when first degree stochastic dominance does not. Therefore in ranking investments the better tool to use would be second degree stochastic dominance because fewer indeterminate cases would be encountered.

Stochastic dominance is justified theoretically by reference to expected utility. Hadar and Russell[2] proved that the only necessary assumption for first degree stochastic dominance is that the investor's utility function has a positive first derivative, that his marginal utility always be positive. The necessary assumption for second degree stochastic dominance is that the first derivative of the utility function is positive and the second derivative is negative, that the investor has positive but diminishing marginal utility.

Second degree stochastic dominance is therefore assumable for "all" investors, and as a result could be used for investment decisions without respect to specific utility functions. There is one fatal drawback to the stochastic dominance technique, however; the entire probability distribution must be known to allow a choice. Less information about the distribution, only the two parameters $\overline{X}$ and $\sigma_X{}^2$, is necessary in the mean-variance approach to choice.

Notes

[1] Described originally in John von Neumann and Oskar Morgenstern, *Theory of Games and Economic Behavior*, 2nd ed. (Princeton, N. J.: Princeton University Press, 1947). A later summary of the technique can be found in R. Duncan Luce and Howard Raiffa, *Games and Decisions*, (New York: Wiley, 1957).

[2] Joseph Hadar and William R. Russell, "Rules for Ordering Uncertain Prospects," *American Economic Review*, March 1969.

Chapter 7 Questions

1. Could utility values be used instead of money payments in the game theory problems?
2. The maximin criterion is called the pessimist's strategy, and the maximax criterion the optimist's. Why?
3. Is a mixed strategy solution feasible when the game situation can only be played one time?
4. How could a utility function be estimated for an individual?
5. Does utility exist for the "non-person" corporation?
6. How much will the use of an expected money payoff by itself (without a measure of dispersion) distort the investment decision process?
7. Could the mode or median be substituted for the mean, and the range be substituted for the variance in a risk decision model?
8. Explain how the concept of efficiency may allow investment decisions to be made without the specific form of a utility function being known.
9. The statistical interaction of returns from two projects is sometimes referred to as the "portfolio effect." Explain the portfolio effect in terms of the standard deviation or variance of total returns.
10. Will diversification always reduce the variance?
11. Show how the formula for the variance of the total return of two projects demonstrates the adage "don't put all your eggs in one bas-

12. Describe examples of a risk-averse person, a risk-neutral person, and a risk-seeker.
13. Should a utility function be logarithmic in mathematical form, a quadratic, or some other mathematical form?
14. Is the certainty equivalent easier to obtain than the specific form of the utility function?

Chapter 7 Problems

1. In a game against nature situation the decision-maker is faced with the possibilities indicated in this matrix of possible payments to the decision maker:

	Decision-maker strategies	
Nature	1	2
A	10	2
B	4	20

Find the decision-maker's optimum choice of strategy using:
a. The maximin method.
b. The maximax method.
c. The mixed strategy method.

2. A decision-maker's attitude toward income can be expressed by the utility function

$$U = 2X - 0.1X^2$$

where U is utility and X is money income. An investment is to be evaluated where the cash income is subject to a statistical distribution with possible values and probabilities:

X	$P(X)$
3	0.2
5	0.5
7	0.3

a. Compute the expected value of X, $E(X)$.
b. Substitute that value in the utility function and compute the utility of that income level.
c. Find the expected utility of the investment by first calculating the utility level for each possible value of X, and then using the probabilities of those utility outcomes and utilities in the expected value formula.

3. Repeat the calculations of problem 3, this time using the utility function

$$U = 3 + 1.5X$$

4. Investment A has these possible cash outcomes and probabilities:

Outcome	Probability
10	0.1
15	0.6
20	0.3

Investment B has these:

Outcome	Probability
12	0.2
14	0.6
16	0.2

Using the efficiency concept can a clear choice be made between A and B?

5. Project A has even chances (0.5 probabilities) of a gain of 50 or a loss of 10, and Project B has a certain outcome of a gain of 18. Choose between A and B.

6. Common stock A has an expected value at the end of the year of $60 per 100 shares and a standard deviation of that value per 100 shares of $20. Common stock B's expected value per 100 shares is $50 and its standard deviation per 100 shares is $16. The correlation coefficient between the values of A and B is 0.4. Calculate the expected value and variance for these combinations:

a. 200 shares of A and 0 shares of B.
b. 0 shares of A and 200 shares of B.
c. 100 shares of A and 100 shares of B.

7. Suppose the correlation coefficient in problem 6 is –0.2. Recalculate the expected values and variances of the combinations.

Chapter 7 References

Borch, Karl H. *The Economics of Uncertainty*. Princeton, N.J.: Princeton University Press, 1968.

Farrar, Donald E. *The Investment Decision under Uncertainty*. Englewood Cliffs, N. J.: Prentice-Hall, 1962.

Fishburn, Peter C. "Utility Theory." *Management Science*, January 1968.

Friedman, Milton, and Savage, L. J. "Utility Analysis of Choices Involving Risk." *Journal of Political Economy*, August 1958.

Hadar, Josef, and Russell, William P. "Rules for Ordering Uncertain Prospects." *American Economic Review*, March 1969.

Jean, William H. "The Extension of Portfolio Analysis to Three or More Parameters." *Journal of Financial and Quantitative Analysis*, January 1971.

Luce, R. Duncan, and Raiffa, Howard. *Games and Decisions*. New York: Wiley, 1957.

Mao, James C. T., and Helliwell, John F. "Investment Decisions Under Uncertainty: Theory and Practice." *Journal of Finance*, May 1969.

Markowitz, Harry. "Portfolio Selection." *Journal of Finance*, March 1952.

—— *Portfolio Selection: Efficient Diversification of Investments*. Cowles Foundation Monograph #16. New York: Wiley, 1959.

Pratt, John W. "Risk Aversion in the Small and in the Large." *Econometrica*, April 1964.

Schlaifer, Robert. *Analysis of Decisions Under Uncertainty*. New York: McGraw-Hill, 1969.

Swalm, Ralph D. "Utility Theory–Insights into Risk Taking." *Harvard Business Review*, November-December 1966.

von Neumann, J., and Morgenstern, O. *Theory of Games and Economic Behavior*, 2nd ed. Princeton, N.J.: Princeton University Press, 1947.

Whitmore, G. A. "Third-Degree Stochastic Dominance." *American Economic Review*, June 1970.

8

CAPITAL BUDGETING UNDER RISK

Deriving a general solution procedure for capital budgeting under risk is complicated because of the dimensions involved. Investment projects normally result in a sequence of cash flows, and each cash flow must be considered as a random variable with some statistical distribution. Then the combination of investment projects also has a statistical distribution, so the "portfolio effect" must be investigated for the combinations of projects.

To simplify the analysis somewhat the selection criterion assumed will use two measures for each situation, the expected present value, $E(PV)$, and the variance of present value, $\sigma^2(PV)$. The expected present value is a desired characteristic, the investor's (the corporation's) utility is an increasing function of $E(PV)$; and the variance of present values is an undesirable characteristic, the investor's utility is a decreasing function of $\sigma^2(PV)$.

Much time must be spent in deriving the formulas for $E(PV)$ and $\sigma^2(PV)$. First the formulas for a single project are presented, and then the formulas for a combination of projects.

In the single project $E(PV)$ and $\sigma^2(PV)$, the entire probability distributions for all the periods' cash flows could be used directly to derive the probability distribution of present values. Since only the summary measures, the mean and variance, of that distribution are to be used in a decision model, a shortcut that will avoid the use of the distribution of present values will be derived. In that shortcut method the *period* means and variances are combined to derive $E(PV)$ and $\sigma^2(PV)$.

Another advantage to working with period means and variances is that sometimes those numbers can be estimated directly with a higher degree of accuracy than the estimate of the entire probability distribution. Some examples of that estimation will be presented below.

To derive $\sigma^2(PV)$ some measure of the statistical dependence of cash flows over time will be necessary. That measure can be expressed in terms of covariances, as the covariance of period one's cash flows with period two's cash flows, for example, or in terms of a correlation coefficient. The correlation coefficient is relatively easier to estimate, and the covariance can then be computed from that estimate.

Depending on the size of the correlation coefficient some easy formulas for the calculation of $\sigma^2(PV)$ can be used. If the correlation between cash flows is zero, the case of independence, a formula similar to taking the present value of the period variances will yield the variance of present values. When the cash flows are perfectly positively correlated, the correlation coefficient equals one, the standard deviation of present values, $\sigma(PV)$, equals the present value of the period standard deviations. For any correlation between these two extremes the longer formula for $\sigma^2(PV)$ must be used.

Once $E(PV)$ and $\sigma^2(PV)$ for a single project are derived there is a choice among decision criteria. The mean and variance may be used directly with the investor's utility function, represented in indifference curve form in the diagrams. Even when the exact utility function is unavailable the efficiency concept can be used to discriminate among single projects.

In the case of risk-neutrality the decision is based solely on $E(PV)$. Risk-neutrality may be assumable for small investment projects under consideration by a large corporation, but should not be assumed for every capital budgeting under risk situation.

A utility-based decision model that is applicable in some situations uses the present value of certainty equivalents. To use this technique, independence over time of cash flows is necessary, but the required information about the investor's utility function is kept to a minimum. Another commonly used procedure, the risk-adjusted discount rate method, is compared with the present value of certainty equivalents.

The analysis must then be expanded to handle multiple investment projects. The $E(PV)$ and $\sigma^2(PV)$ for separate projects are combined, following the same formulas for a mean and variance of a sum of random variables used in Chapter 7. To derive the variance of present values for a combination of projects the correlation coefficient of present values between projects must be known. Again that coefficient may be estimated directly.

A shorter list of decision criteria for combinations of projects is available. The investor's utility function may be used directly to select the optimum combination, the efficiency conditions can be used to limit the choice without reference to the investor's specific utility function, and in the case of risk-neutrality an exact solution to the optimum combination can be found. The present value of certainty equivalents and risk-adjusted discount rate methods are not readily applicable in the combination of projects case.

The Derivation of Present Value Distributions for a Single Project

One approach to deriving the mean of present values, $E(PV)$, and the variance of present values, $\sigma^2(PV)$, is to derive the entire distribution of present values from the distributions of each period's cash flow. To demonstrate this derivation a discrete distribution of the cash flow for each period will be assumed.

For the general case it cannot be assumed that the periods' cash flows are statistically independent. Instead what happens at time two is dependent on what happened at time one, time three on time two, and so forth. One way of describing the statistical independence is by defining conditional probabilities.

The notation X_j will be used here to stand for a particular cash flow at time j. X_j is a random variable that assumes a set of discrete values. If the probability of Xj's occurrence is not dependent on any other event, that probability (called a marginal probability) is $P_j(X_j)$. For all except the first period the probability of X_j is dependent on what happened in the prior period, X_{j-1}. The probability of X_j must therefore be expressed as the conditional probability $P_j(X_j \mid X_{j-1})$.

There are a total of t periods (and cash flows) for an investment project. One possible outcome for the cash flow sequence is the set $(X_1, X_2, \ldots, X_t)$. For that cash flow sequence a present value can be defined, and the probability of that cash flow sequence is the probability of that particular present value.

The probability of the cash flow sequence in terms of the marginal and conditional probabilities is a product:

$$P(X_1, X_2, \ldots, X_t) = P(X_1)P(X_2|X_1) \ldots P(X_t|X_{t-1})$$

(If the cash flows are independent over time, substitute $P(X_j)$ for $P(X_j \mid X_{j-1})$ in the formula.)

A simple example will serve to demonstrate the derivation of the distribution of present values. Assume a two-period project with three possible cash flows each time period. The cash flows and their respective probabilities are summarized in Table 8.1.

TABLE 8.1
Example of Cash Flow Distributions

X_1	$P_1(X_1)$	X_2	$P(X_2 \mid X_1)$
10	0.4	5	0.5
		15	0.3
		25	0.2
20	0.5	5	0.1
		15	0.8
		25	0.1
30	0.1	5	0.1
		15	0.3
		25	0.6

In reading the table it should be remembered that the cash inflow of 15 at time 2 (the event that $X_2 = 15$) can occur with a cash inflow of 10 at time 1, 20 at time 1, or 30 at time 1. If $X_1 = 10$ the probability that $X_2 = 5$ is 0.5, that $X_2 = 15$ is 0.3, and that $X_2 = 25$ is 0.2

The cash flow sequences, the present values of the cash flow sequences computed with an interest rate of 10 percent, and the probabilities of the sequences are summarized in Table 8.2. In Table 8.2 the sequence (10, 5) gives a present value of

TABLE 8.2
Example Distribution of Present Values

Cash flow sequence	Present value	Probability $P(X_1)P(X_2 \mid X_1)$
(10, 5)	13.22	0.20
(10, 15)	21.49	0.12
(10, 25)	29.75	0.08
(20, 5)	22.31	0.05
(20, 15)	30.58	0.40
(20, 25)	38.84	0.05
(30, 5)	31.40	0.01
(30, 15)	39.67	0.03
(30, 25)	47.93	0.06

$$\left[\frac{1}{1+0.10}\right]10 + \left[\frac{1}{1+0.10}\right]^2 5 = 13.22$$

The probability of that sequence is

$$0.4(0.5) = 0.20$$

The listing of present values and probabilities could be used directly in a decision model, either by using the present values as arguments in a utility function and calculating the expected utility with the respective probabilities, or by deriving the mean and variance of present values from the distribution and using those parameters in an expected utility function. Before the distribution of present values is used in such a decision model, however, the amount of computation necessary to derive the distribution should be reviewed.

For the two-period example nine cash flow sequences were possible. If there were m possible cash flows for each period and t time periods for the investment project, the number of cash flow sequences is m^t. If there were ten possible outcomes per period and eight periods, the number of sequences would be

$$10^8 = 100{,}000{,}000$$

That is too much information to consider processing.

Fortunately a shorter method exists to derive the parameters of the present value distribution from the parameters of the periods' distributions.

The Present Value as a Linear Combination of Random Variables

The computation of a present value is mathematically a linear combination of the cash flows. This fact can easily be seen by writing the present value computation in two ways:

$$PV = [\frac{1}{1+r}]X_1 + [\frac{1}{1+r}]^2 X_2 + \ldots = \sum_{j=1}^{j=t} [\frac{1}{1+r}]^j X_j$$

$$PV = a_1 X_1 + a_2 X_2 + \ldots = \sum_{j=1}^{j=t} a_j X_j$$

where

$$a_j = [\frac{1}{1+r}]^j$$

If the X_j are random variables, then the formulas for the mean and the variance of present values can be adapted directly from the mean and variance formulas for a linear combination of random variables. Using the notation Z for the linear combination, the expected value of Z can be found by

$$E(Z) = a_1 E(X_1) + a_2 E(X_2) + \ldots = \sum_{j=1}^{j=t} a_j E(X_j)$$

The mean of present values, $E(PV)$, can be found from the period means, $E(X_j)$, by the formula

$$E(PV) = \sum_{j=1}^{j=t} [\frac{1}{1+r}]^j E(X_j)$$

The mean of present values is the present value of the period means.

This formula holds regardless of the statistical dependence of cash flows over time.

The formula for the variance of Z is a little longer since covariances must be taken into account. Using the notation σ_{ii} to stand for the variance of the ith random variable and σ_{ij} for the covariance of the ith random variable with the jth random variable, the general formula for the variance of the linear combination of random variables is

$$\sigma^2(Z) = \sum_{i=1}^{i=t} \sum_{j=1}^{j=t} a_i a_j \sigma_{ij}$$

If $i = j$ in this formula σ_{ij} is a variance, and if $i \neq j$ σ_{ij} is a covariance. Suppose there are two variables, $t = 2$; then the variance is

$$\sigma^2(Z) = a_1{}^2\sigma_{11} + a_2{}^2\sigma_{22} + 2a_1a_2\sigma_{12}$$

If there are three random variables

$$\sigma^2(Z) = a_1{}^2\sigma_{11} + a_2{}^2\sigma_{22} + a_3{}^2\sigma_{33} + 2a_1a_2\sigma_{12} + 2a_1a_3\sigma_{13} + 2a_2a_3\sigma_{23}$$

There is a covariance term for every pair of random variables. Given t random variables the number of covariances is

$$\frac{t^2 - t}{2}$$

and the number of variances is t.

The covariance σ_{ij} can also be expressed in terms of the correlation coefficient ρ_{ij} and the standard deviations σ_i and σ_j:

ρ_{ij}

$$\sigma_{ij} = \rho_{ij}\sigma_i\sigma_j$$

Since $\sigma_i{}^2 = \sigma_{ii}$; and $\rho_{ii} = 1$; the formula for the variance of the linear combination of random variables can be written as

$$\sigma^2(Z) = \sum_{i=1}^{i=t} \sum_{j=1}^{j=t} a_i a_j \rho_{ij}\sigma_i\sigma_j$$

Now suppose the variance of present values for a t-period project is to be calculated from the period variances (or period standard deviations):

$$\sigma^2(PV) = \sum_{i=1}^{i=t} \sum_{j=1}^{j=t} [\frac{1}{1+r}]^i [\frac{1}{1+r}]^j \rho_{ij}\sigma(X)\sigma(X_j)$$

For a two-period project:

$$\sigma^2(PV) = [\frac{1}{1+r}]^2\sigma^2(X_1) + [\frac{1}{1+r}]^4\sigma^2(X_2) + 2[\frac{1}{1+r}][\frac{1}{1+r}]^2\rho_{12}\sigma(X_1)\sigma(X_2)$$

An example will demonstrate the calculations of $E(PV)$ and $\sigma^2(PV)$. Suppose those parameters are to be derived for a two-period project where an interest rate of 10 percent is used for present calculations. The items of information needed are the parameters of the time 1 cash flow:

$$E(X_1) = 60$$
$$\sigma^2(X_1) = 25$$

the parameters of the time 2 cash flow:

$$E(X_2) = 40$$
$$\sigma^2(X_2) = 64$$

and the correlation coefficient of the two cash flows:

$$\rho_{12} = 0.7$$

The mean of present values is

$$E(PV) = [\frac{1}{1+0.10}]60 + [\frac{1}{1+0.10}]^2 40$$
$$= 54.5$$

The variance of present values is

$$\sigma^2(PV) = [\frac{1}{1+0.10}]^2 25 + [\frac{1}{1+0.10}]^4 64 + 2[\frac{1}{1+0.10}][\frac{1}{1+0.10}]^2$$
$$= 106.4 \qquad (0.7)(5)(8$$

To solve for $E(PV)$ and $\sigma^2(PV)$ for a t-period project the information needed is t period means, t period variances, and

$$\frac{t^2 - t}{2}$$

correlation coefficients (or covariances). For a 10-period project the required items total

$$10 + 10 + \frac{10^2 - 10}{2} = 65$$

This is a considerable improvement over the 100,000,000 cash flow sequences and present values of the preceding section.

Before describing an estimation procedure to derive the period means and variances and the correlation coefficients, two special cases of statistical relation between periods will be discussed. In these two cases a considerably shortened formula for $\sigma^2(PV)$ can be used.

Two Special Cases of the Correlation Coefficient Value

The two special cases occur when the cash flows are independent over time, $\rho_{ij} = 0$, and when the cash flows are perfectly positively correlated, $\rho_{ij} = 1$.

If the cash flows are all independent, the correlation coefficients and the covariances are zero, and the formula for the variance of present values is

$$\sigma^2(PV) = \sum_{j=1}^{j=t} \left[\frac{1}{1+r}\right]^{2j} \sigma^2(X_j)$$

The variance of present values is *almost* the present value of the variances for this case, but the exponent of the present value factor is $2j$, not j.

In the second special case $\rho_{ij} = 1$, and the variance of present values is

$$\sigma^2(PV) = \left[\sum_{j=1}^{j=t} \left[\frac{1}{1+r}\right]^{j} \sigma(X_j)\right]^2$$

For a two-period project with $\rho_{12} = 1$ the variance of present values using the original $\sigma^2(PV)$ formula is

$$\sigma^2(PV) = \left[\frac{1}{1+r}\right]^2 \sigma^2(X_1) + \left[\frac{1}{1+r}\right]^4 \sigma^2(X_2) + 2\left[\frac{1}{1+r}\right]\left[\frac{1}{1+r}\right]^2 \sigma(X_1)\sigma(X_2)$$

$$= \left[\left[\frac{1}{1+r}\right]\sigma(X_1) + \left[\frac{1}{1+r}\right]^2 \sigma(X_2)\right]^2$$

For this case the standard deviation of present values, $\sigma(PV)$, is the present value of the period standard deviations, $\sigma(X_j)$.

In both these special cases only the period variances (or standard deviations) are needed to calculate $\sigma^2(PV)$. For a t-period project there are t parameters that must be provided.

Estimation of Period Means, Variances, and Correlation Coefficients

The required estimates of the period means and variances might be obtained directly from the promoters of the investment project, but their estimates might be improved if a pictorial representation of the distribution were utilized in the estimation process. For example suppose that the estimator thought the distribution followed a pattern such as is represented in Figure 8.1.

Figure 8.1
Normal Distribution of a Cash Flow

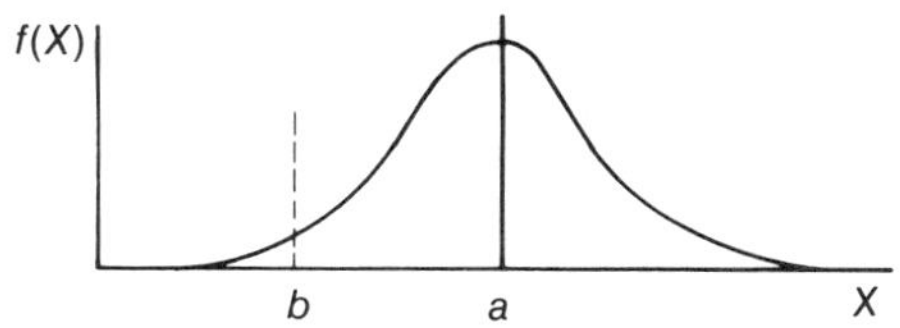

Figure 8.1 is a representation of a Normal distribution, whose characteristics are well-known to anyone who has taken an introductory statistics course. The value a on the diagram represents the middle of the distribution, the median which is also the mean of the distribution. The value b may represent a numerical outcome such that the probability of achieving a value below b is 5 percent. In the Normal distribution the distance between a and b is 1.645 standard deviations. Therefore given the values of a and b the variance can be calculated as

$$\sigma^2(X) = \left[\frac{a-b}{1.645}\right]^2$$

To derive the mean and the variance of the Normal distribution only two point estimates are needed. The value a is the mean, and it might be described as the value such that it is equally likely that an outcome will be above a or that the outcome will be below a. The value b is a "pessimistic" or low value, chosen so that there is only a 5 percent chance of an outcome below b. The variance is obtained from a and b as demonstrated above.

The distribution of a period's cash flow will not always be Normal, of course. In a great many cases the distribution drawn will be close enough to a standard type of statistical distribution that the estimation of the mean and variance can be made from two or three points of the distribution. Another example which is particularly easy to work with is the rectangular distribution, shown in Figure 8.2.

Figure 8.2
Rectangular Distribution of a Cash Flow

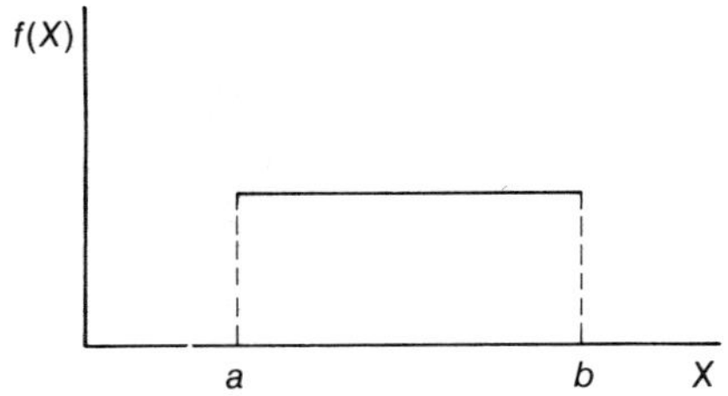

In the rectangular distribution the mean is the midpoint of the range, in Figure 8.2

$$E(X) = \frac{b+a}{2}$$

The variance is

$$\sigma^2(X) = 1/12\, b^2 - 1/6\, ab + 1/12\, a^2$$

Again only two points must be given, a and b, to derive the mean and variance. These points for the rectangular distribution are the end points, the extreme values for the money outcome.

Estimation of the correlation coefficient for two periods' cash flows will necessarily be direct. The investment project expert should have some idea of how outcomes are related over time. A value somewhere between zero and one is reasonable to assume for the coefficient, the closer to one the greater the degree of positive relation between the two periods' outcomes, and the closer to zero the nearer to independent the two outcomes.

One fact that may be an aid to estimation of the correlation coefficient is that the square of the coefficient is the percentage of the variation in the dependent variable explained by the linear relationship between the variables. If the statement could be made, for example, that 50 percent of the variation in period 2's cash flow is attributable to its relationship with the period 1 cash flow, then the correlation coefficient ρ_{12} is estimated as $\sqrt{0.50}$ or about 0.7.

Decision Models for the Single Project

Once $E(PV)$ and $\sigma^2(PV)$ are derived for the investment project those parameters must be used as the basis for an accept-reject decision, or a ranking of projects. Selection of an optimum combination of projects will be deferred to a later section after the $E(PV)$ and $\sigma^2(PV)$ formulas for combinations are derived.

The theoretically correct decision model would use $E(PV)$ and $\sigma^2(PV)$ as the arguments in an investor's (corporation's) utility function. That utility function can be represented by the set of indifference curves (as was done in Chapter 7) shown in Figure 8.3. The two axes are $E(PV)$ and $\sigma^2(PV)$, and moving to the right indicates higher levels of satisfaction.

Figure 8.3
Indifference Curves for Accept-Reject Example

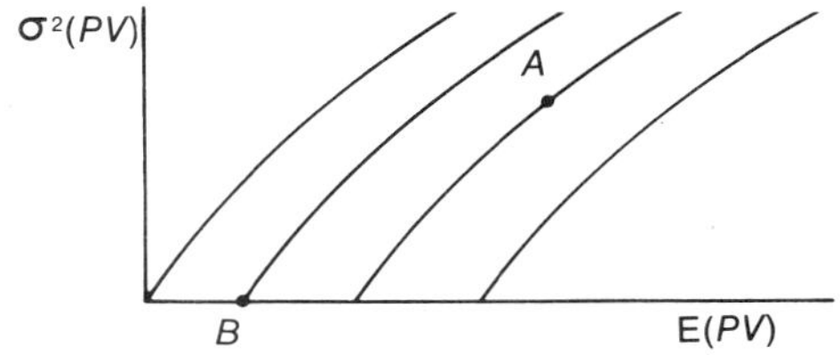

In Figure 8.3 the point A indicates the $E(PV)$ and $\sigma^2(PV)$ for an investment project. The point B represents the price of the project. Since B lies on an indifference curve to the left of the indifference curve that A is on, the investor should accept this project. He improves his satisfaction level by exchanging B for A.

The ranking of two projects with equal prices can be shown by indifference curves as well. In Figure 8.4 $E(PV)$ and $\sigma^2(PV)$ for two projects are shown by the points A and B. Because B is on a higher indifference curve (farther to the right) than A Project B is preferred to Project A.

Figure 8.4
Indifference Curves for Ranking Example

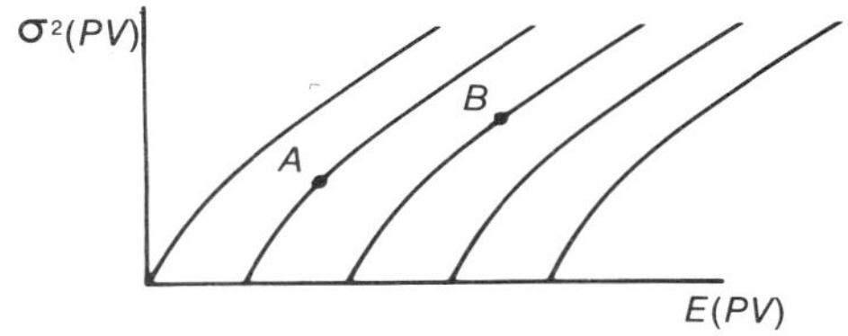

Indifference curves and utility functions are fine in theoretical models but in practice it is very hard to derive an exact utility function for an investor or a corporation. Instead the concept of efficiency can be applied to ranking projects without depending on a specific utility function or set of indifference curves.

Assuming only that $E(PV)$ is a desirable characteristic of an investment project and $\sigma^2(PV)$ an undesirable characteristic, the "north-west corner" rule for dominance used in Chapter 7 can also be used here to eliminate inefficient projects. Suppose Projects A, B, and C with equal prices have $E(PV)$ and $\sigma^2(PV)$ values as indicated in Figure 8.5. A dominates everything to the northwest of it in the diagram, B dominates everything to the northwest of it, and C dominates everything to the northwest of it. Project C is preferred to B because B is northwest of C. C has a higher mean of present values and a lower variance of present values than B. No ranking is possible between Projects A and C.

Figure 8.5
Efficiency Ranking of Projects

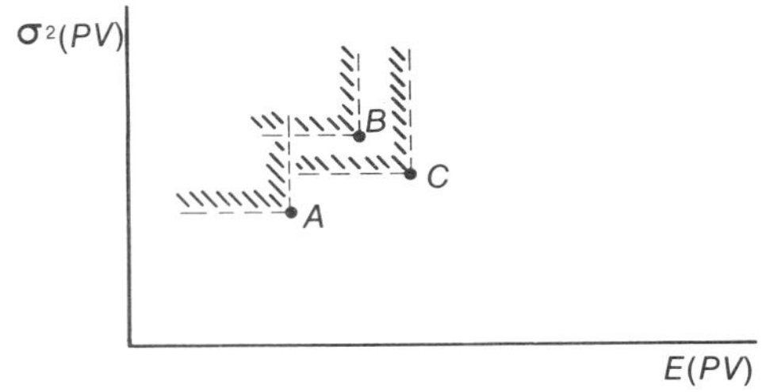

The efficiency analysis does not provide a complete answer to the selection of a single project from a set of projects. Some other means must be used to select between A and C. Applying the efficiency conditions does serve to reduce the choices necessary to the investor or corporation officer.

A somewhat different decision approach to the single project case uses a single number, the present value of certainty equivalents, to summarize the desirability of the project. In this technique a certainty equivalent cash flow is derived for each period, and then the present value of these flows is calculated.

Figure 8.6
Derivation of Certainty Equivalent

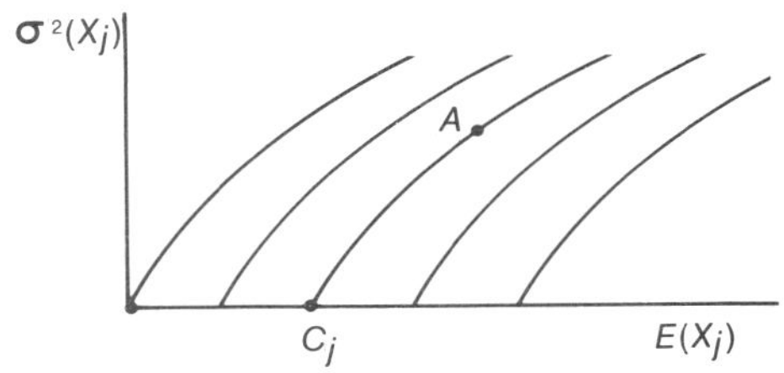

The certainty equivalent is defined by reference to the indifference curve (and utility function) for a period's cash flow parameters, $E(X_j)$ and $\sigma^2(X_j)$, as in Figure 8.6. Those parameters locate the point A in the diagram which is equivalent in the investor's satisfaction level to the certain cash flow C_j.

The derivation of the present value of certainty equivalents therefore requires knowledge of the investor's risk-return preferences at every time point of the project's life. If the t certainty equivalents C_j are found, then the present value of certainty equivalents is found by the formula

$$\sum_{j=1}^{j=t} \left[\frac{1}{1+r}\right]^j C_j$$

The present value of certainty equivalents can be approached in a less formal manner than specifying the entire utility function at each point in time. The certainty equivalent can be a direct subjective estimate by the investor or corporate official based on his knowledge of the distribution of the period's cash flow. If that distribution is summarized by the parameters $E(X_j)$ and $\sigma^2(X_j)$ the calculation of the certainty equivalent could be by some simple formula such as

$$C_j = \frac{a}{\sigma^2(X_j)} E(X_j)$$

where a is an arbitrary constant chosen to adjust the reduction effect of the variance on the mean.

The flexibility of estimation method used for the certainty equivalents may make this decision model desirable. Once a present value of certainty equivalents is calculated it can be compared to the price of the project for an accept-reject decision. The present values of certainty equivalents for projects with the same price can be compared to derive a ranking of projects. Implicit in the technique is the assumption of independence of events between time periods, though.

A commonly used method of handling capital budgeting under risk by business firms is the adjustment of the interest rate used in present value computations to allow for the risk of the project. The risk-adjusted discount rate, k, is then applied to the mean cash flows, $E(X_j)$, to compute a present value:

$$\sum_{k=1}^{j=t} E(X_j) \left[\frac{1}{1+k}\right]^j$$

(Instead of the mean cash flow the mode, the most likely value, is sometimes used in this calculation.)

One advantage of this procedure is that sometimes investment projects can be divided into risk classes, and projects within a risk class would be subjected to the same "hurdle rate" in the evaluation process. The chief executives of a corporation might divide the types of investments into three categories: (1) low risk, (2) medium risk, and (3) high risk, and require a discount rate of 8 percent for the first category, 10 percent for the second, and 12 percent for the third, as an example. A low risk project might be the refinancing of a bond issue, a medium risk project the acquisition of another company, and a high risk project the introduction of a new product.

The major disadvantage of the risk-adjusted discount rate method is its implication that risk increases with time. The rate k in the present value computation must adjust both for the passage of time and the risk characteristics of the cash flows. Suppose the risk-adjusted rate k is compared with a risk-free interest rate r which adjusts only for the passage of time.

The ratio

$$\frac{1+r}{1+k} = R$$

is a risk adjustment factor. If the present value factor $1/1 + k$ is expressed in terms of r and R the result is

$$\frac{1}{1+k} = R\left[\frac{1}{1+r}\right]$$

Now consider the sequence of present value multipliers

$$\left[\frac{1}{1+k}\right], \left[\frac{1}{1+k}\right]^2, \ldots, \left[\frac{1}{1+k}\right]^t$$

Expressed in terms of r and R the sequence of present value multipliers is

$$R\left[\frac{1}{1+r}\right], R^2\left[\frac{1}{1+r}\right]^2, \ldots R^t\left[\frac{1}{1+r}\right]^t$$

The cash flows in the present value computation using a risk-adjusted discount rate are subject to an increasing risk adjustment over time, which implies that risk increases over time, perhaps geometrically as R appears in the sequence. Therefore the use of a simple risk-adjusted discount rate may materially distort the decision process.

It would probably be better to adjust the money values used in the present value computation for risk rather than the interest rate, as is done in the present value of certainty equivalents model.

One special case of decisions under risk, the risk-neutral assumption, simplifies all the analysis by eliminating the variances, $\sigma^2(X_j)$ and $\sigma^2(PV)$, from consideration. If the investor is risk-neutral his decision is based entirely on expected values, the mean of present values $E(PV)$. He selects the investment project with the highest $E(PV)$ so long as it is higher than the price of the project, or he ranks investment projects with equal prices by $E(PV)$.

For the risk-neutral case the capital budgeting procedures of Chapters 5 and 6 are adapted quickly. Instead of the certain cash flows the mean cash flow $E(X_j)$ is substituted in the formulas of those chapters.

The assumption of risk-neutrality may be reasonable for investment projects that are small in relationship to the size of the corporation, or for investments that are small relative to the total wealth of an individual investor. There is a temptation, however, to assume risk-neutrality because it makes computations easier. Such an attitude may lead to incorrect capital budgeting or investment decisions.

Early Abandonment of an Investment Project Example

After an investment project is accepted and underway it is sometimes possible to abandon that project, realizing some scrap or abandonment value. If the project is continued the opportunity cost of continuing is the foregone scrap value that is surrendered to obtain the later cash flows from the project.

The decision to continue an investment project rather than abandon it can be treated as a capital budgeting problem. Suppose, for example, that an investment project with originally projected cash flows of −1,000, 300, 400, 500, 400, 200 could be abandoned at time one (after receipt of the 300 inflow) and a scrap value of 800 obtained. If the project is continued at time one the resulting cash flow sequence is −800, 400, 500, 400, 200. That sequence can be analyzed in terms of a net present value, computed at an interest rate of 12 percent:

$$-800 + 400(0.89286) + 500(0.79719)$$

$$+ 400(0.71178) + 200(0.63552) = 367.55$$

Because the net present value is positive the proper decision is to continue the project. (The same decision could have been determined by computing the internal rate of return, IRR, for the cash flow sequence, 34.44 percent, and comparing that rate with the hurdle rate of 12 percent.)

If the project is continued at time one it may be desirable to check it again at time two, at time three, and so forth. If the set of abandonment values for the various time points (measured in terms of the original project life) are:

Time	1	2	3	4	5
Abandonment value	800	700	500	200	0

then the consequences of continuing at the alternative points can be computed. The net present value of continuing the project at time one has already been computed as 367.55. If the project is continued at time two the net present value obtained will be

$$-700 + 500(0.89286) + 400(0.79719) + 200(0.71178) = 207.67$$

$$(\text{IRR} = 31.44\%)$$

so it should not be abandoned at time two. At time three the net present value from continuing is

$$-500 + 400(0.89286) + 200(0.79719) = 16.58$$

$$(\text{IRR} = 14.83\%)$$

The net present value from continuing at time four is

$$-200 + 200(0.89286) = -21.43$$

(IRR = 0%)

Because this value is negative the project should be abandoned at time four.

Besides being used for a continuing review (post-audit) of investment projects the concept of abandonment value can be used to add some dimensions to the original decision about acceptance of an investment project. If the set of abandonment values were known at the time point when the original acceptance decision was made, the optimum project length could have been determined at the same time.

To start with, suppose the project is to last the full five periods. The net present value for this length is

$$-1{,}000 + 300(0.89286) + 400(0.79719) + 500(0.71178)$$

$$+ 400(0.63552) + 200(0.56743) = 310.33$$

(IRR = 24.08%)

If the project is terminated at time four the cash inflow at time four is 400 plus 200 scrap value, and the net present value is

$$-1{,}000 + 300(0.89286) + 400(0.79719) + 500(0.71178)$$

$$+ 600(0.63552) = 323.94$$

(IRR = 24.89%)

for termination at time three,

$$-1{,}000 + 300(0.89286) + 400(0.79719) + 1{,}000(0.71178) = 298.52$$

(IRR = 25.44%)

If terminated at time two,

$$-1{,}000 + 300(0.89286) + 1{,}100(0.79719) = 144.77$$

(IRR = 20.95%)

When the project is terminated at time one the net present value is negative:

$$-1{,}000 + 1{,}100(0.89286) = -17.85$$

(IRR = 10%)

Using the criterion of maximizing net present value for selecting the investment project length, the four-period length is optimum. (Notice that the internal rate of return criterion would result in a different length, three periods.) It is no coincidence that the optimum abandonment point computed before was time four.

Abandonment value can alter the risk characteristics of an investment project as well. If the outcomes of an investment project over time become unfavorable losses may be cut by early abandonment of the project. Consideration of the abandonment possibility can change an unacceptable project into an acceptable project either through an increase in the expected present value or a reduction in the variance of present value, or both.

To keep the analysis simple suppose a two-period investment project is under consideration that has the possible cash flow sequences and probabilities summarized in the diagram.

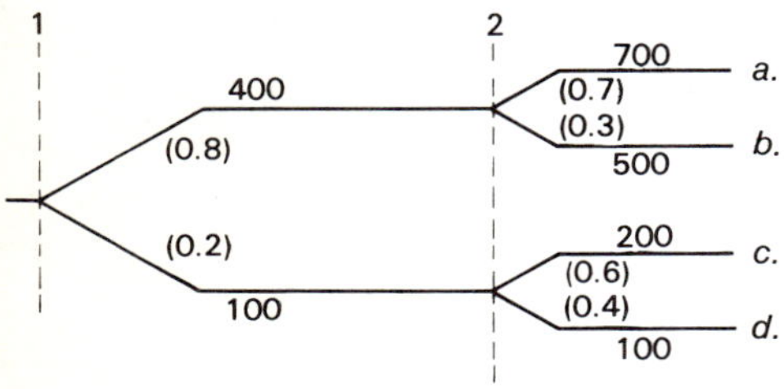

The diagram can be interpreted as meaning that the cash inflow at time one will be 400 with probability 0.8, or 100 with probability 0.2. If the outcome 400 occurs at time one, the cash inflow at time two will be 700 with probability 0.7, or 500 with probability 0.3. If the outcome 100 occurs at time one, the possible outcomes at time two are a cash inflow of 200 with probability 0.6 and 100 with probability 0.4. Therefore there are four possible cash flow sequences in the example as defined above.

If the price of this project at time zero is 600, the listing of the four possible cash flow sequences and the respective probabilities is:

a. −600, 400, 700
probability = 0.8(0.7) = 0.56
b. −600, 400, 500
probability = 0.8(0.3) = 0.24
c. −600, 100, 200
probability = 0.2(0.6) = 0.12
d. −600, 100, 100
probability = 0.2(0.4) = 0.08

The corresponding net present values at an interest rate of 12 percent are:

a. $-600 + 400(0.89286) + 700(0.79719) = 315.17$
b. $-600 + 400(0.89286) + 500(0.79719) = 155.74$
c. $-600 + 100(0.89286) + 200(0.79719) = -351.27$
d. $-600 + 100(0.89286) + 100(0.79719) = -430.99$

These net present values and their respective probabilities can be combined to derive an expected net present value of

$$0.56(315.17) + 0.24(155.74) + 0.12(-351.27) + 0.08(-430.99) = 138.40$$

and a standard deviation of net present value of

$$[0.56(315.17)^2 + 0.24(155.74)^2 + 0.12(-351.27)^2 + 0.08(-430.99)^2 - (138.40)^2]^{1/2} = 268.25$$

These measures in the absence of an abandonment option would be used in the accept-reject decision.

Now suppose abandonment at time one (after the time one cash inflow is received) at a scrap value of 300 becomes possible. If the cash inflow of 400 is realized the project should not be abandoned—the cash inflows possible at time two, 700 and 500, both have values, discounted to time one, greater than 300. If the cash inflow of 100 at time one is realized, the project should be abandoned at that time since 300 is greater than the discounted value of 200 or 100, the only possible cash inflows at time two.

Now the possible cash flow sequences are reduced to three, assuming a rational abandonment decision. The three possible cash flow sequences and probabilities are

a. −600, 400, 700
   probability = 0.56
b. −600, 400, 500
   probability = 0.24
c′. −600, 400
   probability = 0.20

In the third sequence, c′, the cash inflow from the project at time one is 100, and the 300 scrap value is added to make the total inflow of 400.

The net present values are:

a. = 315.17
b. =155.74
c′. $-600 + 400(0.89286) = 242.86$

Using these net present values and the respective probabilities the revised expected net present value is

$$0.56(315.17) + 0.24(155.74) + 0.20(-242.86) = 165.46$$

and the standard deviation of net present value is

$$[0.56(315.17)^2 + 0.24(155.74)^2 + 0.20(-242.86)^2 - (165.46)^2]^{1/2} = 214.16$$

The inclusion of the abandonment alternative in this example both increased the expected net present value and reduced the standard deviation of net present value, both effects acting to make the investment project more desirable.

The determination of the alternative sequences taking the abandonment option into account was made easy in the example because of the numbers chosen for illustration. The sequence c′ resulted because another decision under risk at time one was assumed. With other numbers the abandonment decision at time one might have to be based on both a mean and standard deviation of cash flows at time two compared to the price of continuing, the foregone abandonment value, at time one.

The Mean and Variance of Present Values for Combinations of Projects

Combining projects requires relatively little problems with the formulas for $E(PV)$ and $\sigma^2(PV)$ so long as a correlation coefficient between two projects' present values is defined. To distinguish between projects a subscript must be added in the notation so $E_1(PV)$ will be used for the mean of present values of the first project and $\sigma_1{}^2(PV)$ for the variance of present values of the first project. To identify the correlation coefficient as defined for present values (rather than periods' cash flows) the symbol $\rho_{12}(PV)$ will be used for the correlation of the present values of projects 1 and 2.

To allow for variable size of projects the symbol b_i will be used for the size of the ith project. In most cases with combinations of investment projects the b_i value will be either 0 or 1. That value is 0 if the project is not included in the combination, and it is 1 if the project is included.

The mean present value for a combination of projects, $E_c(PV)$, is computed from the formula

$$E_c(PV) = b_1E_1(PV) + b_2E_2(PV) + \cdots = \sum_{i=1}^{i=n} b_iE_i(PV)$$

where there are n projects to choose from. This formula is simple, of course, because no interaction terms are involved in the expected value of a linear combination of random variables.

For combinations from a set of two projects the variance of present values, $\sigma_c{}^2(PV)$, is calculated as

$$\sigma_c{}^2(PV) = b_1{}^2\sigma_1{}^2(PV) + b_2{}^2\sigma_2{}^2(PV) + 2b_1b_2\rho_{12}(PV)\sigma_1(PV)\sigma_2(PV)$$

For a combination picked from n projects the formula is

$$\sigma_c{}^2(PV) = \sum_{i=1}^{i=n}\sum_{k=1}^{k=n} b_ib_i\rho_{ik}(PV)\sigma_i(PV)\sigma_2(PV)$$

To demonstrate the use of the formulas for $E_c(PV)$ and $\sigma_c{}^2(PV)$ suppose two projects are selected. The first project has a mean of present values of 40 and a variance of present values of 49. The second project has a mean of present values of 30 and a variance of present values of 36. The correlation coefficient between the two projects' present values is 0.3.

The mean present value for the two-project combination is

$$E_c(PV) = (1)40 + (1)30$$
$$= 70$$

The variance of present values for the combination is

$$\sigma_c^2(PV) = (1)^2 49 + (1)^2 36 + 2(1)(1)(0.3)(7)(6)$$
$$= 110.2$$

The two-project combination is a particularly important combination for the corporation's capital budgeting under risk. An investment project under consideration will be added to the existing operations of the corporation if accepted. In the example the first project could be interpreted as the existing operations of the corporation, and the second project as an incremental project, the one under evaluation.

Adding that project to the existing activities of the corporation adds 30 to the expected present value of the corporation's activities. The increase in variance of present values is

$$110.2 - 49 = 61.2$$

Therefore the incremental characteristics of the investment project are the change in mean of 30 and the change in the variance of 61.2. That project should be assessed on the basis of those incremental values. It would be misleading to judge that project on the basis of its individual variance of present values, 36.

When larger sets of projects are defined for a decision model the existing operations of the corporation should always be included as one of the projects. Any set of projects accepted will be added to the existing operations, and will interact statistically (unless the set is independent, and the correlation coefficient is zero) with those existing operations.

Acquisitions of Operating Businesses Example

Occasionally it will be profitable for a corporation to acquire other business firms that are already operating rather than start a new line of business "from scratch." Besides the physical assets acquired, the going concern consists of skilled personnel, a management expertise, and the goodwill inherent in an established project. At times the new parent is able to combine the acquired operations with its original operations and achieve a performance greater than the sum of the parts—the "synergistic effect."

One of the difficulties with evaluating the acquisition of an operating business is the identification of the cash flows resulting from the purchase. To follow consistently the principles of capital budgeting outlined in this and earlier chapters the incremental cash flows after taxes should be used in a present value function, either to derive a total present value, an appraisal value, to compare with the purchase price of the business, or to derive the internal rate of return, the yield, on the purchase price. Usually, however, sufficient information is not available to derive the after-tax cash flows so a substitute measure, the after-tax earnings of the business, must be used in the evaluation.

A second problem that makes adaptation of standard capital budgeting techniques difficult is the infinite life of the business acquired. Instead of acquiring a depreciating or depleting asset with a limited term of usefulness, the operating business normally has no limit to its life. Because of the necessity of forecasting earnings for an infinite period and of evaluating present value functions containing an infinite number of amounts, frequently analysts in the going concern evaluation use a less precise measure such as the payback period to derive an appraisal value. If a seven-year payback period is required by the buyer, for example, the appraisal value would be the sum of the next seven years' estimated earnings. The earnings for seven years are easier to estimate than the earnings from now to eternity.

Two patterns of earnings for an infinite period can be evaluated in a present value function. If earnings per year are expected to remain at a constant amount, C, the present value function for a perpetual annuity can be used to derive

$$PV = \sum_{i=1}^{i=\infty} \frac{C}{(1+r)^i} = \frac{C}{r}$$

If earnings per year are \$1,000,000, and the required rate of return, r, is 12 percent, then the present value of the going concern, the appraisal value, is

$$\frac{\$1{,}000{,}000}{12\%} = \$8{,}333{,}333$$

In the second earnings pattern, earnings grow each period at a rate that is constant for all time. If earnings at time one are C_1, and the growth rate in earnings is g, then the sequence of earnings acquired can be expressed as

$$C_1, C_1(1+g), C_1(1+g)^2, \cdots, C_1(1+g)^k, \cdots$$

The present value of this sequence is

$$PV = \frac{C_1}{(1+r)} + \frac{C_1(1+g)}{(1+r)^2} + \cdots + \frac{C_1(1+g)^{k-1}}{(1+r)^k} + \cdots$$

$$= \sum_{i=1}^{i=\infty} \frac{C_1(1+g)^{i-1}}{(1+r)^i}$$

By using some algebra (the formula for a converging geometric series) this formula reduces to

$$PV = \frac{C_1}{r-g}$$

if r is greater than g.

Suppose a going concern is being evaluated that is expected to have earnings at time one of $1,000,000, and whose earnings are expected to grow at a rate of 6 percent a year forever. If the acquiring corporation's required rate of return is 14 percent, the appraisal value of this going concern is

$$\frac{\$1{,}000{,}000}{14\% - 6\%} = \$12{,}500{,}000$$

No other formulas for an infinite series of earnings result in simple closed expressions that can be easily evaluated.

Because the acquisition is likely to be significantly large in relation to the acquirer's present size, the incremental risk characteristics of the going concern should also be considered in a capital budgeting evaluation. If the measure of risk is to be the standard deviation of annual earnings, then the measure on which evaluation is based should be the change in the standard deviation of earnings.

Suppose the existing operations of the acquiring corporation produce expected earnings of $E(X)$ with a standard deviation of $\sigma(X)$. The acquisition candidate's expected earnings are $E(Y)$ and the standard deviation of earnings is $\sigma(Y)$. If ρ_{XY} is the correlation coefficient between the two earnings then the combined results after the acquisition will be

$$E(X+Y) = E(Y)$$

$$\sigma(X+Y) = [\sigma^2(X) + \sigma^2(Y) + 2\rho_{XY}\sigma(X)\sigma(Y)]^{1/2}$$

If the existing operations of the corporation have these parameters:

$$E(X) = \$5{,}000{,}000$$
$$\sigma(X) = \$1{,}500{,}000$$

and the going concern to be acquired has these:

$$E(Y) = \$1{,}000{,}000$$
$$\sigma(Y) = \$400{,}000$$
$$\rho_{XY} = 0.3$$

then after the acquisition (ignoring any costs of capital) the parameters would be

$$E(X + Y) = \$5{,}000{,}000 + \$1{,}000{,}000 = \$6{,}000{,}000$$

$$\sigma(X + Y) = [(\$1{,}500{,}000)^2 + (\$400{,}000)^2$$

$$+ 2(0.3)(\$1{,}500{,}000)(\$400{,}000)]^{1/2} = \$1{,}664{,}332$$

The incremental characteristics of the candidate for acquisition are the change in expected earnings of \$1,000,000 and the change in standard deviation of earnings of \$164,332.

Even though the standard deviation of the company to be acquired considered in isolation is \$400,000, the increase in standard deviation of the acquirer is \$164,332. This reduction in value is due to the fact that the operations represented by X and Y are less than perfectly positively correlated.

Another factor that may make the acquisition of going concerns relatively attractive is the possibility of advantageous financing means that may be worked out between buyer and seller. The financing decision will not be treated here, but deferred to a later chapter. Instead it is assumed here that the valuation techniques discussed above are used to arrive at an appraisal value which is then used as a basis for bargaining between buyer and seller. Once the price is established in the negotiations, the means of payment forms a separate topic for further negotiation.

Decision Models for the Multiple Project Case

Figure 8.7
Feasible Set of Indivisible Projects

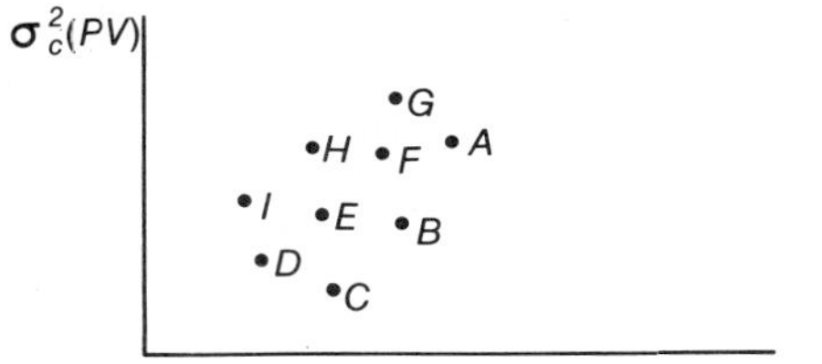

Figure 8.8
Feasible Set of Divisible Projects

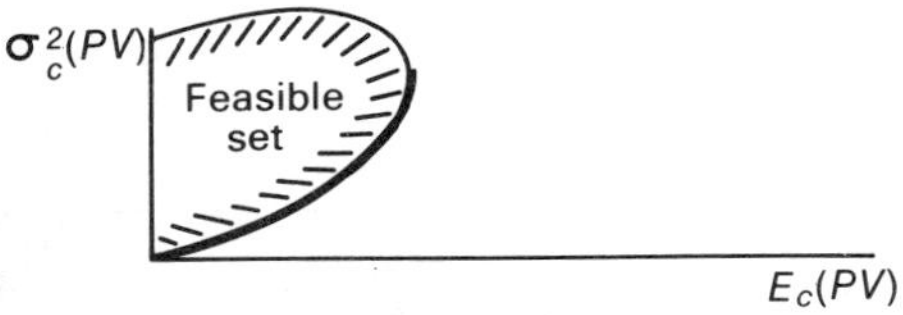

When a budget constraint is combined with the $E_c(PV)$ and $\sigma_c^2(PV)$ information a feasible set of combinations will be generated as shown by the points plotted in Figure 8.7. In this diagram the investment projects are indivisible, all the b_i are zero or one.

Given a set of indifference curves, a utility function for the corporation, a selection from the combination of projects in Figure 8.7 could be made exactly. So long as the corporation is not a risk-seeker the optimum combination would be A, B, or C. The set of combinations (A, B, C) is the efficient set, which can be determined without indifference curves.

If the projects are divisible the feasible set of combinations is a continuous region as shown in Figure 8.8. The set of indifference curves, if available, could be used to select the optimum combination of projects. Even without indifference curves the efficient set can be derived. In Figure 8.8 the efficient set is the southeast border of the feasible set, represented by the bold curve in the diagram.

The special case of the risk-neutral corporation or investor can still be applied in the multiple projects case. The risk-neutral investor seeks the highest expected present value and does not care about the variance. The combination with the highest $E_c(PV)$ is his selection.

The present value of certainty equivalents cannot be easily adapted to the multiple projects case. Adding together present values of certainty equivalents would imply linear period utility functions, which implies a risk-neutral investor. The only accurate alternative is to compute each period's certainty equivalent for each combination, and use these figures to calculate the present value of certainty equivalents for the combination. Since a large number of combinations must be investigated the computations necessary to use the present value of certainty equivalents are prohibitive.

The risk-adjusted discount method is also difficult to adapt to the multiple projects case. The statistical interaction of projects is ignored in this technique, so use of the method would distort the selection process unless the projects are truly statistically independent of each other and the existing operations of the corporation.

Summary

Adaptation of the decision under risk approaches of Chapter 7 to the capital budgeting problem mainly involves calculation of means and variances of present values for individual projects and combinations of projects. The starting point of the calculations is the estimation of the distribution or parameters of the distribution for each period's cash flow.

Two or three point estimates are necessary to determine the mean and variance of such standard distributions as the Normal and the rectangular. Another item of information needed that usually has to be estimated directly is the correlation coefficient between periods. If the means, variances, and correlation coefficients are known, computation of the mean and variance of present values is performed by the evaluation of the formulas given in the text.

Although the decision models for single projects were extensively discussed, those models should not be used by a corporation unless: (1) the corporation has no existing operations the projects will be added to; (2) the project under consideration is statistically independent of the existing operations of the corporation; or (3) the corporation is risk-neutral.

Instead, a single project should be analyzed as an addition to the existing operations of the corporation. The incremental characteristics of the project, the change in the mean of present values and the change in the variance of present values, should be used for judging the project.

In the calculations for the mean and variance of present values one additional statistical measure was required. The correlation coefficient of projects' present values also must be obtained from a subjective estimate to allow computation of the variance for combinations of projects.

Once the parameters of the combinations are calculated, the choice of combinations can be made by reference to the investor's or corporation's utility function if available. Even without a utility function the efficient combinations can be isolated through application of the "mean is desirable, variance is undesirable" rule. In the special case of risk-neutrality an exact solution of the optimum combination can be made by finding the combination that maximizes expected present value.

Chapter 8 Questions

1. Should the corporation engage in continual review of existing investment projects to see if they might profitably be abandoned? Should the corporation engage in a continual review if the motive for the review to see if the person who originally estimated the projects' cash flows was accurate in his estimates?
2. Is the present value of certainty equivalents a more operational (easier to implement) method for evaluating a single investment project than working directly with the mean and variance of present value?
3. Suppose the cash flows of a project are dependent over time. How can the variance of present value be computed?
4. Does the dependence of cash flows over time make any difference in the computation of the mean present value?
5. What is the inherent distortion in the use of risk-adjusted discount rates? Is this procedure always incorrect?
6. How reasonable is the assumption of risk-neutrality in investment project selection in the large corporation?
7. At time one three different cash inflows are possible, at time two four inflows, and at time three six inflows. How many different cash flow sequences are possible for this investment project?
8. What other types of distribution besides the Normal and the rectangular can be used for deriving the variance of a cash flow from a small number of point estimates?
9. When one corporation acquires another, can it be expected that some economies can be effected by joining some administrative tasks together, so that the combined earnings results will be greater than a simple sum of the two earnings streams?
10. The diversification or portfolio effect was one of the primary reasons for the boom in conglomerates of the 1960s. What other reasons were there? Do these reasons still exist in the 1970s?

Chapter 8 Problems

1. A manager in a firm that is known to be risk-neutral must make a choice between two investment projects, A and B, that have the same price. Using the distribution of cash flows the present value distributions of the two projects have been derived as.

A		B	
Present value	Probability	Present value	Probability
800	0.3	600	0.2
1,000	0.4	900	0.5
1,200	0.3	1,400	0.3

a. Which project should the manager choose?
b. If the firm were risk-averse which project should be chosen?

2. Given the distributions below of the cash inflows for the two periods, the assumption that the outcomes are independent over time, and an interest rate of 10 percent, calculate the variance of present values for this project:

Time 1		Time 2	
Cash inflow	Probability	Cash inflow	Probability
100	0.4	0	0.2
200	0.6	200	0.4
		300	0.4

3. The distribution of a cash inflow is assumed to be the Normal distribution. The promoter of the project has come up with two estimated values. The first was chosen so that the probability of a cash inflow less than that value occurring is 0.05. The first value is $30. The second value was chosen because it is in the middle of the distribution, so that the probability of a cash inflow greater than that value is equal to the probability of a cash inflow below that value. The second value, the estimated mean, is $75. Calculate the estimated variance of the cash inflow.
4. The distribution of a cash inflow is assumed to be a rectangular (or uniform) distribution, and two estimates have been provided by an expert. The first estimate, $40, is the lowest possible cash inflow of the distribution, the lower end of the range. The second estimate, $100, is the highest possible cash inflow of the distribution, the upper end of the range. Compute the mean and the variance of this distribution.
5. The board of directors of the corporation has settled on an attitude toward risk that is reflected in this formula for calculation of certainty equivalents from the mean and variance of cash inflows:

$$C_j = \frac{30}{\sigma_{X_j}^{\ 2}} \overline{X}_j$$

Use an interest rate of 10 percent to calculate the present value of certainty equivalents for the investment project with these parameters of cash inflows:

Time 1		Time 2		Time 3	
$\overline{X}_1$	σ_{X_1}	$\overline{X}_2$	σ_{X_2}	$\overline{X}_3$	σ_{X_3}
120	50	80	60	90	70

6. For projects of risk class A the corporation uses a discount rate of 10 percent, and for those of risk class B an interest rate of 14 percent. By accident a project is misclassified as B rather than A. For the present values of the cash inflows of the first three periods derived by the "risk-adjusted discount rate method" how much distortion of the present values results from the wrong classification?
7. A two-period project's cash flows are dependent over time. Each period two different outcomes are possible, time 1 $100 inflow or $20 inflow, and time 2 $80 inflow or $30 inflow. The probability of the $100 outcome at time 1 is 0.6, and the probability of the $20 outcome at time 1 is 0.4. If the $100 outcome occurs at time 1 the probability of the $80 inflow at time 2 is 0.7 and the probability of the $30 inflow

is 0.3. If the $20 outcome occurs at time 1 the probability of the $80 inflow at time 2 is 0.1 and the probability of the $30 inflow is 0.9.

a. Using an interest rate of 10 percent calculate the expected present value and the variance of present value for the project.

b. Suppose it is possible to abandon the project at time 1 after the cash inflow occurs, receiving a scrap value of $50. Under what circumstances should the project be abandoned?

c. If the project would be abandoned only if the unfavorable outcome, a cash inflow of $20 at time 1, occurs, what is the revised expected present value and variance of present value for this project?

8. XYZ Corp. is considering acquiring ABC Corp. Before the acquisition XYZ's mean annual earnings are $800,000 with a standard deviation of $300,000. ABC's mean annual earnings are $400,000, with a standard deviation of $200,000. If the two corporations' activities are combined in an additive fashion (with no synergistic effects), and the correlation between the two earnings streams is 0.5, what will be the new mean annual earnings and standard deviations of earnings?

Chapter 8 References

Archer, Stephen H., and D'Ambrosio, Charles A., eds. *The Theory of Business Finance*. New York: Macmillan, 1967.

Bauman, W. Scott. "Evaluation of Prospective Investment Performance." *Journal of Finance*, May 1968.

Borch, Karl. "Decision Rules Depending on the Probability of Ruin." *Oxford Economic Papers*, March 1968.

Chambers, J. C., and Mullick, S. K. "Determining the Acquisition Value of a Company." *Management Accounting*, April 1970.

Hanssmann, Fred. "Probability of Survival as an Investment Criterion." *Management Science*, September 1968.

Hertz, David B. "Risk Analysis in Capital Investment." *Harvard Business Review*, January-February 1964.

Hillier, Frederick S. "The Derivation of Probabilistic Information for the Evaluation of Risky Investments." *Management Science*, April 1963.

Hillier, Frederick S., and Heebink, David V. "Evaluation of Risky Capital Investments." *California Management Review*, Winter 1965.

Hogarty, Thomas F. "The Profitability of Corporate Mergers." *Journal of Business*, July 1970.

Jean, William H. *The Analytical Theory of Finance*. New York: Holt, Rinehart & Winston, 1970.

Lerner, Eugene M., and Carleton, Willard T. *A Theory of Financial Analysis*. New York: Harcourt, Brace, 1966.

Levy, Haim, and Sarnat, Marshall. "Diversification, Portfolio Analysis and the Uneasy Case for Conglomerate Mergers." *Journal of Finance*, September 1970.

Mao, James C. T. *Quantitative Analysis of Financial Decisions*. New York: Macmillan, 1969.

Moore, Basil J. *An Introduction to the Theory of Finance*. New York: Free Press, 1968.

Myers, Stewart C. "Procedures for Capital Budgeting Under Uncertainty." *Industrial Management Review*, Spring 1968.

Naslund, Bertil. "A Model of Capital Budgeting Under Risk." *Journal of Business*, April 1966.

Peterson, David E. *A Quantitative Framework for Financial Management*. Homewood, Ill.: Irwin, 1969.

Robichek, Alexander A., and Myers, Stewart C. *Optimal Financing Decisions*. Englewood Cliffs, N. J.: Prentice-Hall, 1965.

Robichek, Alexander A., and Van Horne, James C. "Abandonment Value and Capital Budgeting." *Journal of Finances*, December 1967.

Sharpe, William F. *Portfolio Theory and Capital Markets*. New York: McGraw-Hill, 1970.

Van Horne, James C. "Capital Budgeting Decisions Involving Combinations of Risky Investments." *Management Science*, October 1966.

Vickers, Douglas. *The Theory of the Firm: Production, Capital and Finance*. New York: McGraw-Hill, 1968.

12¾ 12¾ — ¼
8¾ 9 + ⅜
16⅞ 16⅞ — ⅛
4⅛ 4⅛ — ⅛
10⅞ 11 + ¼
31¾ 31¾ — ⅛
4⅞ 4⅞ .....
8⅝ 8⅝ — ⅛
1⅞ 2 + ⅛
1¼ 1¼ — ⅛
6½ 6½ .....
13¾ 13¾ ⅛
12⅛ 12⅛ — ⅛
10⅝ 11 — ⅛
14⅝ 14⅝ — ⅝
7¾ 7¾ — ⅛
13 13 + ⅛
12½ 12½ — ¼
2¾ 2¾ — ⅛
4¾ 5 + ¼
27½ 27⅞ + ¼
4⅝ 4⅝ .....
6 6 — ⅛
6¼ 6⅜ — ⅜
10⅛ 10¾ .....
10⅝ 10⅝ — ⅜
45⅞ 45⅞ — ⅜
27½ 27½ .....
25½ 25¾ + ½
16⅞ 16⅞ — ⅛
4⅞ 4⅞ .....
10¼ 10½ + ¼
2¼ 2½ + ¼
38 38 — ½
15½ 15½ —¼
7⅜ 7½ + ¼
23 23⅛ — ⅝
49 49 — ½
41¾ 41¾ — ½
2⅝ 2⅝ .....
12⅜ 12⅜ — ⅜
38¾ 39⅛ —3¼
2⅛ 2⅛ .....
7¾ 7¾ — ¼
4¾ 4¾ .....
23⅜ 23⅝ + ⅛
2¾ 2¾ .....
18½ 19¼ + ⅞
26¾ 26¾ — ⅝
22½ 22½ — ¼
9⅞ 10 — ½
23⅞ 24¼ + ¼
5¾ 5⅞ + ¼
17⅞ 17⅞ — ¾
12 12⅛ .....
⅛ 11⅛ — ⅛
12¾ 12⅞ + ⅛
22⅛ 22⅛ — ¼
37¾ 37⅞ .....
8½ 8½ — ½
7⅞ 7⅞ .....
1¾ 1⅞ .....
24 24 .....
7⅛ 7⅛ — ⅛
13 13⅜ + ⅛
1¼ 1¼ — ⅛
28¾ 28¾ — ⅞
22⅜ 22⅜ — ⅞
13⅛ 13⅜ + ¼
6⅞ 7 .....
8⅛ 8¼ — ⅛
53¾ 63¾ —¼
8 8⅛ — ⅛
13 13 — ¼
18¾ 18¾ .....
35 35 — ½
7 7¼ + ⅛
3⅞ 3⅞ + ⅛
⅛ 26⅛ —1⅛
½ 25⅞ — ⅛
8 — ⅜
6⅜ — ⅛
11⅛ + ⅝
9⅝ + ⅛
23⅜ + ⅛
10⅞ — ⅛
4⅜ — ⅛
10⅝ — ⅛
13½ + ¼
5¼ + ⅛
2 — ⅛
¼ 10½ + ¼
4⅞ .....
2½ + ⅛
27⅜ + ⅛
4⅛ — ¼
8⅝ — ⅛
6 — ⅛
7¾ + ⅛
25⅛ + ⅛
4⅝ — ⅛
8½ + ⅛
20¼ — ⅜
6⅞ — ¼
15 + ⅛
10½ — ⅝
9⅜ + ¼
42¾ + ⅜
21¾ + ⅜
5½ .....
7⅝ — ⅞
19¼ — ⅛
67 +5
32¼ +1¼
6¾ — ⅛
3 ⅞ + ¼
17¾ — ¾
5½ — ⅛

CarPL pf 5 z190 73 72 72½ + ⅜
Carousel Fsh 4 2 1⅞ 1⅞ — ⅛
CarrierCp wt 39 16⅜ 15¾ 15⅞ + ⅛
Carro Dv .99f 11 9 8⅞ 8⅞ .....
Castle A .80 1 18 18 18 .....
Castleton Ind 31 2⅝ 2⅜ 2⅝ + ¼
Castlewd Int 6 16⅜ 16 16 — ¼
CaVitron Cp 24 16½ 16 16⅛ + ⅜
CBWL H .15e 22 6¾ 6⅝ 6⅝ .....
CelluCraft 8 6 6 .....
CenMe pf3.50 z60 46 46 46 .....
Cen Sec 1.30e 15 9⅝ 9½ 9½ — ⅛
Centry El .60 6 49⅝ 49½ 49⅝ + ⅛
CentryInd .24 2 8½ 8⅜ 8¼ ... .
Certified Cp 20 8 7¾ 7⅞ ... ⅛
Ickertron Cp 54 4 3⅞ 3⅞ ... .
Chad Mill .40 23 11¾ 11¼ 11⅜ — ⅝
ChampHo .10 300 104¾ 99⅝ 99⅝—3⅞
an Ind 4¾ 4⅝ 4¾ .....
Ickhart Co .15e 66 29 281 28¼ +1
Charter Med 29 11¾ 11⅜ 11½ — ⅜
CHB Foods 13 9¼ 9 9 — ¼
achmExp . $e 7 10 18 10 .....
.KHERRY Burr 8 ¼ 16 16⅛ + ¼
Chi Rivt 1.60 1 25⅝ 25⅝ 25⅝ — ⅛
Child World 7 31 30¾ 30¾ + ⅛
Christia Cos 34 7¼ 6½ 6⅞ — ¼
Cl CvFd .43e 4 21 20⅞ 21 a- 1
CIMKGGrp wt 47 4¾ 4⅝ 4⅝ — ⅛
CIC Corp 22 22 21½ 22 + ¼
Cinerama 8133⅛ 3 3| - 1
Circ
e K .22 68 37⅞ 37½ 37⅞ + ¼
CitSv AR a 28 11-16 11-16 11 16—1-16
Citzn Finl .16 11⅜ 10⅞38⅞ — ⅜
CKIZMtg 1.33e 12 14⅜ a3 14⅛ + ⅛
acltizMtglik wt 2 2⅛ 2 2 ⅛
CityGsFla .50 1 8¾ 8¾ 8¾ .....
Clark Cable 2 3½ 3¼ 3½ + ⅛
ClarkeGr .20 6 20¼ 20 20⅛ .....
larkson Ind 16 21¾K ¼⅛⅛ 21½ + ⅛
Clarostat 13 7⅞ 7⅝ 7⅞ + ⅜
Clary Corp $2 7⅜ 7 $⅜ + ⅜
Clary Corp $2 7⅜ 7 $⅜ + ⅝
INTON Mer 24 15⅛ 14½ 14¾ + ⅛
Clopay .53t 6 15⅞ 15½ 15½ — ¼
CMI Corp 20 6⅞ 6⅝ 6⅝ .....
CMI Inv Cp 33 7 8 76 76 138
CMI
IV WT ¼⅝ ½⅝⅝⅝⅝ 45 45⅜ + ⅜
Co Bul
d Cos 39 3⅝ 13 13 — ⅜
Codesco .15e 26 18⅜ 18⅛ 18⅜ + ⅛
Coff Mat .37e 32 23⅛ $2⅝ 23 — ⅜
Cohen Hatfd 1 6⅛ 6⅛ 6⅛ — K
Cohu E
ec .10 7 8 7⅞ 8 + ⅛
Colt Intl 301 27⅞ 26¾ 26¾ — ⅜
Cole Natl .44 10 26⅜ 2 ⅞ 26⅛ + ¼
:olComl .10e 37 22¾ 22⅜ 22⅜ — ¼
ColComl .10e 37 22¾ 22⅜ 22⅜ — ¼
Colon Snd .30 29 9 9 9 — ⅛
ColwllCo .21e 14 27¼ 26⅝ 27 8— ½
aM 2.61e 2$ 28⅝ 28⅜K ¼—⅜ — ¼
Icolwl Mtg wt 25 8⅜ 8¼ 8¼ — ¼
Combin Com 44 34½ 33½ 34 + ⅜
Combcstn Eq 116 32¾ 31⅞ 32½ + ⅞
Cominc .70 1 30¾ 30¾ 30¾ — ¼
IckomlAilia .21 5 16½ 16¼ 16¼ — ½
Coml Met .60 4 13 12⅞ 12⅞ — ⅛
Commodor 24 16 15¾ 16 + ⅜
CUNHlth Fac 18 12⅛ 1¾ 11¾ — ⅜
ComPsych Ct 1632 30¾ 30¾ —1¼
ComPS 1.56 4 26¼ 26 26¼ + ⅜
Compolnd .36 11 14⅞ 14⅝ 14⅞ + ⅜
eh Des 4 6⅛ 6 — ⅛
ConpuDyne 7 2¾ 2⅝ 2⅝ .....
Comput Eq 8 3¾ 3⅝ 3⅝ .....
Comput Inst
5 3 2⅞ 3 .....
Comput Invst 25 11½ 10⅝ 10⅝ — ⅞
Conchemco 16 21 20½ 20⅝ — ¼
Concord Fab 7 4¾ 4⅝ 4¾ + ⅛
Condec Corp 56 10⅝ 10¼ 10¼ — ¼
Connlly Con 5 4 4 4 .....
Connrex .24r 18 13 12¾ 12¾ + ⅛
Conroy Inc 27 14¼ 14 14 — ¼
Con Cdn Far 2 1 1 1 .....
Con Nat Sh A 12 5½ 5½ 5½ .....
Con Oil Gas 18 5⅛ 4⅞ 4⅞ — ⅛
Cons Ref .10e 5 16¼ 16 16 — ¼
ConsltDes .40 2 11¼ 11⅛ 11⅛ — ⅛
Consyne Cp 10 20⅞ 20½ 20½ — ¼
Cont Mater 22 2⅝ 2½ 2½ — ⅛
Cont Tel wt 70 5 4⅞ 5 .....
Cook Elec .30 100 15½ 15 15⅜ + ⅜
Cook Ind 12 11⅝ 11½ 11⅝ + ⅛
CookPntV .60 5 21⅜ 21⅛ $1⅜ + ⅛
Cooper Jarrt 5 10½ 10⅜ 10⅜ + ⅛
Cordon Intl 26 11 10¾ 10¾ — ½
Core Labs 9 13¾ 13½ 13½ — ½
Corrn Blk .74 1 36 36 36 — ¼
Courtld .12e 10 4⅛ 4 1-16 4⅛+3-16
CoxCble Com 11 34 33¾ 33¾ — ¼
Craig Corp 17 4⅝ 4½ 4½ .....
CramerE .33t 27 8½ 8¼ 8¼ — ⅜
Creative Mgt 42 14¾ 14½ 14½ —⅛
CreoleP 2.20 105 18⅜ 17⅞ 18¼ + ¼
Crest Foam 15 6 6 6 — ⅛
Crestmont 3 3⅜ 3⅜ 3⅜ .....
Crompton .80 4 25 25 25 .....
Cross AT .40 16 59⅝ 59 59 —⅜
CwnCPt 1.18f 5 22⅛ 21¾ 21¾ — ½
Crystal Oil 94 11½ 10⅝ 10⅞ + ⅜
Cubic Cp .20e 21 17 16¾ 16 ⅞+ ¼
Curtis Math 2 4⅞ 4¾ 4⅞ + ⅛
CutterA .44 57 34½ 34½ 34½ + ¼
CutterB .44 4 29¼ 29 29¼ + ¼
D
Daltch .26e 8 10¼ 10⅛ 10⅛ .....

Electrog .60 3 15 14¾ 15 .....
Elect Assist 15 4⅞ 4¾ 4¾ .....
Elect Comp 14 2⅞ 2⅞ 2⅞ .. ..
ElectrEn .50t 2 9¾ 9¾ 9¾ + ¼
Elect Resch 2 4⅞ 4⅞ 4⅞ .....
Electron .60b 13 39⅛ 39⅛ 39⅛ .....
Electrospce 84 13⅞ 12¾ 12⅞ — ¾
Elgin Nat wt 33 ¾ ⅝ ⅝ .....
El Tronics 19 17⅛ 16⅞ 16⅞ — ⅛
Emenee Cp 2 5¼ 5⅛ 5⅛ — ¼
Entdon Inc 36 5½ 5⅛ 5⅛ — ¼
EpkoSho .64a 13 15¼ 15⅛ 15¼ + ¼
Equity Fd wt 10 25 24⅛ 24⅛ — ⅝
EquityNat In 65 9 8½ 8½ — ⅜
Ernst A .37t 3 6⅜ 6⅜ 6⅜ .....
Ero Ind 20 11⅛ 10⅝ 10⅝ — ½
Esgro Inc 35 7¼ 6⅝ 6⅝ — ¼
Espey Mfg 3 4¾ 4⅝ 4⅝ .....
Esquire Rad 18 16⅛ 15⅝ 15⅝ .....
Essex Chem 6 4 3⅞ 4 .....
Euthencs .31t 3 9⅞ 9¾ 9¾ — ¼
EvansAr .10e 4 11 11 11 .....
Executne .24 32 18¾ 18¼ 18¼ — ¼
F
Fab Ind 34 14½ 13¾ 14½ + ⅝
Fabien .40a 1 9½ 9½ 9½ + ⅛
Fabri Ce .03e 12 22¾ 22½ 22½ — ¼
Fabrics Natl 5 3½ 3¼ 3¼ .....
Fair Tex Mill 8 9⅞ 9⅝ 9¾ + ¼
Fairfld Noble 20 8 7¾ 8 + ⅛
Falcon Sbd 93 14¼ 13½ 13½ — ⅜
FamilyDlr St 52 49½ 49 49¼ +1¼
FamDolSt wi 8 25⅛ 24¼ 24¼ — ⅜
Family Rec 5 4⅛ 4 4 .....
Fanny Farm 5 17⅝ 17⅜ 17⅜ — ½
Fashion Fab 20 28⅛ 27¾ 27¾ — ⅝
Fed Resrces 36 3 2¾ 2¾ — ¼
FedMart .40b 1 18⅛ 18⅛ 18⅛ .....
Felmont Oil 24 14¾ 14½ 14⅝ .....
Felsway .32 26 20¾ 19¾ 19¾ — ¾
Fibrebord wt 19 12 11¾ 11⅞ .....
FidelGr 3.11e 13 35⅝ 35¼ 35½ — ⅛
FidelcoGr wt 6 10⅜ 10⅜ 10⅜ .....
Field Plastic 4 4⅞ 4¾ 4⅞ + ¼
Filmways 1 6⅞ 6⅞ 6⅞ — ⅛
FlltrDyn .01e 40 31⅛ 30⅝ 30⅝ — ¾
FinSanBa .20 18 25½ 25 25 — ¼
Finl Gen .24b 44 11⅞ 11½ 11¾ + ⅛
FinGenA .30b 22 11⅝ 11⅜ 11½ — ⅜
Fst Conn .80a 1 16 16 16 + ⅛
Fst Den 1.70e 19 19¾ 19¼ 19¼ — ⅝
Fst Denv wt 17 2¾ 2⅝ 2⅝ — ⅛
Fst Hartford 27 4¾ 4⅛ 4¾ + ½
FstHart pf.25 2 12 12 12 + ⅛
FirstNtl Real 20 1½ 1½ 1½ .....
FstS&LnS .36 84 27¼ 25⅞ 27¼ +2¼
FstWisM .51e 5 30¼ 30⅛ 30⅛ + ⅛
FischrP 1.06t 180 33¾ 32¼ 32⅞ +1⅛
Fishman .40b 2 11⅝ 11⅝ 11⅝ .....
Flagg Ind 24 9⅞ 9½ 9½ — ⅜
Flight Safty 5 22⅞ 22¾ 22¾ — ⅜
Flock Ind 70 19⅝ 18½ 18⅞ — ⅜
Fla Capital 26 5⅜ 5 5 — ⅛
Fluke Mf .53t 18 23¼ 22⅞ 22⅞ — ⅜
Fly Tiger wt 187 26¼ 25½ 25½ + ⅝
Foodrm .07p 15 6½ 6¼ 6¼ — ⅛
Ford Can 2a z60 94 92½ 92½ — ¾
Forest Cit .25 1 27⅝ 27⅝ 27⅝ + ¼
ForestLb .44f 29 13¾ 13½ 13⅝ + ⅛
FoxStaPh .52 1 47¼ 47¼ 47¼ — ⅛
FPA Corp 3 11⅞ 11⅝ 11⅝ — ⅜
Frankl M .20 16 47 45⅞ 45⅞ —1⅛
FranksN n.32 18 19⅛ 18¾ 18¾ — ¼
Fresnillo .20e 3 15½ 15¼ 15⅜ .....
Friend Frost 2 4½ 4½ 4½ .....
Frier Ind 20 5¾ 5⅜ 5⅜ — ½
Frontier Air 46 12⅜ 11⅞ 11⅞ — ⅝
Front Air wt 43 8⅞ 8¼ 8½ — ⅛
G
Gabriel Ind 8 13⅛ 13 13 — ⅛
Garan Inc .21 26 17 16⅝ 17 + ¼
Garcia Corp 13 18⅝ 18¼ 18¼ — ⅛
Garland .15e 20 13⅞ 13⅛ 13½ + ⅛
Gate Spt Gds 36 5½ 5⅜ 5½ + ⅛
Gayld Ntl .30 1 8 8 8 .....
Gaynor Stafd 14 14¼ 14 14¼ .....
Gearhart .24 71 14⅞ 14½ 14⅝ + ⅞
Gen Alloys 7 2⅞ 2¾ 2⅞ + ⅛
Gen Buildrs 3 4⅞ 4¾ 4⅞ .....
G Cinema .32 11 53 62½ 52½ + ¼
GenEduc Svc 35 7⅞ 7½ 7½ — ⅜
Gen Interiors 2 6⅝ 6⅝ 6⅝ — ⅛
Gen Mtg .97e 45 9⅛ 8⅞ 9 + ⅛
Gen Plywood 8 3⅜ 3¼ 3¼ .....
Gen Recreat 16 8⅛ 8⅛ 8⅛ .....
Gen Resrch 44 19½ 17⅝ 18 —1⅛
Genge In .25f 6 8½ 8½ 8½ — ⅛
Geon Ind 18 25¾ 25⅝ 25¾ + ⅜
GerberSc Ins 7 12½ 12½ 12½ — ¼
Giant Fd .50a 13 28¾ 28⅛ 28⅛ — ⅞
Giant Strs Cp 10 23¾ 23½ 23⅝ .....
Giant Yel .40 59 9 7-16 9⅛ 9 5-16 .....
Gilbert Cos 8 2⅜ 2⅜ 2⅜ .....
Gladding Cp 28 11¼ 10⅝ 10⅝ — ⅜
Glasrock Prd 69 8⅝ 8⅜ 8½ .....
Glen Ger .15t 11 8⅝ 8¼ 8⅝ + ⅛
GlobeSec Sys 16 23 22¾ 22¾ — ¼
Gloucster En 19 15⅞ 15¼ 15⅞ + ⅝
Goldblatt .36 30 9¼ 8½ 8¾ — ½
Goldn W Mob 14 19¼ 19 19 — ¼
Good LS Co 28 22⅜ 21⅝ 21¾ — ¾
Goodway 40 3¾ 3⅜ 3⅝ + ⅛
Gorin Str .50 6 7⅝ 7½ 7½ .....
GormRup .80 9 25¼ 25 25 + ¼
Gould Inc wt 30 12¾ 12⅛ 12⅛ — ⅝
Grainger .50 41 59¾ 58⅞ 59⅛ — ⅝
Grand Auto 6 20⅞ 20¾ 20¾ + ⅛
Granite Mgt 8 8⅜ 8⅛ 8¼ .....
Grass Val .10 19 10 9⅝ 9¾ — ¼

PART FOUR

LOAN AND SECURITY FORMS

A precondition to choosing a set of funds sources, a capital structure for the corporation, is a knowledge of what forms of legal contracts are available between the corporation and its capital suppliers. Those contracts are the loan and security forms that are described in Part IV.

The content of Part IV is therefore primarily descriptive, with only a few formulas for the computation of specific costs of capital of the funds sources being used. The specific cost of capital of a fund source can be used for a preliminary discrimination among sources. The adjective "specific" is used to limit that cost of capital to one particular contractual arrangement. The "cost of capital" is the interest rate that makes the net present value of all the after-tax receipts and outlays due to the financing contract equal zero. The cost of capital is therefore the fund source analogue to the internal rate of return of investment projects, the fund use. A superficial capital structure criterion would be to choose the set of financing sources that will minimize the average cost of capital. A correspondingly oversimplified scheme of optimization for the corporation's entire set of financial activities would be to maximize simultaneously the overall internal rate of return on assets while minimizing the overall cost of capital.

The capital sources are divided by time length of the contract and presented in two chapters. The first chapter is concerned with short and intermediate-term sources, and the second with long-term sources of funds. The short and intermediate-term sources include direct loans, commercial paper and note security sales, and the leasing of assets. Under the long-term sources four basic types of securities are discussed—bonds, preferred stock, common stock, and convertibles and warrants. Of course innovative financial officers may combine security forms in a package financing or devise new security forms if a purchaser can be found.

9

SHORT AND INTERMEDIATE-TERM SOURCES OF FUNDS

A corporation has a variety of fund sources that can be classified by period of use. Short-term funds are defined here as those which will be used for time periods of less than one year, intermediate-term funds for time periods between one year and ten years, and long-term funds for periods longer than ten years. The distinction is somewhat arbitrary between short and intermediate-term, but is more meaningful between long-term and short-term.

Equity instruments, common and preferred stock, warrants, and convertible securities, are sold for long-term purposes, and the usual inference is that these securities are perpetual in nature—the period of funds use is infinite. If debt securities are long-term they are called bonds, if intermediate-term, notes, and if short-term, commercial paper. Direct loans are normally short or intermediate-term. Debt may be "subordinated" to other debt forms, which means that the subordinated debt-holders' claims to income and/or assets in case of liquidation are inferior to other debt-holders' claims.

This chapter is concerned with short and intermediate-term sources of funds, and long-term sources are described in Chapter 10. The forms of the loan agreements or security indentures are many, presenting some definite problems in the financial management of the fund source allocation.

"Automatic" Short-Term Sources

Certain sources of short-term funds are considered automatic in origin, without a separate loan application and transaction being necessary. These sources are mostly trade credit, accounts payable, but some significant accruals of expenses may occur in individual business firms. Accounts payable originate from a purchase of merchandise, and accrued expenses come from the method of periodic payment of certain expenses.

Trade credit is not entirely automatic since an explicit arrangement with the supplier is usually necessary when the account is originally opened. A supplier may refuse to sell on open account if he doubts that the balances will be paid promptly, but once established each transaction does not have to be approved separately.

To stimulate prompt payment of invoices a cash discount is frequently stated in the invoice terms. Terms such as 2/10, n/30 are used to indicate that a 2 percent discount can be taken by the purchaser if the invoice is paid within ten days of the invoice date. If payment is delayed beyond the tenth day the original amount of the invoice is due, and must be paid by 30 days from the invoice date. Most firms could be expected to pay by the tenth day since the cost involved in the extra 20 days of credit is so high. 2 percent for 20 days of additional credit is approximately 36 percent a year.

Whether a cash discount is necessary or how large the discount should be will depend on the supplier's assessment of his customers' willingness and ability to pay promptly. If the supplier's terms are applied uniformly to all his customers, one customer may find that the cost of additional credit beyond the cash discount period is ridiculously high, while another customer may decide it is worth the cost.

The use of trade credit by a purchaser may involve some implicit costs beyond any explicit cash discounts foregone. Since extending credit results in accounts receivable investment for the supplier, the price of the goods may be increased to allow for the carrying costs of the accounts. It might be possible, for example, for a customer to agree to pay on a C.O.D. (collect on delivery) basis in return for a discount from the regular price of the merchandise. If the regular terms are net/30, a discount of 1 percent from the regular price for payment on delivery would amount to an annual interest allowance of 12 percent. Carrying the argument still further it might be possible to arrange C.B.D. (cash before delivery) terms, and achieve further discounts from the regular price of the merchandise. Such C.O.D. and C.B.D. arrangements would probably only be practical when the buyer of the merchandise is a major customer of the supplier, so that negotiations and amendments to the regular prices and terms are worthwhile to both parties.

Besides the implicit cost through the price of the merchandise being adjusted to allow for credit, there are other implicit costs to the use of trade credit. The existence of one kind of debt may alter the price of other types of debt. An excessive accounts payable balance may result in a higher charge for short-term bank loans, for example.

A less-often recognized form of automatic credit comes from the accrual of expenses such as wages, utilities, and even taxes. Wages are not paid as the services are performed, but are accumulated and paid weekly, semi-monthly, or monthly. If wages for a half-month pay period were $10,000, for example, the average accrual of wages and therefore the amount of credit granted by employees would be $5,000. If the company could switch to a monthly payroll period, the size of the monthly paycheck would be $20,000, increasing the average accrual to $10,000. Of course such a move might be resisted by employees, creating more difficulties than the additional credit is worth to the management.

Other automatic accruals come from those expenses such as utilities where payment occurs after the service is rendered. Part of the collection of corporate income taxes occurs after the corporation makes the taxable income, so accrued corporate income taxes can be considered a short-term source of funds that is automatic with the making of profits. The corporation does not have the option of changing the size and period of this accrual.

Short-Term Unsecured Loans

A business firm may be able to borrow on an unsecured basis if its credit rating is high enough. The most likely source of short-term unsecured loans is a commercial bank, although other financial institutions such as insurance companies and finance companies make such loans. Individual firms may have access to special sources such as individuals or government agencies.

The loan may be made in the form of a single loan, negotiated to cover a fixed period of time such as six months, or in the form of a line of credit or a revolving credit arrangement. The line of credit is an agreement whereby the lender stands ready to lend any amount up to the limit stated in the agreement at any time during a fixed period, perhaps a year. The borrower will presumably use the line of credit only as needed, and the size of the loan is therefore entirely flexible. The revolving credit arrangement is typically a longer-term arrangement whereby the borrower makes a series of borrowings and repayments under the same agreement, perhaps borrowing to finance inventory expansion during one time of the year, repaying (cleaning-up) the loan later in the year, and then borrowing again the next year.

Calculating the cost of borrowed funds may be complicated somewhat by some standard practices that have evolved particularly with bank loans. For example, the interest payment may be deducted in advance—the discount method of computing interest may be used. A company borrowing $100,000 for six months at a stated rate of 8 percent may find that the bank deducts the $4,000 interest at the time of the loan, making the proceeds of the loan only $96,000, with $100,000 as the amount that is paid at the end of the loan's term. In this case the actual interest rate is 8.33 percent, which can be calculated as

$$\frac{\$\ 4{,}000}{\$96{,}000}(2) = 8.33\%$$

The interest charge is divided by the proceeds of the loan, and then multiplied by the number of loan periods in a year.

Another frequently encountered complication with bank loans is the compensatory balance requirement. The bank may require that a certain percentage of the loan, for example 15 percent, be left on deposit with the bank. If the compensatory balance must be kept in the borrower's checking account where no interest on the balance can be paid, the compensatory balance results in a considerable increase in the true interest cost of the loan. Suppose a company again borrows $100,000 from the bank at a stated interest rate of 8 percent, and this time the interest is not deducted in advance, but the bank requires a 15 percent compensatory balance to be kept in the borrower's checking account. The true proceeds of the loan are $85,000, so the actual interest rate is

$$\frac{\$\ 4{,}000}{\$85{,}000}(2) = 9.41\%$$

If the compensatory balance could be kept in the form of a time deposit where the bank pays interest on the balance, the actual interest rate on the loan would be reduced. The size and the form of the compensatory balance are subject to negotiation between the bank and the borrower, of course.

If the lender is committed to extending variable amounts of loans under a line of credit or revolving credit arrangement, usually a fixed fee will be charged for the commitment. The commitment fee is typically between ½ and 1 percent of the amount of the line of credit or revolving credit maximum, and interest is charged separately on the actual amount borrowed. The interest rate charged may be variable in the contract, particularly for the longer term arrangements, but is usually tied to some interest rate such as the bank's "prime rate" or the Federal Reserve discount rate.

Most commercial banks have published prime rates that are supposed to be the lowest interest rate the banks will charge, normally only for their "prime" customers. The prime rate tends to serve as a basing-point for the bank's structure of interest rates charged on various loans. If the prime rate for an example bank is 8 percent, the rate charged on its best short-term business loans will be 8 percent, for a slightly riskier category of borrower perhaps 8½ percent, a still riskier category 9 percent, and so on. The individual bank establishes its own prime rate, but usually due to competitive pressures most banks in a given geographical area will have the same prime rate. Most of the time banks nationwide will have the same posted prime rate.

Because of the Federal Reserve's close control over commercial banks' aggregate reserves and lending capacity, the prime rate of banks serves as an indicator of the central bank's current monetary policy and the state of the nation's economy. While banks may not normally change their prime rates more often than once or twice a year, there have been periods when rapidly changing economic conditions have resulted in frequent and large changes in those rates as shown in Figure 9.1. Along with the price of money (the interest rate) business firms have found the availability of loan funds from banks varies over time. Accordingly, in planning for loan sources, the corporation's financial managers must engage in a certain amount of economic forecasting to estimate the cost and availability of short-term loans in the future. The alternatives are to arrange intermediate-term loans or to depend on other sources of short-term loans than commercial banks.

Figure 9.1
The Historical Record of the Prime Rate

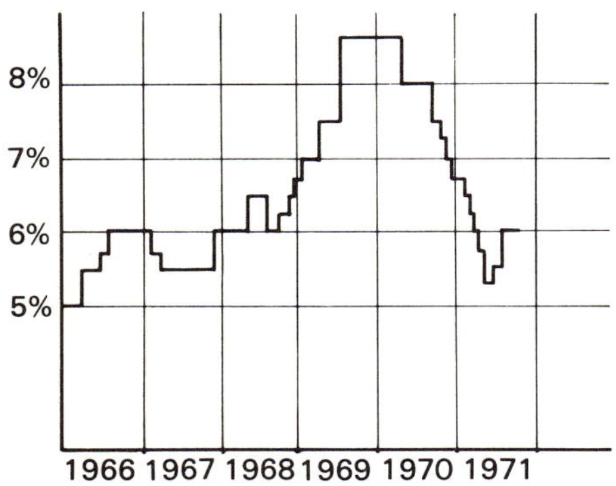

Commercial banks are the largest suppliers of short-term unsecured loans to business. Other financial institutions, such as finance companies, tend to specialize in other loan forms. For larger business firms the sale of debt securities is a reasonable alternative to direct borrowing.

Commercial Paper

Commercial paper is a short-term unsecured debt security, sold publicly or by direct placement in varying denominations, with maturity lengths that vary generally from 15 to 270 days. The paper itself is a promise to pay a certain amount at maturity to the holder, and ranks legally as an unsecured loan.

Commercial paper is issued on a discount basis—for example, if \$100,000 is to be paid the holder at the end of six months, and the yield to the holder is to be 8 percent, the buyer of the commercial paper will pay \$96,154 to the seller:

$$\frac{\$\ 3{,}846}{\$96{,}154}(2) = 8\%$$

The commercial paper may be sold directly by the issuer, or it may be sold through a dealer. Normally a dealer's facilities are used if the size of the issue is small, or if the issuing firm is less well known in the financial markets. Larger and more frequent issuers of commercial paper usually find it worthwhile to maintain a sales office of their own.

The paper is graded by Dun & Bradstreet's National Credit Office according to that reporting service's assessment of the credit-worthiness of the issuer. The highest rating given is "prime." Commercial paper sold through a dealer does not bear the endorsement of the dealer, although there is probably some implicit approval of the issuer felt by the buyer in that situation. Accordingly commercial paper dealers may perform some grading of their own before agreeing to sell a firm's paper.

To sell commercial paper successfully at a reasonable interest rate the corporation must be a very large well-known company, with an impeccable credit reputation. Accordingly the commercial paper issuers are small in number, probably less than 700 firms, and are mostly finance companies or sales finance subsidiaries of large manufacturing or retail corporations.

Commercial paper at one time was a limited market in which only a very few corporations issued securities, but it grew in importance with the prolonged periods of tight money policy by the Federal Reserve in the latter 1960's. The amount of commercial paper outstanding grew from less than $5 billion in 1960 to more than $38 billion in 1970 as corporations discovered this alternative to normal borrowing from banks and other financial institutions. The default by Penn Central on its commercial paper in the late spring of 1970 caused some degree of confusion in the commercial paper market, as lenders became more concerned with the investment quality of issues they had taken for granted before. The net result was a short-term decrease in the volume of paper outstanding, but the volume soon rose to its former level.

The purchasers of commercial paper include banks, other financial organizations, and non-financial corporations desiring to employ temporarily excess cash. The maturity date of commercial paper can frequently be designed to meet the buyer's requirements, so that commercial paper may be considered at times to be a better investment medium than even short-term U.S. government securities since no transaction cost would be incurred by the holder even for a very short holding period.

For the very large firm the issue of commercial paper may be an alternative to short-term loans from banks. Usually the yield on commercial paper is slightly below banks' prime rates, although the yield will fluctuate daily as the market supply and demand conditions change. The prime rate of banks is relatively steady, so even the very large firm may prefer the certainty of charges and availability of bank loans through a line of credit to the uncertain availability of funds through the commercial paper market.

Secured Loans

To provide additional assurance of the repayment of a loan lenders will in some circumstances require the pledge of specific assets as security. The normal expectation is that if the borrower is unwilling or unable to repay the loan the lender can simply foreclose on the pledged asset, sell it, and get sufficient proceeds from the sale to cover the loan balance.

Frequently, however, the pledged assets for a secured loan are not readily converted into cash, usually due to the specialized nature of the assets. Machines and buildings designed for a special purpose or partly finished manufacturing goods-in-process are sometimes pledged for secured loans, even though the market value of those assets under forced-sale conditions might be very low. In this case the security agreement may simply serve as a threat—the lender can close the business down by removing the pledged asset if the borrower is slow in making his required payments.

The usual expectation is that the pledged asset must be readily convertible into cash. Accordingly various forms of security are commonly used for loans: marketable securities, accounts receivable, inventories, and plant and equipment, depending on the nature of those assets in the individual firm.

Marketable securities may be pledged against a loan rather than being sold by the borrower for various reasons. The securities might have been acquired at a lower price than the current market price, so that if the securities were sold the company would be liable for taxes on the profit. If the voting rights attached to the marketable securities are important sale might be considered impractical. Of course, if the company expects the market price of the securities to rise in the future, sale now would be undesirable.

When marketable securities are pledged, the size of the loan in proportion to the market value of the securities will vary as the type of security varies. A lender may be willing to lend up to 90 percent of the value of U.S. government securities, for example, but only 50 percent of the value of common stocks. Usually the percentage will vary with the possible drop in market value over the term of the loan.

Accounts receivable are sometimes used as security for short-term loans, even though the administrative costs to the lender make the interest rate that must be charged on the loan rather high. Normally duplicate accounts receivable ledger records must be maintained by the lender, so that when an individual account is paid the lender can remove that account from the pledged balances. When the loan is originally initiated the lender may find it desirable to undertake some audit procedures to verify that the account balance actually exists, and that the account shows reasonable promise of being paid promptly. If the assigned receivables are handled on a "non-notification" basis, the payments on account are still made to the borrowing company, and it is desirable for the lender to be able to verify that the amounts collected from customers are all reported. Since these costs are all to be added to a basic lending charge, the total cost of this type of secured loan is likely to be high.

"Factoring" of the accounts receivable, sale of the accounts to a financial institution, the factor, may be preferable to using the accounts receivable as security for loans, particularly when the borrowing company needs funds on a continuing basis. In some lines of business, for example the clothing manufacturing industry, the sale of seasonal merchandise to small retail stores results in very large and very slow-paying accounts receivable in relationship to the other assets of the business firm. Rather than tie up large amounts of capital in accounts receivable it has become commonplace in those industries to factor the accounts. The costs are high, possibly, since the factor's discount on the face amount of the receivables must be large enough to cover the bookkeeping and auditing expense, the bad debt expenses (if sold on a nonrecourse basis), and the factor's cost of funds while waiting for payment. These expenses otherwise would all have to be born by the selling company, however, and since factors are usually larger and more creditworthy companies it is possible that those expenses would be less if paid by the factor than the seller. On balance it may be cheaper to factor accounts receivable for some business firms.

Inventories are easier to use as security for loans if the inventory is a standard product, salable without further conversion, and is easily identifiable as pledged property. Usually raw material inventories such as grain, wool, steel and other metals qualify easily for loans if means can be worked out to assure the lender continually that the collateral still exists. A fairly complex set of warehousing arrangements have been worked out in the various states to provide that assurance. If the pledged inventories have been stored in a public warehouse, for example, the goods can only be removed on the receipt of written permission (the endorsed warehouse receipt) of the lender.

Another example of inventory loans is found in the new car inventories of automobile dealers. Automobiles are readily identifiable by serial numbers, and require an official certification of title. If the lender is forced to foreclose, the new cars can usually be readily sold to other dealers at very small price concessions. Accordingly a high percentage of the wholesale (factory) price of a new car inventory can usually be borrowed by the dealer.

An extension of the idea of inventory loans is the "consignment inventory" arrangement. A consigned inventory is still owned by the seller, and title to the item passes only when the retailer sells it to the customer. In consignment arrangements the repossession of the inventory does not require a legal foreclosure proceeding since the title has not passed from the seller.

Other assets may be pledged for short-term loans, but usually a mortgage of equipment or real estate comes about in an intermediate-term or long-term loan or debt security. The mortgage is usually arranged at the time of the purchase of the asset.

The pledging of assets as security for loans should reduce the ability of the firm to borrow on an unsecured basis. Unsecured lenders sometimes regard the unpledged assets of the firm as implicit collateral for their loans, assuming that if the borrower is unwilling or unable to make the required interest and principal payments bankruptcy proceedings can be instigated and those assets will be seized by the courts and sold to satisfy creditors claims. If some of the assets are pledged this reduces the "pool of assets" available for use in satisfying the general creditors' claims. As will be seen in a later section, seizure and sale of assets to satisfy debts does not work so easily because of the complexity of bankruptcy laws and court procedures.

Restrictive Covenants In the Loan Agreement

When the lender is not convinced that the borrowing corporation is a prime credit risk, some restrictive covenants may be included in the loan agreement that constrain the corporation's management from certain actions that may endanger the lender's security. Those restrictions may be stated as working capital maintenance, asset acquisition and preservation requirements, restriction of additional debt, and dividend payment limitation.

The purpose of the covenants is not only to insure that the borrower has enough cash to pay the lender's loan when it comes due, but to forestall other creditors' of the corporation having to take prior legal action (possibly bankruptcy proceedings as described in the following section) which would endanger the lender's loan. In other words one lender has to worry about other lenders' actions.

The maintenance of working capital at a minimum total is intended to insure that ordinary accounts payable and accruals can be paid on time, allowing the borrower corporation to continue normal operations. Preservation of fixed assets may have the same motivation, allowing the corporation to continue generating revenue. Preservation may also be desired for the idea of having some assets that can be seized and sold to satisfy the claim. Limiting the acquisition of additional assets is an obvious attempt to keep the corporation from spending cash and possibly incurring additional debt.

The restriction on additional debt presumably limits the chances of other creditors "foreclosing." The restriction may take the specific form of prohibiting the issuing of any more claims superior to that of the lender, such as secured debts with a pledge of significant amounts of assets. The limitation on dividends is an added move toward preservation of the corporation's cash.

The imposition of restrictive covenants in a loan agreement is obviously important to the borrower. More effort may be devoted to bargaining about the covenants than to the interest rate and the schedule of repayments. Excessive limitations on the corporation's activities may cause a reconsideration of the loan application by the borrower.

Insolvency, Extension, and Bankruptcy

Occasionally a business firm finds itself unable to meet its fixed obligations, and must therefore go through some procedures for delaying the payment or scaling down the size of the debts. If the difficulties are small and temporary, possibly due to the firm's inability to realize a sale of some asset at the time originally scheduled, it may be possible to arrange a voluntary extension or composition of claims with a group of creditors and thereby forestall more serious legal action. An extension is an agreement to delay payment for some period of time, while a composition involves a reduction in the size of the claims of creditors.

These agreements are entirely voluntary, and individual creditors are not bound by the agreements of other creditors. The agreements may be reached as a result of legal action under the jurisdiction of a state court, but are more likely to be the result of private negotiation.

The firm itself may seek a legal extension of the time schedule of debt payments by petitioning for an "arrangement" through the federal district courts under Chapter XI of the federal Bankruptcy Act. If this voluntary petition is accepted by the court and the plan for payment submitted is allowed, the court will appoint a referee to supervise negotiations with creditors, and if necessary a receiver or trustee to administer the plan of payment. The rights of secured creditors cannot be abridged under this arrangement, but unsecured creditors can be bound to the terms if a majority of those creditors accept the plan. Usually the voluntary action under Chapter XI forestalls a more serious legal action, bankruptcy, which may result in reorganization and recapitalization of the debtor company, or possibly in liquidation of the assets and dissolution of the company.

Creditors can bring bankruptcy proceedings against the debtor company through the federal district courts under the other provisions (usually Chapter X) of the Bankruptcy Act. In this action the court assumes control over the operations of the debtor company while legal action is being considered and taken. The objective is to preserve the assets of the company, usually through continuing the operations of the business, while a plan for reorganization or liquidation is being devised.

The usual assumption is that the firm is worth more as a going concern than would be realized through a forced sale of its assets. This assumption is used during the period of court deliberation, but is also inherent in most of the approved plans for reorganization. Most of the time a company going through bankruptcy will not be liquidated, but will continue in operation under a revised capital structure. If the court decides the firm should be liquidated rather than reorganized, the distribution of cash proceeds of liquidation follows a rule of priorities established according to the legal characteristics of the debts.

The general priority to cash distributions in liquidations follows this order:

1. Special priority claims.
2. Secured debt.
3. Unsecured (general) debt.
4. Subordinated debt.
5. Equity securities.

Special priority claims includes wages in arrears to employees of the firm not in excess of $600 per person, taxes due various government units, and the administrative and other expenses incurred in the bankruptcy proceedings. After these claims are paid the secured debt holders will receive the proceeds of the sale of the pledged assets, and if that is insufficient to satisfy the secured claims, the remainder of the debt is moved down to the unsecured category. Unsecured or general debt may have priority with respect to the class of subordinated debt if such subordinated debt exists. Subordinated debt still has prior claim to the various classes of equity securities. Within each class of priority listed there may be some additional distinction made due to the terms of the loan agreement or security agreement. For example, preferred stock usually has priority with respect to common stock in liquidation, and a corporation would have different classes of subordinated debt.

Suppose a corporation with book values as shown below is declared bankrupt and undergoes liquidation:

Assets		Liabilities and equity	
Pledged assets	$ 4,000,000	Secured debt	$ 3,000,000
Other assets	6,000,000	Unsecured debt	2,500,000
		Subordinated debt	1,000,000
		Equity	3,500,000
	$10,000,000		$10,000,000

The pledged assets are sold for $2,000,000 and the other assets for $3,000,000. The amount of special priority claims is $100,000. The distribution of cash would proceed as follows:

The special priority claims are paid in full, $100,000.
Secured creditors receive $2,000,000 from the pledged assets, and become general creditors for the remaining $1,000,000.
The total unsecured or general debt is now $3,500,000, and the remaining cash available for distribution is $2,900,000, so unsecured creditors receive 29/35 of their claims, or about 83 cents on the dollar.
Subordinated debt holders and equity holders receive nothing.

In this example none of the creditors receive full payment of their claims. Secured creditors receive a total of $2,828,571 against the claim of $3,000,000, and unsecured creditors receive $2,071,429 against the claim of $2,500,000.

For the subordinated creditors to receive anything in liquidation, the proceeds of the sale of assets would have to exceed $5,600,000 (the total claim of the special priority claims, the secured creditors, and the unsecured creditors). For the equity holders to receive cash in this liquidation the proceeds of the asset sale would have to exceed $6,600,000.

If the corporation is reorganized to continue in business, determination of the new capital structure will involve two separate problems. First the value to be placed on the new concern must be determined, and then a capital structure must be designed that will be viable—that will compensate the creditors of the firm to as full an extent as possible, but will not involve such a high schedule of fixed charges as to throw the firm back into insolvency.

The basic valuation mechanism generally used is to capitalize the expected earnings stream of the firm at some reasonable rate. Both the expected earnings and the capitalization rate are estimates, of course. Suppose that in the bankrupt corporation it was determined that an annual stream of earnings before interest and taxes of $1,200,000 could be reasonably expected following reorganization. If the capitalization rate chosen were 15 percent, the firm's appraisal value would be

$$\frac{\$1{,}200{,}000}{15\%} = \$8{,}000{,}000$$

Now a capital structure must be designed that will allow the firm to continue in existence indefinitely. A large number of different types of securities might be involved in the chosen combination, but it is assumed for example purposes here that the capital structure simply consists of $3,000,000 debt and $5,000,000 equity. According to the absolute priority rule the former secured debt holders would receive the new $3,000,000 debt, the former unsecured debt holders would receive $2,500,000 of the new equity, the former subordinated debt holders would receive $1,000,000 of the new equity, and the former equity holders would receive the remaining $1,500,000 of equity.

If the estimated values are actually the value at which the new securities can be sold, the only ultimate losers in this recapitalization are the former equity holders. Of course there may be significant time lags before a creditor receives his settlement, and the inconvenience, uncertainty, and delay of payment involved in the bankruptcy proceedings may represent real costs to the creditor. Accordingly lenders to a business firm certainly prefer to avoid lending where an appreciable probability of insolvency exists. To avoid the disruption and delay of bankruptcy, important creditors will often voluntarily delay pressing their claims to allow the debtor company time to "work things out."

Intermediate-Term Loans

If a loan is between one year and ten years in length it may be classified as intermediate-term. Actually, since long-term direct loans are so seldom made, the time definition could be further simplified to say that an intermediate-term loan is any loan with maturity longer than one year. Exact distinctions cannot always be made since the renewal or extension of a short-term loan may fit it into an intermediate-term category. The revolving credit plan or line of credit discussed earlier may be an intermediate-term loan.

The source of intermediate-term loans is usually a commercial bank—although insurance companies sometimes make large direct loans—specialized finance companies may be a source, and occasionally a borrowing firm will fit the requirements so that it can obtain funds directly from an agency of the U.S. government such as the Small Business Administration.

Finance companies sometimes make intermediate-term loans to businesses, although the loan is usually a secured one, tied to the purchase of equipment. Normally the finance companies are short-term lenders, such as in the case of an inventory-secured or accounts receivable-secured loan.

Insurance companies are good sources of intermediate-term loans for the larger borrowers. The asset size of the typical life insurance company is so large that the company can easily make large loans without incurring a significant degree of risk in its investment portfolio. The form of the loan from an insurance company may be a debt security rather than a loan, and the debt securities may be marketable notes, as discussed below, or may be nonmarketable.

The Small Business Administration is an agency created to make loans to small business firms when those firms cannot otherwise obtain credit at reasonable interest rates. In recent years this agency has been the channel of federal funds to ghetto businesses, where the loan serves a social wefare purpose rather than a strictly business purpose. Most other federal government programs are aimed at particular needs that cannot be filled by private credit sources—such as loans made to finance defense or aerospace production. Therefore agencies of the federal government are not a general source of intermediate-term loans, only a source that may be tapped under particular circumstances.

Security is more likely to be required for the intermediate-term loan than for the short-term, mainly because the longer time period of payment tends to make that type of loan somewhat riskier. The types of assets pledged are typically long-term, semipermanent assets, such as equipment, buildings, and other real estate.

Other restrictions than the pledge of specific assets are likely to be required by lenders of intermediate-term funds. The restrictions may include a limitation on dividend payment or loans to shareholders, the maintenance of a minimum working capital total or current ratio, a prohibition on further borrowing by the firm, limits on the acquisition or sale of fixed assets, and other financial restrictions. Occasionally the restrictions included in the loan contract will specify that certain individuals must be kept as officers of the firm or members of the board of directors, and sometimes creditors are even given formal voting rights. The existence of such restrictions may be costly to the firm if the restrictions inhibit profitable decisions and operations.

The repayment provisions of an intermediate-term loan may call for periodic payments of interest with a lump-sum payment of the principal amount at the end of the loan period. Installment payments, either of level amounts or of varying amounts, may be required, and in this case the average term of the loan is less than the stated term. If the installment payments are level amounts, the size of the payment required to amortize the loan can be computed using present value tables, or by special installment payment tables.

Intermediate-Term Debt Securities

Larger business firms may elect to sell intermediate-term debt securities, usually called "notes," as an alternative to direct loans. If the notes are privately placed—sold directly to an institution such as an insurance company—the firm normally is not required to register the securities with the Securities and Exchange Commission (SEC). However if public sale is contemplated, the note issue usually comes under the jurisdiction of the SEC.

For securities issues of term longer than 270 days (the dividing point for commercial paper) where the sales are interstate in nature, the SEC requires financial data to be filed with it, and prospective purchasers of the security issue must be furnished with certain financial information about the company in the form of a prospectus. The amount of information and legal formality required for registration sometimes makes it worthwhile for a firm to alter its plans for a public issue. More important sometimes is the *public* disclosure of financial data in the prospectus that might possibly give some competitive advantage to a competitor.

If the decision is made to go ahead with a public issue of intermediate-term notes, the services of an investment banker are usually necessary to facilitate the offering. An investment banker is a specialized financial institution whose main function is to provide advice and expertise in selling security issues. The investment banker will help to plan the terms of the security offering, provide legal and accounting assistance to meet the requirements of the SEC registration, and usually act as a sales agent for the security issue. In addition the investment banker may fulfill an underwriting function, where the underwriter guarantees the sale of the security issue at a fixed price.

The amount of services rendered by the investment banker will determine the fee charged. If underwriting is part of the contract the total charge by the investment banker may be considerably higher than if the investment banker only sells the security issue on a "best-efforts" basis. The cost of issue of an intermediate-term note issue may be significantly large to the firm since it must be spread over a much shorter term than in a long-term bond issue. Accordingly intermediate-term loans may be more practical an alternative than intermediate-term debt securities.

Leasing as an Alternative to Intermediate-Term Loans or Securities

If a business firm needs financing in connection with the acquisition of a specific asset the alternative of leasing the use of that asset should be investigated. In this case the leasing arrangement is frequently called "100 percent financing," since the user of the asset does not make an appreciable equity investment in the asset.

Leasing is commonly used as a means of obtaining the use of data processing equipment, and of office space or other real estate where purchase of an entire parcel would not be feasible. Many other items of equipment can now be leased with the development of specialized leasing institutions that frequently are subsidiaries of banks and insurance companies. Airlines sometimes lease their aircraft, trucking companies part of their rolling stock, and railroads can obtain the use of railroad cars in this manner.

Leasing when thought of superficially may not look as if it should be an economic alternative to borrowing and buying an asset. The lease charges, after all, must include the same costs of depreciation, maintenance, and an imputed return on capital no matter who owns the asset. If a leasing company owns the asset, the charge for the asset will also include some allowance for profit, possibly making the real cost of leasing greater.

However, there are certainly cases where economies of scale can result in a lower cost of leasing than borrowing and buying. If the leasing company is a large purchaser of that type of asset, such as an automobile leasing company purchasing hundreds of cars directly from a manufacturer, the company may be able to obtain some sort of volume discount on the initial purchase price that could be passed on partially to the user. The leasing company may be able to borrow funds at a lower cost than the user company, due either to the size of the institution or to more frequent and therefore less costly access to the capital markets. Occasionally a case of irrational pricing may be found—a leasing company may have miscalculated the expected life of the asset in question and therefore be using too long a depreciation period in its pricing.

One other reason is sometimes used for leasing that has to do with concealing borrowing from other creditors and prospective stockholders. If the user company borrows to buy the asset, the debt incurred must be shown in full in the financial statements, possibly resulting in a higher cost of further borrowing or an evaluation that the common stock of the corporation has become riskier. If the asset is leased, however, the full value of the lease payment liability is not shown on the financial statements. An annual payment of $100,000 for ten years, for example, would be sufficient to amortize a loan of $671,000 if an interest rate of 8 percent is charged. If there is a loan of $671,000 to the firm, it must be shown in full on the balance sheet as a liability, but if the $100,000 payment is for a lease contract, the $671,000 would not appear as a liability. There actually is no real difference in the degree of financial obligation involved unless the lease contract has an escape clause which provides for early termination. In spite of this similarity the only disclosure of lease obligations currently required in accounting statements is a footnote to the balance sheet indicating the size of the annual lease payment if the size is deemed "material." It would seem that a desirable change in accounting principles rulings would be to show the capitalized value of lease payment obligations as a type of liability on the balance sheet.

An Example of the Lease-or-Buy Decision

Sometimes the corporation has the alternative of renting the use of an asset, leasing it, rather than being required to purchase the asset to obtain its use. Where the use of the asset is very short-term, such as the rental of a car for an executive on a business trip, or where only a portion of an asset unit is to be used, as in the rental of an office in an office building, the obvious choice is to lease rather than buy. In other cases, however, the choice is not so obvious.

The two major types of lease are the financial lease and the operating lease. In the operating lease use of the asset is only for short periods of time, and the lease obligations (payments) are short-term in nature. In a financial lease, on the other hand, the contract calls for a long-term series of payments by the user, usually equivalent to the economic life of the asset in question. The reasonable alternative to the financial lease therefore is to buy the asset.

A financial lease requires no appreciable investment by the user, but a set of periodic payments that are similar to installment payments on a loan. Actually financial leases are sometimes called "100 percent financing" because of the similarity to borrowing all the purchase price of the asset and repaying the loan over the life of the asset.

Since the lease payments charged by the owner of the asset include amounts for the economic depreciation of the asset, an allowance for the carrying cost of the investment of funds (an imputed interest charge) in the asset, and some profit, the appropriate comparison for a leasing opportunity is with a combination of borrowing and buying the asset. Because the user corporation has some other assets and equity it is possible to assume for comparison purposes that an amount equal to the purchase price would be borrowed to buy the asset.

Suppose for example that the corporation has the opportunity of leasing an item of equipment for a five-year period, paying \$800 at the end of each year. The corporation is responsible for maintenance of the equipment during the lease. Because the corporation acquires no "salvage value interest," has no rights to the asset after expiration of the lease, the entire amount of the lease payment is an expense for tax purposes. If the corporation is subject to a tax rate of 45 percent, the after-tax lease payments are

$$\$800\,(1 - 0.45) = \$440$$

a year.

The corporation could acquire the use of the equipment by buying it for \$3,600. If the equipment is purchased, the \$3,600 will be borrowed on a loan agreement that calls for repayment of \$720 and accumulated interest at 10 percent each year. The total cash payments required on a five-year loan are:

Time	**1**	**2**	**3**	**4**	**5**
Payment on loan principal	\$720	\$720	\$720	\$720	\$720
Interest for the year	36	28.80	21.60	14.40	7.20
Total loan payment	\$756	\$748.80	\$741.60	\$734.40	\$727.20

These loan payments must be adjusted for taxes, which will depend on the depreciation expenses allocated on the corporation's tax return. Suppose the estimated scrap value of the equipment is \$100 at the end of five years, and the \$3,500 depreciation is allocated over the five years on a sum-of-the-years-digits basis. That is, depreciation for the first year is 5/15 of \$3,500, for the second year 4/15 of \$3,500, and so forth. The depreciation expenses for tax purposes will therefore be:

Time	1	2	3	4	5
Depreciation expenses	$1,166.67	$933.33	$700.00	$466.67	$233.33

The tax savings due to the depreciation expenses are 45 percent of the depreciation amounts:

Time	1	2	3	4	5
Tax savings	$525	$420	$315	$210	$105

The tax savings due to the interest expenses are 45 percent of $36, 45 percent of $28.80, and so forth. The computation of the net after-tax cash outlays due to the borrow-buy decision is:

Time	1	2	3	4	5
Before-tax loan payment	$756.00	$748.80	$741.60	$734.40	$727.20
Scrap value of equipment					–100.00
Depreciation tax savings	–525.00	–420.00	–315.00	–210.00	–105.00
Interest tax savings	–16.20	–12.96	–9.72	–6.48	–3.24
Net after-tax cash outlays	$214.80	$315.84	$416.88	$517.92	$518.96

The comparison of leasing with borrow-buying for the example evolves therefore into comparing the cash flow sequence: 440, 440, 440, 440 with the sequence: 214.80, 315.84, 416.88, 517.92, 518.96. It is unnecessary to consider maintenance costs of the equipment since they are borne by the corporation in either case, and the benefits derived from the equipment use are the same in either case.

Suppose that an interest rate of 12 percent is appropriate for evaluation of the cash outlay sequences. Since the $440 outlay is the same for each of the five years, the present value factor from Table 3 is used to derive a present value of

$$\$440\,(3.60478) = \$1{,}586.11$$

for the leasing outlay. For the borrow-buy arrangement the present value factors of Table 2 are used for the present value of

$$\$214.80(0.89286) + \$315.84(0.79719) + \$416.88(0.71178) + \$517.92(0.63552) + \$518.96(0.56743) = \$1{,}363.92$$

Because the computed amounts are the present values of *outlays*, the borrow-buy arrangement should be the choice in this example.

The choice of an appropriate interest rate for evaluation of lease or borrow-buy alternatives is not obvious. Although in the example funds could be borrowed at a before-tax rate of 10 percent (an after-tax rate of 5.5 percent), the interest rate used in the computation of present values was much higher, 12 percent after taxes. The rate of 12 percent is intended here to approximate the corporation's overall cost of capital, the aggregate cost of incremental funds to the corporation including equity sources.

Summary

Before the choice of financing sources is discussed it is necessary to identify the common alternatives open to the average corporation. The short and intermediate-term debt financing includes both loan forms and security forms, and within each category the nature of security required differs.

The major sources of short-term funds are accounts payable and accruals, direct loans from a bank or other financial institution, and sale of commercial paper (for the large corporation). Specific security may be required in the short-term loan, and other restrictive covenants may be included in the loan agreement depending on the lender's assessment of the borrower's financial capabilities. The terms established in the loan agreement are also conditioned on the legal environment of the debtor-creditor relationship, particularly the set of federal statutes governing bankruptcy.

Intermediate-term financing forms include direct loans, sale of notes, and financial leases. Specific security and restrictive covenants are more likely in the case of intermediate-term loans, since the longer time span presumably increases the lender's risk exposure. The extreme form of secured loan is the financial lease where title to the asset does not pass from the fund supplier, the lessor. The leasing arrangement was analyzed with respect to the borrow and buy alternative to determine the relative "cost" of the lease. Some of the other indirect benefits of leasing such as the financial disclosure requirement were discussed in the chapter.

The short and intermediate-term funds sources are all debt forms. Equity sources of funds are long-term in nature, and are described in the next chapter along with long-term debt forms.

Chapter 9 Questions

1. If lease obligations should be disclosed in the financial statements in the form of an equivalent liability, how should the benefits of the use of the item leased be shown?
2. Why might an insurance company making an intermediate-term loan to a corporation insist on a note or bond security form rather than a simple loan agreement?
3. Does the bank's publication of a fixed prime rate avoid negotiations with each borrower on the interest rate?
4. Besides concealing the true interest rate on loans, are there any

other reasons for a bank to require a compensatory balance in a loan agreement?
5. What types of retail inventory would serve as collateral for a secured loan?
6. If secured loans are so expensive to administer for the lender, resulting in higher interest charges to the borrower, why do corporations borrow on a secured basis?
7. How important to the lender is specific security in the short-term and the intermediate-term loan?
8. Would it be worthwhile for a creditor to volunteer extension of the payments on a loan rather than force the borrower into a formal bankruptcy?
9. Does the existence of large amounts of accounts payable and accruals increase the perceived risk of other lenders to the corporation? Are they likely to increase their interest charges accordingly? Is there an implicit cost of trade credit and accruals as a result?
10. Direct placement of intermediate-term notes with a financial institution such as a life insurance company will save some issue costs. Will a part of this savings be offset by a higher interest charge by the institution to compensate for lack of marketability of the securities?
11. What advantages are there to direct placement of a note issue over public sale?
12. Why is the federal government in the money-lending business?
13. Another motive for leasing rather than borrowing and buying assets is that the long-term lease payment obligation does not have to be fully disclosed on the corporation's balance sheet. What is the current status of the required disclosure according to the Accounting Principles Board of the American Institute of Certified Public Accountants? Is the leasing arrangement really equivalent to concealed borrowing that may mislead the other creditors of the corporation?

Chapter 9 Problems

1. A construction equipment dealer is having some problems with the size of investment in inventories necessary relative to the amount of capital available. The product in question is a standard scraper that usually sells for $2,000 a unit. The dealer's choices are to: (1) arrange floor financing with his local bank where each scraper is specific collateral for a loan; (2) engage in a consignment sales arrangement with one supplier; and (3) reduce the size of inventory, hoping that customers will be willing to wait for back-ordered scrapers.

If the dealer could attain his ideal inventory it would average 20 scrapers, purchased from the lowest-priced supplier at $1,600 a unit. Given an adequate inventory level the dealer expects to sell 100 scrapers a year. His bank has offered a floor financing plan whereby it will loan 80 percent of the $1,600 purchase price at an annual interest rate of 10 percent. The dealer will have to arrange additional financing for the remaining 20 percent, paying 14 percent a year to this other lender.

To arrange a consigned inventory of scrapers the dealer will have to agree to handle only those scrapers of the IFU Corp. Unfortunately

IFU's price for the scraper is $1,700 a unit. If IFU's deal is accepted, though, the dealer will have no investment in the scraper inventory.

The third alternative is to reduce the average inventory level to 10 scrapers. If this is done the dealer estimates his annual sales will drop to 90 units. To raise the funds to carry this inventory the dealer will have to go to the local loan shark who charges an annual interest rate of 20 percent.

Assuming that all other revenues and costs remain the same, compare the three inventory financing plans and select the best one for the construction equipment dealer.

2. The period of compounding of interest in loan contracts is an often neglected variable in computing effective interest rates. For example, suppose a corporation has a choice between borrowing arrangements with its bank. In the first arrangement the loan is for a three-month period with the expectation that the loan will be renewed at the end of each three-month period, and will finally be repaid at the end of one year. In the second arrangement the loan is explicitly for a one-year period with principal and interest due at the end of the year. The same annual interest rate, 8 percent, is specified in each borrowing contract, but in the first contract interest is compounded four times and in the second one time. On a $100,000 loan what will be the difference in the total interest charges under the two arrangements?

3. A bank on a one-year loan charges a stated interest rate of 6 percent, but the interest is handled on a discount basis (is deducted from the loan proceeds) and the bank requires a compensatory balance of 10 percent of the stated loan amount. What is the true rate of interest on this loan?

4. Suppose that a corporation wanted to disclose the nature of the long-term lease obligation it has entered into with an equipment leasing company. The lease contract calls for an annual payment of $12,000 for eight years. The corporation uses a capitalization rate of 6 percent for long-term contracts. How large should the equivalent present liability be to account for the series of lease payments?

5. A corporation goes into bankruptcy proceedings with the following balance sheet values of assets and claims:

Assets		Liabilities and owners' equity	
Current assets	$ 400,000	Current liabilities	$ 200,000
Equipment, net	600,000	Long-term debt (secured by plant)	800,000
Plant (pledged to secure debt)	1,000,000	Long-term debt (unsecured)	500,000
Other assets	200,000	Subordinated debt	300,000
		Common stock	400,000
	$2,200,000		$2,200,000

a. The court decides to liquidate the corporation, so the assets are sold and the proceeds used to pay claims against the corporation. There are no special priority claims, and the proceeds of the asset sales are:

Current assets	$ 350,000
Equipment	200,000
Plant	500,000
Other assets	150,000
Total	$1,200,000

How much should the owners of each of the types of claims receive in the final cash distribution?

b. Instead of liquidation the court decides on a reorganization and recapitalization. The new capital structure will be:

Long-term debt (secured by a pledge of the plant)	$ 400,000
Long-term debt (unsecured)	500,000
Subordinated debt	200,000
Common stock	800,000
	$1,900,000

How much of each new security form should the old claim-holders receive in this reorganization plan?

6. An automobile dealer offers two alternatives to customers: a four-year lease of a car at an annual rental payment of $2,000 with return of the car to the dealer at the end of the four-year period; or the sale of the car at a purchase price of $5,000. In either case the customer is responsible for repairs, license, and taxes. The estimated salvage value of the car at the end of four years is $800.

a. Compute the dealer's imputed interest rate charge on the financial lease arrangement.

b. Suppose the customer is a business firm that has a 10 percent cost of capital, uses a straight-line depreciation method, and subject to a 40 percent corporate income tax rate. Find the net present value of the leasing arrangement as an alternative to purchase of the car.

Chapter 9 Reference

Adler, M., "Administration of Inventory Loans Under the Uniform Commercial Code," *Journal of Commercial Bank Lending* April 1970. Agemian, Charles A. "Maintaining an Effective Bank Relation-

Agemian, Charles A. "Maintaining an Effective Bank Relationship," *Financial Executive*, January 1964.

Brosky, John J. *The Implicit Cost of Trade Credit and Theory of Optimal Terms of Sale*. Credit Research Foundation, 1969.

Colquitt, Sidney B., Jr. "Compensating Balances–Original Intent and Future." *Journal of Commercial Bank Lending*, September 1968.

Ferrara, W. L. "Capital Budgeting and Financing or Leasing Decisions." *Management Accounting*, July 1968.

Hayes, Douglas A. *Banking Lending Policies: Issues and Practices*. Ann Arbor, Mich: University of Michigan Press, 1964.

Krause, Sidney. "Chapters X and XI–A Study in Contrasts." *The Business Lawyer*, January 1964.

Mitchell, G. B. "After-Tax Cost of Leasing," *Accounting Review*, April 1970.

Rogers, Robert W. "Warehouse Receipts and Their Use in Financing." *Bulletin of the Robert Morris Associates*, April 1964.

Sayer, S. F. "Many Faces of Collateral." *Credit and Financial Management*, February 1970.

Schadrack, F. C., Jr. "Demand and Supply in the Commercial Paper Market." *Journal of Finance*, September 1970.

Weintraub, Benjamin, and Harris, Levin. *Practical Guide to Bankruptcy and Debtor Relief*. Englewood Cliffs, N. J.: Prentice-Hall, 1964.

10
EXTERNAL SOURCES OF LONG-TERM FUNDS

When seeking outside funds for expansion, the corporation has a wide variety of security types that can be issued. Debt securities include all the varieties of bonds that can be designed by a clever financial manager, and the equity securities include common stock and preferred stock, as well as those security types that may ultimately lead to new common stock issues, warrants and convertible bonds or convertible preferred.

Within this chapter the descriptions of the various security types will first be presented, and then a measure of the costs due to the terms of the security issue will be derived. This cost, the specific cost of capital, is an interest rate that equates the present value of the series of cash payments required to the present proceeds of the security issue. Because the cash payments used in the calculation are specific to the single security issue being considered and do not include other effects such as a change in the market price of common stock when a new bond issue is sold, the specific cost of capital will serve only as a rough initial approximation to the "overall" cost of capital of the issue that will be used in a later chapter on the optimum capital structure of the firm.

Besides the description of security types and the formulas for the specific costs of capital the steps in issuing securities will be presented. The requirements of the Securities and Exchange Commission (SEC), the services of the investment banker, and the functions of the organized securities markets will be amplified to establish the institutional background of new security issues.

Bonds

A bond is the representation of a long-term promise to pay interest to the holder of the security at regular intervals, usually semiannually, and to repay the principal amount of the bond at some fixed date. The principal amount, the par value, of a bond is normally $1,000, but a corporation can issue other denominations as desired. Normally bonds are marketable securities, although corporations sometimes issue nonmarketable bonds in direct placement transactions.

The rights of the bondholder are described in a legal document called the indenture. Those rights are specified explicitly and at great length in the indenture, and include such things as the amount and time of payment of interest and principal, the claim on assets and income of the corporations, the trustee appointed under the indenture, and the circumstances that will result in the issuing corporation being in default.

The trustee appointed acts as the legal agent of the bondholders to insure that the terms of the indenture are carried out. If the issuing corporation defaults on its obligations, the trustee is supposed to prosecute the legal steps taken to secure the bondholders' rights. Typically the trustee appointed will be a large bank.

Bonds may be classified as to the claim on assets specified in the indenture. A secured bond, for example, is a bond where specific assets of the corporation are pledged against the bond's repayment. If the assets pledged are real estate or other fixed property, the usual terminology is a mortgage bond. A debenture on the other hand is a bond issue where no specific security is pledged. A subordinated debenture is one where the bondholder's claim is subordinated to some other classes of creditor—usually to all other creditors of the firm, although several levels of subordination may be employed.

In all cases of bond issues except the income bond, the periodic interest payment is a definite obligation that must be met or the corporation will be considered in default, and the principal amount will become immediately due and payable. The income bond is a relatively rare form of bond issue today, where payment of interest is required only if the net income of the corporation is sufficient to cover that interest. Income bonds were used extensively in the 1930s in the reorganization of bankrupt railroads, but a corporation would not normally be able to issue and sell such limited obligations at a reasonable yield today.

The bonds included in an issue may be all due and payable at a fixed time in the future, such as 20 years from the date of issue, or the repayment may be on a semi-installment basis through a sinking fund or serial bond arrangement. If a sinking fund is required in the indenture the corporation must make payments into the fund on a specified regular basis. An independent trustee is normally appointed to administer the sinking fund. The usual use for the payments into the sinking fund is to repurchase some of the bond issue, either on an open market or through recall of individual bonds selected through a random process. Alternatively the sinking fund proceeds may be used to accumulate funds in an investment program (invested in U.S. government securities, for example), to be liquidated at the end of the bond issue's term to provide a major part of the funds to repay the bond issue. Sinking funds are less common now than earlier, because the usual assumption now is that a bond issue will be repaid with the proceeds of a new bond issue—making the capital provided from long-term bond issues a permanent part of the capital structure of the corporation.

A serial bond issue is one in which the due dates of bonds are varied according to the identification number of the bond. Numbers 00001 through 00500 may be due five years from the issue date, numbers 00501 through 01000 six years from the issue date, and so forth. The individual bondholder will know in advance when his bond comes due under this system, so the net effect of a serial bond issue is that the corporation has issued a set of securities with varied maturities. From the issuer's viewpoint the bond issue may be considered to be a long-term installment debt with periodic payments of both interest and principal.

The indenture of a bond issue usually specifies a set of call provisions, the terms whereby the issuer can recall the bond issue before the normal expiration of the term. If a bond issue is called, normally the bondholder will receive a call premium, some amount in excess of the par value of the bond and accumulated interest. The amount of the call premium typically declines as the time of call comes closer to the end of the original term of the issue. For example, the issue may be callable at 106 in the fifth through the seventh year, at 105 in the eighth through the tenth year, and so forth. The 6 percent call premium is supposed to compensate the bondholder for the inconvenience of having to reinvest his funds early when he surrenders his bond.

In times of high interest rates the call provision included in the indenture become of particular importance to bond buyers. If the issue is callable, it is quite likely that the issuer will exercise that privilege when interest rates fall, calling the old bond issue and selling a new issue to refinance. Frequently the call provisions are written and described in terms of a period of "call protection," where the call is specifically prohibited prior to some minimum period from the issue date. The description "five years of call protection" means that the bond issue cannot be called before it has been outstanding five years. Of course the issuing corporation could theoretically repurchase all or part of the bond issue in the open market anyway during this period, but the corporation would have to pay the going market price for the bonds.

Call provisions are viewed as one-sided protection for the issuing corporation that may result in the disadvantage of the bondholder. If an issue is callable, the issuer is likely to call it if interest rates drop sufficiently below the coupon rate, and the bondholder will be forced to reinvest his funds at the lower interest rates. If on the other hand interest rates rise above the coupon rate, the issuer will be happy to keep the issue outstanding to its original maturity date. In this case the bondholder cannot take advantage of the higher interest rates–if he sells his bond it will be at a lower price than par, or if he holds the bond the rate earned is lower than current market rates of interest.

Because of the nature of fluctuating market rates of interest, the call provisions, the period of call protection and the size of the call premium, have become as significant as the coupon rate of interest in the design of bond issues. If little call protection is included in the indenture, the issuer may have to pay a measurably higher coupon rate.

Bonds are usually sold in \$1,000 denominations, and the coupon rate (or nominal rate) is expressed as a percentage of par. An 8 percent bond, for example, will pay \$40 interest twice a year in the usual case. If the yield to maturity is to be exactly 8 percent the buyer will pay \$1,000. If the yield is greater than 8 percent the price paid must be less than \$1,000, or if the yield is less than 8 percent the price is greater than \$1,000. Calculation of the price may be made by present value computations if the assumption is made that the bond will not be called early. If the bond is a 20-year issue, the price, the present value, is found by evaluating the present value function for a given value of r, the yield to maturity:

$$\text{Price} = \sum_{i=1}^{i=40} \frac{\$40}{(1+\frac{r}{2})^i} + \frac{\$1{,}000}{(1+\frac{r}{2})^{40}}$$

Usually it is not necessary to evaluate a present value since bond tables (such as *Investors Bond Values Table,* Boston: Financial Publishing

Company, 1962) are available to facilitate calculations. If the yield of the 8 percent bond is 7.9 percent, for example, the price of the example bond must be $1010.

In the case of a callable bond the yield may be calculated to the date the issue first becomes callable, to an arbitrary date somewhat later, or to the maturity date of the issue. If in the example the bond issue is callable at 106 after five years, the present value (price) would be calculated under the call date rule as

$$\text{Price} = \sum_{i=1}^{i=10} \frac{\$40}{(1+\frac{r}{2})^i} + \frac{\$1{,}060}{(1+\frac{r}{2})^{40}}$$

since there are ten six-month periods in five years. An extensive example of when a corporation should exercise its call provision is presented in the appendix to the chapter.

The issuer's specific cost of capital will differ from the bondholder's yield because of the tax deductibility of the interest charges and issue or call premium costs. To calculate that cost of capital each of the cash flows above would be adjusted to an after-tax basis, and the interest rate derived that would equate the present value of the cash outflows to the present cash inflow.

Preferred Stock

Preferred stock is legally considered to be a form of ownership of the corporation where certain preferences are given to the holder in return for some limitations on the usual ownership rights. The payment of dividends on preferred stock is considered a distribution of earnings, so the dividend amount is not tax deductible as bond interest is. Accordingly corporations have a powerful incentive to issue bonds rather than preferred stock when limited-income securities are to be sold.

Dividends on preferred stock do not have to be paid by the corporation when earnings are insufficient to cover those dividends. Those dividends must be paid, however, before any dividends can be paid on common stock. Normally the indenture covering the preferred issue specifies that the dividend obligation is cumulative—if the preferred dividend is passed one period that amount is added to the total to be paid the following period. If the preferred issue were noncumulative, the passed dividend would never be paid.

The amount of dividends paid on preferred stock is normally limited to a specified rate per share, expressed either as a set dollar amount or as a percentage of the par or stated value of the share. Occasionally a corporation may issue a participating preferred stock, where the preferred holder may share in any extra distribution of dividends on common stock above a certain level. Participating features are relatively rare.

Preferred stockholders usually have preference to common stockholders in liquidation distributions. The amount of the preference is stated in the indenture, and is usually the par value of the stock plus any dividends in arrears. This preference in liquidation pertains under bankruptcy proceedings as described in the previous chapter, so a preferred stock is ranked ahead of common stock for distribution of cash in liquidation or for issue of new securities in reorganization.

Preferred stock does not normally have voting rights, although the indenture may specify occasions where preferred stockholders could exercise such rights temporarily. Those occasions might include times when the preferred dividend is in arrears, when new bond issues (having a prior claim to preferred) are being considered, or when dissolution or merger of the corporation is being considered. At certain times during bankruptcy proceedings preferred stockholders legally acquire voting rights irrespective of the indenture terms.

Preferred stock may be a permanent part of the capital structure of the corporation, or there may be provisions for retirement of the issue included in the indenture. Retirement may be systematic through a sinking fund or serial retirement arrangement, or it may be optional through a call provision in the indenture. If the stock is callable the call price will include some premium over the par or stated value and accumulated dividends to compensate the holder for his inconvenience.

The specific cost of capital of preferred stock is approximately equal to the stockholder's yield since the dividend is not tax deductible to the issuing firm. It would be equal if the cost of issuing, the selling and other expenses, were zero. In the case of cumulative, nonparticipating preferred stock where no provision for retirement is included in the indenture, the dividend is a perpetuity, so the specific cost of capital can be computed by dividing the annual dividend by the proceeds of the stock sale. If the issuing corporation netted \$100 per share on a \$7 dividend preferred stock, the specific cost of capital would be

$$\frac{\$7}{\$100} = 7\%$$

If the preferred stock included a participation clause, determination of the specific cost of capital would follow the procedures described below for common stocks. Calculation of the cost of capital if the preferred is convertible into common stock will be treated in a separate section on convertible securities.

Common Stock

Common stock is the security that represents the holder's proportionate share of the residual ownership of the corporation. Common stock may have a par value or stated value per share, but that value is essentially only a bookkeeping number and normally has no other valuation significance. The number of shares issued and outstanding determines what interest one common share represents. If 100,000 shares are outstanding, each share represents 1/100,000 of the residual ownership of the corporation.

As residual owners common stockholders do not usually engage in the active management of the corporation, but participate indirectly through the election of representatives. Common stockholders elect the board of directors of the corporation, the highest executive group, and vote directly on certain major decisions such as mergers, major security issues, executive stock option plans, and like matters. The specific matters that must be brought before the stockholders are usually delineated in the corporation laws of the state in which the corporation is chartered, in regulations of the Securities and Exchange Commission, and in the corporate charter.

Common stockholders may receive the residual income of the corporation if the board of directors declare dividends. The board of directors may elect to retain part or all of earnings, but if this decision is contrary to stockholders' wishes at least theoretically a new board of directors can be elected at the next annual stockholders meeting.

The common stockholder is not normally liable for the debts of the corporation because under the usual legal interpretation the corporation exists as a legal person, able to enter into contracts as a separate entity. This limited liability feature means that the maximum amount a common stockholder can lose is the amount paid for his stock.

In some states common stockholders have preemptive rights, the right of first refusal on any additional common stock issues. Preemptive rights are supposed to protect the individual stockholder's proportionate share in the corporation, to avoid potential dilution of earnings and possibly voting control. In those states where preemptive rights are not required, those rights may be specified in the corporate charter.

Distribution of earnings to the common stockholders usually is in the form of cash dividends paid quarterly or at other regular intervals to the stockholder registered as the owner on the date of record for the dividend. The ownership lists are sometimes maintained by an outside institution, the transfer agent or registrar. A cash dividend, for example, may be declared on May 1, to be paid June 1 to stockholders of record at the close of business on May 14.

Occasionally the corporation may declare dividends in some other form than cash, such as the distribution of shares of stock in a subsidiary company. These distributions are known as spin-offs, and are usually tax-free to the recipient.

Rather than pay cash dividends some corporations have adopted the policy of paying stock dividends, whereby additional shares are issued to stockholders on a proportional basis to the number of shares owned on the date of record. In a 5 percent stock dividend a stockholder who already held 100 shares of stock would receive 5 additional shares. The stockholder receives no cash in the transaction, unless provision is made for payment of cash in lieu of fractional shares, and owns the same proportion of the corporation after the stock dividend. No tax is paid by the shareholder at the time of the receipt of the additional shares.

To realize any cash income the stockholder must sell part of his holdings of common stock. For tax purposes his cost of the original shares is reallocated among the larger number of shares, so for example, if the stockholder above had paid a net price of $21 a share for his 100 shares, his reallocated cost basis for 105 shares would be $20 a share. If he sold the 5 shares received in the dividend for $30 a share, his cash income would be \$150 but his capital gain for tax purposes would only be \$50.

Payment of a stock dividend rather than no dividend may be designed to facilitate the partial sale of holdings by the stockholder to generate cash income while maintaining "round-lot" (multiples of 100 shares) holdings. The holder of 100 shares above would still have 100 shares after he sold the 5 shares received in the stock dividend. This motivation for stock dividends is weak, but still stronger than assuming that stockholders are naive enough to believe they are receiving anything more than additional pieces of paper in a stock dividend.

Corporations hold annual (or for small corporations perhaps more frequent) stockholder meetings where election of the board of directors is regularly scheduled, and when other matters that require a vote of stockholders are considered. Because most stockholders cannot be physically present, proxies to vote their shares of stock are solicited by management, or by dissident groups. The solicitation and recording of proxies is regulated by the Securities and Exchange Commission.

Two types of voting arrangements are in general use for elections of the board of directors, simple majority and cumulative voting. Under the simple majority rule, each position on the board is elected separately in sequence, and one share has one vote in each election. Therefore the group holding a majority of shares can elect its candidates to all the positions on the board.

Cumulative voting arrangements have been designed to allow minority representation on the board of directors. Under this scheme each share of stock has as many votes as the number of directors to be elected. If there are 9 members of the board to be elected, each share of stock has 9 votes which can be cast for a single candidate or split among several candidates. Accordingly a minority group can be assured of electing a number of candidates if they hold the number of shares that is the solution of this equation:

$$\text{number of shares} = \frac{\text{total shares outstanding} \times \text{number of directors sought}}{\text{total number of directors} + 1} + 1$$

If nine directors are to be elected, 1,000,000 shares of common are outstanding, and the minority group wants to elect three directors, the minority group must control

$$\frac{1{,}000{,}000(3) + 1}{9 + 1} = 300{,}001 \text{ shares}$$

Some states require cumulative voting, and corporate charters may specify it in other states. To avoid minority representation, in some cases the terms of board members have been staggered so they do not all come up for election in one year, and sometimes the numbers of members of the board is changed to accomplish the goal.

Occasionally the common stock of a corporation will be classified, with the usual distinction on the basis of voting. For example Class A common will have no voting power, but Class B does. The motive of this form of classification is to maintain control of the corporation without having a majority of the common equity. It would be possible to have classifications based upon dividend rate, preference to assets in liquidation, or other factors as well.

The Cost of Capital of Common Stock

Because common stock is perpetual and dividends may therefore be paid for an infinite period of time, the calculation of a specific cost of capital for common stock is possible under very restrictive assumptions. When the common is considered as a contract requiring the corporation to pay dividends forever, two time patterns of dividend size, a constant dividend level and a dividend that grows at a constant rate, will allow numerical solution of the cost of capital. If it is assumed that the corporation has an option as to the time that common stock is issued, a limited term of cash payments is inferred and a solution can again be obtained.

If the dividend is assumed to be constant for all future time, the formula for a perpetuity can be used to solve for the specific cost of capital. Symbolically, if D is the per-period dividend amount, P is the net proceeds of the stock sale, and k is the specific cost of capital, then

$$P=\sum_{t=1}^{t=\infty}\frac{D}{(1+k)^t}=\frac{D}{k}$$

Therefore

$$k=\frac{D}{P}$$

If a common stock is sold at a net proceeds of \$30 a share and the corporation expects to pay an annual dividend of \$2 a share, the cost of capital is

$$\frac{\$2}{\$30}=7.5\%$$

In the second time pattern the amount of dividend paid grows at a constant rate every period. If D_O is used for the base dividend quantity, the amount paid at time zero, and g is the rate of growth of the dividend amount, then the dividend at time t can be expressed as

$$D_t=D_o(1+g)^t$$

If the base dividend is \$1 and the growth rate is 5 percent, the dividend at time 2 would be

$$D_2=\$1\ (1+0.05)^2=\$1.0625$$

The present value of the infinite series of dividend payments for the constant growth rate case is s of dividend payments for the constant growth rate case is

$$P_0 = \sum_{t=1}^{t=\infty} \frac{D_0(1+g)^t}{(1+k)^t}$$

(The first dividend paid is D_1, at the end of the first period. The base dividend amount, D_0, is not paid to the stock purchaser who paid the net amount of P_0.) The expression on the right is a converging geometric series in $[1 + g/1 + k]$ if k is greater than g, and therefore a simple expression can be derived for the present value:

$$P_0 = \frac{D_0(1+g)}{k-g}$$

The specific cost of capital can be solved for:

$$k = \frac{D_0(1+g)}{P_0} + g$$

The cost of capital is the sum of the "current" dividend yield,

$$\frac{D_0(1+g)}{P_0}$$

and the growth rate g. In the numerical example if the proceeds of the stock sale were \$21 a share the cost of capital would be

$$k = \frac{\$1(1+0.05)}{\$21} + 0.05 = 10\%$$

Extension of the infinite holding period analysis to other time patterns of dividend payment usually presents insuperable mathematical difficulties. The number of types of infinite series that have solutions is limited. Accordingly, for most analyses of common stocks where an infinite time period must be used, a constant growth rate is assumed.

An opportunity cost type of analysis may be used that will avoid the use of an infinite series of dividend payments—that will terminate the series at some reasonable point. In this model it is assumed that the corporation has the option of issuing the common shares now or of delaying the issue to some fixed time in the future. If the stock is issued now the corporation foregoes the cash that could have been received if the stock were issued at the future time. The opportunity cost of present issue is the estimated future cash proceeds.

If the future point to be used as a reference is time n, the proceeds of a stock sale at that time, P_n, is included as a cash outlay in the present value equation:

$$P_0 = \sum_{t=1}^{t=n} \frac{D_t}{(1+k)^t} + \frac{P_n}{(1+k)^n}$$

The set of cash outlays then includes the dividends to be paid through time n and the net price of the stock at time n.

Suppose the common stock if sold now would net \$30 a share, a dividend of \$1.50 is to be paid at the end of the first year, and the estimated proceeds per share if the stock sale is delayed to the end of the first year (after the dividend is paid) are \$31. The present value equation evaluated would be

$$\$30 = \frac{\$1.50}{(1+k)} + \frac{\$31}{(1+k)} = \frac{\$32.50}{(1+k)}$$

The specific cost of capital is

$$k = 8\,{}^{1}/_{3}\%$$

In each of the three methods presented, the specific cost of capital to the firm would be equal to the before-tax yield (internal rate of return) of the investor if the net proceeds of the security issue were equal to the price paid by the investor. Dividends paid are not tax-deductible to the corporation.

The future issue price as an imputed cash outlay will be used again below in both the cost of capital of warrants and the cost of capital of convertible securities. The estimation problems involved in determining a future price are severe, but no greater than estimating the future course of dividend payments for an infinite time period.

Warrants

Next to be considered as a long-term source of funds to the corporation is the issue of warrants to buy common stock. The warrant gives the holder the right to buy common stock from the corporation at a fixed price (the exercise price) at any time during a specified period of time. Usually one warrant gives the holder an option on one share of common stock.

The warrant may be perpetual, with no expiration date, but the usual practice is to limit the option to some reasonable period of time such as five years. If the warrant is to be outstanding for longer periods of time, sometimes the exercise price will be scheduled to change at certain times. For example the exercise price might be \$30 a share for the first five years, \$35 for the second five years, and so forth.

One of the most publicized warrants of a large corporation in recent years was the 5-year warrant issue of American Telephone and Telegraph in May, 1970, sold in combination with a large debenture issue. The exercise price of the warrant is \$52, and the warrants were sold at the time when the price of the common stock was about \$50 a share. The net proceeds of the warrant issue were approximately \$11 per warrant.

One analysis and justification of the \$11 price of that warrant was based on a projected value for the ATT common stock of \$75 a share by May, 1975. A holder who exercised at the expiration date could purchase the share of common at \$52 and then sell at \$75, realizing \$23 difference. The price of \$11 in May, 1970, would result in a cash inflow before taxes of \$23 five years later. To solve for the warrant holder's yield, the present value equation

$$\$11 = \frac{\$23}{(1+r)^5}$$

must be solved for r. The solution to the nearest whole percent is

$$r = 16\%$$

If the investor exercised the warrant in May, 1975, and sold the share of common stock simultaneously for \$75, his realized before-tax yield would be 16 percent per year.

Of course that solution is for a single estimated future value of the option, and in a more complete analysis other possible values for the common stock in May, 1975 should be taken into account, perhaps to the extent of deriving a statistical distribution of yields.

Another assumption built into the derivation of the 16 percent yield is that the warrant will not be exercised prior to its expiration date. This assumption is the result of considering the probable market price of the warrant as its theoretical value changes with the variations in market price of common. The theoretical value of the warrant is the difference between the exercise price of the warrant and the market price of the common stock. The theoretical value as a function of that market price is graphed in Figure 10.1. Here the exercise price is \$20 a share, so the theoretical value of the warrant is zero when the common is \$20 or less, and increases \$1 for each \$1 increase in the market price of common above \$20.

Figure 10.1
The Theoretical Value of a Warrant

The warrant holder can be assured that the market price of the warrant will never fall below the theoretical value during the term of the warrant. If it did so, professional arbitragers could in that case buy warrants, exercise them, and sell the common for a profit. Their actions would tend to raise the price of warrants and lower the price of the common stock, reestablishing the relationship between the market price of the warrants and their theoretical value.

Because of the built-in leverage possibilities the warrant may have a market value in excess of its theoretical value. If an investor paid only the theoretical value of the warrant, the investment characteristics of the warrant might be extraordinarily desirable when compared to that of the common stock. Disregarding the time factor for the moment, suppose that an investor is considering the purchase of a warrant exercisable at \$20 a share when the current market price of the common is \$25. If the investor pays only the theoretical value of \$5 for the warrant, he can buy five warrants or one share of common for the same outlay, \$25. Suppose the possible future values of the common at the time the warrant would be exercised are as listed below:

Common price per share	Profit if one share of common is purchased	Profit if five warrants are purchased	
0	−25	−25	Warrants not exercised
10	−15	−25	
20	−5	−25	
30	5	25	
40	15	75	
50	25	125	

The profits differ in the two investment choices, but in only two cases would the warrant purchase give worse outcomes than the stock purchase. For the higher prices the gain from the warrant purchase is much greater than the stock purchase. Although an exact choice between the two alternatives could not be determined without probabilities of the future stock prices and the investor's utility function, it is probable that most investors would choose the warrants. If so, the price of the warrants would tend to rise above the theoretical value.

The example could be changed to demonstrate the preference even more strongly if the market price of the common stock at the time of the investment decision were changed to \$20 or some smaller figure. In that case the theoretical value of the warrant is zero, so the purchaser would risk nothing if the warrants were purchased at that value. He has no possibility of loss, but possibility of gain if the market price of the common goes above \$20 a share. That is the type of investment everyone dreams of.

The conclusion is that the market value of a warrant tends to behave in relationship to the theoretical value as shown in Figure 10.2. At low common prices the market value is greater than the theoretical value, and this difference diminishes at higher prices. The market value is never below the theoretical value for any common stock price.

Figure 10.2
Market Value and Theoretical Value of a Warrant

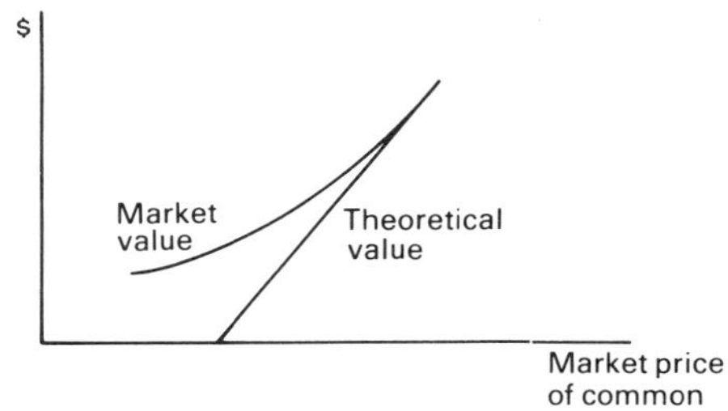

The warrant should probably not be exercised prior to the expiration of the exercise period. Even if a warrant holder desires dividend income or wants the voting power of common, he should sell the warrant and use the proceeds of the sale to buy common stock rather than exercise the warrant. This conclusion is based upon the presumption that the market price of the warrant is above its theoretical value.

Suppose for example that the warrant is exercisable at \$20 when the market price of the common stock is \$30. The theoretical value of the warrant would therefore be \$10. Suppose that the actual market value of the warrant is \$12, giving a small premium of \$2 for the leverage possibilities of the warrant. Now if the warrant holder wanted to acquire one share of common stock he could (1) exercise the warrant, giving \$20 to the corporation for that newly issued share, or (2) sell the warrant for \$12, add \$18 more and buy the share on the open market. The second method saves \$2. Of course transaction costs and possible capital gains taxes on the warrant sale are ignored in the example.

It seems likely then that warrants can be expected to be exercised only near the end of their term, or near to the time when changes in the exercise price are scheduled. Corporations that issue perpetual warrants may therefore expect that exercise will occur *far* into the future!

Warrants are usually issued as "sweeteners" in packages of securities, as for example in combination with a debenture issue to insure the sale of the issue. Therefore identification of the proceeds of the warrant may be difficult. The calculation of the specific cost of capital of a warrant utilizes the proceeds of the warrant, P_0, the exercise price specified, P, and the estimated price of common stock at the time of exercise, P_n:

$$P_0 = \frac{P_n - P}{(1+k)^n}$$

The issuer receives P_0 now, and foregoes the difference in market price and the exercise price at time n because those shares of stock are committed to the warrant holder and cannot be sold otherwise. The circumstances are similar to the third case in common stock analysis discussed above.

Warrants may be a specially desirable means of financing for the small growing corporation that has difficulty in raising funds and in meeting periodic interest payments. The warrant contract does not require any periodic cash outlays until after exercise, and then only optional payments, dividends on common stock. Of course the issue of warrants means eventual dilution of control and income when the additional common shares are issued.

Convertible Securities

Corporations sometimes issue preferred stock or bonds that are convertible at the option of the holder into a certain number of shares of common stock. The conversion privilege changes the character of these securities considerably, making it worthwhile to treat them separately.

In addition to the regular features of preferred stock or bonds the indenture will specify the rate of exchange of common stock for the security. Usually the exchange proportion is expressed as a price of common stock in terms of the par value of the convertible security. If a $1,000 convertible debenture's conversion price is 50, that means the bond can be exchanged for 20 shares of common stock. To find the number of shares of common stock obtainable for a convertible security the par value of the convertible should be divided by the conversion price.

The indenture may specify a sliding scale of conversion prices over time, 50 for the first four years, 55 for the next four years, and so on. It is theoretically possible for the conversion privilege to expire at some point, but this is not customary.

The time of conversion into common stock can be partially controlled by the issuer through inclusion of a call provision in the indenture. Suppose, for example, that a $1,000 par value convertible bond has a conversion price of 50, and is callable at 106. If the bond is called, the holder has the option of surrendering his bond for $1,060, or converting and receiving 20 shares of common stock. If the market price of the common is greater than $53 a share, the bondholder should choose to convert. Of course if the market price of the common were below $53, the call by the issuer would not result in conversion but in retirement of the issue.

Another time that conversion is in a sense forced is when the term of a convertible bond issue expires. If the convertible bond issue from above is a 20-year issue, and if the market price of the common is over $50 a share at the end of the 20-year period, the holder should convert at that point rather than accept the $1,000 repayment of principal. Since preferred stocks are not normally limited in term, this semi-forced conversion should not occur with a convertible preferred stock.

Voluntary conversion by the holder is hard to predict, but may be analyzed in a manner similar to that used for warrants. The value of a convertible bond is compared to two other values; a theoretical "straight" bond value—the value of the security if the conversion privilege were not included, and the value of the corresponding number of shares of common stock.

Because investors are normally willing to pay some premium for the conversion privilege the issuing corporation can pay a lower coupon interest rate on a convertible bond than would be required on a nonconvertible bond of the same quality. If the going interest rate is 8 percent on a nonconvertible issue, for example, a convertible issue with a coupon rate of 6 percent might be sold at par, depending on the conversion terms. The price of a 6 percent coupon 20-year bond when market yields are 8 percent might then behave over time as shown in Figure 10.3.

Figure 10.3
Bond Value of the Convertible

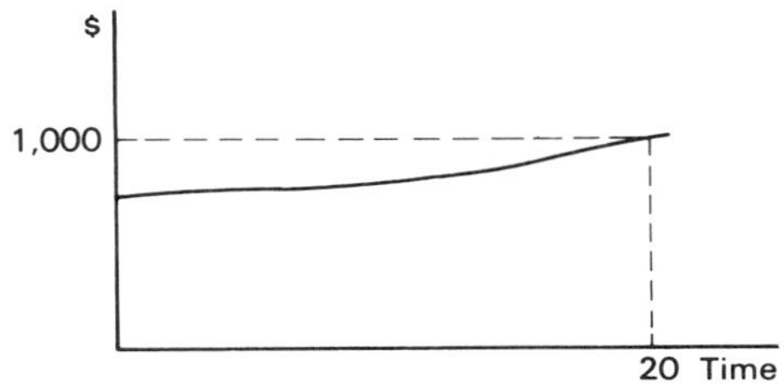

The equivalent common stock value of the convertible is a multiple of the projected price per share of common stock. If the conversion price is 50, the multiple is 20 shares. Assuming a growth in the price of common stock over time, the stock value of the convertible is shown in Figure 10.4.

Figure 10.4
Stock Value of the Convertible

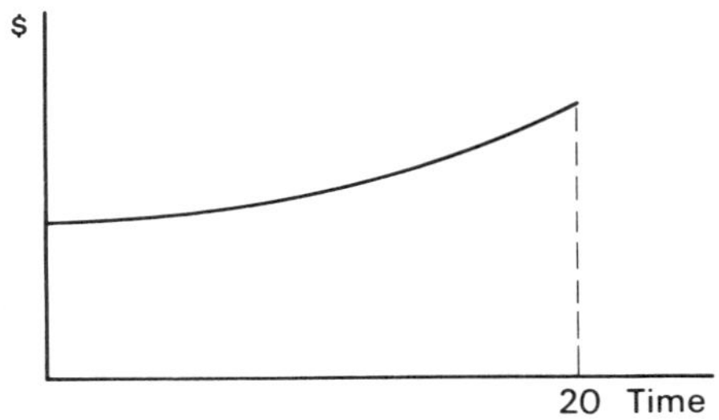

The market value of the convertible will always be at least as great as the common stock value: otherwise an arbitrager could profit by buying the convertible bond, converting, and then selling the common stock. The market value of the convertible will exceed the bond value because the convertible holder has all the advantages of a bond holder, guaranteed interest and repayment of principal, and in addition the possible gain from the conversion privilege. Accordingly the behavior of the market price of the convertible over time in relation to the two theoretical values should be as shown in Figure 10.5.

Figure 10.5
Bond Value, Stock Value,
and Market Value of the Convertible

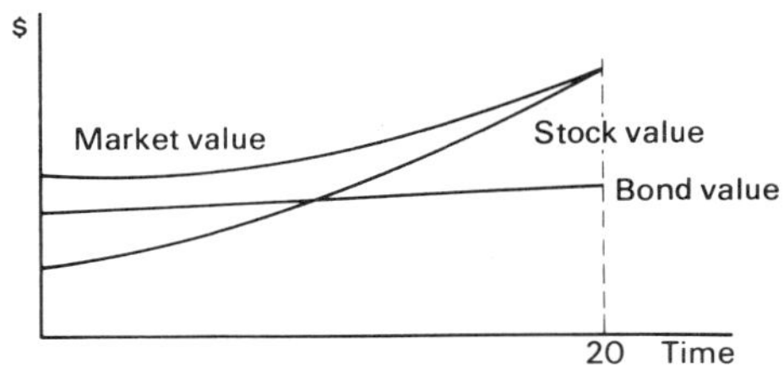

If the market value of the convertible bond is always greater than the equivalent common stock value, it would not pay the investor to convert. If he desired common stock, perhaps because of a higher dividend or voting rights, he should sell the convertible bond and use the proceeds to buy the common stock. Ignoring transaction costs and possible capital gains taxes, the investor would be better off by the amount of the spread between the market value of the convertible and the value of the equivalent number of common shares. The conclusion is that the conversion privilege should not be exercised prior to the end of the term of the bond.

Since convertible preferred in most cases is a perpetual security with no "end of term," voluntary conversion by the holder may never occur.

Unless the issuing corporation has a policy of forcing conversion by a call of the security, the conversion time depends upon an expiration of the conversion privilege. In any case the appropriate equation for calculation of the explicit cost of capital will include the estimated value of the common shares issued in conversion as the last cash outlay. The proceeds of the convertible issue, P_0, the net after-tax periodic interest or dividend payments, D_t, and the estimated value of the equivalent common shares at time of conversion, P_n, are combined into

$$P_0 = \sum_{t=1}^{t=n} \frac{D_t}{(1+k)^t} + \frac{P_n}{(1+k)^n}$$

The specific cost of capital is the value of k that satisfies this equation.

Corporations that issue convertible securities may be influenced to do so by the lower interest or dividend payments up to the time of conversion. During that period the cash-short corporation may effect significant savings due to the spread between nonconvertible coupon rates and convertible coupon rates. Of course the corporation may "pay later" when the dilution from conversion occurs.

The procedures for issuing the various securities that might be used by a corporation are quite likely to involve first of all meeting legal requirements. The agency of the federal government most interested in security issues is the Securities and Exchange Commission.

The Role of the Securities and Exchange Commission

The Securities and Exchange Commission (SEC) was formed in the 1930s as an attempt to control some of the abuses prevalent in the securities markets that contributed to the great crash of 1929. In a series of acts of Congress beginning with the Securities Act of 1933, the commission has been given a broad spectrum of regulatory powers over corporations, brokerage firms, and organized securities markets.

Companies issuing securities of term longer than 270 days that may be sold interstate are required to register those issues with the SEC. Exceptions to this rule are securities of railroad companies and privately placed issues. A certain amount of financial information (less for issues smaller than $300,000) must be filed with the SEC, and approval of the prospectus that summarizes information for the prospective buyer must be obtained from the SEC. The SEC does not try to prohibit the sale of risky securities, but simply insists that relevant information must be provided to the investor.

Organized securities exchanges must be registered with the SEC, and securities dealers and their officers must be licensed by the SEC. This places those institutions and individuals under the jurisdiction of the SEC's rulings, as well as providing for continuing regulation of corporations not registering new issues. Both those companies with securities listed on organized exchanges and those traded over-the-counter with more than 750 shareholders and over $1 million assets are subject to continuing regulation, including the periodic filing of financial information with the SEC that may be inspected by members of the public. Failure to comply with SEC regulations could result in severe difficulties for a corporation, brokerage firm, securities salesman, or exchange.

In addition to these general regulatory powers the SEC supervises proxy solicitations of stockholders, regulates investment advisers' activities, acts as an advisor in the proceedings under Chapter X of the Bankruptcy Act, controls the financial structure of certain public utility holding companies, and serves as an information gathering system for studies of securities and security markets.

Besides the SEC, a company's financial operations may come under the jurisdiction of state regulatory commissions, and certain types of firms are regulated by other agencies of the federal government, such as railroads by the Interstate Commerce Commission.

Securities Exchanges and the Listing of Securities

Two national exchanges, the New York Stock Exchange and the American Stock Exchange, and several regional exchanges exist for the organized trading of securities. If a company's securities are not listed for trading on an organized exchange, transactions can still be made on an over-the-counter (OTC) basis. Trading is active enough in some OTC issues that certain brokerage firms do a considerable portion of their business in these issues, and prices of the more important OTC stocks are reported on a regular basis by the financial press.

The organized exchanges have certain requirements that must be met before the securities of a corporation will be listed for trading. These requirements are designed to discriminate in favor of large, established businesses, and usually include a minimum total net income for some period of time, a certain number of shares outstanding with a minimum number of public holders, an established previous market value per share and in aggregate, and a minimum size of assets or sales. To continue the listing smaller minimums must be maintained, and certain financial information must be provided stockholders and the exchange. Many corporations that could meet the requirements have chosen not to have their securities listed, perhaps preferring the anonymity of unlisted securities.

The exchanges are most well known for the trading of common stock, but other securities are listed and traded as well. Bonds, preferred stocks, convertible securities, and in some cases warrants are also traded. (The New York Stock Exchange does not normally list warrants, so some corporations whose stock is listed on that exchange have warrants listed on the American Stock Exchange.)

Transactions in listed securities must normally be consummated through brokerage firms that "have a seat" on the exchange. An exception to this rule is found in the "third market" where large blocks of securities are sometimes directly traded between financial institutions. The commissions charged by the brokerage firms are set by the exchange, subject to the approval of the SEC.

The operations in listed securities approximate an auction market rather than a negotiated market. Because of the usual large volume of purchases and sales of an individual security, sellers and buyers simply place an order through the brokerage firm specifying a price and quantity desired, and this order is transmitted to the floor specialist in the exchange who then matches buy and sell orders to complete the transaction. The specialist may maintain a small inventory of the particular security to facilitate the transaction, but the effect is that of an auction market.

In OTC transactions, on the other hand, the number of transactions is much smaller and the effect is that of a negotiation with offer and counter-offer. Some brokerage firms will "make markets" in certain unlisted securities, holding an inventory and standing willing to buy shares at a certain price, the bid price, or to sell shares at another price, the asked price. To compensate the broker for the risk of maintaining the illiquid inventory sometimes the bid-asked spread becomes quite high. A difference of as much as 20 percent for small corporations with low prices and low transactions volume is not uncommon.

The spread between bid and asked price may make the transactions cost of trading in OTC stocks very large to the investor. Suppose an investor purchased a stock at the asked price of $5, and then for some reason sold the stock the same day at the bid price of $4.50. Besides the commissions that might be charged by his brokerage firm, the investor would be out the 50 cent spread for a total "in-and-out" cost in excess of 10 percent.

Saving investors' transactions costs may therefore be a reasonable motive for corporations to seek listing for their securities on an organized exchange. The liquidity benefits to the investor may result in a higher general market value for the securities.

The Role of the Investment Banker in Issuing Securities

When the corporation management decides that a security issue is desirable, the services of an investment banker should be sought. The investment banker is a specialist financial organization that will advise the corporation in designing the security's terms, possibly assist or undertake the sale of the securities, and may guarantee (underwrite) the sale of the securities at a fixed price. In spite of the similarity of names an investment banker is not a commercial bank—in the U.S. commercial banks are forbidden to act as investment bankers. The investment banker is normally the part of a brokerage firm that specializes in new security issues.

The advice of a specialist institution is desirable because the usual corporation does not issue new securities on a continuous basis, and therefore would not find it economic to maintain a staff of experts in the field. The advice may take other forms than just designing appropriate coupon rates of interest or dividends and conversion rates, but may include such things as how to meet the SEC and other agencies' registration and information requirements. The investment banker may even arrange private placements of the issue if that is feasible.

For those firms such as public utilities that issue new securities more often, the advising function may be less important, and the issuer may go to a competitive bidding to obtain a selling effort rather than negotiating directly with a single investment banker. Many public utility firms are required to use competitive bidding by the state public utility regulatory commissions, because it is thought that the bidding will result in a lower sales cost than negotiation. In competitive bidding the security issue is advertised to the investment bankers who then submit sealed bids for the selling fee, or if the issue is to be underwritten a purchase price for the entire security issue. The bids are then opened on the advertised date, and the best bid accepted.

Particularly when a large security issue is to be underwritten groups of investment bankers may form a temporary syndicate to spread the sales activity and the risk. The syndicate is formed only for the period involved in the issue, and is dissolved as soon as the bid is rejected or the securities are sold.

In a general public offering the selling efforts of the investment banker may be on a "best-efforts" basis, a pure agency arrangement, or the investment banker may guarantee the sale at a fixed price through accepting an underwriting function. The fee charged for underwriting can be expected to vary as the nature of the security, the size of the issue, and as the degree of stability or uncertainty in the markets changes.

Rights Offerings and Other Issue Methods

The issuer may decide that the best method for selling new securities is not a private placement or a public sale, but is to offer the new securities for subscription by existing stockholders through a "rights offering." The states that have preemptive rights laws on the books require that any new equity securities must be offered first to existing common stockholders before being placed on sale to the public. In other states the corporate charter may specify the preemptive right.

The procedure for a rights offering, voluntary or involuntary, is best illustrated by an example. Suppose a corporation has 1,000,000 shares of common stock outstanding and wishes to sell an additional 200,000 shares. If the present market price of the common is $30 a share, the offering price will be set somewhat lower, say $24, to insure the sale. The existing shareholders on a record date will be given the right to buy one new share at $24 for each five shares they already hold. The rights can be exercised at any time before the expiration date, which is usually set about one month from the announcement.

The rights to buy are normally detachable, meaning that the right can be sold separately from the common stock during the period of the offering. Therefore, the stockholder has the alternative of selling the rights if he does not wish to buy more common stock. The theoretical value of each right in the numerical example would be $1.20 when the market price of the common is $30, since it takes 5 rights plus $24 to get one share of common stock. Of course, since the market price of the common stock will probably fluctuate during the offering period the actual market price of the rights will fluctuate also, but more widely.

Since the rights become worthless after the expiration date, the corporation can assume that effectively all the rights will be exercised by that date unless the market price of the common falls below the exercise price. No great amount of selling costs or underwriting fees are incurred, and accordingly the rights offering is probably the best method to sell new common stock. The fact that the offering is at a discounted price from market is not significant since the buyers receiving the discount are the common stockholders, the residual owners of the corporation.

Occasionally corporations will offer bonds or preferred stock on a rights basis to common stockholders, but usually the rights offering of these securities is used only when other securities such as warrants or convertibles are issued in a combination offer.

One other method of issuing securities other than a sale is the direct issue of securities for the purchase of assets. A plant or other real estate may be purchased by issuing bonds or notes directly to the seller, but the more common case is that of the acquisition of another company. In these cases the terms and types of securities must be adjusted to satisfy the seller, and the services of the investment banker are less vital. If the securities are to be marketable, however, registration with the SEC and other agencies is obligatory.

Summary

Many variations can be found in long-term security forms that are available to the capital-seeking corporation. Within the bond category classification can be made on the basis of interest payment obligation, repayment schedule, call feature, lien against assets of the corporation, subordination of rights to other security-holders, and conversion privilege.

While preferred stock is legally considered as an ownership form rather than a debt form, from the aspect of the issuing corporation or the common stockholders it may be viewed as a form of perpetual debt, where the annual dividend amount is the payment for use of the funds by the corporation. The dividend amount is not tax-deductible, however, so preferred stock is usually thought to be a more expensive method of raising funds than a debt issue.

Besides preferred and common stock the other security forms, warrants and convertibles, are analyzed as equity sources of funds. Both warrants and convertibles usually result in a savings of cash payments by the corporation for some period of time, so these issues are more likely to be used by the small growth corporation.

Some of the legal requirements (SEC registration), security sale methods, and provisions for listing of securities were described in this chapter. The choice of an optimum financing mix is deferred to a later chapter, after the development of an understanding of the debt and equity markets, the corporation's financial market environment, in the next section of the book. This chapter's purpose was to establish the factual description of alternatives open to the corporation.

APPENDIX TO CHAPTER 10

The Bond Refinancing Decision

When bonds are sold by a corporation the indenture (contract spelling out the responsibilities of the corporation and the rights of the bondholders) calls for the payment of a fixed amount of interest every period with the repayment of the principal to occur at the end of term of the issue. Most indentures, however, allow the issuing corporation to pay off the bondholders earlier by the exercise of a "call provision." To compensate bondholders partially for the inconvenience of having to surrender their bonds before their original term expires, the issuer must pay an extra amount, the call premium, over the par value and accrued interest. Typically this premium is expressed as a percentage of the par value, so if a $1,000 bond with a 6 percent call premium is called, the issuer must pay the holder $1,060 plus any accrued interest.

The call provision is included in the indenture so that the issuer will not get "locked into" the payment of unnecessarily high interest rates if prevailing interest rates fall after the bonds are sold. The amount interest rates must fall to make it worthwhile for the corporation to call the old bond issue and refinance by selling a new issue will depend on the size of the call premium and the expenses of selling the new issue. The possible refinancing defines a set of cash flows that can be analyzed in a capital budgeting context.

To define the set of cash flows on an after-tax basis the provisions of the tax code must be kept in mind. When an old issue is called, any unamortized expenses from that issue and the amount of the call premium are treated as expenses for tax purposes at that time. The issue costs of the new issue must be amortized over the life of that issue.

To illustrate the computations of the cash flows due to refinancing suppose a corporation has an outstanding issue of 20-year bonds with a coupon interest rate of 8 percent payable annually, and the principal amount of the issue is $1,000,000. The bonds were sold at par on January 1, 1971, and the issue cost at that time was $40,000, amortizable on a straight-line basis ($2,000 per year) for tax purposes. The issue is callable at 106, the call premium is 6 percent of par.

Now suppose the corporation can call and refinance that bond issue with a new $1,000,000 issue with a coupon interest rate of 6.5 percent on January 1, 1973. If the new issue is an 18-year issue, it will cover the same period as the old issue, maturing December 31, 1990. The selling costs of the new issue are $36,000 (to be amortized for tax purposes at $2,000 a year).

First the net cash outlay after taxes on January 1, 1973 must be determined. The cash outlays before taxes are the total of the call premium, $60,000, and the $36,000 selling expenses of the new issue, or $96,000. For tax purposes the call premium of $60,000 and the $36,000 unamortized issue costs of the old issue are expenses, a sum of $96,000. If the corporation is subject to a 40 percent tax rate, the net after-tax outlays on January 1, 1973 can be calculated as

$96,000	(before-tax outlays)
−38,400	(tax savings from expenses, 40% of $96,000)
$57,600	(after-tax outlay)

The computations of the annual cash flows can be made in much the same way. The before-tax outlay on interest expenses would be reduced $15,000 per year, the difference between interest of $80,000 before the refinancing and $65,000 after refinancing. The annual expenses for tax purposes before the refinancing are the sum of $80,000 interest and $2,000 amortization of issue costs, $82,000. After the refinancing the expenses shown on the tax return will be the sum of $65,000 interest and $2,000 amortization of issue costs, 67,000. The difference in expenses for tax purposes is also $15,000, so the net reduction in after-tax annual outlays is

$15,000	(before-tax outlays)
− 6,000	(reduction in tax savings, 40% of $15,000)
$ 9,000	(after-tax reduction in outlays)

The $9,000 annual savings is realized for each of the 18 years of the bond issues' lives. At the end of the last year the repayment of the $1,000,000 is the same under the old bond issue or the new bond issue.

The refinancing opportunity can be summarized in terms of cash flows as an outlay of $57,600 at time zero (January 1, 1973) to achieve inflows of $9,000 at time 1 (December 31, 1973) through time 18 (December 31, 1990).

This stream of cash flows should be evaluated as an investment project under certainty since no doubt exists as to the size of the flows. Because the cash inflows are regular in size (identical for times 1 through 18) an internal rate of return could be used as a summary measure of the refinancing's benefits. The solution of the internal rate of return to a computer degree of accuracy is:

$$\$57,600 = \sum_{i=1}^{i=18} \frac{\$9,000}{(1+r)^i}$$

If the present value of the $9,000 annual cash savings is to be computed for comparison with the outlay (price) of $57,600, a question that obviously comes to mind is what interest rate to use in the computation. Among other rates that could be defined are:

1. The rate the corporation can earn on zero risk alternative investments;
2. The overall marginal cost of capital to the corporation;
3. The after-tax cost of capital of the new bond issue.

The third alternative is probably the best rate to use on theoretical grounds. The capital structure of the corporation is not being changed appreciably since the \$57,600 outlay is small. The bond refinancing does not affect the amount of funds available for purchase of other investments. The difficulty involved is deriving the after-tax cost of capital of the new bond issue if a fine degree of accuracy is desired.

If the old bond issue is ignored, the net proceeds of the new bond issue are \$964,000, the \$1,000,000 sales price minus the \$36,000 issue cost. Each year the net after-tax outlay for interest is \$38,200. The before-tax interest outlay is \$65,000, but the annual expense for tax purposes is \$65,000 plus \$2,000 amortization of issue costs. The net outlay per year is therefore

\$65,000	(before-tax outlay)
–26,800	(tax savings from expenses, 40% of \$67,000)
\$38,200	(net after-tax outlay)

This outlay is made for times 1 through 17, and at time 18 the net outlay is \$1,038,200 since the principal must be repaid at that time.

The after-tax cost of capital of the new bond issue is the solution of the present value function:

$$\$964{,}000 = \sum_{i=1}^{i=17} \frac{\$38{,}200}{(1+r)^i} + \frac{\$1{,}038{,}200}{(1+r)^{18}}$$

An approximate solution could have been obtained by adjusting the coupon interest rate on the issue to an after-tax basis:

$$6.5\%(1-0.4) = 3.9\%$$

without much loss in accuracy.

Because the present value tables at the end of the book do not go to such accuracy, this after-tax cost of capital will be rounded off in the computations to 4 percent. The present value of a \$9,000 annuity received every year for 18 years can be calculated by abstracting the present value factor of 12.65930 from Table 3 at the back of the book, and multiplying it by \$9,000:

$$12.65930(\$9{,}000) = \$113{,}883.70$$

Since \$113,883.70, the present value of the cash savings of times 1 through 18 is greater than the present outlay, \$57,600, the refinancing is desirable.

The same result would have been obtained by comparing the yield on the refinancing, 14.19 percent, to the hurdle rate of 3.94 percent (or 4 percent).

One assumption that was made that may alter the results of the analysis appreciably was the length of term of the new bond issue. Suppose the new bond issue had been a 20-year issue instead of an 18-year issue. The old issue would have matured December 31,1990, but the new issue now matures December 31, 1992. The issue costs must be amortized over a longer period, and account must be taken of the difference in cash flows on December 31,1990 (time 18), December 31, 1991 (time 19), and December 31, 1992 (time 20).

In this revised example the net after-tax outlay at time zero is the same, \$57,600. For times 1 through 17 the after-tax reductions in outlays become \$8,920. The before-tax savings in interest costs are still \$15,000, but the expenses shown for tax purposes go from \$82,000 (\$80,000 interest plus \$2,000 amortization of issue costs incurred January 1, 1971) to \$66,800 (\$65,000 interest plus \$1,800 = 1/20 \$36,000 amortization of issue costs incurred January 1, 1973), a difference of \$15,200. The calculation of the after-tax reduction in outlays for times 1 through 17 (December 31, 1989) is

\$15,000	(before-tax outlays)
− 6,080	(reduction in tax savings, 40% of \$15,200)
\$ 8,920	(after-tax reduction in outlays)

At time 18 the \$8,920 reduction in outlays is augmented by the \$1,000,000 reduction due to not having to pay off the original bond issue at that time. The total reduction, inflow, at time 18 is therefore \$1,008,920.

At time 19 the corporation must make an outlay for interest of \$65,000 before taxes that is due to the refinancing. The expenses for tax purposes at that time are \$66,800, the interest plus the amortization of issue costs, so the net *increase* in outlays at time 19 is

\$65,000	(before-tax increase in interest outlay)
− 26,720	(increase in tax savings, 40% of \$66,800)
\$38,280	(net after-tax increase in outlays)

At time 20 the bond issue must be repaid as well as the final interest payment made, so the net *increase* in after-tax outlays at that time is \$1,038,280.

Under the revised refinancing plan the set of cash flows derived is

time 0	time 1 through time 17	time 18	time 19	time 20
−\$57,600	\$8,920	\$1,008,920	−\$38,280	−\$1,038,280

The internal rate of return for the refinancing is solved from:

$$\$57{,}600 = \sum_{i=1}^{i=17} \frac{\$8{,}920}{(1+r)^i} + \frac{\$1{,}008{,}920}{(1+r)^{18}} - \frac{\$38{,}280}{(1+r)^{19}} - \frac{\$1{,}038{,}280}{(1+r)^{20}}$$

$r = 18.22\%$

The present value of the cash flows of time 1 through time 20 at a rate of 4 percent using the present value factors of Tables 2 and 3 at the end of the book is

$$\$8{,}920(12.16567) + \$1{,}008{,}920(0.49363) - \$38{,}280(0.47464) - \$1{,}038{,}280(0.45639) = \$114{,}431.13$$

Although not much difference is realized in the present value by the revision of the time period covered, a considerable difference in the internal rate of return results. Presumably this is due to the large variations in cash flows at times 18 through 20.

Some additional dimensions could be introduced to the refinancing decision that might more nearly approximate reality, but would complicate the analysis significantly. For example, if a bond issue is refinanced now, that issue cannot be refinanced next year if interest rates drop still further. If a series of future interest rates is forecast, a set of mutually exclusive investment projects corresponding to the times of refinancing could be defined. Then the problem is the selection of the best one of the set of projects, the optimum time to refinance. Such an analysis will not be done here, however.

Chapter 10 Questions

1. Does a sinking fund provision in the bond indenture reduce the risk to the bond buyer?
2. If the call provision in the indenture only works to the disadvantage of the bond buyer, why don't the buyers insist on complete call protection for the life of the issue?
3. If interest on bonds were not tax-deductible for the corporation would this result in a general switch from bonds to other securities for corporations' capital raising?
4. If a corporation sells warrants with no expiration date, are the proceeds of the issue really cost free?
5. Why would a warrant holder exercise his warrants prior to their expiration date?
6. Does the high degree of leverage (response to changes in the common stock price) of warrants automatically make them desirable for the speculator?
7. How would convertible bonds be classified as to the degree of risk to the owner relative to the other securities of the same corporation?
8. Under what circumstances will the low coupon rate of the convertible bond outweigh the eventual dilution in common stock for the issuing corporation?
9. If convertible bonds are "nearly" common stock, why should there be any limit to the amount a corporation can sell of them?
10. What are the advantages of preferred stock as a financing instrument?
11. Would it be better for a corporation to sell ordinary preferred stock or convertible preferred stock?
12. Suppose a corporation has two classes of common stock, voting

and nonvoting. Should the lack of voting rights make the second class of stock less valuable?

13. How does cumulative voting make minority representation on the board of directors more attainable?

14. How much distortion can be expected in the computation of the specific cost of capital of common stock from the assumption of a constant rate of growth of dividends?

15. Is the growth in market price of common stock likely to be at a steady rate? Does this invalidate the use of an estimated future price in calculating the specific cost of capital of common stock?

16. Describe the role of the SEC in policing the securities markets.

17. Why are an investment banker's services worth paying a fee? Are such services worth a fee when a rights offering method is used?

18. Why is it generally desirable for a corporation to seek listing of its securities on an organized security exchange?

19. Are the information disclosures required by the SEC and the stock exchanges reasonable, or does this constitute an invasion of the corporation's privacy?

20. If a bond issue is refinanced does that preclude a further refinancing if interest rates fall again?

21. If a bond issue is called and refinanced, does the call premium serve to compensate the holder of the old issue for his inconvenience in finding a new investment? What about the fact that the bondholder has to reinvest at a lower interest rate?

Chapter 10 Problems

1. A 20-year bond issue is sold at par with a coupon interest rate of 7 percent, and total issue costs are 4 percent of the issue. These issue costs are immediately deducted from the cash proceeds of the issue, and are amortized over the life of the issue on a straight-line basis for tax purposes. The corporation's income tax rate is 40 percent. Compute the specific cost of capital for this bond issue.

2. A preferred stock issue with a stated dividend rate of $8 per share is sold at a price of $100 a share. The issue costs are 5 percent, and the corporation's income tax rate is 45 percent. What is the specific cost of capital for this issue of preferred stock?

3. The corporation sells an issue of common stock for a net (after issue costs) proceed of $40 a share. The last dividend paid was $2 a share, and that dividend is expected to grow at a rate of 10 percent a year forever. What is the specific cost of capital for this common stock issue?

4. Another corporation sells common stock now for a net price of $50 a share. No dividends are paid now and the corporation does not intend to pay any in the foreseeable future. However, a stock analyst has come up with two estimates of a future price of that stock, $70 a share three years from now, and $90 a share five years from now.

a. Compute the specific cost of capital using the $70 estimate.

b. Compute the specific cost of capital using the $90 estimate.

c. What is the implied cost of capital for the two-year segment from time three to time five?

5. A corporation sells warrants to buy common stock at a net price of $10 each. Each warrant gives the holder the right to buy one share of common stock for $20. The warrants expire four years from now. The present price of the common stock is $18 a share, and the estimated future prices of the common at various time points are:

Time	1	2	3	4
Estimated price of common	24	30	38	50

What is the specific cost of capital for this warrant issue?

6. The corporation sells a 20-year issue of 5 percent coupon, $1,000 par value convertible bonds. The conversion price is 20, meaning that one bond can be exchanged for 50 shares of common stock. The corporation income tax rate is 40 percent. The present market price of the common stock is $10 a share, and that value is expected to grow at the rate of 10 percent a year forever. What is the specific cost of capital for this convertible issue?

7. A corporation sells a 30-year bond issue with a coupon rate of 9 percent at par. Issue costs were very small so they can be ignored in this problem. The bond issue is callable at 107 after five years. Suppose interest rates fall and the corporation calls the bond issue to refinance at the lower rate as soon as it can.

   a. Calculate the bondholders' before-tax yield for the five-year holding period.

   b. The corporation's tax rate is 40 percent. Calculate the realized specific cost of capital for the issue.

Chapter 10 References

Boness, A. James. "A Pedagogic Note on the Cost of Capital." *Journal of Finance*, March 1964.

Bowlin, Oswald D. "The Refunding Decision: Another Special Case in Capital Budgeting." *Journal of Finance*, March 1966.

Brigham, Eugene F. "Analysis of Convertible Debentures." *Journal of Finance*, March 1966.

"Direct Placement of Corporate Debt." *Economic Review*, Federal Reserve Bank of Cleveland, March 1965.

Elsaid, Hussein H. "The Function of Preferred Stock in the Corporate Financial Plan." *Financial Analysts Journal*, July-August 1969.

Gordon, Myron J. *The Investment, Financing and Valuation of the Corporation.* Homewood, Ill.: Irwin, 1962.

Hayes, Samuel L., III, and Reiling, Henry B. "Sophisticated Financing Tool: The Warrant." *Harvard Business Review*, January-February 1967.

Nelson, J. Russell. "Price Effects in Rights Offerings." *Journal of Finance*, December 1965.

Reilly, F. K. "An Analysis and Reconciliation of Bond Refunding Decision Models." *Marquette Business Review*, Summer 1969.

Robichek, Alexander A., and McDonald, John G. "The Cost of Capital Concept: Potential Use and Misuse." *Financial Executive*, June 1965.

Shelton, John P. "The Relation of the Price of a Warrant to the Price of its Associated Stock." *Financial Analysts Journal*, May-June and July-August 1967.

Traum, S. S. "Accounting and Tax Aspects of Issuing Convertible Debenture Bonds." *New York Certified Public Accountant*, December 1967.

Van Horne, James C. "New Listings and Their Price Behavior." *Journal of Finance*, September 1970.

Vinson, C. E. "Pricing Practices in the Primary Convertible Bond Market." *Quarterly Review of Economics and Business*, Summer 1970.

Weil, Roman L., Segall, Joel E., and Green, David. "Premiums on Convertible Bonds." *Journal of Finance*, June 1968.

Wilt, Glenn A., Jr., and Fahlgren, George W. "Some Aspects of Issuing Corporate Securities." *Arizona Business Bulletin*, May 1968.

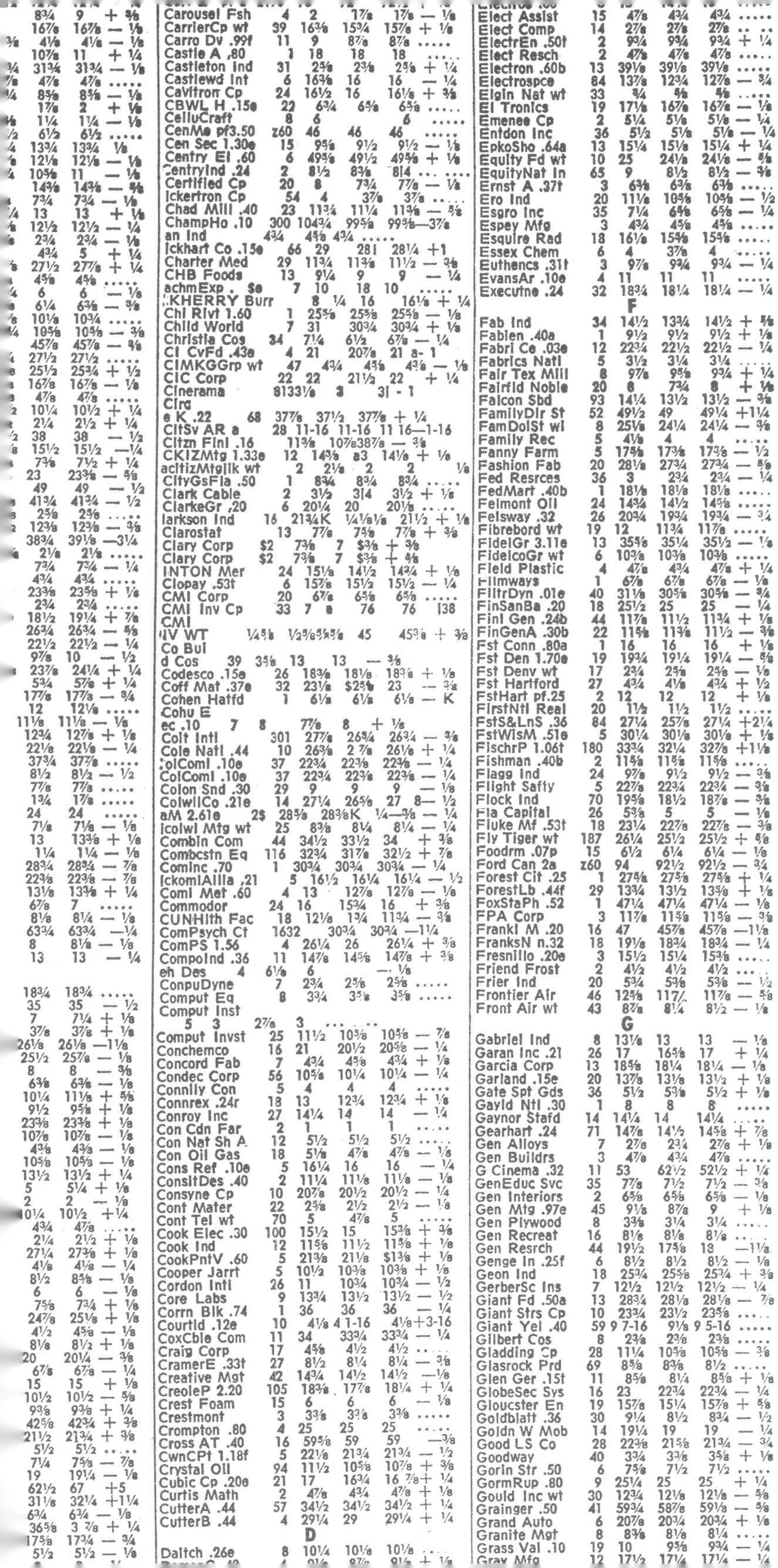
Carousel Fsh 4 2 1⅞ 1⅞ — ⅛
CarrierCp wt 39 16¾ 15¾ 15⅞ + ⅛
Carro Dv .99f 11 9 8⅞ 8⅞ .....
Castle A .80 1 18 18 18 .....
Castleton Ind 31 2⅝ 2⅜ 2⅝ + ¼
Castlewd Int 6 16⅜ 16 16 — ¼
Cavitron Cp 24 16½ 16 16⅛ + ⅜
CBWL H .15e 22 6¾ 6⅝ 6⅝ .....
CelluCraft 8 6 6 .....
CenMe pf3.50 z60 46 46 46 .....
Cen Sec 1.30e 15 9⅝ 9½ 9½ — ⅛
Centry El .60 6 49⅝ 49½ 49⅝ + ⅛
CentryInd .24 2 8½ 8⅜ 8¼ .....
Certified Cp 20 8 7¾ 7⅞ — ⅛
Ickertron Cp 54 4 3⅞ 3⅞ .....
Chad Mill .40 23 11¾ 11¼ 11⅜ — ⅝
ChampHo .10 300 104¾ 99⅝ 99⅝—3⅞
an Ind 4¾ 4⅝ 4¾ .....
Ickhart Co .15e 66 29 28¼ 28¼ +1
Charter Med 29 11¾ 11⅜ 11½ — ⅜
CHB Foods 13 9¼ 9 9 — ¼
achmExp . $e 7 10 18 10 .....
KHERRY Burr 8 ¼ 16 16⅛ + ¼
Chi Rivt 1.60 1 25⅝ 25⅝ 25⅝ — ⅛
Child World 7 31 30¾ 30¾ + ⅛
Christia Cos 34 7¼ 6½ 6⅞ — ¼
Cl CvFd .43e 4 21 20⅞ 21 a- 1
CIMKGGrp wt 47 4¾ 4⅝ 4⅝ — ⅛
CIC Corp 22 22 21½ 22 + ¼
Cinerama 8133⅛ 3 3l - 1
Circ
e K .22 68 37⅞ 37½ 37⅞ + ¼
CitSv AR a 28 11-16 11-16 11 16—1-16
Citzn Finl .16 11⅜ 10⅞38⅞ — ⅜
CKIZMtg 1.33e 12 14⅝ a3 14⅛ + ⅛
acitizMtglik wt 2 2⅛ 2 2 ⅛
CityGsFla .50 1 8¾ 8¾ 8¾ .....
Clark Cable 2 3½ 3¼ 3½ + ⅛
ClarkeGr .20 6 20¼ 20 20⅛ .....
larkson Ind 16 21¾K ¼⅛⅛ 21½ + ⅛
Clarostat 13 7⅞ 7⅝ 7⅞ + ⅜
Clary Corp $2 7⅜ 7 $⅜ + ⅜
Clary Corp $2 7⅜ 7 $⅜ + ⅜
INTON Mer 24 15⅛ 14½ 14¾ + ⅛
Clopay .53t 6 15⅞ 15½ 15½ — ¼
CMI Corp 20 6⅞ 6⅝ 6⅝ .....
CMI Inv Cp 33 7 8 76 76 l38
CMI
IV WT ¼⅝ ½⅝⅝⅝ 45 45⅜ + ⅜
Co Bul
d Cos 39 3⅝ 13 13 — ⅜
Codesco .15e 26 18⅜ 18⅛ 18⅜ + ⅛
Coff Mat .37e 32 23⅛ $25⅝ 23 — ⅜
Cohen Hatfd 1 6⅛ 6⅛ 6⅛ — K
Cohu E
ec .10 7 8 7⅞ 8 + ⅛
Colt Intl 301 27⅞ 26¾ 26¾ — ⅜
Cole Natl .44 10 26⅝ 2 ⅞ 26⅛ + ¼
ColComl .10e 37 22¾ 22⅜ 22⅜ — ¼
ColComl .10e 37 22¾ 22⅜ 22⅜ — ¼
Colon Snd .30 29 9 9 9 — ⅛
ColwilCo .21e 14 27¼ 26⅝ 27 8— ½
aM 2.61e 2$ 28⅝ 28⅜K ¼—⅜ — ¼
lcolwl Mtg wt 25 8⅜ 8¼ 8¼ — ¼
Combin Com 44 34½ 33½ 34 + ⅜
Combcstn Eq 116 32¾ 31⅞ 32½ + ⅞
Cominc .70 1 30¾ 30¾ 30¾ — ¼
lckomlAilla .21 5 16½ 16¼ 16¼ — ½
Coml Met .60 4 13 12⅞ 12⅞ — ⅛
Commodor 24 16 15¾ 16 + ⅜
CUNHlth Fac 18 12⅛ 1¾ 11¾ — ⅜
ComPsych Ct 1632 30¾ 30¾ —1¼
ComPS 1.56 4 26¼ 26 26¼ + ⅜
Compolnd .36 11 14⅞ 14⅝ 14⅞ + ⅜
eh Des 4 6⅛ 6 — ⅛
ConpuDyne 7 2¾ 2⅝ 2⅝ .....
Comput Eq 8 3¾ 3⅝ 3⅝ .....
Comput Inst
5 3 2⅞ 3 .....
Comput Invst 25 11½ 10⅝ 10⅝ — ⅞
Conchemco 16 21 20½ 20⅝ — ¼
Concord Fab 7 4¾ 4⅝ 4¾ + ⅛
Condec Corp 56 10⅝ 10¼ 10¼ — ¼
Connlly Con 5 4 4 4 .....
Connrex .24r 18 13 12¾ 12¾ + ⅛
Conroy Inc 27 14¼ 14 14 — ¼
Con Cdn Far 2 1 1 1 .....
Con Nat Sh A 12 5½ 5½ 5½ .....
Con Oil Gas 18 5⅛ 4⅞ 4⅞ — ⅛
Cons Ref .10e 5 16¼ 16 16 — ¼
ConsltDes .40 2 11¼ 11⅛ 11⅛ — ⅛
Consyne Cp 10 20⅞ 20½ 20½ — ¼
Cont Mater 22 2⅝ 2½ 2½ — ⅛
Cont Tel wt 70 5 4⅞ 5 .....
Cook Elec .30 100 15½ 15 15⅜ + ⅜
Cook Ind 12 11⅝ 11½ 11⅝ + ⅛
CookPntV .60 5 21⅜ 21⅛ $1⅜ + ⅛
Cooper Jarrt 5 10½ 10⅜ 10⅜ + ⅛
Cordon Intl 26 11 10¾ 10¾ — ¼
Core Labs 9 13¾ 13½ 13½ — ½
Corrn Blk .74 1 36 36 36 — ¼
Courtld .12e 10 4⅛ 4 1-16 4⅛+3-16
CoxCble Com 11 34 33¾ 33¾ — ¼
Craig Corp 17 4⅝ 4½ 4½ .....
CramerE .33t 27 8½ 8¼ 8¼ — ⅜
Creative Mgt 42 14¾ 14½ 14½ —⅛
CreoleP 2.20 105 18⅜ 17⅞ 18¼ + ¼
Crest Foam 15 6 6 6 — ⅛
Crestmont 3 3⅜ 3⅜ 3⅜ .....
Crompton .80 4 25 25 25 .....
Cross AT .40 16 59⅝ 59 59 —⅜
CwnCPt 1.18f 5 22⅛ 21¾ 21¾ — ½
Crystal Oil 94 11½ 10⅝ 10⅞ + ⅜
Cubic Cp .20e 21 17 16¾ 16 ⅞+ ¼
Curtis Math 2 4⅞ 4¾ 4⅞ + ⅛
CutterA .44 57 34½ 34½ 34½ + ¼
CutterB .44 4 29¼ 29 29¼ + ¼
D
Daltch .26e 8 10¼ 10⅛ 10⅛ .....

Elect Assist 15 4⅞ 4¾ 4¾ .....
Elect Comp 14 2⅞ 2⅞ 2⅞ .....
ElectrEn .50t 2 9¾ 9¾ 9¾ + ¼
Elect Resch 2 4⅞ 4⅞ 4⅞ .....
Electron .60b 13 39⅛ 39⅛ 39⅛ .....
Electrospce 84 13⅞ 12¾ 12⅞ — ¾
Elgin Nat wt 33 ¾ ⅝ ⅝ .....
El Tronics 19 17⅛ 16⅞ 16⅞ — ⅛
Emenee Cp 2 5¼ 5⅛ 5⅛ — ¼
Entdon Inc 36 5½ 5⅛ 5⅛ — ¼
EpkoSho .64a 13 15¼ 15⅛ 15¼ + ¼
Equity Fd wt 10 25 24⅛ 24⅛ — ⅝
EquityNat In 65 9 8½ 8½ — ⅜
Ernst A .37t 3 6⅜ 6⅜ 6⅜ .....
Ero Ind 20 11⅛ 10⅝ 10⅝ — ½
Esgro Inc 35 7¼ 6⅝ 6⅝ — ¼
Espey Mfg 3 4¾ 4⅝ 4⅝ .....
Esquire Rad 18 16⅛ 15⅝ 15⅝ .....
Essex Chem 6 4 3⅞ 4 .....
Euthencs .31t 3 9⅞ 9¾ 9¾ — ¼
EvansAr .10e 4 11 11 11 .....
Executne .24 32 18¾ 18¼ 18¼ — ¼
F
Fab Ind 34 14½ 13¾ 14½ + ⅝
Fabien .40a 1 9½ 9½ 9½ + ⅛
Fabri Ce .03e 12 22¾ 22½ 22½ — ¼
Fabrics Natl 5 3½ 3¼ 3¼ .....
Fair Tex Mill 8 9⅞ 9⅝ 9¾ + ¼
Fairfld Noble 20 8 7¾ 8 + ⅛
Falcon Sbd 93 14¼ 13½ 13½ — ⅜
FamilyDlr St 52 49½ 49 49¼ +1¼
FamDolSt wl 8 25⅛ 24¼ 24¼ — ⅜
Family Rec 5 4⅛ 4 4 .....
Fanny Farm 5 17⅝ 17⅜ 17⅜ — ½
Fashion Fab 20 28⅛ 27¾ 27¾ — ⅝
Fed Resrces 36 3 2¾ 2¾ — ¼
FedMart .40b 1 18⅛ 18⅛ 18⅛ .....
Felmont Oil 24 14¾ 14½ 14⅝ .....
Felsway .32 26 20¾ 19¾ 19¾ — ¾
Fibrebord wt 19 12 11¾ 11⅞ .....
FidelGr 3.11e 13 35⅝ 35¼ 35½ — ⅛
FidelcoGr wt 6 10⅜ 10⅜ 10⅜ .....
Field Plastic 4 4⅞ 4¾ 4⅞ + ¼
Filmways 1 6⅞ 6⅞ 6⅞ — ⅛
FiltrDyn .01e 40 31⅛ 30⅝ 30⅝ — ¾
FinSanBa .20 18 25½ 25 25 — ¼
Finl Gen .24b 44 11⅞ 11½ 11¾ + ⅛
FinGenA .30b 22 11⅝ 11⅜ 11½ — ⅜
Fst Conn .80a 1 16 16 16 + ⅛
Fst Den 1.70e 19 19¾ 19¼ 19¼ — ⅝
Fst Denv wt 17 2¾ 2⅝ 2⅝ — ⅛
Fst Hartford 27 4¾ 4⅛ 4¾ + ½
FstHart pf.25 2 12 12 12 + ⅛
FirstNtl Real 20 1½ 1½ 1½ .....
FstS&LnS .36 84 27¼ 25⅞ 27¼ +2¼
FstWisM .51e 5 30¼ 30⅛ 30⅛ + ⅛
FischrP 1.06t 180 33¾ 32¼ 32⅞ +1⅛
Fishman .40b 2 11⅝ 11⅝ 11⅝ .....
Flagg Ind 24 9⅞ 9½ 9½ — ⅜
Flight Safty 5 22⅞ 22¾ 22¾ — ⅜
Flock Ind 70 19⅝ 18½ 18⅞ — ⅜
Fla Capital 26 5⅜ 5 5 — ⅛
Fluke Mf .53t 18 23¼ 22⅞ 22⅞ — ⅜
Fly Tiger wt 187 26¼ 25½ 25½ + ⅝
Foodrm .07p 15 6½ 6¼ 6¼ — ⅛
Ford Can 2a z60 94 92½ 92½ — ¾
Forest Cit .25 1 27⅝ 27⅝ 27⅝ + ¼
ForestLb .44f 29 13¾ 13½ 13⅝ + ⅛
FoxStaPh .52 1 47¼ 47¼ 47¼ — ⅛
FPA Corp 3 11⅞ 11⅝ 11⅝ — ⅜
Frankl M .20 16 47 45⅞ 45⅞ —1⅛
FranksN n.32 18 19⅛ 18¾ 18¾ — ¼
Fresnillo .20e 3 15½ 15¼ 15⅝ .....
Friend Frost 2 4½ 4½ 4½ .....
Frier Ind 20 5¾ 5⅝ 5⅝ — ½
Frontier Air 46 12⅝ 11⅞ 11⅞ — ⅝
Front Air wt 43 8⅞ 8¼ 8½ — ⅛
G
Gabriel Ind 8 13⅛ 13 13 — ⅛
Garan Inc .21 26 17 16⅝ 17 + ¼
Garcia Corp 13 18⅝ 18¼ 18¼ — ⅛
Garland .15e 20 13⅞ 13⅛ 13½ + ⅛
Gate Spt Gds 36 5½ 5⅜ 5½ + ⅛
Gayld Ntl .30 1 8 8 8 .....
Gaynor Stafd 14 14¼ 14 14¼ .....
Gearhart .24 71 14⅞ 14½ 14⅝ + ⅞
Gen Alloys 7 2⅞ 2¾ 2⅞ + ⅛
Gen Buildrs 3 4⅞ 4¾ 4⅞ .....
G Cinema .32 11 53 62½ 52½ + ¼
GenEduc Svc 35 7⅞ 7½ 7½ — ⅜
Gen Interiors 2 6⅝ 6⅝ 6⅝ — ⅛
Gen Mtg .97e 45 9⅛ 8⅞ 9 + ⅛
Gen Plywood 8 3⅜ 3¼ 3¼ .....
Gen Recreat 16 8⅛ 8⅛ 8⅛ .....
Gen Resrch 44 19½ 17⅝ 18 —1⅛
Genge In .25f 6 8½ 8½ 8½ — ⅛
Geon Ind 18 25¾ 25⅝ 25¾ + ⅜
GerberSc Ins 7 12½ 12½ 12½ — ¼
Giant Fd .50a 13 28¾ 28⅛ 28⅛ — ⅞
Giant Strs Cp 10 23¾ 23½ 23⅝ .....
Giant Yel .40 59 9 7-16 9⅛ 9 5-16 .....
Gilbert Cos 8 2⅜ 2⅜ 2⅜ .....
Gladding Cp 28 11¼ 10⅝ 10⅝ — ⅜
Glasrock Prd 69 8⅝ 8⅜ 8½ .....
Glen Ger .15t 11 8⅝ 8¼ 8⅝ + ⅛
GlobeSec Sys 16 23 22¾ 22¾ — ¼
Gloucster En 19 15⅞ 15¼ 15⅞ + ⅝
Goldblatt .36 30 9¼ 8½ 8¾ — ½
Goldn W Mob 14 19¼ 19 19 — ¼
Good LS Co 28 22⅝ 21⅝ 21¾ — ¾
Goodway 40 3¾ 3⅜ 3⅝ + ⅛
Gorin Str .50 6 7⅝ 7½ 7½ .....
GormRup .80 9 25¼ 25 25 + ¼
Gould Inc wt 30 12¾ 12⅛ 12⅛ — ⅝
Grainger .50 41 59¾ 58⅞ 59⅛ — ⅝
Grand Auto 6 20⅞ 20¾ 20¾ + ⅛
Granite Mgt 8 8⅜ 8⅛ 8¼ .....
Grass Val .10 19 10 9⅝ 9¾ — ¼

PART FIVE

THE DEBT AND CAPITAL MARKETS

When designing a capital structure or arranging financing sources, the corporation's financial officers must bargain with a capital supplier or set terms on the security offering that will allow it to be sold successfully. This means that the size of offering, the yield to the holder, and the repayment schedule must be in line with competing securities. Otherwise the corporation may pay more than is necessary for the capital, or may be unable to raise the funds.

To design the security offering or loan arrangements, the financial officers must know the current state of the securities markets. The required knowledge is not just a listing of yields for individual securities, but includes the whole spectrum of interrelationships among securities.

In this section of the book the securities markets are analyzed from the aspect of an investor, a viewpoint external to the financial management of the corporation. The investor's attitudes toward risk and the size of expected returns, when considered in the aggregate, establish the structure of interest rates and security yields, and the availability of funds.

For debt and equity capital the sources include certain financial institutions as well as individuals. The aims and operations of the financial institutions are conditioned on the corporate tax structure, government regulations, and the desires of the institutions' owners. The actions of individual investors are also dependent on the U.S. tax code, but are only slightly affected by government regulation.

To facilitate the exposition, the chapters in this section are divided into the debt market and the equities market. The debt market includes both loan transactions and the sale of debt securities. The difference between the debt and equities markets is sufficiently great that the participants in the two markets are almost separate. Individual investors seldom make loans to corporations or buy corporate bonds, and very few financial institutions hold corporate equities.

11

THE DEBT MARKETS

When a corporation must raise funds through loans or by sale of debt securities, a thorough knowledge of the market environment is necessary for success in planning the type of financing, the amount, the timing, and the negotiation with the capital supplier. In this chapter the debt markets in the United States are described.

The usual suppliers of debt capital to the operating corporation are financial institutions such as commercial banks. Except for times of abnormally high interest rates (such as during 1970), individuals do not purchase many corporate debt securities or make direct loans to corporations. Instead individuals who purchase dollar-denominated investments (debt rather than equity securities) do so for the most part through financial intermediaries. They make deposits in their bank or savings and loan, buy insurance policies, or contribute to pension funds. The financial intermediary, the bank, savings and loan association, insurance company, or pension fund, buys the corporate debt security or makes the direct loan to the corporation. Accordingly the first part of this chapter contains an explicit description of the activities of the common types of financial intermediaries.

After the discussion of the debt market participants, the next topic is the structures of interest rates that are commonly distinguished. The division used here is (1) the term structure of interest rates, (2) the cyclical structure of interest rates, and (3) the risk structure of interest rates.

In the term structure of interest rates analysis is of how rates vary by maturity length (term) of the debt security. For example 5-year notes may have a yield of 6 percent and 20-year bonds a yield of 7 percent. Closely related to the term structure is the cyclical structure of interest rates, how interest rates vary with the level of business activity, the stage of the business cycle. Short-term funds may require an interest rate of 4 percent in a recession, and an interest rate of 9 percent in prosperity. Interest rates also vary by the degree of financial risk perceived by the investor. To a prime borrower a bank may lend funds at 6 percent interest, but on a riskier type of loan the charge would be 10 percent.

A lender must be able to discriminate among borrowers, to grade with respect to financial risk. The final portion of this chapter is on external financial analysis of a corporation from the aspect of prospective suppliers of debt capital. The analysis may be based on study of the borrowing corporation's published financial statements, on privately furnished statements, or on a specialized financial rating service's assessment of the credit rating of the corporation. A financial manager must be aware of how his corporation compares to other corporations that may also be seeking funds from the debt capital supplier.

Financial Intermediaries in the Abstract

A financial intermediary differs from other business firms in that its purpose is the acquisition of intangible property in the form of securities rather than the acquisition of physical assets. The financial intermediary's product is credit, not some manufactured good. The true financial intermediary grants loans and buys securities from firms and individuals, using funds derived from other firms and individuals.

The financial intermediary issues claims on itself to obtain funds. The claims it issues may take the form of stocks, bonds, direct borrowing, deposit liabilities, or other liabilities, depending on what type of institution it is. A commercial bank, for example, issues claims in the form of common stock, and possibly some preferred stock or debentures, but the bulk of the claims on the commercial bank take the form of deposit liabilities, time deposits, and demand deposits. The largest part of claims against an insurance company take the form of policy reserves, those amounts that are actuarially due to policyholders.

The claims acquired by the financial intermediary may take the form of securities issued by a business firm, debt securities of government units, certifications of indebtedness such as notes and mortgages, or other forms. Those claims will vary with the type of financial intermediary, commercial banks for example hold mostly short-term loans to business firms and individuals, while savings and loan associations hold mostly long-term mortgages against real estate.

The financial intermediary serves the economic role of a distributing mechanism for private savings and investment. An individual or business firm, for example, with accumulated money buys the claims issued by the financial intermediary, and the financial intermediary in turn uses the money to acquire other claims issued by a third party.

The intermediary serves three distinct purposes that justify its existence. First it provides professional management in the selection of the claims it purchases—a bank specializes in judging worthy credit risks, selecting whom to lend to. The second major result of the financial intermediary's activities is the diversification of investments (the claims purchased) and the resulting reduction of risk in the portfolio of assets. An individual security may be quite risky when considered in isolation, but as shown in Chapter 7, a collection of risky securities may have a smaller degree of risk due to the "portfolio effect" of diversification. The third purpose of the financial intermediary is the absorption of the residual risk from the portfolio. The bank is supposed to bear the risk of its loans, not the depositors in the bank.

Intermediaries may be organized on a "mutual" basis, a form of cooperative in which most of the claimholders share in the profits of the enterprise, or it may be organized as a profit-making enterprise in which a separate group of owners earn the profits above those revenues that are necessary to meet the return on other claims. Both forms of organization are found in insurance companies and savings and loan associations, but most financial intermediaries are not mutuals. Even a mutual company may find itself separately liable for a form of corporate income taxes.

Since most financial intermediaries are organized as corporations the corporate income tax structure has some influence on their investments. The federal tax rates on ordinary income are 22 percent on the first $25,000 and 48 percent on income over $25,000 (as of the date this book was written). The corporate tax rate on long-term capital gains is 30 percent. Interest on municipal bonds is tax exempt, and 85 percent of dividend income is exempt from tax (100 percent if the intermediary owns more than 80 percent of the subsidiary corporation). If the intermediary chose investments purely on the basis of federal taxation, the ranking of investments would be (1) municipal bonds, (2) common or preferred stocks held for dividend income, (3) assets such as common stock held for long-term capital gains, and (4) corporate or other debt or bonds held for interest income.

Financial intermediaries are traditionally regulated in their activities by some governmental agency. The regulation may be from an agency of the federal government, such as the Federal Home Loan Bank system or the Comptroller of the Currency, or from an agency of a state government, such as a state banking commission or insurance commission. The major reasoning behind the regulation is usually the protection of interests of the claimholders of the intermediary, such as the depositors or the policyholders. In some instances of federal government regulators, the objective of the regulation is to achieve some economic goal such as control over the money supply of the country, promotion of the housing industry, or promotion of black capitalism.

As a response to regulation and also to good business practices, the financial intermediaries tend to select investments to coordinate with the form of their liabilities. If liabilities are short-term in nature, such as deposits withdrawable on demand, then the intermediary would invest a large portion of its assets in a short-term form. This matching of the time-nature of assets and liabilities is not exact, however, since the intermediary can usually anticipate that withdrawals will be offset to some extent by new deposits.

The capital structure of the intermediary probably exerts a greater influence on the investment policy. If organized on a stock company basis the amount of equity in relationship to the total assets may vary from as low as 3 percent to as much as 30 percent. An intermediary with a 3 percent equity cannot suffer much loss on its portfolio of assets before its equity would disappear.

Commercial Banks

Commercial banks can be viewed as financial intermediaries because the ability of an individual bank to extend loans depends upon its ability to attract deposits. Commercial banks are unique, though, because those institutions are the only ones that create money in the process of buying claims. When a commercial bank makes a loan or buys a bond from a person, a deposit balance is created that is usually counted as money by economists. The deposit that is created or increased in size is normally a checking account balance that is spendable by the owner.

Because they are money-creators, commercial banks have come under some special controls by an agency of the federal government, the Federal Reserve System. Individual banks and the banking system are controlled in the amount of expansion of assets and liabilities possible through a system of required reserves. Commercial banks are required to have reserve balances equal to a percentage of time deposits and demand deposits, or they face penalties. The eligible assets that count as reserves are currency and deposits owned in the Federal Reserve Bank. The commercial bank's balance in the Federal Reserve serves as its "funds" to be used as the basis for the expansion of loans and other earning assets. To attract additional funds a bank must sell some asset, induce depositors to increase the size of their deposits, or sell additional securities. Accordingly the commercial bank's individual ability to acquire earning assets is based upon the claims it can sell, just as any other financial intermediary.

Commercial banks are possibly subject to three levels of regulation depending on their organization. A nationally chartered bank comes under the jurisdiction of the Comptroller of the Currency, and since national banks must be members of the Federal Reserve System those banks are subject to regulation by the System. State-chartered banks are controlled in their operations to some extent by state banking commissions. Membership in the Federal Reserve System is optional for state banks, so that form of regulation may not be applicable.

Because the demand deposit liabilities of a commercial bank are transferable by check, it is possible that the volume of that form of claim issued may be highly volatile for some banks. Time deposits are not transferable by check, so the size of those claims issued can usually be considered to be relatively stable. The commercial bank's investment policy may therefore be conditioned on the composition of its deposit liabilities—the higher the proportion of time deposits, the less need for liquidity in assets.

Other liabilities of the commercial bank are usually small in size and therefore ignored in the usual analysis. Occasionally a bank will be found that has issued some form of intermediate-term or long-term debentures, preferred stock, or has engaged in some significant short-term borrowing. During the tight money period of 1969-1970, several larger banks engaged in some innovative financing, borrowing Eurodollars through foreign subsidiaries and issuing commercial paper through affiliated nonbank companies. Banks that are members of the Federal Reserve System have the privilege of borrowing directly from the Federal Reserve, although such borrowing cannot be on a continuing basis and therefore is not supposed to be used to finance expansion of assets.

The size of owners' equity in relationship to total assets varies between 3 percent and 10 percent with possibly a normal ratio of 6 percent. This low ratio may seem to constrain commercial banks' choices of assets to those with little possibility of loss, but losses may be offset to some extent by increased nominal yields on the loans. For example, suppose a bank expected an average return on consumer loans of 8 percent. If the average default loss on one category of consumer loans was 3 percent then the bank could charge a nominal (stated) interest rate of 11 percent on that category, expecting an average yield after defaults of 8 percent.

A bank's assets can be graded by degree of liquidity, with the least liquid category being loans since loans are not normally marketable. Within the loan category, the sooner the loan is scheduled to be repaid the higher would be the degree of liquidity. In the case of installment loans payments are received periodically over the term of the loan, so even three-year installment loans would rate as fairly liquid assets. Normally a bank's loan portfolio would contain a large amount of consumer installment loans, in most cases secured by a lien on durable goods such as automobiles. Short-term business loans, usually unsecured and payable in full at maturity date, are the largest part of a bank's loan portfolio. Banks can make intermediate-term loans, and even long-term real estate mortgages are held by banks. A large portion of the real estate mortgages are VA or FHA insured, and therefore can be sold if necessary.

The degree of liquidity in holding marketable securities depends not only on the speed with which the security can be sold, but also on the cost of the sale transaction. Cost here includes the sales commission paid the broker and the difference between the price received for the security and its original acquisition price. Banks are usually allowed to carry bonds on their books at original cost, not recognizing the possible lower market value until the actual sale is made. Therefore banks normally prefer not to sell bonds that have depreciated since purchase, because they would then have to recognize the loss from the security sale.

Usually the shorter the term to maturity of a bond the less chance there is for a capital loss, and therefore the more likely the bank would sell that bond if additional funds were needed. Banks traditionally hold Treasury Bills in some volume as "secondary reserves" because those securities are highly liquid and some interest return can be earned. In the past banks held appreciable quantities of longer-term U.S. government securities, but with wide swings in market rates of interest, the prices of that type of security have changed as well, indicating that those longer-term securities are not very liquid.

Banks also hold municipal bonds in some significant degree. The primary motive here is tax-free income, and sometimes the securities held are locally-issued, giving the bank a convenient way of acquiring the bonds without going through a municipal bond dealer or having to assess the credit-worthiness of the municipality. Municipal securities are probably not considered as very liquid assets by the bank's management because those securities' degree of marketability may not be very high.

Banks then, in general, make loans to business firms and individuals, and hold most short-term U.S. government securities and long-term municipal bonds. A bank could possibly hold small amounts of corporate bonds or even corporate stock, but cannot be considered as a significant corporate security holder.

Savings and Loan Associations and Mutual Savings Banks

The other major deposit-accepting financial institution is the savings and loan association, or in the New England area the mutual savings bank. Savings and loan associations may be "mutual" in organizational form, in which case depositors technically own the association. The stock company form is allowed for state-chartered savings and loan associations.

Savings deposits form the major source of funds for these institutions, and the deposits are very similar to time deposits in commercial banks. Interest is paid on the deposit balance, and withdrawal of the deposit without prior notice is usually possible. These financial institutions would therefore seem to need a high degree of liquidity in their asset portfolios.

Savings and loan associations and mutual savings banks invest most of their funds in real estate mortgages, which are not considered generally marketable unless they are of the VA or FHA insured form. Those institutions do maintain some liquid reserves in the form of currency, deposits in commercial banks, and U.S. government securities. Members of the Federal Home Loan Bank System can borrow from the System to meet liquidity needs. This borrowing is normally of a short-term nature, although the Federal Home Loan Bank has extended longer-term loans at times to member associations.

There may be two possible levels of regulation for these institutions, from the Federal Home Loan Bank for member institutions, and from state regulatory associations. The investments of these institutions are limited to real estate loans, so they cannot be considered as a general source of funds for business loans or security purchase.

Life Insurance Companies

Because of the nature of fund requirements and asset portfolios differs, life insurance companies and fire and casualty insurance companies will be described separately, beginning with the life companies.

Life insurance companies may be organized on a mutual basis or as a stock company. In either case their activities are regulated by state insurance commissions who may prescribe closely the investments allowable. The state regulating the activities may not be only the state in which the company is incorporated, but states in which policies are sold may also regulate the activities of the company to protect policyholders.

Life insurance companies obtain their funds from a long-term contract, the insurance policy. If the policy calls for a level premium payment over the period of the contract, an excess over the actuarial requirement to cover the expected death payments is accumulated over the early years of the contract. If the insurance is of the term variety, the size of the annual premium is based on the actuarial expectation of death benefits. In either case some amount to allow for operating expenses and profit is included in the premium.

Because life insurance companies deal with large numbers of people, the amount of cash necessary to meet policy pay-offs is predictable with a high degree of accuracy. However borrowing against the cash surrender value of policies, cancellation of policies, or failure of its agents to sell an adequate number of new policies could cause cash flow difficulties for a life insurance company.

A life insurance company must therefore keep some highly liquid assets in its portfolio, although the bulk of the portfolio may be in a relatively illiquid form. Because policy obligations are normally expressed in fixed dollar quantities, life insurance companies have typically invested in fixed-income, fixed-maturity-value assets such as loans and bonds. Most state insurance commissions have required such investment forms, allowing only a small percentage of equity investments unless those investments were used for variable-annuity insurance contracts.

Because the need for liquidity is limited, life insurance companies typically buy long-term bond issues, either corporate or government, or make long-term mortgage loans. Since the average size of the companies is so large, individual companies may be able to absorb quite large securities issues, make loans on large real estate projects, or make major intermediate-term loans to business firms without assuming an amount of risk that is significant in relation to the size of the insurance company. These companies may be subject to a requirement in some states that they purchase only corporate bonds from a selected list of eligible issues, where the selection is on the basis of evaluation by the regulating commission or by one of the recognized rating services. However, the insurance companies are not confined to marketable issues, so large corporations can sometimes arrange a direct placement of a bond issue with an insurance company or group of companies.

Fire and Casualty Insurance Companies

The insurance policies written by fire and casualty insurance companies are short or intermediate-term protection against damages from fire, accident, collision, or other casualty losses. The premiums are usually collected in advance of the period of coverage. The amount of an individual claim will not necessarily be equal to the amount of the policy coverage, and the total amount of claims during a time period are not as predictable as in the case of life insurance policies.

The company may be a mutual or stock company operated for the profit of the common stockholders. The premiums charged for protection may be controlled by state insurance commissions, and the investment portfolio of the company may be regulated as well.

The fire and casualty insurance company has a greater need for liquidity than a life insurance company, but many of these companies hold large amounts of common stock in their investment portfolios. The holdings of equities may be partially justified on the basis of purchasing power considerations since the amount of claim on a casualty loss could be expected to vary as the price level changes. Even in a mutual company "owner's equity" is large in proportion to total assets for a financial institution, so the greater variation in market value of common stocks can be absorbed. The preferential tax treatment given dividend receipts provides a further incentive to hold stocks rather than bonds.

Fire and casualty companies do very little lending either on a term basis or through real estate mortgages. The typical portfolio of assets consists of cash, government bonds, corporate bonds, preferred stocks, and common stocks—almost all are marketable securities. The assets of fire and casualty insurance companies look much like a conservatively-oriented balanced mutual fund, with a slightly higher degree of liquidity maintained.

Pension Funds There are a wide variety of pension funds operating in the United States today, and only "private" pension funds will be discussed here. The Social Security system is not considered as equivalent to a private pension fund because the contributions to the system are made in the form of a tax on income, the funds of the system are invested only in specified U.S. government securities, and the pension benefits paid are not based on an actuarial computation of contributions made to the fund. For much the same reasons the Civil Service Retirement System and state and local government retirement systems are separated from private pension funds.

Very few of the private pension funds in the United States are regulated by government agencies, although suggestions for bringing union-sponsored funds under some sort of federal control have been made from time to time. Funds administered by life insurance companies are regulated in investment policy through state insurance commissions' regulation of the company, but funds administered by other private companies are limited in their investment policies only by the financial constraints of the pension agreements.

A pension agreement may call for contributions by an individual on a voluntary basis, where the benefits paid are based on the investment performance of the fund during the accumulation period. An alternative plan may require a fixed schedule of benefits to be paid, altered only by the size of the periodic contributions and the time length covered by the accumulation. In this case the size of benefits is usually computed using a very conservative expected return, such as 5 percent, on the investment program. A common type of pension is one established by an employer, in which the size of the contribution is at the option of the employer, and any deficiencies in the fund's capacity to make the required pension payments are made up by further payments by the employer. This latter case can be called a non-fully-funded plan, and it usually arises when the employer maintains control over the fund and therefore determines the investment policy of the fund. Labor unions frequently insist that control over the pension fund be given to the union itself, presumably insuring that the fund will survive in spite of any possible failure of the employer firm.

A wide variety of investment practices can be expected from private pension funds. The pension fund may hold common stocks, government or corporate bonds, real estate mortgages, and in some cases engage directly in real estate investments. Tax features should not be a criterion in the fund's investment portfolio because income to the funds is not taxed.

Finance Companies Another significant type of financial intermediary in the U.S. economy is the finance company, an institution that specializes in extending relatively small, short, or intermediate-term loans to businesses and individuals. Included in this category are consumer finance companies, sales finance companies, and industrial finance companies.

Consumer finance companies specialize in making small unsecured loans to individuals, typically under the requirements expressed in states' small loan acts where maximum interest rates on certain size loans are set. The usual size of loan is between $300 and $1,000, and repayment is on an installment basis. In case of default on payments the finance company may try to collect through garnishment of wages. Borrowers use the loan proceeds for various purposes, meeting small emergencies, Christmas shopping expenditures, payment of taxes, and the like. There may be some discernible seasonal pattern to loan volume, but the random variation in loan balances is high. Accordingly a consumer finance company's need for funds can be expected to fluctuate.

A sales finance company makes loans to individuals (and occasionally to business firms) to finance the purchase of durable items such as automobiles, appliances, and furniture. The loans are usually secured by a pledge of the item purchased, and are repaid on a level installment basis. The size and term of loan is larger than that of the consumer finance company. The level of loan requirements should be related to the level of durable goods purchased, and will therefore fluctuate seasonally and randomly.

Industrial finance companies are less homogeneous as a group since different specialties as to type of loan can be expected. One company may extend secured loans on accounts receivable, another secured loans on inventories, and others on other types of security. The common factor is that the loans are secured by some type of business asset.

Finance companies are not regulated in their investment activities except that maximum interest rates allowed on consumer small loans are typically established by state laws. Some other state laws regarding usury (setting maximum interest rates that can be charged) may have some application in individual circumstances. The companies are stock companies, organized for the profit of common stockholders.

Finance companies raise a large part of their funds by various borrowing operations. Long-term debentures are issued, and several forms of short-term borrowings are made by the typical firm. The smaller firms tend to depend on loans from banks to cover their variable needs, and the large, well-established companies sell commercial paper for those purposes. The commercial paper market has traditionally been dominated by finance company issues, although other firms have been induced into raising funds this way during times of scarce credit.

Other Institutions

Some other financial institutions have not been included in the descriptions above because they do not fit the strict definition of financial intermediary used here. Mutual funds, for example, are a device for collective ownership of a large number of securities, but the claims issued by the mutual fund are simply pro-rata titles to the claims owned by the mutual fund. Only in the case of a leveraged mutual fund that has issued bonds or preferred stocks would the nature of the claims issued differ from the claims purchased by the fund. Mutual funds invest mostly in corporate equities, so they are discussed in the next chapter.

Another major category of financial institution that is not included as a financial intermediary is the personal trust, where securities are held in the name of a trust, the trust is operated by a trustee, and the income is distributed to trust beneficiaries. Again in this case the claim against the trust is effectively a claim on the assets of the trust.

Analysis of Short-Term Liquidity

A short-term lender to a business firm is naturally concerned with the prospects of prompt repayment of the loan and interest by the borrower. The ability of the borrower to repay is only vaguely related to the profits of the firm during the term of the loan, but depends on the generation of sufficient cash from operations or other sources to meet the obligation.

There are three approaches to determining the short-term liquidity of a company: balance sheet ratio analysis, projections of net cash generation from income statement data, and cash budgets prepared internally by the borrowing company. The first two methods can be utilized by an external analyst using published data for the most part, but the third appraisal of short-term liquidity is an internally generated document, and may represent additional requirements imposed in the loan application by the lender.

Ratio Analysis

The accounting information presumed available for this approach is the last balance sheet and the income statement for the most recent accounting period. The portion of the balance sheet containing the current assets and current liabilities listings is to be related to the corresponding quantities reported in the cash flows portion of the income statement.

To illustrate the ratio analysis the following portion of the balance sheet of a hypothetical firm will be used:

Balance Sheet of ABC as of December 31, 1971

Current Assets		Current Liabilities	
Cash	50	Accounts payable	100
Marketable Securities	100	Accrued expenses payable	100
Accounts receivable	200		
Inventories	150		
Total	500	Total	200

The applicable portion of the income statement is:

Income Statement of ABC for year ended December 31, 1971

Credit sales		2400
Cash sales		200
Total sales		2600
Cost of goods sold		
Inventory Dec. 31, 1970	350	
Purchases (all credit)	1000	
	1350	
Inventory Dec. 31, 1971	150	
Cost of goods sold	1200	

The first ratio in analyzing short-term liquidity is the "current ratio," defined as

$$\frac{\text{Total Current Assets}}{\text{Total Current Liabilities}}$$

For ABC the current ratio is 2.5.

The numerator of the ratio, total current assets, is the sum of cash on hand and those assets that will normally be converted into cash in the following year. Marketable securities could be sold to raise cash if needed. Accounts receivable balances on December 31 will presumably be collected during the post-balance sheet period. Inventories will be sold and collected for.

The denominator, total current liabilities, is the total of recorded short-term debts at the date of the balance sheet. Accordingly the current ratio is sometimes loosely described as the ratio of funds sources to funds requirements. Of course the problem with this interpretation is that the firm does not cease operations on the balance sheet date, but continues to acquire inventories, sell merchandise, collect receivables, pay payables, and incur other expenses.

If the balances reported on the balance sheet are typical of the usual amounts of receivables, inventories, and so forth, the current ratio can give a measure of coverage, or of the margin of safety in meeting current obligations that the firm maintains. The margin of safety does depend on the relative speed of conversion to cash inflows and outflows of the account balances shown. It is probable, for example, that it will take a longer time to convert inventories into cash inflows than the time when accounts payable are due. The conversion time of accounts receivable will be closer to the conversion time of accounts payable.

Because of the two-stage conversion process of inventories, first to accounts receivable and then to cash, the inventory balance is sometimes eliminated from the current ratio formula to yield the "acid-test" or "quick ratio." The acid-test ratio is defined as

$$\frac{\text{Total Current Assets} - \text{Inventories}}{\text{Total Current Liabilities}}$$

For ABC the acid-test ratio is 1.75.

In the acid-test ratio the conversion times of the numerator and denominator are more nearly matched, although there may be discrepancies between the due date of payables and that of receivables.

Whether the current ratio or the acid-test ratio is calculated, it is usually desirable to get some idea of the conversion times of assets and liabilities. The estimate of conversion time is based upon calculation of some "turnover" ratios, where flow quantities from income statement items are compared to balances from the balance sheet.

The "accounts receivable turnover ratio" is calculated as

$$\frac{\text{Credit Sales}}{\text{Accounts Receivable}}$$

Since ABC's credit sales for 1971 as shown on the income statement were \$2,400 the value of this ratio is 12. The reciprocal of this ratio is the average age of accounts receivable, so ABC's average age of receivable is 1/12 of a year, or one month. This last statement implicitly assumes that credit sales occurred at a constant rate over time in 1971, and that the December 31 balance is typical of other dates.

Credit sales may not be attainable as a separate number from total sales on an income statement, even though it is listed separately in the example statement. An estimate might have to be made of the proportion of credit sales in the total sales figure, possibly based on normal practices in ABC's industry. There might not be much distortion caused if total sales were substituted for credit sales in the definition of this turnover ratio.

An "inventory turnover ratio" can be calculated to give a measure of the average age of merchandise on hand:

$$\frac{\text{Cost of Goods Sold}}{\text{Inventory}}$$

Since ABC's cost of goods sold is \$1,200 the inventory turnover ratio for ABC is 8. This result indicates that the average age of inventory is 1/8 of a year, 1½ months.

The same qualifications need to made regarding the numerator and denominator in this ratio. Cost of goods sold may not be available from the published income statement, and may have to be obtained by other means such as estimation from a gross sales figure. The inventory balance on the balance sheet date may not be representative of the balance on other dates of the year. Because of the detail presented here on the income statement, the balance on December 31, 1971 can be seen to be atypical, or at least questionable, since the December 31, 1970 balance was \$350.

An estimate of the age of accounts payable can be derived from the "accounts payable turnover ratio," defined as

$$\frac{\text{Credit Purchases}}{\text{Accounts Payable}}$$

On ABC's income statement total credit purchases for 1971 were \$1,000, so the accounts payable turnover ratio would be 10. The reciprocal of this ratio is 1/10, indicating the average age of accounts payable is 1/10 of a year, or 1.2 months. The usual qualifications of availability and accuracy of the numerator and denominator apply to this ratio.

The five ratios described here are summaries of past transactions involving working capital, and *may* be indicative of future transactions. The ratios may be used as absolute measures of liquidity, or may be compared with the ratios for comparable companies to give a comparative measure of liquidity. Common financial ratios for various industries are available from financial reporting services such as Robert Morris Associates or Dun and Bradstreet.

One of the major difficulties with use of the working capital ratios for analysis of a firm's short-term liquidity is the possibility of "window-dressing" transactions by the firm in question. For example ABC may normally have balances of $350 for inventory and $300 for accounts payable. Combined with the other balances shown in the balance sheet above this would give a current ratio of

$$\frac{700}{400} = 1.75$$

instead of 2.5. The higher current ratio might have been achieved by deferring merchandise purchases of $200 that normally would have occurred in December, 1971 until the first few days of January, 1972. This deferral of purchases is perfectly legitimate for ABC, but it does result in a misleading value for the current ratio. If the management of ABC thought the statements dated December 31, 1971 would be used for analysis by credit-grantors or lenders they might decide to "window-dress" by such actions as deferring purchases.

Cash Flow Approximation

To analyze the ability of the firm to pay its obligations in the short run, a net balance of cash inflows over cash outlays during the next period would be a desirable figure to have. Unless a great deal of "insider" information about the affairs of the firm is known such a forecast cannot be accurately made. Instead a crude measure of net cash generation from operations in the preceding period can sometimes be derived from income statement information.

The "cash flow" figure is derived by adding back depreciation charges to the net income for the period. Depreciation is the major noncash expense recorded on most firms' books, and there is usually little relationship between the size of the depreciation charge and actual expenditures for renovation and replacement of the depreciating assets in the short run.

The use of this measure of cash flow for prediction purposes must assume unchanged operations of the firm in the following period. The implication is also made that the firm's acquisition of new assets, payment of old liabilities, and payment of dividends or other changes in capital structure are optional with the firm's management. The firm's cash flow may already be committed, for example, to the purchase of new machinery, and the external analyst may be unable to discover such commitments.

Other Sources of Short Run Information and Evaluations

Fortunately there are sources of external judgments regarding the credit-worthiness of most business firms. One of the most well-known financial reporting services, Dun & Bradstreet, Inc., summarizes information about individual business firms, and these reports are available to subscribers on a fee basis. Smaller business firms may be evaluated by local credit bureaus. In both cases the degree of information available to the service varies, and the informational content of the service's report can therefore be expected to vary.

If the external party desiring information about a company's prospects has sufficient bargaining power, the company may be requested to furnish special statements such as a cash budget or other specialized projection. A bank, for example, may require that a loan applicant furnish a cash forecast for the following year as a part of the formal application for a loan. The preparation of the forecast would of course be the responsibility of the employees of the firm, and should therefore be more accurate than any external analyst's projections.

The Term Structure of Interest Rates

Figure 11.1
Yields on Government Obligations

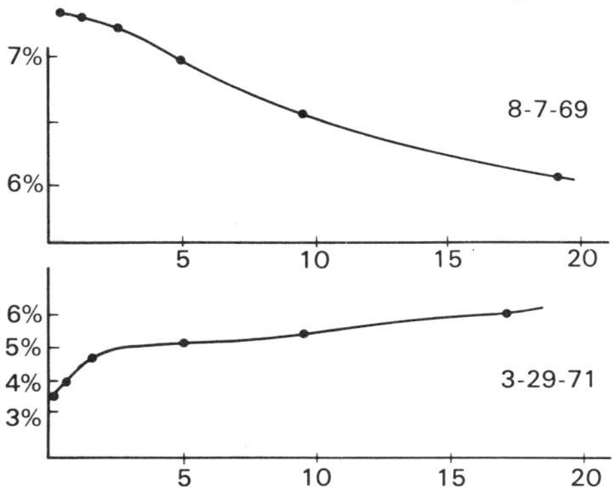

Figure 11.2
Yields on Corporate Debt Securities

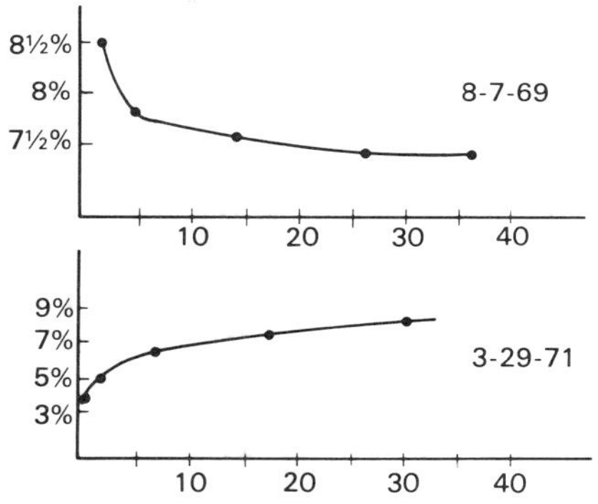

Figure 11.3
Definition of Interest Rates

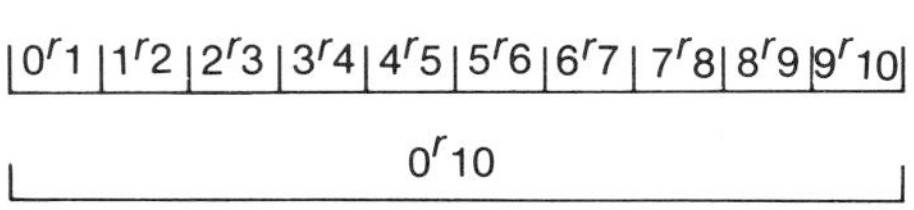

Interest rates vary by time to maturity, term, of security. Whether rates on short-term securities should be lower than rates on long-term securities has intrigued economists for years.[1] Financial institutions, in planning investment portfolios of debt securities, are influenced in their choices by the existing term structure of interest rates as well as their forecasts of future term structures. The relation between short and long-term rates is of interest to the corporation financial manager as well, because one of the decisions that must be made in debt financing is what term security to sell. That decision will be based in part on relative interest rates.

The term structure of interest rates is not constant over time, as shown in Figures 11.1 and 11.2. In Figure 11.1 are plotted the yields on representative federal government issues. (Because the longer-term issues are low coupon issues selling at a discount from par value, a part of the yield from holding those issues is subject to the lower capital gains tax rate, biasing the before-investor-tax yields downward.) On August 7, 1969, the yield curve was downward sloping, but on March 29, 1971, the yield curve was upward sloping.

Some representative interest rates paid by private corporations on newly issued securities are shown in Figure 11.2. Since the securities are new issues there should be no bias in the rates due to investor taxes. Again, though, the yield curve was downward sloping on August 7, 1969, and upward sloping on March 29, 1971.

Many explanations are possible for the slope of the yield curve, but only one, the "unbiased expectations theory," will be presented here. Briefly the unbiased expectations theory states that the interest rate on a long-term security is an average of the expected short-term interest rates during the life of the long-term security.

Suppose for example the long-term security is a ten-year bond, and the short-term interest rates are those on one-year securities. To demonstrate the theory a total of eleven interest rates must be used, the rate on the ten-year bond, designated as $_0r_{10}$, the rate on a one-year security that runs from time zero to time one, $_0r_1$, the rate on a one-year security that runs from time one to time two, $_1r_2$, and so on. To identify the interest rates two subscripts must be used, the first identifying the time point the interest rate begins to apply, the second identifying the time point ending the rate's applicability. For the ten-year time period the interest rates used are shown in Figure 11.3.

The relationship between the long-term rate $_0r_{10}$ and the one-period rates $_tr_{t+1}$ is given by the equation:

$$(1 + {_0r_{10}})^{10} = (1 + {_0r_1})(1 + {_1r_2} \ldots (1 + {_9r_{10}})$$

If each of the one-period rates is known the compound interest factor $(1 + {}_0r_{10})$ is the geometric average of the one-period compound interest factors $(1 + {}_tr_{t+1})$.

Suppose the one-period interest rates were known:

${}_0r_1 = 5\%$;
${}_1r_2 = 4\%$;
${}_2r_3 = 7\%$;
${}_3r_4 = 10\%$;
${}_4r_5 = 5\%$;
${}_5r_6 = 6\%$;
${}_6r_7 = 4\%$;
${}_7r_8 = 7\%$;
${}_8r_9 = 4\%$;
${}_9r_{10} = 8\%$;

From those rates the long-term interest rate could be computed:

$$(1 + {}_0r_{10})^{10} =$$
$$(1.05)(1.04)(1.07)(1.10)(1.05)(1.06)(1.04)(1.07)(1.04)(1.08)$$

$${}_0r_{10} = 6.2\%$$

According to the unbiased expectations theory the long-term interest rate is 6.2 percent because the expected short-term interest rates are 5 percent, 4 percent, 7 percent, and so forth.

The short-term interest rates ${}_tr_{t+1}$ are not actually measurable at time zero with the exception of the first rate, ${}_0r_1$. If the two observed interest rates are

${}_0r_1 = 5\%$ ${}_0r_{10} = 6.2\%$

the unbiased expectations theorists would say that evidently investors (the market) expect short-term interest rates to be higher than 5 percent during the life of the ten-year bond.

The analysis does not have to be made in terms of short-term rates applicable to only one period. For example the ten-year bond rate could be analyzed in terms of a three-year rate, ${}_0r_3$, covering the period from time zero to time three, and a forward rate, ${}_3r_{10}$, covering the period from time three to time ten. The ten-year bond rate would then be defined by the equation

$$(1 + {}_0r_{10})^{10} = (1 + {}_0r_3)^3(1 + {}_3r_{10})^7$$

If the observed interest rates are 7 percent ($= {}_0r_{10}$) on the 10-year bond and 5.5 percent ($= {}_0r_3$) on a three-year security, the unbiased expectations explanation of those rates would be based on the expected future interest rate ${}_3r_{10}$ being higher than the three-year rate of 5.5 percent, as it must be to satisfy the equation.

The unbiased expectations explanation of a rising yield curve as shown in the March 29, 1971, parts of Figures 11.1 and 11.2 would be that investors generally expected short-term rates to rise in the future. The falling yield curve parts (August 7, 1969) of those figures are explained by the statement that investors expected short-term interest rates to decline in the future.

The next question is why investors expect interest rates to change over time. A partial explanation can be found in the cyclical structure of interest rates, how interest rates vary with the level of aggregate business activity.

The Cyclical Behavior of Interest Rates

Interest rates tend to increase during periods of business expansion and decrease in recession. The natural tendencies of interest rates are probably intensified by monetary policy actions of the Federal Reserve and fiscal policy actions by the federal government. In the abstract "the" interest rate is the price of money, and supply-demand diagrams can be used to demonstrate the determination of an equilibrium interest rate as in Figure 11.4.

Figure 11.4
Supply and Demand for Money

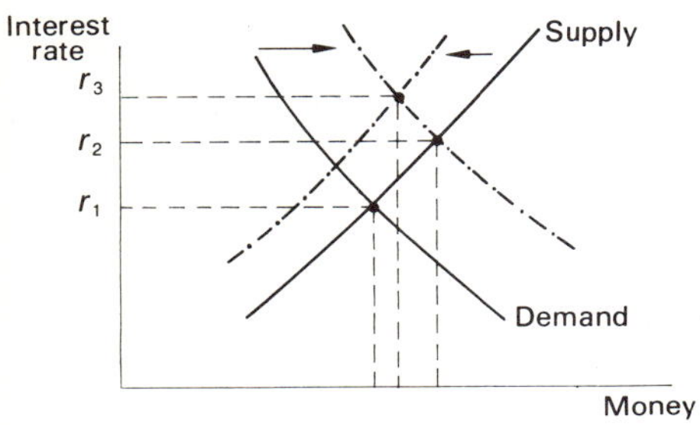

In Figure 11.4, r_1 is the beginning equilibrium interest rate, the rate where the supply and demand quantities of money are equal. If a business expansion occurs, the demand for money may shift to the right (increase) and a new higher equilibrium interest rate, r_2, result. If the business expansion results in inflation, the Federal Reserve may step in and reduce the aggregate reserves of the banking system, causing a shift of the supply curve to the left (a decrease) which results in a still higher equilibrium rate of interest, r_3. The reverse sequence can also be shown on the diagram, a recession causes a shift to the left of the demand curve, lowering interest rates, and if the Federal Reserve takes positive actions to increase bank reserves the supply curve shifts to the right, further lowering interest rates.

The usual theoretical economic analysis is in terms of an overall interest rate, but the cyclical movement of interest rates can be seen in time series of specific interest rates. One relatively stable interest rate of wide interest is the published prime rates of commercial banks. In Figure 11.5 the prime rate from 1966 through 1971 is shown again.

Figure 11.5
Prime Rates of Banks

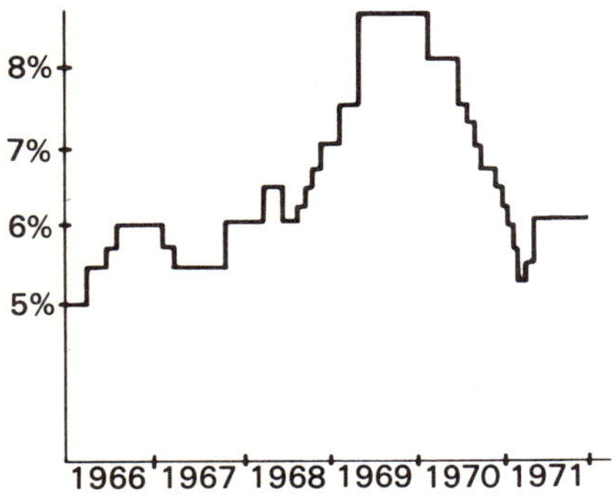

The cyclical behavior of this key interest rate can be seen from Figure 11.5. The prime rate probably understates the actual interest rate charged on bank loans somewhat in times of high published rates because banks can raise the effective interest rate by requiring larger compensatory balances and using somewhat higher standards for qualification as a prime borrower. It was said, for example, during the period of 1969 and 1970 when the published prime rate was 8.5 percent that the actual rate was about 10 percent for the best customers, that the banks for public relations didn't dare post a higher prime rate than 8.5 percent.

The year 1969 also showed how fast interest rates could rise in a short period of time due to the combination of business expansion and Federal Reserve restraint. The fall in the next year was even faster when recession developed and the Federal Reserve took dramatic action to supply banks with reserves.

The change in long-term rates was not as dramatic as shown by the plot of yields on new issues of Aa rated corporate bonds for the same periods in Figure 11.6. The lower variability of long-term interest rates is predictable from the theory of the term structure of interest rates presented above, since investors in long-term issues are well aware of the possible cyclical behavior of short-term interest rates.

To predict interest rates one must be aware of the likely course of aggregate business activity and the response of the Federal Reserve and federal government to that activity. Much time and effort is spent by business economists in such forecasting activity for financial institutions and large corporations. How accurate their forecasts are, particularly of resulting interest rate levels, is open to question.

The Risk Structure of Interest Rates

The third component of interest rates is the level of the interest rate with respect to the perceived risk of the capital supplier. Risk in this connection is the possibility of receiving some yield other than the nominal yield. The nominal yield is the yield computed on the assumption that all the interest payments will be made on time and the bond principal value will be repaid at maturity. An investor paying $1,000 for a bond that pays $80 interest annually has a nominal yield of 8 percent.

Figure 11.6
Yields on New Issues of Aa Corporate Bonds

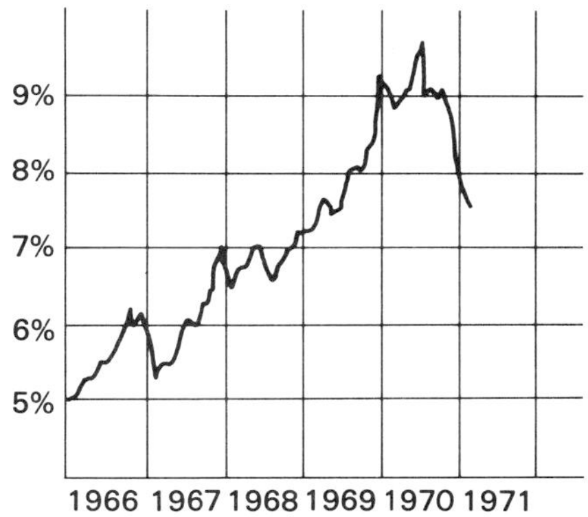

The buyer of a bond may not actually realize the nominal yield. The issuing corporation may default on the interest payments, either delaying them or failing to pay at all, or default on the payment of principal. The holder of the bond could realize a return greater than the nominal yield if the bond is called early at a premium, or if he sells the bond at a premium during a period when interest rates are low. If he sold the bond at a discount during high interest periods, his yield is less than the nominal yield. Therefore the nominal yield is just one yield that is possible for the bond-holder.

To approach the risk structure systematically a separation of "interest-rate risk" from "business risk" must be made. Interest-rate risk refers to the possibility of realizing other than the nominal yield due to changes in the prevailing level of interest rates. Examples of realized interest-rate risk are when the bond-holder sells at a discount that is due to higher prevailing rates than the nominal yield, at a premium due to lower prevailing rates, or when his bond is called by the issuer corporation. Business risk is therefore the possibility of the issuer's default on interest or principal payments.

Figure 11.7
Distribution of Possible Yields Illustrating Business Risk

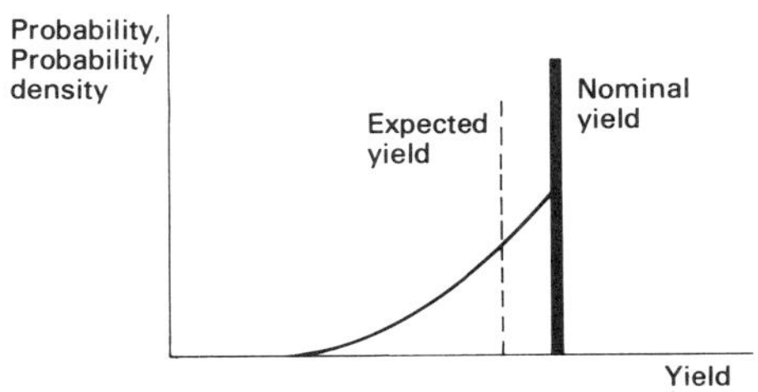

The distribution of possible yields when business risk is considered is skewed to the left, as shown in Figure 11.7. Because there is some probability of default, a probability that the bond-holder will receive less than the nominal yield, the expected yield is somewhat less than the nominal yield.

The expected yield on bonds should be greater than the interest rate available on risk-free securities. Assuming that bond-holders are risk-averse investors, to accept some degree of risk their expected return must be greater than the risk-free interest rate. For analysis of business risk the risk-free rate for comparison could be the highest rated private bond available, Aaa under Moody's rating system, where the degree of business risk is negligible.

In Table 11.1 the spread in nominal yields for Aaa through Baa, "lower medium grade obligations," are shown. Comparable figures are not available for *expected* yields, of course. The "risk spread" in yields during the period shown ranged from 1.61 percent to 0.94 percent.

TABLE 11.1
Selected Bond Yield Averages for Industrial Bonds

	Aaa	Aa	A	Baa
Nov. 1969	7.21	7.37	7.72	8.15
Dec. 1969	7.58	7.69	7.95	8.58
Jan. 1970	7.76	7.85	8.14	8.84
Feb. 1970	7.73	7.84	8.12	8.76
March 1970	7.61	7.79	7.95	8.57
April 1970	7.58	7.76	8.01	8.65
May 1970	7.76	7.92	8.25	8.82
June 1970	8.16	8.35	8.64	9.05
July 1970	8.19	8.32	8.69	9.22
Aug. 1970	7.83	8.03	8.56	9.32
Sept. 1970	7.79	7.97	8.55	9.29
Oct. 1970	7.75	7.92	8.50	9.22
Nov. 1970	7.75	7.96	8.47	9.28
Dec. 1970	7.31	7.51	8.06	8.92
Jan. 1971	7.01	7.18	7.64	8.46
Feb. 1971	6.68	6.91	7.31	8.04

Source: *Moody's Bond Record,* March 1971, published by Moody's Investors Service, Inc.

To analyze the degree of risk and the amount of risk spread applicable to a single security may be difficult since the bond-holder, likely to be a financial institution, holds a portfolio of bonds rather than a single security issue. Through diversification the holder's standard deviation of yield on the portfolio should be less than the standard deviation of the yield on a single bond issue.

For example suppose a bond-holder has an existing portfolio of bonds with expected yield of 8 percent and standard deviation of yield of 3 percent. Another bond issue becomes available with expected yield of 8 percent and standard deviation of yield of 5 percent when considered in isolation. If the correlation coefficient of yields between the individual issue and the bond-holder's present portfolio is 0.3, then the possible expected yields and standard deviation of yields that can be generated by including some of the new bond issue in the portfolio are shown in Figure 11.8:[2]

Figure 11.8
Possible Bond Portfolio Yields, First Example

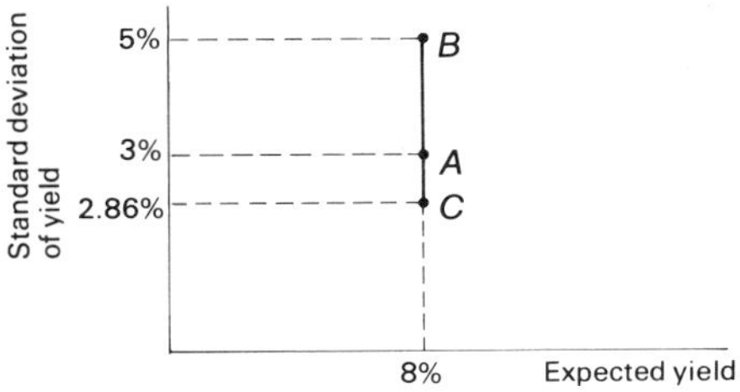

In Figure 11.8 point *A* represents the bond-holder's standard deviation of yield and expected yields before including any of the new bond issue in the portfolio, point *B* the standard deviation and expected yield if the portfolio consisted only of the new bond issue, and point *C* the portfolio results that could be obtained if the new issue is combined with the old portfolio in proportions to obtain the lowest standard deviation. Point *C* is attained when the portfolio is composed of 18 percent of the new bond issue and 82 percent of the old portfolio.

Any point on the solid line connecting *A*, *B*, and *C* in Figure 11.8 is attainable, so the optimum point should be *C* where the standard deviation of yield is 2.86 percent.

The example illustrates the difficulty in isolating the portfolio risk of an individual bond issue. By including this new issue in the portfolio the standard deviation is reduced from 3 percent to 2.86 percent. The incremental risk of the new bond issue in this example is therefore not the 5 percent standard deviation of yield.

The result of 2.86 percent for the standard deviation of return for the bond-holder in the example was based upon equal expected yields of the new issue and the old portfolio. Suppose the expected yield on the new issue were 9 percent instead of 8 percent, and all the other numbers of the example were unchanged. The possible portfolio combinations of the revised example are shown in Figure 11.9.

Figure 11.9
Possible Bond Portfolio Yields, Revised Example

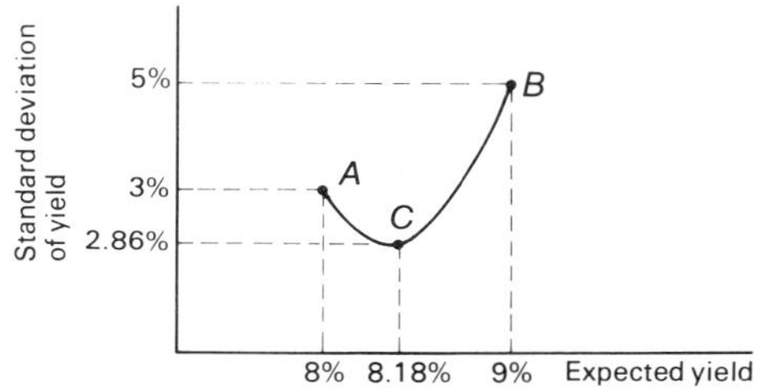

In Figure 11.9 the bond-holder would not necessarily choose point *C* to get the minimum standard deviation, but could choose any point between *C* and *B* and be still considered risk-averse. Therefore the incremental risk in the revised example depends on the bond-holder's actual choice of portfolio mix. It may be the 5 percent standard deviation of yield or some lower number. A more sophisticated economic model to resolve the incremental risk measurement difficulty is presented in the chapter appendix.

The setting of interest rates to allow for the incremental risk is the establishment of the nominal yield on the debt security, the rate that will be realized by the lender or bond-holder if the debtor does not default on his payments, as those rates listed in Table 11.1. If the incremental risk is judged as "high" the lender will require a high nominal yield, therefore hopefully increasing the expected yield.

External Analysis of Long-Term Debts

In assessing the financial risk of individual bond issues some sort of financial analysis is required. A purchaser of 20-year bonds, for example, expects to receive interest payments twice a year for twenty years, and then receive the repayment of the principal amount of the bond. Accordingly the prospective bond purchaser is interested in the financial prospects of the issuer over this long period of time.

The emphasis in analysis therefore shifts from net cash flows to the profitability of the firm. A business can operate for a few years with no profits, but to survive for the longer period profits are necessary.

A basic type of ratio is usually calculated based upon current operations of the firm—a coverage ratio to relate the earnings stream to the fixed charges associated with the debt servicing payments. If the bond issue is not a serial issue or one in which a sinking fund must be built up, the current cash requirements are the annual interest payments. The "number of times bond interest is earned" ratio is defined as

$$\frac{\text{Earnings Before Interest and Taxes}}{\text{Bond Interest}}$$

Earnings before interest and taxes is used as the numerator of the fraction because interest payments have "priority" over taxes. Interest payments are tax deductible.

The coverage ratio required will of course vary with the type of industry the firm is in. A ratio of 3 for a public utility, for example, would be adequate for the utility's bond issue to be considered low risk, high quality. But a coverage ratio of 3 for a company in a more cyclical industry such as steel production might be considered more risky. In general a ratio between 5 and 10 for the "average" manufacturing firm may be expected to yield a low-risk designation for the bond issue. Such a high number is necessary to yield an adequate "margin of safety," since the period projected is many years in the future.

The number of times bond interest is earned ratio does not consider repayment of the bond issue explicitly. The assumption may actually be made that this bond issue will be repaid from the proceeds of another issue at maturity date. In the case of a serial bond issue or a sinking fund issue the ratio may be altered to account for those required payments. Because those repayment amounts are not tax deductible the coverage ratio would be defined as

$$\frac{\text{Earnings Before Interest and Taxes}}{\text{Bond Interest} + \dfrac{\text{Sinking Fund Payment}}{1 - \text{tax rate}}}$$

Other types of ratios could be calculated that would compare the size of bond issue to fixed assets or to the book value of owners' equity. This type of ratio would emphasize the repayment of principal rather than the meeting of current interest payments.

Collateral for a bond issue, either the pledge of a specific asset in the case of a mortgage bond issue or the general pledge of assets in a debenture, may have very little real meaning to the bond-holder. First, a default on the bond issue would in most cases result in the issuing firm's going into a bankruptcy proceeding, where the courts are quite likely to insist on a reorganization of the firm, a restructuring of security issues, rather than dissolution of the firm. Even in the case of a mortgage bond issue the trustees of the indenture can initiate proceedings to seize the pledged assets, but then the question of salability of those assets arises. Frequently pledged assets are special purpose buildings or equipment that cannot be readily sold at reasonable prices. Accordingly collateral for long-term bond issues is usually deemphasized in assessing the risk characteristics of those issues.

A great deal of reliance is placed on professional bond rating services by prospective bond purchasers. Two financial services, Moody's Investors Service, Inc., and Standard & Poor's Corporation, regularly evaluate every public bond issue of significant size in the United States. The ratings achieved by those services are considered reliable enough that state regulatory commissions regularly refer to those ratings in establishing eligible lists of securities for their financial institutions to hold.

The two services use a slightly different letter code, but usually their ratings coincide as indicated in this partial listing of corporate bond grades:

Moody's	Standard & Poor's
Aaa	AAA
Aa	AA
A	A
Baa	BBB
Ba	BB

The services rate municipal bond issues as well as corporate bonds.

The two services do not attempt to describe the ratings techniques used in terms of a formula. They evidently combine an extensive analysis of financial statements with subjective judgments about the prospects of the industry, the quality of management, and other applicable factors. Because of the large numbers of analysts employed and the many years of experience of the two services, their rating results can be expected to be highly accurate.

Summary

Supplies of debt capital, short or long-term, to the nonfinancial corporation come mainly from financial institutions that act as intermediaries between savers and borrowers. For short-term loans the usual source is the corporation's commercial bank, although other institutions may be used and the corporation may rely partially on the commercial paper market. Longer-term debt securities may be sold in a public offering or privately placed with a financial institution. The usual buyer of corporate bonds will be an insurance company or pension fund, with appreciable numbers of individuals buying corporate bonds only in times of high interest rates.

The interest rates charged and the amounts of funds available from lenders depend first of all on the lender's assessment of the borrower's credit-worthiness. This assessment may be based on analysis of the borrower's financial statements but is more likely based on the specialist financial reporting services' information. The degree of business risk perceived by the lender will to some extent determine the spread between the nominal rate charged on the debt security and the rate available in the market on risk-free securities. If the degree of business risk is significant the lender will base his computations on the expected yield, a quantity somewhat less than the nominal yield, and the standard deviation of yield or other measure of variation considered in a portfolio context.

Besides business risk the lender (and borrower) has to contend with interest-rate risk—the possibility that prevailing yields for that type of security in the market will change, causing a capital gain or loss on the marketable security. Interest rates vary by the state of the business cycle and Federal Reserve monetary policy.

The borrowing corporation faces a choice of what maturity length debt to issue, and therefore the term structure of interest rates must be considered. At times short-term rates are lower than longer-term rates, but at other times the relationship is reversed. If the unbiased expectations theory is used to explain the term structure of interest rates, a higher long-term rate is the result of investors' expectations that short-term interest rates will rise above the existing level during the life of the long-term security. If the long-term rate is lower than present short-term rates, investors expect interest rates to fall in the future.

So interest rates in the debt markets are based on at least three factors, the business risk due to the borrower's financial characteristics, the general level of interest rates in the economy, and the term of the particular security. A corporation planning to borrow or issue debt securities must take all these factors into account when deciding whether to accept a capital-supplier's offer.

In the appendix to this chapter some additional theory regarding risk classification in a portfolio context is summarized. An individual security issue can be classified either by its yield's correlation with a market index of yield or by the excess return of the security, the expected return minus the risk-free interest rate.

Notes

[1] A good description of the term structure literature as well as other theories of interest rates can be found in James C. Van Horne, *Function and Analysis of Capital Market Rates* (Englewood Cliffs, N.J.: Prentice-Hall, 1970).

[2] If a is the fraction of the portfolio put into the new bond issue and $(1 - a)$ the fraction in the old combination of securities, then the standard deviation of yields is computed by the formula

$$\sigma = [a^2(5)^2 + (1-a)^2(3)^2 + 2a(1-a)(0.3)(5)(3)]^{1/2}$$

and the expected yield by the formula

$$E = a(8) + (1 - a)8$$

APPENDIX TO CHAPTER 11

The Risk Premium on Debt Securities and Risk Classifications

The difference between the expected yield on a risky security and the yield that can be obtained from a risk-free security is the risk premium. For example if the expected yield on a particular corporate bond is 8 percent and the yield on risk-free (possibly government bonds) securities is 5 percent, then that corporate bond's risk premium is 3 percent. Risk premium is not defined in terms of nominal yields, so the actual measurement of risk premiums is difficult. Nominal yields are quoted in the financial presses for securities, but the expected yield is less than the nominal yield if the security yield has some risk attached.

The risk premium for individual securities has been derived in theoretical models by Sharpe, Lintner, and Mossin.[1] In these models the individual security is analyzed with respect to its role in a portfolio of many securities. The concluding expression for the risk premium is based on the assumption that all prices of securities and their resulting yields are in equilibrium.

In this model the yield on the ith security (the one being investigated) is R_i, the yield on the risk-free security is R_f, and the yield on the portfolio of risky securities is R_m. Both R_i and R_m are stochastic variables with some statistical distribution, so the expected yield of the ith security is $E(R_i)$ and the expected yield on the portfolio of risky securities is $E(R_m)$.

The results of the model are expressed also in terms of the variance of the yield of the portfolio of risky securities, $\sigma^2(R_m)$, and the covariance of the yields of the ith security and the portfolio of risky securities, $\mathrm{Cov}(R_i R_m)$. In equilibrium the risk premium of the ith security is

$$E(R_i) - R_f = \frac{[E(R_m) - R_f]}{\sigma^2(R_m)} \mathrm{Cov}(R_i R_m)$$

The quantity

$$\frac{\mathrm{Cov}(R_i R_m)}{\sigma^2(R_m)}$$

is suggested as a measure of volatility of the ith security. That quantity is a measure of the variability in return of the ith security relative to the variability in return of the portfolio of risky securities.

The quantity $[E(R_m) - R_f]$ is the risk premium for the portfolio of risky securities. When divided by the variance,

$$\frac{[E(R_m) - R_f]}{\sigma^2(R_m)}$$

the ratio is called the aggregate reward to variability measure since the numerator is the risk premium, the reward, and the denominator is the measure of variability of return. The ratio can be interpreted as the market price of variability (or risk).

The numerator of the volatility measure, $\mathrm{Cov}(R_i R_m)$, serves as a measure of the individual security's variability. The risk premium for the ith security is therefore a "price times quantity equals total value" expression. The market price of variability is market determined, and the amount of variability is a characteristic of the individual security.

To illustrate how this valuation equation could be used suppose that the average return on corporate bonds for a period of time was determined to be

$$E(R_m) = 8.5\%$$

and the risk-free return on bonds (measured by reference to federal government bonds) was

$$R_f = 6\%$$

If the variance of return on the set of corporate bonds was

$$\sigma^2(R_m) = 0.0016$$

then the market price of variability is

$$\frac{E(R_m) - R_f}{\sigma^2(R_m)} = \frac{8.5\% - 6\%}{0.0016} = 15.625$$

To predict the risk premium for an individual security the covariance $\text{Cov}(R_i R_m)$ must be known. Rather than estimate covariances directly it is easier to decompose it into its parts:

$$\text{Cov}(R_i R_m) = \rho_{im}\sigma(R_i)\sigma(R_m)$$

and estimate the parts. $\sigma(R_m)$ is already determined to be 0.04. The standard deviation of the ith security is somewhat higher, suppose 0.09. The correlation between the ith security's yield and the yield on all corporate bonds should be relatively high, 0.8 for the example. The covariance is therefore

$$\text{Cov}(R_i R_m) = (0.8)(0.09)(0.04) = 0.00288$$

The risk premium for the ith security should therefore be

$$15.625(0.00288) = 4.5\%$$

Since the risk-free interest rate R_f is 6%, the expected return on the ith security must be

$$4.5\% + 6\% = 10.5\%$$

if the prices and returns are in equilibrium.

The individual security in the example would be classified as relatively risky because of its high expected yield, or possibly because of its individual standard deviation of return, $\sigma(R_i)$, of 9 percent. A more exact measure of risk in the market context is the volatility measure

$$\frac{\text{Cov}(R_i R_m)}{\sigma^2(R_m)} = \frac{0.00288}{0.0016} = 1.8$$

Because this measure is greater than one the security can be characterized as "riskier than the market average."

Sharpe[2] has suggested that securities with volatility indices greater than one be classified as "aggressive" and those with indices less than one be classified as "defensive." In equilibrium this classification can be made on the basis of comparing the expected yield on the security with the expected yield of the portfolio since if

$$\frac{\text{Cov}(R_i R_m)}{\sigma^2(R_m)} > 1$$

then $E(R_i) > E(R_m)$. Of course the classification could also be expressed in terms of the risk premiums because

$$[E(R_i) - R_f] > [E(R_m) - R_f]$$

under the same circumstances.

Notes

[1] William F. Sharpe, "Capital Asset Prices: A Theory of Market Equilibrium under Conditions of Risk," *Journal of Finance*, September 1964; John Lintner, "Security Prices, Risk, and Maximal Gains from Diversification," *Journal of Finance*, December 1965; and Jan Mossin, "Equilibrium in a Capital Asset Market," *Econometrica*, October 1966. A reconciliation and clarification appears in Eugene F. Fama, "Risk, Return and Equilibrium: Some Clarifying Comments," *Journal of Finance*, March 1968.

[2] William F. Sharpe, *Portfolio Theory and Capital Markets* (New York: McGraw-Hill, 1970).

Chapter 11 Questions

1. Because of the large amount of fixed obligations, any variability in returns from assets will be magnified in the return on equity of a financial intermediary. Does this leverage effect make investing in the common stock of a financial institution more or less desirable to an investor?
2. If the services of professional analysts such as the bond rating services and stock brokers are available, why should an individual lender or investor ever bother to perform an independent analysis of a corporation?
3. The competition for deposits among banks is restrained by the Federal Reserve's regulations establishing maximum interest rates on time deposits. How can banks compete in other ways for those deposits?
4. Interest cannot legally be paid by banks on demand deposits. Do other services performed for depositors constitute an implicit interest payment?
5. If a bank invests in nonmarketable assets such as loans, in theory the bank may not be able to meet all its demand liabilities. What stops a general wave of bankruptcy from occurring in the commercial banking system then?
6. If a savings and loan association invests such a large proportion of its assets in long-term residential mortgages how can it preserve the liquidity of its deposits?
7. When interest rate levels in the economy change, the savings and loan associations and mutual savings banks have potentially very large changes in profits. Why?
8. A life insurance company's cash requirements are usually estimable with a very high degree of accuracy. What effect should this have on the investments of these companies?
9. Why is it necessary for state regulatory commissions to regulate the investment practices of life insurance companies?

10. The existence of the Federal Deposit Insurance Corporation for banks and the Federal Savings and Loan Insurance Corporation for savings and loans means that the small depositor (up to $20,000) doesn't have to worry about the safety of his funds. Does the existence of the FDIC and FSLIC mean that the institution's managers can engage in a more aggressive investment policy?

11. A fire and casualty insurance company has two sources of income, from underwriting and from the investment portfolio. Many of these companies' insurance rates are regulated by state commissions. Is it likely that the commission will take investment income into account in setting insurance rates and therefore penalize good portfolio selection and reward poor portfolio management?

12. If a finance company has a wide seasonal variation in the demand for loans, its seasonal need for funds might be met by selling commercial paper. Why is it usually considered necessary that the finance company maintain a line of credit with commercial banks as well?

13. Why aren't all pension funds regulated by a state or federal commission? Is it possible that after an employee retires he will be informed by his former employer that the size of his pension has been reduced or even eliminated?

14. What other ratios besides those described in the chapter could be from the balance sheet and income statement to measure:

a. Short-term liquidity?
b. Long-term liquidity?
c. Profitability?
d. Efficiency of Operations?

15. What other devices can be used to "window-dress" the end of period financial statements?

16. Should deviation from a normal ratio value, as determined from industry averages, always indicate significantly different operations of the corporation being analyzed?

17. Does a ratio simplify analysis over a technique using the two numbers in unadjusted form?

18. Why may the cash flow of a corporation be a more significant figure than the corporation's earnings?

19. Do professional security analysts have access to more information than individual investors?

20. What other explanations of the term structure of interest rates are possible?

21. How can the manager of the corporation's marketable securities portfolio take advantage of an upward-sloping yield curve? How about a down-sloping yield curve?

22. What is the explanation of high interest rates during a recession?

23. Do interest rates always reflect investors' expectations of inflation as well as their other expectations?

Chapter 11 Problems

1. A bank manager is trying to solve the problem of the appropriate level of secondary reserves which are to be invested in Treasury bills. The normal balances of the principal balance sheet accounts are:

Assets		Liabilities and capital	
Reserve deposits in the Federal Reserve	52	Demand deposits	300
		Time deposits	400
Cash in vault	30	Capital	100
Marketable securities	218		
Loans	500		
	800		800

The bank must maintain reserve deposits in the Federal Reserve equal to 12 percent of demand deposits and 4 percent of time deposits. The immediate liquidity policy is to keep cash in vault at 30 at all times.

Based on past experience the largest seasonal drain from demand deposits will be 80 and from time deposits 50. It is considered desirable to maintain loans at their normal balance and handle the seasonal deposit drain from the liquidation of secondary reserves (part of marketable securities). What is the minimum level of secondary reserves when balances are normal?

2. The corporate tax rate on ordinary income above $25,000 is 48 percent, and on long-term capital gains it is 30 percent. Eighty-five percent of the dividends from preferred stock or common stock are excluded in the computation of a corporation's taxable income. A financial institution has a choice between making loans where the interest income is fully taxable or investing in securities with some degree of tax shelter. The interest rate, the before-tax yield, on loans is 8 percent. Ignoring risk characteristics, compute the minimum before-tax yield necessary on these alternatives to loans:

a. Municipal securities held for interest income.
b. Preferred stocks held for dividend income.
c. Common stocks held for dividend income.
d. Common stocks or other assets held for capital gains.

3. Because of the 48 percent corporate income tax rate, it is sometimes said that the federal government bears 48 percent of the risk of corporations' investments. Using a security investment with this distribution of possible taxable profits:

Taxable profit	Probability
100	0.1
200	0.1
300	0.8

calculate the mean and standard deviation of:

a. Taxable profits.
b. Federal income taxes on the profit.
c. After-tax profits of the corporation.

4. The last financial statements for Subject Corp. were as follows:

Balance Sheet as of December 31 (amounts in $000)

Current assets		Current liabilities	
Cash	1,500	Accounts payable	3,000
Accounts receivable	3,400	Accrued taxes	500
Inventories	3,100	Long-term liabilities	
Marketable securities	500	Bonds (8%, due 1992)	6,000
Fixed assets		Owners' equity	
Equipment	9,200	Preferred stock (7%)	3,000
Accumulated depreciation	(2,100)	Common stock	8,300
Buildings	10,200	Retained earnings	11,900
Accumulated depreciation	(1,400)		
Land	8,300		
	32,700		32,700

Income Statement for the year ended December 31 (amounts in $000)

Sales		25,300
Cost of goods sold		
Beginning inventory	2,900	
Purchases	17,200	
Total	20,100	
Ending inventory	3,100	
		(17,000)
Gross profit on sales		8,300
Expenses		
Wages	3,200	
Depreciation	1,200	
Interest	480	
Miscellaneous expenses	320	
		(5,200)
Net income before taxes		3,100
Corporate income taxes		(1,500)
Net income after taxes		1,600
Dividends on preferred stock		(210)
Dividends on common stock		(400)
Increase in retained earnings		990

Calculate the following:
a. Current ratio.
b. Acid-test ratio.
c. Accounts receivable turnover ratio.
d. Inventory turnover ratio.
e. Accounts payable turnover ratio.
f. Cash flow.

5. (Refer to problem 4.) On December 30 Subject Corp. purchased $1,200,000 of merchandise on open account. If that purchase had been deferred to January 2 of the following year, some of the December 31

account balances would have changed. Recalculate, assuming the purchase was deferred, the following:

a. Current ratio.
b. Acid-test ratio.
c. Inventory turnover ratio.
d. Accounts payable turnover ratio.

Chapter 11 References

Altman, Edward J. "Financial Ratios, Discriminant Analysis and the Prediction of Corporate Bankruptcy." *Journal of Finance*, September 1968.

Bierman, Harold, Jr. "Measuring Financial Liquidity." *Accounting Review*, October 1960.

"Corporate Pension Funds and Capital Markets." Federal Reserve Bank of Cleveland. *Monthly Review*, November 1966.

Finley, J. A. "Life Industries Changing Portfolio in 1960's." *Commercial and Financial Chronicle*, November 21, 1968.

Foulke, Roy A. *Practical Financial Statement Analysis*. 5th Ed. New York: McGraw-Hill, 1961.

Hart, O. H. "Life Insurance Companies and the Equity Capital Market." *Journal of Finance*, May 1965.

Hurley, E. M. "Business Financing by Business Finance Companies." *Federal Reserve Bulletin*, October 1968.

Innocenti, R. E. "Stock-Bond Split Decision for Pension Funds." *Financial Analysts Journal*, November 1969.

Johnson, A. W. "Interpretation of Financial Statements." *Financial Analysts Journal*, November 1968.

Kellog, C. M. "Insurance Company Investments." *Best's Insurance News*, September 1968.

Meigs, A. J. "Changing Role of Banks." *Journal of Finance*, May 1965.

Pogue, Thomas F., and Soldofsky, Robert M. "What's in a Bond Rating." *Journal of Financial and Quantitative Analysis,*, June 1969.

Rosen, L. S., and Decoster, D. T. "Funds Statements: A Historical Perspective." *Accounting Review*, January 1969.

Shapiro, R. "Financial Intermediaries, Credit Availability and Aggregate Demand." *Journal of Finance*, September 1966.

Van Horne, James C. *The Function and Analysis of Capital Market Rates*. Englewood Cliffs, N.J.: Prentice-Hall, 1970.

12 THE EQUITIES MARKETS

The market for corporate equities can be separated into the primary market where newly-issued securities are sold and the secondary market where existing securities are traded. While a corporate financial manager may seem to be interested mainly in the primary market where new shares may be sold, his responsibility to the shareholders of the corporation requires his attention to be directed to the secondary market as well. The objective of financial (and other) management should be to maximize the well-being of the corporation's owners, and that objective will require taking account of the market value of the corporation's outstanding securities. The major participants in the equities markets are individuals, mutual funds, and certain financial intermediaries such as insurance companies and pension funds. About 15 percent of the individuals in the United States are direct owners of common stocks, but many more individuals own stocks through the collective form of mutual funds and through their claims on financial intermediaries.

The investment behavior of individuals is based partially on the institutional framework of the U.S. tax system. Certain forms of investment are promoted through tax incentives (perhaps inadvertently), and the form of income sought from direct security investment by individuals is conditioned on that form's treatment for taxes. When the average individual buys common stocks, for example, his objective is likely to be capital gains rather than dividend income.

Analysis of individual securities is continually performed both by individual investors and professional financial analysts. The basic idea of both groups is to find a security whose appraisal value is greater than the present market price. Hopefully once the security is purchased the "market" will reevaluate the security and a capital gain will result. If an overvalued security is found, it is a candidate for a short sale or elimination from the portfolio.

The appraisal value is reached by the application of procedures familiar from earlier chapters. In the absence of any consideration of risk the present value of the estimated stream of future dividends is the appraisal value. The future stream of dividends depend on the corporation's current earnings, earnings retention policy, and its investment opportunities. Without all this information most analysts have to be content with applying a price-earnings multiplier to current earnings. The multiplier may be based on an absolute standard or on current price-earnings multiples in the market.

When risk measures are taken into the appraisal process, each security must be considered as part of a portfolio. Some simplification of the required formulas is possible by use of the Sharpe-Lintner valuation formula, introduced in the appendix to Chapter 11. In this formula only the means and variances of the security under question, the market average of securities, and the risk-free security must be taken into consideration.

The analysis performed will not be any better than the information on which it is based. Accordingly as much published and unpublished data about the corporation under study as possible must be gathered. Since so much depends on accounting earnings, the analyst should be fully aware of the accounting treatment given depreciation and other expense amortization, as well as the revenue realization principles used.

Since some investors seek to avoid the problem of choosing individual securities for their investment portfolios by buying mutual funds, the evaluation of mutual fund performance is another problem that arises. The methods of evaluation are similar to those of appraising common stocks, and in fact the shares of a mutual fund can be considered as another common stock. The Sharpe-Lintner formula forms the basis of the most sophisticated evaluation methods.

Federal Income Taxes of Individuals

Three levels of income taxes are commonly imposed on the income of individuals: federal, state, and city income taxes. Because of the wide variability of rates and provisions it will not be possible to cover state and city taxes adequately, and therefore only the main provisions of the federal income tax code will be reviewed.

Income received by the individual may consist of wages or salaries, dividends, interest, unincorporated business income, capital gains, rents, royalties, pensions, and annuities. Some variety of special treatment is given to types of income such as dividends, interest on municipal securities, long-term capital gains, and income from mineral production. Special adjustments are made for such payments as contributions of the individual to self-employment retirement plans.

The computation of taxes due follows a four-step procedure if no special treatment items are reported by the taxpayer. First, the income from various sources is added to arrive at "adjusted gross income." From that total two subtractions are made to arrive at "taxable income." The first subtraction is an allowance for personal exemptions, and the second is either an amount equal to the standard deduction or the total of itemized deductions.

The allowance for personal exemptions is $750 beginning in 1973. A man with a wife and two children filing a joint return would therefore be able to deduct $3,000 for personal exemptions.

The taxpayer has the option of using the standard deduction or itemizing deductions, whichever will give the higher total deduction. If he uses the standard deduction the amount of the standard deduction beginning in 1973 is the lower of 15% of adjusted gross income, or $2,000.

The deductions that can be itemized in lieu of the standard deduction include a portion of medical and dental expenses, most state and local government taxes paid, charitable contributions, interest expenses, and some other miscellaneous deductions. Usually it is to the advantage of individuals to itemize deductions if house payments are being made because of the high interest charges and property taxes incurred. Itemized deductions form the basis of certain tax-avoidance techniques, as will be demonstrated later in the chapter.

Once taxable income is computed the tax rates applicable are presented in Table 12.1. Rates are differentiated by the marital status of the taxpayer, with three categories, married, unmarried, and head of household. A head-of-household rate is applicable to a single person maintaining a residence with one or more other related individuals living there—typically a widow or widower with children.

TABLE 12.1
Federal Income Tax Rates

Taxable income	Tax on column 1	% on excess	Taxable income	Tax on column 1	% on excess
Married individuals filing joint returns					
...	...	14	36,000	10,340	45
1,000	140	15	40,000	12,140	48
2,000	290	16	44,000	14,060	50
3,000	450	17	52,000	18,060	53
4,000	620	19	64,000	24,420	55
8,000	1,380	22	76,000	31,020	58
12,000	2,260	25	88,000	37,980	60
16,000	3,260	28	100,000	45,180	62
20,000	4,380	32	120,000	57,580	64
24,000	5,660	36	140,000	70,380	66
28,000	7,100	39	160,000	83,580	68
32,000	8,660	42	180,000	97,180	69
			200,000	110,980	70
Heads of households					
...	...	14	36,000	11,280	48
1,000	140	16	38,000	12,240	51
2,000	300	18	40,000	13,260	52
4,000	660	19	44,000	15,340	55
6,000	1,040	22	50,000	18,640	56
8,000	1,480	23	52,000	19,760	58
10,000	1,940	25	64,000	26,720	59
12,000	2,440	27	70,000	30,260	61
14,000	2,980	28	76,000	33,920	62
16,000	3,540	31	80,000	36,400	63
18,000	4,160	32	88,000	41,440	64
20,000	4,800	35	100,000	49,120	66
22,000	5,500	36	120,000	62,320	67
24,000	6,220	38	140,000	75,720	68
26,000	6,980	41	160,000	89,320	69
28,000	7,800	42	180,000	103,120	70
32,000	9,480	45			
Unmarried individuals					
...	...	14	20,000	5,230	38
500	70	15	22,000	5,990	40
1,000	145	16	26,000	7,590	45
1,500	225	17	32,000	10,290	50
2,000	310	19	38,000	13,290	55
4,000	690	21	44,000	16,590	60
6,000	1,110	24	50,000	20,190	62
8,000	1,590	25	60,000	26,390	64
10,000	2,090	27	70,000	32,790	66
12,000	2,630	29	80,000	39,390	68
14,000	3,210	31	90,000	46,190	69
16,000	3,830	34	100,000	53,090	70
18,000	4,510	36			
Married individuals filing separate returns					
...	...	14	22,000	7,030	50
500	70	15	26,000	9,030	53
1,000	145	16	32,000	12,210	55
1,500	225	17	38,000	15,510	58
2,000	310	19	44,000	18,990	60
4,000	690	22	50,000	22,590	62
6,000	1,130	25	60,000	28,790	64
8,000	1,630	28	70,000	35,190	66
10,000	2,190	32	80,000	41,790	68
12,000	2,830	36	90,000	48,590	69
14,000	3,550	39	100,000	55,490	70
16,000	4,330	42			
18,000	5,170	45			
20,000	6,070	48			

In addition to the tax rates presented in the table there is a maximum marginal tax rate on "earned income" of 50%, and an additional 10% tax on certain tax preference items.

Suppose the federal income taxes due for an individual, married with two children, are computed. His income consists solely of a salary of $15,000. The personal exemption allowance would be $3,000, and if the standard deduction is used it would be $2,000 (the lower of 15% of $15,000 or $2,000). Deductions would be itemized if they total more than $2,000. The following deductions are assumed:

Medical and dental expenses	$ 300
State and local taxes paid	900
Charitable contributions	200
Interest paid	1,300
	$2,700

$2,700 is greater than $2,000, so the taxpayer itemizes deductions.

From adjusted gross income of $15,000, $3,000 personal exemption allowance and $2,700 itemized deductions are subtracted, leaving $9,300 taxable income. The tax from Table 12.1 is:

Tax on $8,000	=	$1,380
22% of $1,300	=	286
		$1,666

Besides the federal income tax of $1,666, the individual will be subject to a social security tax, and possibly state and city income taxes as well.

Some Examples of Tax Planning and Tax Avoidance

Special treatment is given certain income sources and expenditures. The first $100 of dividend income is excluded in the computation of adjusted gross income, and all interest income from municipal bonds is excluded (is tax-free).

A self-employed individual can exclude from adjusted gross income payments to a qualifying retirement plan (a "Keogh Act" plan) up to 10% of income or $2,500, whichever is lower. Accordingly tax can be delayed on that amount of income until the person begins to draw retirement benefits after the age of 59-1/2. The earnings of the retirement fund is not taxed either, the tax being imposed only upon payment of the benefits. Because such a long interval of time exists between receipt of the income and the tax on the retirement benefits, a strong incentive exists for self-employed individuals to contribute to such retirement plans.

An employer's contributions to a pension fund are not taxed as income to the employee, nor is the income generated within the fund taxed. Therefore employees through their union's negotiations frequently prefer increased pension benefits to increased direct wages because of the tax treatment.

A long-term (asset held more than six months) capital gain is treated differently from ordinary income under the tax code. The taxpayer has the option of considering only half the gain as income, subject to the tax rates in Table 12.1, or of using a maximum tax rate of 25% on the first $50,000 of long-term capital gains. In addition a portion of the capital gain may come under a special tax imposed for the first time in the Tax Reform Act of 1969, a 10% tax on a specified list of tax-preference items.

The list of tax-preference items includes the excluded half of long-term capital gains, some part of percentage depletion, excess investment interest, excess amortization, and other items as well. For computation of the 10% tax-preference tax, the individual can deduct $30,000 plus the income taxes due that year from the total of tax preference items.

For the very high-income taxpayer the *marginal* rate of taxes on long-term capital gains would be 36.5%. For lower bracket taxpayers it will be less, possibly as low as 7%. In the computation of the 36.5% marginal tax rate, the taxpayer's other capital gains are assumed larger than $50,000, and his other tax-preference items total more than $30,000 plus his income taxes on income. Therefore an incremental $1 in long-term capital gains is subject to a regular tax of 35cents (50cents at a 70% tax rate) plus an amount of 1.5cents under the 10% tax-preference items tax. His tax-preference amount on the capital gain is 50cents, the excluded portion of the gain, which is reduced by the income tax due on the gain of 35cents, leaving 15cents subject to the 10% tax.

The highest possible tax rate on long-term capital gains is therefore 36.5%, which is considerably less than the top rate of 70% for ordinary "nonearned" income. For lower bracket taxpayers, the effective rate of tax on long-term capital gains will be less than 36.5%, of course, and always less than ordinary income tax rates. The conclusion is that it will always be advantageous to the individual taxpayer to receive income as a long-term capital gain rather than as ordinary income.

Income received from mineral production is subject to special rules regarding allowances for depletion of the mineral deposit. As an alternative to basing depletion allowances on the original cost of the mineral deposit, a special percentage computation is possible based on the value of the mineral production. The rate allowable in oil and gas production for example is 22% of the value of production with a limitation of 50% of the net income from that production. The amount of depletion charged by the percentage method may be considered to be partly a tax-preference item subject to an additional 10% tax. The 22% depletion allowance does not automatically mean that 22% of oil and gas production revenue is tax-free, but that the revenue does have certain tax advantages that other income does not.

Mineral exploration carries an additional tax advantage, in that intangible drilling expenses can be treated as a current expense and do not have to be capitalized and subsequently amortized. This write-off of intangible drilling expenses is one way of converting ordinary income into a lower-taxed form of income.

For example suppose a wealthy individual who pays very high tax rates (70% on ordinary income) decides to drill an oil well. He spends $100,000, of which $80,000 is counted as intangible drilling expenses. Now suppose sufficient production is achieved from the well to justify a sales price of $100,000. His cost basis of the well is $20,000, so he has a capital gain of $80,000. If the holding period is longer than six months he has converted $80,000 of ordinary income into a long-term capital gain, possibly saving $26,800 in income taxes [$80,000(0.70 – 0.365) = $26,800]. This savings is achieved without the use of the 22% depletion allowance entering into the computation since he did not hold the well long enough to produce an appreciable quantity of oil. If he had held the well for production of oil, those income receipts would have been subject to the special depletion allowance treatment.

Other tax-avoidance and tax-delaying techniques are possible due to the special depreciation methods allowable by the tax code. For example on new residential rental property the "double-the-declining-balance" method or the "sum-of-the-years-digits" method can be for calculating depreciation for tax purposes, so long as the amount of depreciation charged does not exceed 200% of that which would be charged if the straight-line method of computing depreciation were used. The use of accelerated depreciation delays tax on income to later periods, and may result in certain circumstances in the conversion of ordinary income into long-term capital gains, thereby "avoiding" some tax on income.

An example will help to demonstrate the accelerated depreciation tax treatment. Suppose an apartment house costing $200,000 is constructed on land worth $50,000. The gross rentals from apartments will be $40,000 per year, and *cash* operating expenses are $15,000 per year. The "cash flow" generated by the apartments would then be

$40,000	rentals
– 15,000	cash operating expenses
$25,000	cash flow

If the straight-line depreciation method were used, under an assumed 40-year life for the building, the annual depreciation charge would be 2½% of $200,000 (land is not depreciable), or $5,000. The net income using the straight-line method, which might be called the "true income," is

$25,000 – $5,000 = $20,000

For tax purposes the double-the-declining-balance method would be elected. Under this method the straight-line percentage is doubled and applied to the declining net value of the asset. For the example the first year's depreciation would be $10,000 (5% of $200,000), the second year's $9,500 (5% of $190,000), and so forth. For tax purposes therefore the net income shown for the first year will be

$25,000 – $10,000 = $15,000

The $5,000 of excessive depreciation is a "tax shelter" in this example. Of course the amount of tax shelter will decline over time, eventually becoming negative if the building is held long enough by the investor.

So far the residential rental property has been shown to be a tax-delaying device for the owner. Tax is avoided under certain conditions of the sale of the building. If the building is sold before the end of 16 2/3 years (200 months), a part of the excessive depreciation of the accelerated method over the straight-line method must be considered ordinary income at that time rather than a long-term capital gain. Suppose for example that the building and land were sold for $245,000 at the end of the first year. The book value for tax purposes might seem to be:

200,000	original cost of building
– 10,000	accumulated depreciation
190,000	net value of building
50,000	cost of land
240,000	total

yielding a long-term capital gain of $5,000, but the tax code would require in this case that the $5,000 be treated as ordinary income if it is applicable to the depreciable property. If the gain can be identifiable as being due to appreciation in the value of the land, it would be treated as a long-term capital gain.

If the building and land were sold after 16 2/3 years the gain over tax book-value would evidently qualify as a long-term capital gain subject to the lower tax rates. Of course any gain attributable to increases in the value of the land would be treated as an ordinary long-term capital gain so long as the land is held over six months.

Another tax-avoidance measure is frequently encountered that uses the itemized deductions provisions for interest and state and local taxes paid. Typically this itemized deduction route involves the debt-financed purchase of undeveloped land, with a period of holding aimed at a long-term capital gain.

For example suppose that a piece of land is purchased for $100,000. The buyer arranges an 80 percent term loan on the land that calls for the payment of 8 percent interest annually with repayment of the loan principal at the end of five years. If property taxes are 2 percent of $100,000, or $2,000 a year, the buyer would have itemized deductions of $8,400 a year while he held the land. The $8,400 is applied against ordinary income, of course. The buyer hopes that the land will appreciate in value and that he can then sell it and treat any proceeds in excess of $100,000 as a long-term capital gain. If his appreciation were exactly 8.4 percent per year he would have converted $8,400 of ordinary income into a long-term capital gain. It is possible that the $8,400 would fall under the 10 percent tax-preferences tax, diminishing slightly the tax advantages of this investment.

This section is intended to illustrate some provisions of the federal income tax laws that affect individuals' investment planning and management. The tax laws are changed by Congress periodically, and the interpretation of those laws varies as court decisions are delivered on particular issues. Therefore competent tax advice should be sought from a tax lawyer or tax accountant when specific tax planning is undertaken.

The tax code results in at least three incentives that bias individual investment programs in ways that are significant for an understanding of the equities markets. First the tax deferral of pension fund payments and income probably diverts some funds away from individual investment programs into the institutionalized form of a pension fund. The tax deduction through itemization of interest and property taxes makes home ownership less expensive than renting when the house payment is the same size as the rental payment. In addition the chance to achieve a high degree of leverage through the low down payment typically required allows the home owner to hedge against inflation. Counterbalancing this bias toward home ownership are the tax shelters built into the ownership of rental housing. If a sufficient number of investors are attracted into providing apartments for rent, rental rates should tend to be lower than in the absence of the tax shelter. The existence of two basic tax rates, one on ordinary income and a lower rate on long-term capital gains, means that considerable efforts will be made toward converting income into the lower-taxed form. Even if elaborate conversion schemes such as the oil well drilling and vacant land purchase examples are not engaged in, the average investor is more likely to buy common stocks or other equities rather than debt securities because of the greater chance of capital gains.

Present Value Analysis of Common Stocks

In analyzing a common stock for potential purchase the emphasis here is placed on potential capital gains rather than dividend income. The desired objective is to buy stocks that will appreciate materially in price over some reasonable period of time, at which point the capital gain is realized through the sale of the stocks. Because of the different tax treatment for long-term capital gains, it will usually be desirable to anticipate at least a six-month holding period for the selected stocks.

The theoretical models for valuing a common stock presented in earlier chapters were based on an infinite holding period where the income receipts took the form of dividends paid. In the case of a constant rate of growth of dividends the present value of the stream of dividends was represented by

$$P_0 = \sum_{i=1}^{i=\infty} \left[\frac{1+g}{1+r}\right]^i = \frac{D_0(1+g)}{r-g}$$

In equation (12-1) P_0 is the present value of the dividend stream at time zero, D_0 is the base dividend quantity (the amount paid just prior to the acquisition of the stock), g is the rate of growth per period of dividends, and r is the required rate of return of the evaluator of the common stock. If, for example, a stock was under consideration where a base dividend of \$1 has just been paid, the dividend is expected to grow at a rate of 6 percent per period, and the required rate of return is 10 percent, equation (12-1) would yield a present value of

$$\frac{\$1(1+0.06)}{0.10-0.06}=\$26.50$$

This present value of \$26.50 is an appraised value of that common stock, and is not necessarily equal to the current market price of that stock.

As time passes the appraisal value will grow at the same rate as the dividend. The present value computed at time one, P_1, would be

$$P_1=\sum_{i=2}^{i=\infty}\frac{D_0(1+g)^i}{(1+r)^{i-1}}=\frac{D_0(1+g)^2}{r-g}$$

That is, the purchaser of the stock at time one would receive the first dividend at time two, one period from his purchase time. For the numerical example the first dividend received would be \$1.1236, which is

$$D_0(1+g)^2=\$1(1+0.06)^2$$

Equation (12-2) can be compared with equation (12-1), yielding the result that

$$P_1=(1+g)P_0$$

This result would obviously apply to any two successive time periods. Therefore the appraisal value increases at the same rate g over the time that the dividend increases.

If investors in the stock markets use a present value approach in their analyses of stocks, the price that will result for an individual stock will tend toward the present value computed by equation (12-1). Of course this equality of present value and price assumes the investors have the same expectations regarding growth of dividends and the same required rate of return.

The individual stock purchaser in this constant growth rate situation has the option of taking his return in the form of capital gains or dividends, depending on his holding period. Suppose he buys a stock at time zero and holds the stock for one period, selling immediately after he receives the dividend. The dividend received at time one is $D_0(1+g)$, and the price received for the stock at time one is $P_0(1+g)$. His yield on the investment can be found by solving the equation

$$P_0=\frac{D_0(1+g)+P_0(1+g)}{1+r}$$

for r. The solution is

$$r = \frac{D_0(1+g)}{P_0} + g$$

which is the same as if equation (12-1) were solved for r. The required rate of return is the yield to the investor if the price is equal to the appraisal value, the present value.

In the numerical example a buyer of the common stock at \$26.50 at time zero would receive a dividend of \$1.06 at time one. The market price at time one after the payment of the dividend would be \$28.09. The investor would therefore receive a total cash inflow of \$29.15 at time one if he sold the stock. His profit would be \$2.65, 10 percent of his initial investment of \$26.50.

The use of the interest rate r in this idealized market situation requires some additional qualification. The required rate of return or yield to the stockholder is before personal income taxes, and therefore the analysis should be modified before being put to more extensive use to account for the differential tax treatment of capital gains and dividend income.

The model results are also based on the constancy of the rate of growth of dividends. If g is not a constant, but perhaps a decreasing function of time the results of equation (12-1) will be modified. A derivation of an analogue to equation (12-1) is beyond the scope of this book, but the resulting expression for the present value of a stock would include terms that would combine the current dividend and the growth factor. The form of the relationship between the present value and the current dividend and growth rate will not be specified, but present value should be an increasing function of both the dividend and the growth rate.

Retention Policy, Return on Retained Earnings, and the Growth Rate

In theoretical present value models considered to this point, emphasis has been placed on dividends rather than earnings per share because only dividends result in an explicit cash payment to the shareholder. If earnings are retained the result *may* be an increase in the market value of the stock of some corresponding amount, but this result depends on an additional factor not considered so far, the company's rate of return on retained earnings. This rate of return can be combined with a rate of retention of earnings to derive the growth rate in dividends.

Suppose the target company has an initial earnings per share at time zero of E_0, and the company has adopted a policy of retaining the fraction b of earnings, thereby paying dividends equal to $(1 - b)$ of earnings. If the company earns an after-tax rate of return on retained earnings of k, then the earnings at time one would be

$$E_1 = E_0 + E_0(b)(k) = (1+bk)E_0$$

The earnings at any point in time, E_t, would be

$$E_t = (1+bk)^t E_0$$

The growth rate in earnings per share is bk.

The base dividend quantity is

$$D_0 = (1-b)E_0$$

and any period's dividend could be expressed in terms of the earnings at that time

$$D_t = (1-b)E_t$$

If equation (12-4) is substituted in equation (12-6)

$$D_t = (1-b)(1+bk)^t E_0$$

Then the expression from equation (12-5) for E_0 is substituted

$$D_t = (1+bk)^t D_0$$

and the result is that

$$g = bk$$

The growth rate of dividends is equal to the product of the retention rate and the rate of return on retained earnings. The growth rate in dividends is equal to the growth rate in earnings per share if b and k are constants.

Suppose for the example that earnings per share for the period ended at time zero, E_0, were \$4, the retention rate, b, were 0.75, and the rate of return on retained earnings, k, were 8 percent. The earnings at time zero are allocated \$1 to dividends and \$3 to retained earnings. The company would earn 8 percent additional on the \$3 retained, increasing earnings per share at time one to \$4.24. Twenty-five percent of \$4.24 would be paid as dividends at time one, \$1.06, and \$3.18 retained. Earnings per share and dividends would increase by 6 percent each time period, which could be calculated from tracing the dollar figures through each time point or by multiplying 0.75 by 8 percent.

Growth in dividends can be shown therefore to be the result of an earnings retention policy and the operating results of the company as expressed in the rate of return on retained earnings. Within some reasonable range a company can determine what its growth rate (of dividends and earnings per share) will be. If it could be assumed that the retention rate and the rate of return on retained earnings could be held constant over all future time, then a constant growth rate would be achieved.

The market value of the company's stock will not necessarily increase by the *amount* of retained earnings even though the *rate of growth* in market price is equal to the rate of growth of retained earnings. In the numerical example the amount of retained earnings at time one is \$3.18, but the increase in market price between time zero and time one is only \$1.59. The discrepancy in dollar figures is due to the fact that the company only earns 8 percent on retained earnings while the market capitalization rate, the required rate of return of stockholders, is 10 percent.

Had the example company earned the same rate of return on retained earnings as the market capitalization rate, 10 percent, the increase in market price would have been equal to the amount of retained earnings. To illustrate this point the earnings at time zero, E_0, should be changed to \$2.50, the retention rate, b, to 0.6, and the rate of return on retained earnings, k, to 10 percent. The company pays \$1 dividends at time zero and retains \$1.50. Earnings therefore increase to \$2.65 at time one, and a dividend at time one of \$1.06 is paid. Earnings of \$1.59 are retained at time one, which is exactly equal to the increase in market price between time zero and time one (that increase is still equal to \$1.59 because the base dividend of \$1 and the growth rate in dividends of 6 percent are unchanged).

To translate a dollar of retained earnings into a dollar of increase in market price in this model therefore requires an additional assumption that the company can invest retained earnings and receive a yield which is equal to the stockholders' required rate of return. If k is less than r, then the stockholder's capital gain will be less than the amount of retained earnings; if k is greater than r, the capital gain will be greater than the amount of retained earnings; and if k is equal to r, the capital gain will equal the amount of retained earnings.

The point to which this discussion has been leading is the use of earnings per share by itself as a measure of the income of the stockholder. If the price of the stock would increase by exactly the amount of retained earnings, then the total income of the stockholder, the dividend plus the capital gain, would equal the earnings per share of the company. This equality has been shown to be only a special case in the constant growth rate model. Current earnings per share therefore cannot be used alone in analyzing and appraising common stocks. Some weight must be given to the retention rate and the company's rate of return on incremental capital, retained earnings.

Appraisal Value Based on Earnings Per Share and Its Growth Rate

The usual practice followed in evaluating common stocks is to use two measures of the individual stock, current earnings per share and the anticipated growth rate of earnings per share over the near-term future, in combination with a simple price-earnings multiple as a capitalization factor to arrive at an appraisal value for a common stock. The method relies heavily on absolute standards for the price-earnings ratio in its simplest form, but can easily be modified to reflect current average market capitalization rates.

The price-earnings (p-e) multiple is a number which is multiplied times "normal" current earnings per share to yield a value of the share of stock. If the p-e multiple or ratio is 10 and earnings per share adjusted for any unusual items is \$2, the product would give an appraisal value of \$20 a share. Because current earnings are known the problem in this method of appraisal is the selection of the p-e multiplier.

The p-e multiple is varied by the growth rate assumed for earnings per share. The growth rate is a future growth rate, perhaps that rate to be maintained over the next seven years. The estimate is usually based on the past growth rate in earnings, modified to represent the analyst's subjective evaluation of the company's potential.

The choice of the appropriate p-e multiplier to fit the assumed growth rate may be according to some absolute standard determined in advance. For example a set of p-e multipliers suggested for use in this type of evaluation is contained in the following table, abstracted from Benjamin Graham, David L. Dodd, and Sidney Cottle, *Security Analysis*, 4th Ed., McGraw-Hill, 1962, p. 538:

Expected growth rate	Price-earnings multiplier
0%	8.5
2.5%	13.5
5%	17
7.2%	20
10%	23.5
14.3%	31
20%	41.5

If a stock were expected to grow at an annual rate of 5% for the next seven years and current earnings per share were \$3, the appraisal value using the multiplier from this table would be

$$17(\$3) = \$51$$

Rather than use an absolute set of p-e multipliers as shown above, it may be possible to derive a multiplier from other stocks that have similar characteristics to the one under analysis. For example, suppose the stock being analyzed is XYZ Steel Corp. common, with current earnings per share of \$4.20. An analyst might try to find a "steel company" p-e multiplier by investigating the current prices and earnings per share of a group of comparable steel companies. If the group multiplier turned out to be 11, this multiplier would then be used to derive the appraisal value of

$$11(\$4.20) = \$46.20$$

for XYZ Steel Corp.

The use of average industry p-e multipliers implies several assumptions about the elements of the appraisal. First, reliance is placed on actual market p-e ratios, which can of course change over time. The assumption of homogeneity is built in, that the particular company being analyzed is typical of that industry group with the same exact growth prospects as the other members of that group.

If in the example XYZ Steel Corp. had a current market price of $42, a p-e ratio of 10 might indicate that investors think the company is not typical of the other steel companies. The market's assessment of XYZ may be a result of the conclusion that its growth rate in earnings will be lower than other steel companies.

Market p-e ratios for various industries tend to change over time as investor enthusiasm about industry growth rates in earnings changes. A person who has followed the stock markets over a period of years can cite many "fads" in industries. At various times airlines, color television manufacturers, conglomerates, birth control pill makers, computer soft-ware companies, cable television corporations, nursing home operators, mobile home manufacturers, and pollution control companies have had above average p-e ratios because growth prospects seemed extraordinarily high. The stock market's appraisal of those growth prospects, as measured by industry p-e ratios, has changed, though, and will probably continue to change in the future. A speculator or investor should probably spend an appreciable amount of time trying to "psych-out" the market; to predict what will be the next fad or hot industry on the exchanges.

Besides changes in industry p-e ratios the general level of stock prices changes over time, not necessarily as earnings change. Therefore, there have been appreciable changes in p-e ratios for the general market, as measured perhaps by the p-e ratio for the 30 stocks included in the Dow-Jones Industrial Index or by some other aggregative index.

The investor in common stocks therefore faces three levels of determinants of market prices when selecting particular stocks to buy: the general level of stock prices, industry stock prices, and the price levels of particular stocks.

Analysis of Common Stocks Under Risk

Because the future retention rate and earnings on retained earnings are uncertain, the stream of future dividends and future market prices should be treated as random variables. A valuation model for a common stock should therefore take account not only of the expected future dividend or expected future price, but the standard deviation of the dividend or price as well.

Rather than going through an elaborate mean-variance utility-based model using certainty equivalents or other techniques, the usual adjustment for risk is performed on the capitalization rate r, the investor's required rate of return. If the investor judges the risk of Stock A to be higher than that of Stock B, then a rate of 12 percent might be used in evaluating A and a rate of 10 percent for B when each stock is evaluated in isolation (the portfolio effect is ignored). If the risk-adjusted discount rate is applied to the future stream of expected dividends, some distortion due to the geometric nature of the risk adjustment over time may be experienced. If the risk-adjusted discount rate is applied to a single future price, however, no inherent distortion should result.

Suppose the investor is making a one-year investment in a single common stock and must choose between Stock A and Stock B. Neither stock pays a dividend, and the investor's brokerage firm has come up with the estimates of the prices one year from now of:

$E(\text{A price}) = 40$
$\sigma(\text{A price}) = 8$
$E(\text{B price}) = 38$
$\sigma(\text{B price}) = 5$

By comparing the two standard deviations the investor may be able to develop the different capitalization rates, 12 percent and 10 percent, based on his subjective attitude toward risk and his knowledge of rates of return available on other securities. The appraisal values of the two stocks computed by the present value method are

$$\$40\left[\frac{1}{1+0.12}\right] = \$35.71$$

and

$$\$38\left[\frac{1}{1+0.10}\right] = \$34.55$$

If the two stocks are equally priced (say \$30 now) the conclusion is that the investor should buy Stock A.

The analysis is incomplete, however, since the possible portfolio effects are ignored. No consideration has been given to the possible interaction of the stock prices with other securities the investor may already hold, to the possibility of combining some of Stock A with some of Stock B, or to the other investments available to the investor.

The Sharpe-Lintner model discussed in the appendix of the preceding chapter may be modified to use in evaluating a common stock in a portfolio context. The valuation equation expressed in yields was:

$$E(R_i) = R_f + \frac{E(R_m) - R_f}{\sigma^2(R_m)} \operatorname{Cov}(R_i R_m)$$

where $E(R_i)$ is the expected yield of the ith security, $E(R_m)$ is the yield on the market average of securities, R_f is the yield on a risk-free security, $\sigma^2(R_m)$ is the variance of the yield of the market average, and $\operatorname{Cov}(R_i R_m)$ is the covariance of the ith security's yield with the yield on the market average. The Sharpe-Lintner equation expresses market equilibrium conditions so the $E(R_i)$ value computed from the equation is what the yield on the particular stock should tend to be. If the investor estimates an expected yield higher than $E(R_i)$ from the equation he should buy that stock. If his estimate is lower he should not buy it, but possibly should sell it short.

To apply the model, some additional information is necessary. The market variables may be estimable from historical data, using the reasoning that investors expect what happened in the past to hold true in the future. That is, the average annual return on common stocks in the past will be used as the estimate of $E(R_m)$, the future expected return.

Fortunately some empirical data is available on stock yields from an extensive study by Lawrence Fisher and James H. Lorie in 1968.[1] In the post World War II period, 1946-1965, they found the average annual rate of return on New York Stock Exchange-listed common stocks to be 15.1 percent with a standard deviation of return of 19.8 percent. For evaluation of Stock A the figures

$$E(R_m) = 15.1\%$$

and

$$\sigma(R_m) = 19.8\%$$

will be used.

The yield on a risk-free security, R_f, can be based on current data. Suppose this yield is 6 percent.

The next step is to derive $\text{Cov}(R_iR_m)$ for Stock A. This covariance can be decomposed into

$$\text{Cov}(R_iR_m) = \rho_{im}\sigma(R_i)\sigma(R_m)$$

The standard deviation used above for Stock A is the standard deviation of the future price, 8, which must be converted into a standard deviation of return.

To convert a future price, P_1, and a present price, P_0, into a one-period yield, r, the formula is

$$r = \frac{P_1}{P_0} - 1$$

Since P_1 is the random variable in the equation the expected value of r, $E(r)$, can be derived from the expected future price, $E(P_1)$, by the equation

$$E(r) = \frac{E(P_1)}{P_0} - 1$$

The standard deviation of return, $\sigma(r)$, is derived from the standard deviation of the future price, $\sigma(P_1)$, by

$$\sigma(r) = \frac{\sigma(P_1)}{P_0}$$

For Stock A, then, the standard deviation of return is

$$\sigma(R_i) = \frac{8}{30} = 26\tfrac{2}{3}\%$$

The correlation coefficient of the yield of the particular security with the market yield, ρ_{im}, can be estimated by considering the percentage of the variation in R_i explained by the variation in R_m. Suppose Stock A moves closely with the market so the percentage of explained variation is 64 percent. The square root of 64 percent is 0.8, the estimate of ρ_{im}.

The covariance $\mathrm{Cov}(R_i R_m)$ for Stock A is therefore

$$0.8(26\ 2/3\%)(19.8\%) = 0.04224$$

Combining the numbers and evaluating the Sharpe-Lintner equation, the expected return for Stock A should be

$$\frac{40}{30} - 1 = 33\tfrac{1}{3}\%$$

This computed expected return of 15.8 percent can then be compared to the investor's estimated expected return computed from the expected future price:

$$E(R_i) = 0.06 + \frac{0.151 - 0.06}{(0.198)^2}(0.04224) = 15.8\%$$

Because the investor's expected return is greater than the prediction from the Sharpe-Lintner equation he should purchase Stock A.

Another way of using the Sharpe-Lintner equation is to predict the future price of the stock. If the market values assumed above are equilibrium values, a purchaser of Stock A at the price of \$30 should have an expected return of 15.8 percent by holding the stock one year. That return will be realized if the future price is

$$\$30(1 + 15.8\%) = \$34.74$$

Therefore \$34.74 is the estimate of the future price of the stock.

Of course to estimate the future price in this manner the assumption must be made that the present price, \$30, of Stock A is an equilibrium value, that that price represents investors' general expectations about the future prospects of the company. In coming up with the estimate of \$40, the investor or his brokerage firm may be working on the basis of some other information or estimates not generally available to investors.

The Availability of Information to the Outside Analyst

The analysis of a corporation's financial status by an outsider is complicated because of the limited amount of data that will normally be available. The financial statements that are described in an accounting class, the income statement, balance sheet, and source and use of funds statement are prepared for internal use in the firm, and are not generally available to outsiders. Publicly held corporations are required by the Securities and Exchange Commission to furnish abbreviated income statements and balance sheets to stockholders, but the informational content of these "published" statements may be minimal. For example, a simple number that is basic to financial analysis such as "cost of goods sold" is frequently aggregated with selling and other expenses, and therefore not distinguishable in the income statement furnished to stockholders. This reluctance to disclose on the part of the corporation is understandable, since competitors, customers, and even politicians might be able to use this information to the disadvantage of the corporation.

The analyst will probably not be able to rely exclusively on published information, but will need to seek additional information. More detailed financial statements that follow a prescribed format are filed with the Securities and Exchange Commission, and are available for inspection by members of the public. These statements, such as the "10-K" report, contain much more detailed information, and are probably worth the serious analyst's efforts to inspect. Certain other federal regulatory authorities also receive standardized financial statements that are then available for public inspection. For example, the Federal Communications Commission would have reports filed for telephone and broadcasting companies.

There are several other sources of information that can be utilized under certain circumstances. As mentioned before, summary analyses of credit-worthiness and of bond ratings are available from financial reporting services. Trade associations and financial publications can be used in some cases to obtain additional information about a company. The major stock brokerage firms have staffs of analysts who prepare reports on major companies on a sporadic basis.

Measurement of Earnings and Accounting Principles

For the most part the analysis of this book has considered revenue, expenses, and earnings as an exactly determinable quantity. However, net income shown on financial statements is a quantity that is a result of several estimations where there is some possible variety of result. The most obvious estimation in determining net income is the amount of depreciation charges, but there are many other cases where adoption of a different account treatment will alter net income and the resulting earnings per share of the company.

For example, suppose a company is organized and conducts a business for four years producing a particular product. Machinery is initially purchased for the sum of $1,000,000, and the machinery will be exactly used by the end of the four years, and must therefore be depreciated over the four-year period. The sales revenue per year is $2,000,000, and the cash expenses including corporate income taxes are $1,500,000 per year. The corporate income taxes included in the $1,500,000 are based in part upon some method of depreciation adopted for tax purposes, but the method used for taxes does not have to be used for preparation of the other financial statements.

If straight-line depreciation is used in the financial statements, the net income for each of the four years would be calculated as

Sales revenue	2,000,000
Cash expenses	1,500,000
Net cash generated	500,000
Depreciation charged	250,000
Net income	250,000

Assuming the company had 100,000 shares of common stock outstanding, earnings per share would be $2.50 each of the four years.

If the accountants used the sum-of-the-years-digits method to compute depreciation, the net income and earnings per share for each of the four years would be shown as

	Year 1	Year 2	Year 3	Year 4
Net cash generated	500,000	500,000	500,000	500,000
Depreciation charged	400,000	300,000	200,000	100,000
Net income	100,000	200,000	300,000	400,000
Earnings per share	$1	$2	$3	$4

The example demonstrates the importance of the accounting method used to compute depreciation. With the straight-line method, earnings are level during the four-year period, but with accelerated depreciation earnings show a growth rate that might look very impressive to someone who did not look beyond earnings per share. Total earnings for the four-year period is the same for either method, of course, but if investors place a high premium on growth of earnings per share, the second method might actually result in a higher market price for the company's stock.

There are many other cases where earnings can be reallocated over time depending on an accounting method. Two of the most troublesome cases for external analysis are where certain expenses are capitalized at the time incurred and then amortized later, and where income is received in advance of services rendered, as in the case of a franchise fee received by a franchising company.

When large expenditures are made to acquire an asset, it is not always necessary to capitalize the entire acquisition cost and then amortize over the life of the asset. For example, an oil production company may find it necessary to spend $200,000 to develop an oil well, including the cost of the lease, the expense of drilling the well, and the pipe, pump, and other equipment necessary to produce the oil. If these expenditures are all capitalized and amortized on a straight-line basis over a 20-year period, an amortization expense of $10,000 per year will be shown on the income statement. On the other hand the company could elect to write off as an expense in the year incurred the entire drilling expense, and a part of the cost of the lease and equipment expenditures. In this latter case if the immediate write-off is assumed to be $120,000 and the straight-line is used to amortize the remainder, expenses for the year of acquisition would be $124,000, and for the following years $4,000. Obviously a difference in earnings per share would result in the two cases.

A franchising company, perhaps selling franchises to operate hot dog stands, typically receives a flat sum for the franchise either in cash or in the form of an installment contract payable over a few years. The company itself may be committed to perform services such as management assistance or advertizing for the franchisee over a considerable period of time. In some cases such services are supposed to be paid for by a continuing fee based on the sales volume of the franchise outlet, but there may not be an exact matching of the amount of continuing fee with the amount of services provided.

The initial sales price of the franchise may be recorded as income in the year of the sale. For a company selling a large number of franchises, this practice would tend to inflate net income for the expansion period over what would be shown if the sales price were amortized over some reasonable period. In some franchise operations, where payment for the franchise is by installment rather than in a lump-sum, the possibility of default on the installment contract has led to a modification of recording income only as payments are received to avoid the "bad-debt" overstatement of income. (A number of franchising companies found that prices of their stock fell drastically in 1970 when they changed accounting methods to the installment basis. Earnings per share were lowered significantly in most cases by this accounting change.)

Two more cases of accounting treatment changes that have had significance for growth conglomerate companies in recent years should be mentioned. The first has to do with reporting "diluted" earnings per share as an allowance for outstanding convertible securities and warrants. The other major item is the use of the "purchase" method or the "pooling of interests" method in income computations of merged corporations.

If a corporation has convertible securities or warrants outstanding, it is generally expected that *eventually* a number of additional common shares will be issued in exchange. At the time of issue of these shares the new shareholders will receive equal (per share) rights to retained earnings and future dividends. Cash dividends paid prior to this exercise of the warrant or conversion privilege go only to actual common stockholders, not to potential holders.

Earnings per share figures are adjusted to a diluted basis by assuming that conversion or exercise has already occurred for at least some of the convertible or warrant issues. For example, suppose a corporation has 1,000,000 shares of common stock and $10,000,000 (par value) of 6 percent convertible debentures outstanding. The debentures are convertible at 50, so the bond issue if entirely converted would result in an additional 200,000 common shares being issued. If net income for the current year is $3,000,000, then the undiluted earnings per share are $3. To compute earnings per share on a fully diluted basis the net income of $3,000,000 must be adjusted for the reduced interest charges (net of corporate income taxes), and then divided by the larger number of common shares. Assuming the corporate income tax rate is 50 percent, the new net income figure would be

$$
\begin{array}{ll}
\$3{,}000{,}000 & \\
\underline{+\ \ 300{,}000} & (50\%\ \text{of}\ \$600{,}000) \\
\$3{,}300{,}000 &
\end{array}
$$

The fully diluted earnings per share becomes

$$\frac{\$3,300,000}{\$1,200,000} = \$2.75$$

Usually both figures, \$3 undiluted and \$2.75 diluted, would be reported for the company. Care must be taken however to determine whether *all* the convertible securities and warrants are assumed to be changed into common stock in the computation of diluted earnings per share.

Corporations that have acquired other corporations by the exchange of common stock have had in the past the option as to the treatment of combined operations on a "purchase" basis or a "pooling of interests" basis. In the purchase method the price of the acquisition is recorded on the books with the difference between the price and the net book value of the acquired firm being recorded as goodwill, to be amortized over some period of time. In the pooling of interests method, the price of the acquisition is not recorded: instead the net book value of the acquired firm is used as the price of the addition with no resulting goodwill.

An example will serve to illustrate the differences in accounting treatment. Suppose A acquires B by issuing 200,000 shares of common stock that has a market value of \$40 a share at the time of acquisition. Before the transaction occurs the balance sheet totals of the two firms are

A			
Assets	\$20,000,000	Liabilities Owners' equity	\$ 6,000,000 14,000,000
B			
Assets	\$12,000,000	Liabilities Owners' equity	\$ 7,000,000 5,000,000

A's stock is exchanged for B's stock, and A acquires the assets and assumes the liabilities of B. If the pooling of interests method is used for the merger, the new firm's balance sheet would appear as

A + B			
Assets	\$32,000,000	Liabilities Owners' equity	\$13,000,000 19,000,000

In this method book values are simply transferred, and no good will is recorded. The net effect is as if A purchased B for a price of \$5,000,000.

In the purchase method the transaction price used is the market value of the new shares issued, \$8,000,000. Accordingly the new balance sheet would have these totals

A + B			
Assets	$32,000,000	Liabilities	$13,000,000
Goodwill	3,000,000	Owners' equity	22,000,000

Goodwill of $3,000,000 is recorded as the excess of the purchase price over book value of B. If the goodwill must be amortized over some time period, say 40 years on a straight-line basis, then net income will be reduced by the amount of the amortization each year, $75,000.

The examples presented here are intended to indicate some possible effects of accounting practices on reported earnings per share. Accounting practices do change over time, and it is worthwhile for the analyst to spend effort to determine the accounting bases used in computation of the earnings per share. The Securities and Exchange Commission periodically changes its allowable accounting methods, usually based upon the recommendations of the Accounting Principles Board of the American Institute of Certified Public Accountants.

Investment Through Mutual Funds

Rather than evaluate individual securities and maintain a portfolio of stocks and bonds themselves, many investors prefer to leave the portfolio management to a mutual fund. A mutual fund is a form of investment trust organized to invest in a portfolio of securities. The mutual fund buys, holds, and sells securities, and the investor purchases shares in the mutual fund. The income received by the mutual fund is distributed to shareholders, and is not taxed to the mutual fund but only as income to the shareholders.

An open-end mutual fund is one where the mutual fund will sell shares and repurchase shares at any time. A closed-end fund on the other hand does not sell new shares after the initial offering, and does not normally repurchase shares except in cases where the fund is terminated after a fixed period of time. Shares of a closed-end fund may be purchased and sold on an organized exchange or over the counter. Naturally in that case the price of the closed-end fund will not necessarily be equal to the "net asset value," the total market value of the securities held by the fund, divided by the number of shares of the fund.

The price at which the open-end mutual fund shares are sold or purchased is based upon the net asset value on the day of the transaction. A fee may be added to the net asset value to establish the sales price if the fund is a "load fund." A no-load fund is one where this fee is not charged. Sometimes in either case a small fee is charged on redemption of the shares.

Besides the load fee or other transaction charges, the management of the mutual fund collects a management fee which is based upon the average total assets of the fund. Normally this charge is less than 1 percent per year.

Mutual funds can be found that invest in almost any type of security. There are funds that invest only in municipal bonds, corporate bonds, common stocks, convertible securities, and other specialized securities.

A "balanced fund" for example is expected to buy a mixture of stocks and bonds. An "aggressive" or "growth" fund buys these types of securities. A "hedge fund" (which has some restrictions imposed on ownership of the fund's shares) may engage in short-selling and the purchase or sale of security options, and could therefore be expected to be the most speculative form of mutual fund.

The management of a mutual fund enjoys the economies of scale presumably, spreading the costs of security and market analysis over a large portfolio, and getting volume discounts on trading fees. Additionally the investor should benefit from the wider diversification of the portfolio of stocks possible.

The investor must still make a choice of a particular mutual fund as well as deciding when and what amounts to buy. The usual basis for selection of the mutual fund is past performance, which is measured in several different ways.

The most widely reported and used measure is the comparison of the fund's actual return with a well-known stock market index such as the Dow-Jones 30 Industrials or the Standard and Poors 500 Stocks index. If during a year the Dow-Jones (adding back dividends) goes up 5 percent and the mutual fund has a return of 10 percent to shareholders, then that fund is said to have outperformed the market. Such realized return figures are reported monthly for a large number of mutual funds by *Fundscope* and *Institutional Investor*.

Measuring the past performance of mutual funds strictly on the basis of a realized return over one time segment does not measure all the mutual fund is supposed to accomplish for the investor, however. The mutual fund through superior selection of securities and diversification should have a higher average return or lower standard deviation of returns or both than the market. The usual test is the performance of the mutual fund against a random selection of stocks represented by an aggregate index like the Standard and Poor 500. Both the average return and standard deviation of return are tested through variations of the Sharpe-Lintner formula.

To test a mutual fund's performance the variable R_i in the formula is redefined to be the return on the individual mutual fund. The realized average return over a period of time for the fund is compared to the value $E(R_i)$ computed from the formula

$$E(R_i) = R_f + \frac{E(R_m) - R_f}{\sigma^2(R_m)} \text{Cov}(R_i R_m)$$

Each of the variables on the right side of the equality is a realized value for the period under study.

Suppose for example that monthly data for the last four years is available for use in evaluating a mutual fund. First is the market index data with an average realized return of 14 percent and a standard deviation of return of 8 percent. The mutual fund's average realized return is 16 percent with a standard deviation of 10 percent. The correlation coefficient between the return on the mutual fund and the return on the market index is 0.6. During this four-year period the risk-free rate of interest is 9 percent.

The covariance of the formula is

$$\begin{aligned}\text{Cov}(R_i R_m) &= \rho_{im}\sigma(R_i)\sigma(R_m)\\ &= 0.6(10\%)(8\%)\\ &= 0.0048\end{aligned}$$

Evaluating the entire Sharpe-Lintner equation, the predicted return on the mutual fund based on market index performance, the risk-free interest rate, and the degree of correlation between the fund's performance and the market performance is

$$\begin{aligned}E(R_i) &= 9\% + \frac{14\% - 9\%}{(8\%)^2}(0.0048)\\ &= 12.75\%\end{aligned}$$

Because the actual average return is greater, 16 percent, the conclusion of this evaluation is that this mutual fund's performance was superior to a random selection of securities' performance. Based on this past performance an investor should choose this mutual fund for future performance rather than select a random portfolio of common stocks.

Mutual funds can be ranked by the excess return as well. The fund demonstrated above has an excess return of

$$16\% - 12.75\% = 3.25\%$$

If a second fund has an excess return of 4 percent, the second fund is superior to the first. So far no financial reporting service regularly

So far no financial reporting service regularly reports mutual funds' performances on the basis of both mean return and standard deviation of return.[2] If the investor is unable to find such an evaluation of mutual funds in the future the data can be easily gathered and the equation evaluated without too much effort. Perhaps the increased accuracy over comparing past realized returns alone will be worth the time spent.

The two other simpler methods of analysis have been suggested. In the first [3] the mutual fund's reward to variability ratio is compared to the market index's reward to variability ratio or to another fund's ratio. The reward to variability for a mutual fund is the average realized return minus the risk-free interest rate. This difference is divided by the mutual fund's standard deviation of return (its variability) to derive the reward to variability ratio. For the mutual fund analyzed above, the ratio is

$$\frac{16\% - 9\%}{10\%} = 0.7$$

The example market index reward to variability ratio is

$$\frac{14\% - 9\%}{8\%} = 0.625$$

Because the mutual fund's ratio is higher, it outperformed the market. If another mutual fund's reward to variability ratio was 0.75, it outperformed the first mutual fund.

The last measure[4] is the reward to volatility ratio. The reward is the same, the difference between the fund's average realized return and the risk–free rate of interest, but the divisor is the mutual fund's volatility index. The volatility index is

$$\frac{\mathrm{Cov}(R_i R_m)}{\sigma^2(R_m)}$$

For the example mutual fund, the volatility index is

$$\frac{0.0048}{0.0064} = 0.75$$

The reward to volatility ratio is therefore

$$\frac{16\% - 9\%}{0.75} = 0.0933$$

The reward to volatility index for the market is

$$\frac{14\% - 9\%}{1} = 0.05$$

since

$$\frac{\mathrm{Cov}(R_m R_m)}{\sigma^2(R_m)} = 1$$

The mutual fund outperformed the market on this test as well. In selecting a mutual fund, the one with the highest reward to volatility index is preferred.

Neither of these two latter methods of evaluation methods is currently performed by the financial reporting services. Therefore the investor trying to select a mutual fund must collect his own data and perform his own calculations.[5]

Summary

The equities market is a complex organization that cannot be fully analyzed and described. Individuals and institutions buy, hold, and sell securities from the profit motive, hoping through superior knowledge, calculation, or luck to derive a net income from those activities. Their actions are conditioned on the tax environment.

Analysis of individual securities requires a basis of accurate information about past performance and if possible future earnings prospects.

An appraisal value may be developed from the present value of future dividends or market prices, but risk must be accounted for somehow. If only one period of holding is assumed, the risk adjustment may be consistently accomplished through the interest rate required. When the security is to form part of a portfolio, a variation of the Sharpe-Lintner can be used to appraise the security.

The problem with selection of mutual funds is that selection must be based exclusively on past performance. Several measures of performance were presented, based upon the Sharpe-Lintner formula.

Notes

[1] Lawrence Fisher and James H. Lorie, "Rates of Return on Investments in Common Stock: The Year-by-Year Record, 1926-1965," *Journal of Business*, July 1968.
[2] Empirical analysis of mutual funds' past performance using this method was first performed in Michael C. Jensen, *Risk, the Pricing of Capital Assets, and the Evaluation of Investment Portfolios* (Doctoral dissertation at the University of Chicago, July 1967).
[3] Used in William F. Sharpe, "Mutual Fund Performance," *Journal of Business*, January 1966.
[4] Used in Jack L. Treynor, "How to Rate Management of Investment Funds," *Harvard Business Review*, January-February 1965.
[5] A comparison of the three evaluation techniques can be found in William F. Sharpe, *Portfolio Theory and Capital Markets* (New York: McGraw-Hill, 1970), Chapter 8, or in Keith V. Smith, *Portfolio Management* (New York: Holt, Rinehart & Winston, 1971), Chapter 11.

Chapter 12 Questions

1. The major tax loopholes are centered on the differential tax rates on long-term capital gains. What economic or social rationale can be used for those lower rates?
2. Describe the devices by which ordinary income can be translated into capital gains income.
3. If taxes can simply be deferred to later periods, the individual can gain by investing those funds in the meantime. What are the major devices for delaying tax payments?
4. Do the differential individual tax rates between ordinary income and long-term capital gains provide an incentive for corporations to retain earnings rather than pay dividends?
5. How can the future growth rate of dividends on a particular common stock be estimated?
6. How can the corporation's after-tax rate of return on retained earnings be estimated?
7. If the return on an individual common stock has varied with the market return 50 percent of the time in the past, is there any reason to expect it to vary that way in the future?
8. Do market prices of common stocks reflect those stocks' intrinsic values?
9. When several thousand security analysts are engaged in reviewing the prospects of individual companies is there any reason for an individual investor to try to analyze a particular common stock for investment?
10. How can the market capitalization rate for dividends be measured?
11. What is the relationship between the market capitalization rate for dividends and the market price-earnings ratio?

12. "If all companies would adopt a cash basis of accounting rather than the accrual basis, the ambiguity of earnings per share would be eliminated." Comment.

13. How can the financial statements of one company that uses accelerated depreciation be compared with those of another company that uses straight-line depreciation?

14. What are the latest pronouncements of the Accounting Principles Board of the American Institute of Certified Public Accountants?

15. Does a corporation have to use the same bases (as for example depreciation method) for its tax return as for its public financial statements?

Chapter 12 Problems

1. Blue Point, Inc., common stock has a dividend that is growing at 4 percent a year. The last dividend paid was $1.50 a share, and the market capitalization rate for dividends is 12 percent. Calculate:
   a. The present price per share.
   b. The estimated price per share two years from now.
   c. The estimated price per share five years from now.

2. Red Point, Inc., retains 40 percent of earnings, and its after-tax return on retained earnings is 14 percent.
   a. What is the growth rate of Red Point's dividend?
   b. The market capitalization rate for dividends is 12 percent. If Red Point one year retains $1 per share of earnings what should be the capital gain per share that year?

3. Black Point, Inc., buys an airplane for use as a charter freight carrier. The plane is to be used for eight years and will be junked then at zero scrap value. The freight charter revenues will be $100,000 per year and the cash operating expenses will be $60,000 a year. The corporation income tax rate is 22 percent. The corporation has 10,000 shares of common stock outstanding. Calculate earnings per share for the eight-year period, depreciating the $160,000 cost of the airplane:
   a. Using the straight-line method with an eight-year life.
   b. Using the straight-line method with a six-year life.
   c. Using the sum-of-the-years-digits method with an eight-year life.
   d. Using the sum-of-the-years-digits method with a six-year life.

4. Green Point, Inc., has 200,000 shares of common stock outstanding and a $1,000,000 6 percent coupon convertible bond issue outstanding. The conversion terms are at a price of 40 (25 shares for each $1,000 bond). Green Point's earnings before interest and taxes are $400,000 a year, and the corporate tax rate is 45 percent.
   a. Calculate earnings per share undiluted.
   b. Calculate earnings per share on a fully diluted basis, assuming the bond issue is converted to common stock.

Chapter 12 References

Brealey, Richard A. *An Introduction to Risk and Return from Common Stocks.* Cambridge, Mass.: MIT Press, 1969.

Cohen, K. J., and Pogue, J. A. "Some Comments Concerning Mutual

Fund Versus Random Portfolio Performance." *Journal of Business*, April 1968.

D'Ambrosio, Charles A. *A Guide to Successful Investing*. Englewood Cliffs, N. J.: Prentice-Hall, 1970.

Fisher, Lawrence, and Lorie, J. H. "Rates of Return on Investments in Common Stocks," *Journal of Business*, January, 1965.

Fisher, Lawrence, and Lorie, J. H. "Some Studies of Variability of Returns on Investments in Common Stocks." *Journal of Business*, April 1970.

Francis, Jack Clark, and Archer, Stephen H. *Portfolio Analysis*. Englewood Cliffs, N. J.: Prentice-Hall, 1971.

Gordon, Myron J. *The Investment, Financing and Valuation of the Corporation*. Homewood, Ill.: Irwin, 1962.

—— "Dividends, Earnings and Stock Prices." *Review of Economics and Statistics*, May 1959.

Hawkins, J. W. "Analysis of the New Capital Gains Provisions of the Tax Reform Act of 1969." *Journal of Taxation*, May 1970.

Jensen, M. C. "Performance of Mutual Funds in the Period 1945-1964." *Journal of Finance*, May 1968.

Latané, Henry A., and Tuttle, Donald L. *Security Analysis and Portfolio Management*. New York: Ronald, 1970.

Outlaw, L. J. "Gains on Sale of Real Estate." *Taxes*, July 1968.

Phillips, L. C. "Impact of the New Tax Reform Law upon Corporate Decisions and Earnings." *Financial Analysts Journal*, May-June 1970.

Sharpe, William F. *Portfolio Theory and Capital Markets*. New York: McGraw-Hill, 1970.

Smith, Keith V. *Portfolio Management*. New York: Holt, Rinehart & Winston, 1971.

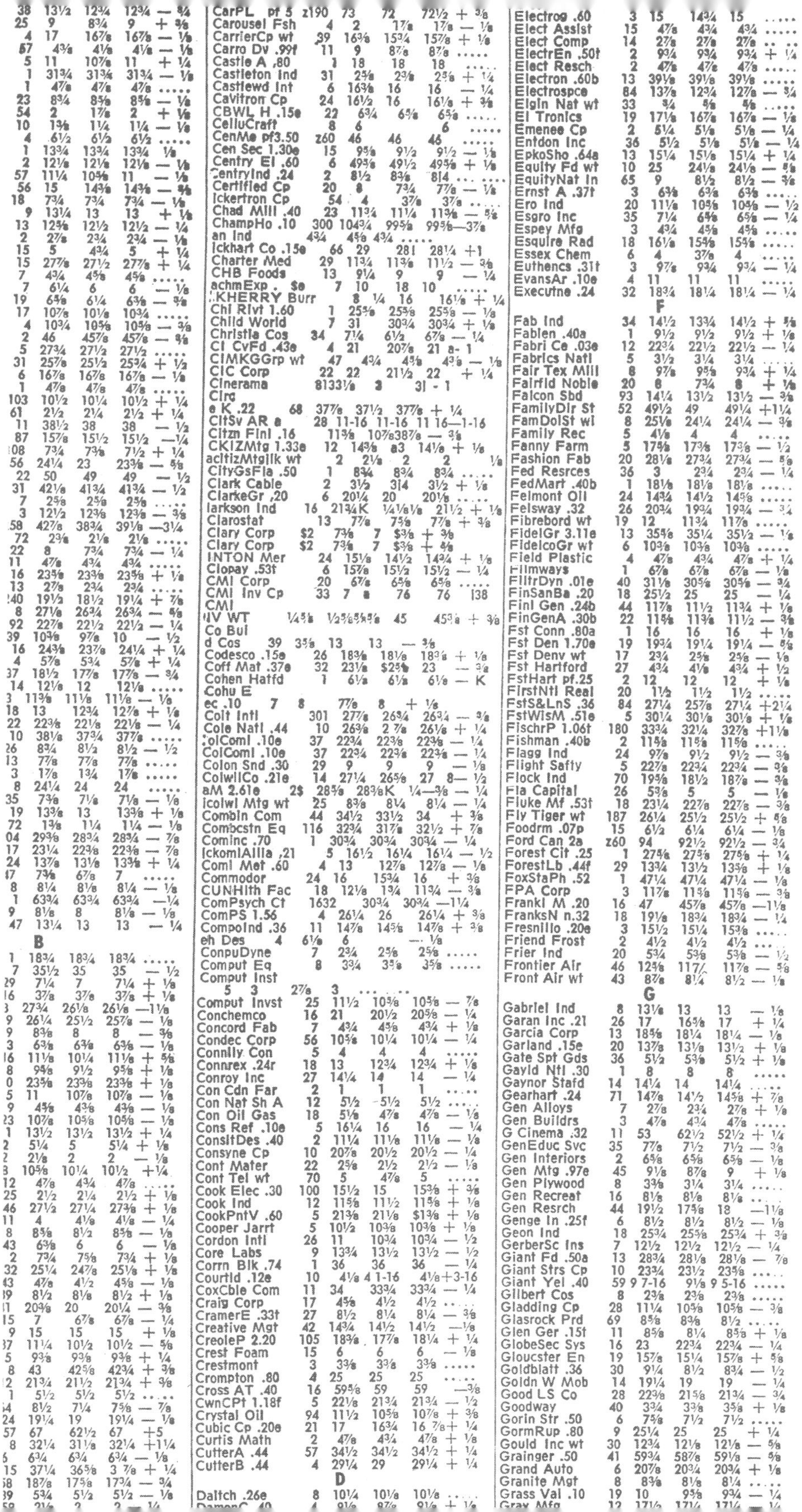

PART SIX

CAPITAL STRUCTURE AND DIVIDEND POLICY

With Part VI the optimization of the corporation's financial activities is resumed. The emphasis in this part, on the selection of capital sources, corresponds somewhat to the emphasis of Parts II and III of the book where the theoretical models for asset selection were presented. In Part VI, the funds sources are combined in models to derive the optimum capital structure and dividend policy.

The usual objective assumed in capital structure decisions is the maximization of the market value of common stockholders' shares. This goal substitutes for the risk-return characteristics of an income stream the objective evaluation of that income stream in the securities markets. Instead of considering an individual stockholder's attitude toward return and risk, the analysis can be based on "average" attitudes, as expressed in market evaluations.

The market value criterion can be applied to those corporations large enough that their securities are traded in an organized market. But for small corporations and for corporations whose stock is closely held, the market value criterion may be meaningless. For those corporations an optimization on the basis of income characteristics is presented in Chapter 13. The income characteristics described in Chapter 13 also serve as a basis for the market evaluation presented in the following chapter.

When an individual security is evaluated in a market context, the existence of other risky securities as well as risk-free securities must be realized in the models used. Although normally only positive holdings of a security in a portfolio are considered, an individual investor is free to issue securities, hold a negative amount of a security, as well. For risky securities the issue is handled by the device of short-selling, and for the risk-free security by borrowing. That is, if an investor sells short 1,000 shares of ABC Corp. he holds −1,000 shares of that security. When the investor borrows $100,000 he must treat the interest payment and principal repayments as certain quantities, and therefore he holds −$100,000 of risk-free security.

The models used for evaluation of individual securities in Chapter 14 explicitly allow an investor to borrow, use personal leverage, to expand his portfolio of securities. Under various assumptions about corporation and individual income taxes, the securities of corporations with identical income streams from assets but differing capital structures are evaluated in a theoretical market to determine whether the capital structure chosen affects the market value of common stocks. The ultimate conclusion of Chapter 14 is that an optimum capital structure does exist that depends among other items on the tax rates of individual investors.

An extension of the model is shown in Chapter 15 where the earnings retention-dividend payment policy is studied. As a side result of the model the cut-off or hurdle rate to be used in capital budgeting is derived. Chapter 15 is concluded with some practical considerations about dividend policy.

13

OPTIMUM CAPITAL STRUCTURE—EARNINGS CRITERION

Now that the securities market environment has been explored, a return can be made to the financial problems of the corporation's management. The major problem remaining to be considered is that of capital structure design, the choice of financing sources and determination of a dividend policy.

Dividend policy is an integral part of the capital structure design since the alternative to dividend payment is earnings retention. Earnings retention is one way in which the corporation's equity capital can be expanded. Nonpayment of cash dividends is therefore an alternative to the other sources of equity capital, new common stock issues, the sale of preferred stock, and after conversion or exercise occurs, convertible securities and warrants.

In planning capital expansion or modification of an existing capital structure the corporation's asset acquisition plans, the capital budgeting choices, are considered as fixed. In most examples to be treated in this section of the book, the capital structure is optimized for a certain quantity of assets producing a revenue whose size or statistical distribution is known. Beginning each model with a known cash inflow to the corporation will allow attention to be focused on the capital structure design problem.

The capital structure then determines the distribution of the corporation's earnings from assets among the creditors, the government in the form of corporate income taxes, payments to owners of senior equity securities, and residual earnings that may be used for dividends on common stock or retained. The income distribution result of the capital structure may have an effect on the total market value of the common stock or the value per share.

In this chapter the income distribution is studied, and the market value effects of capital structure are treated in Chapter 14. In both chapters the structure is optimized with respect to the residual owners of the corporation, the common stockholders. The criterion of earnings per share is used here, and the criterion of market value per share is presented in the next chapter.

For any particular capital structure the earnings per share of common stock is a linear function of the earnings from assets. It will be relatively easy, therefore, to derive a statistical distribution for the earnings per share from the statistical distribution of earnings from assets. In the following models three basic types of securities will be used, debt (bonds), preferred stock, and common stock. The interest on bonds is tax-deductible, but dividends on common stock and preferred stock are not. Interest payments, corporate income taxes, and preferred dividends must be subtracted before the residual earnings "belonging to" common stockholders is derived.

Earnings before Interest and Taxes—Earnings per Share

In studying the income characteristics that result from various capital structures the linear relationship between earnings before interest and taxes (*EBIT*) and earnings per share (*EPS*) must be developed. *EBIT* is the net operating income for the corporation before interest payments and corporate income taxes are deducted. After those deductions are made the true net profit for the period must still be allocated between preferred stock outstanding and common stock outstanding. Each of the deductions, interest, corporate income taxes, and dividends on preferred stock depends on the corporation's capital structure, as does the final divisor, the number of common shares.

The general formula to relate *EPS* to *EBIT* is

$$EPS = \frac{(EBIT - \text{Interest})(1 - \text{Tax rate}) - \text{Preferred dividend}}{\text{Number of common shares}}$$

From *EBIT* the total interest payments are deducted, and the remainder is taxed. After taxes are deducted the dividend payment on preferred stock must also be subtracted before the remainder can be allocated among the common shares outstanding.

The resulting relationship between *EPS* and *EBIT* is linear if a constant tax rate is assumed. The linearity will become more obvious when some numerical examples are demonstrated. Three numerical examples will be used in this section, each a possible capital structure for a corporation needing \$2,000,000 total capital where the corporate tax rate is 40 percent.

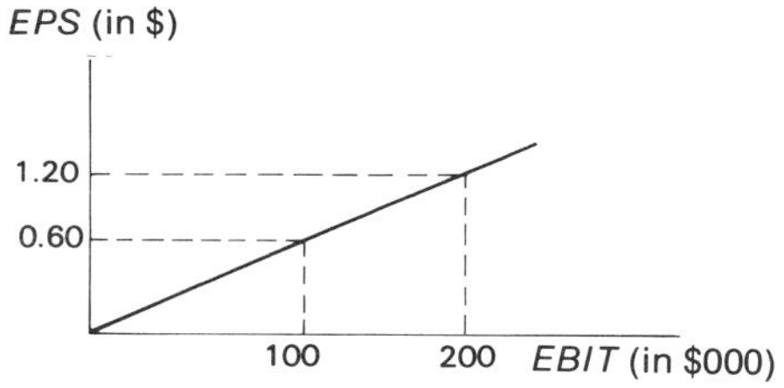

Figure 13.1
EPS as a Function of *EBIT* Structure A

The first structure, A, is one where the corporation sells only common stock, 100,000 shares at a net price of \$20 a share. Since no bonds or other debt are used interest payments are zero. Preferred dividends are zero for the same reason. The equation for structure A is therefore

$$EPS = \frac{(EBIT)(1 - 0.4)}{100{,}000}$$

The equation is graphed in Figure 13.1.

In the second capital structure, B, 60,000 shares of common stock are issued at \$20 a share, and \$800,000 of bonds are sold with an interest rate of 9 percent. Since the total before-tax interest charges are \$72,000,

$$EPS = \frac{(EBIT - \$72{,}000)(1 - 0.4)}{60{,}000}$$

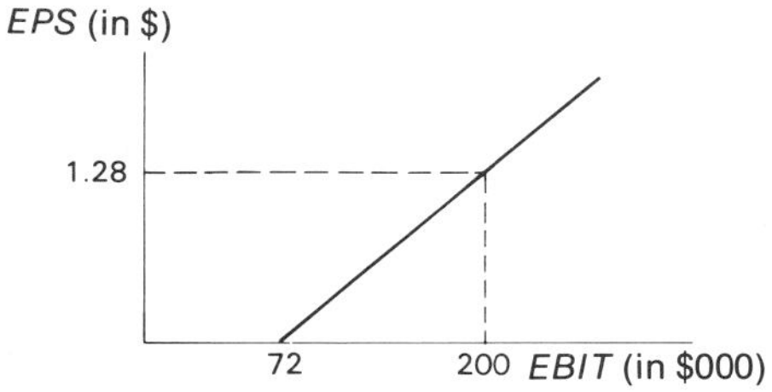

Figure 13.2
EPS as a Function of *EBIT* Structure B

Structure B is shown in Figure 13.2.

For the third capital structure, C, 50,000 shares of common stock are sold at \$20 a share, and \$1,000,000 of preferred stock with a 7½ percent stated dividend rate[1] is issued. The total preferred dividend is \$75,000, and the resulting equation for structure C is

$$EPS = \frac{(EBIT)(1 - 0.4) - \$75{,}000}{50{,}000}$$

The equation for structure C is graphed in Figure 13.3.

Breakeven Comparisons of Capital Structures

Two capital structures can be compared for desirability by computing the point at which equal results will be attained. That is, at what level of *EBIT* will the *EPS*'s be equal? That point is the breakeven point, and at other levels of *EBIT* one or the other structure will yield a higher *EPS* figure.

The comparison can be done graphically as for A and B in Figure 13.4, which is just the combination of Figures 13.1 and 13.2.

The breakeven point is at an *EBIT* level of $180,000, where both structures yield an *EPS* of $1.08. The breakeven point can be solved from the two *EPS* equations:

Set *EPS* of A equal to the *EPS* of B, and solve for *EBIT*

$$\frac{(EBIT)(1 - 0.4)}{100{,}000} = \frac{(EBIT - \$72{,}000)(1 - 0.4)}{60{,}000}$$
$$EBIT = \$180{,}000$$

Substitute this value in one of the equations and solve for *EPS*

$$EPS = \frac{(\$180{,}000)(1 - 0.4)}{100{,}000} = \$1.08$$

From Figure 13.4 it is obvious that for any *EBIT* less than $180,000 structure A would be better, and for *EBIT* greater than $180,000 B would be better. A preliminary decision between these two capital structures could therefore be based on the estimate of *EBIT*. This decision should not be based just on a point estimate of *EBIT* since *EBIT* would normally be expected to vary. From the diagram it can be seen that the steeper sloped line, B, will have a greater degree of variability in *EPS* for a given variability in *EBIT*. The effect of capital structure on variability of *EPS* will be shown more extensively below.

The next pair of structures to be compared is A and C. Graphically the diagrams of Figures 13.1 and 13.3 are combined in Figure 13.5.

The breakeven *EBIT* level is computed again by setting the two structures' *EPS*'s equal, and solving for *EBIT*:

$$\frac{(EBIT)(1 - 0.4)}{100{,}000} = \frac{(EBIT)(1 - 0.4) - \$75{,}000}{50{,}000}$$
$$EBIT = \$250{,}000$$

At that level of *EBIT* the *EPS* of each capital structure is $1.50.

Figure 13.3
EPS as a Function of *EBIT* Structure C

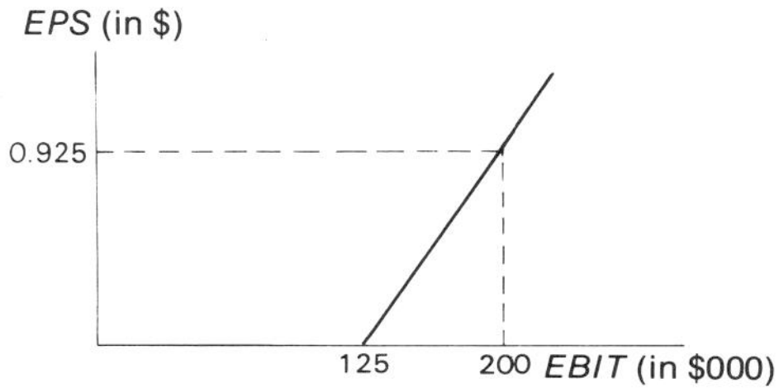

Figure 13.4
Comparison of Structures A and B

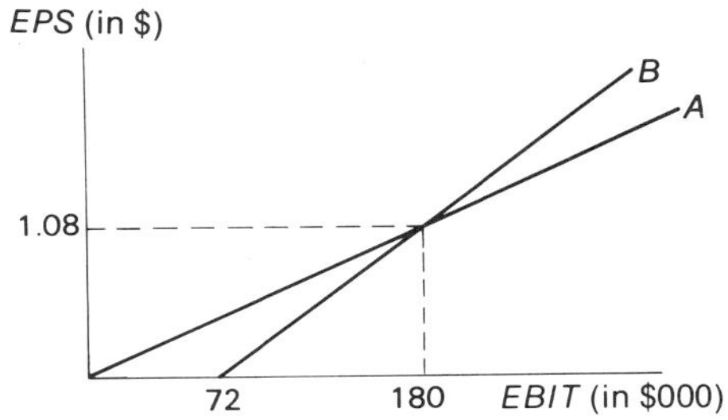

Figure 13.5
Comparison of Structures A and C

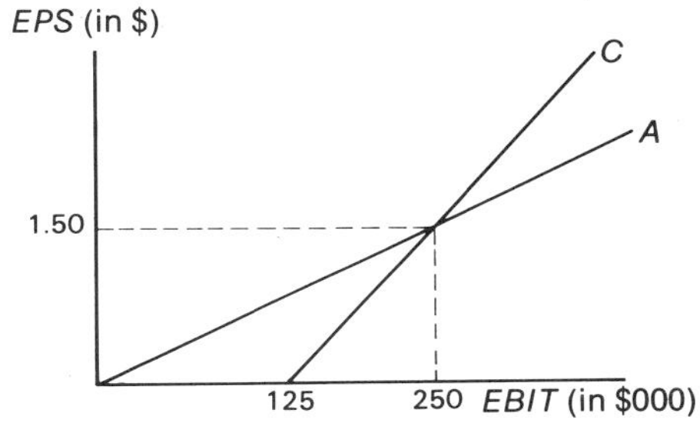

Figure 13.6
Comparison of Structures B and C

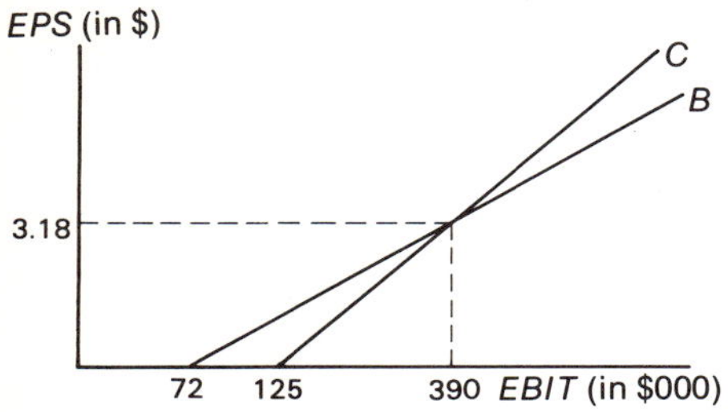

For *EBIT* lower than \$250,000 structure A with all common stock is better than structure B with a mixture of preferred and common stock. For *EBIT* above \$250,000 structure B is better.

The third pair of capital structures that can be made from the three structures is B and C. The diagram for comparison, the combination of Figures 13.2 and 13.3 is shown in Figure 13.6.

The breakeven point is found by solution of the equation:

$$\frac{(EBIT - \$72{,}000)(1 - 0.4)}{60{,}000} = \frac{(EBIT)(1 - 0.4) - \$75{,}000}{50{,}000}$$
$$EBIT = \$390{,}000$$

At that *EBIT* the *EPS* for each of the two capital structures is \$3.18.

All three capital structures can be compared simultaneously by combining the *EPS-EBIT* relationships in a single diagram, Figure 13.7.

Figure 13.7
Comparison of Structures A, B, and C

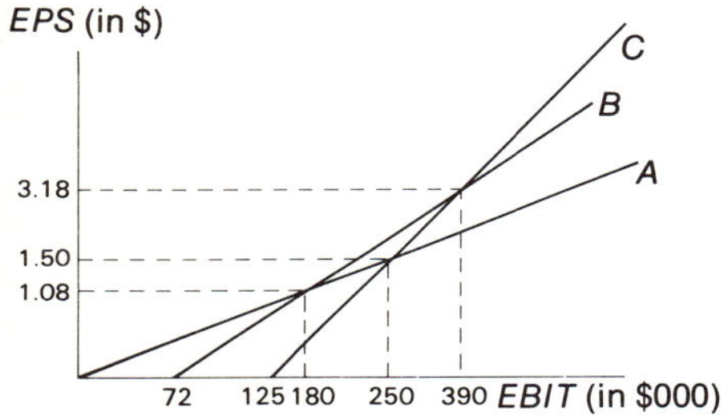

If the estimates of *EBIT* could be treated as certain quantities the relationships in Figure 13.7 could be used to reach these conclusions:
For *EBIT* less than \$180,000, A is best.
For *EBIT* between \$180,000 and \$390,000, B is best.
For *EBIT* greater than \$390,000, C is best.

It would be better to consider the possible variation in *EBIT* and the resulting variation in *EPS* before reaching final conclusions as to the optimum capital structure, however.

Variability Comparisons of Capital Structures

A first approach to analyzing capital structures with respect to variability in *EBIT* and the resulting variability in *EPS* is to use a class of estimates of *EBIT* that do not involve a complete statistical distribution of values. One such class of estimates would include three values for *EBIT*, the most likely value, the lowest possible value, and the highest possible value.

Suppose for the three-structure example that the most likely value of *EBIT* is \$300,000, the lowest possible value is \$200,000, and the highest possible value is \$400,000. The range of possible variations is therefore

$$\$400{,}000 - \$200{,}000 = \$200{,}000$$

For each capital structure four values of *EPS* can be calculated, the most likely, the lowest possible, the highest possible, and the range of outcomes. For structure A those calculations are:

$$\text{Most likely } EPS = \frac{(\$300{,}000)(1 - 0.4)}{100{,}000} = \$1.80$$

$$\text{Lowest possible } EPS = \frac{(\$200{,}000)(1 - 0.4)}{100{,}000} = \$1.20$$

$$\text{Highest possible } EPS = \frac{(\$400{,}000)(1 - 0.4)}{100{,}000} = \$2.40$$

Range of *EPS* = \$2.40 – \$1.20 = \$1.20

For structure B the results are:

$$\text{Most likely } EPS = \frac{(\$300{,}000 - \$72{,}000)(1 - 0.4)}{60{,}000} = \$2.28$$

$$\text{Lowest possible } EPS = \frac{(\$200{,}000 - \$72{,}000)(1 - 0.4)}{60{,}000} = \$1.28$$

$$\text{Highest possible } EPS = \frac{(\$400{,}000 - \$72{,}000)(1 - 0.4)}{60{,}000} = \$3.28$$

Range of *EPS* = \$3.28 – \$1.28 = \$2.00

The results of structure C are:

$$\text{Most likely } EPS = \frac{(\$300{,}000)(1 - 0.4) - \$75{,}000}{50{,}000} = \$2.10$$

$$\text{Lowest possible } EPS = \frac{(\$200{,}000)(1 - 0.4) - \$75{,}000}{50{,}000} = \$0.90$$

$$\text{Highest possible } EPS = \frac{(\$400{,}000)(1 - 0.4) - \$75{,}000}{50{,}000} = \$3.30$$

Range of *EPS* = \$3.30 – \$0.90 = \$2.40

The efficiency rules of Chapter 7 could be modified and applied at this point to allow some choice among these capital structures for the assumed *EBIT* estimates. If the most likely *EPS* is labelled "expected return" and the range of *EPS* is called "risk," then structure C could be eliminated from further consideration because it is dominated by structure B. That is, structure B has a higher expected return, \$2.28 versus \$2.10, and a lower amount of risk, \$2.00 versus \$2.40. Therefore B eliminates C from the contest. No dominance results between A and B since B has both a higher expected return and a higher amount of risk.

Another class of estimates of *EBIT* may be used in analyzing the capital structures. Rather than the slightly cruder measures of the most likely value and the range of *EBIT*, estimates of the mean or expected value of *EBIT* and the standard deviation of *EBIT* may be made. Corresponding calculations of the expected value of *EPS* and the standard deviation of *EPS* for each capital structure can then be performed.

Since *EPS* is a linear function of *EBIT*, the formulas for the mean and the standard deviation of a linear function of a random variable may be used. If X is a random variable with mean of $E(X)$ and standard deviation $\sigma(X)$, and

$$Z = a + bX$$

then

$$E(Z) = a + bE(X)$$

and

$$\sigma(Z) = b\sigma(X)$$

The calculation of the expected *EPS*, *E*(*EPS*), can be performed by substituting *E*(*EBIT*) in the *EPS* equation. The *EPS* equation can be rewritten as

$$EPS = \frac{(-\text{ Interest})(1 - \text{Tax rate}) - \text{Preferred dividend}}{\text{Number of common shares}} + \frac{(1 - \text{Tax rate})}{\text{Number of common shares}} (EBIT)$$

Therefore $\sigma(EPS)$ can be calculated from the formula

$$\sigma(EPS) = \frac{(1 - \text{Tax rate})}{\text{Number of common shares}} [\sigma(EBIT)]$$

Now suppose the expected value *E*(*EBIT*) is \$280,000, and the standard deviation $\sigma(EBIT)$ is \$80,000. For structure A the results in *EPS* are:

$$E(EPS) = \frac{(\$280{,}000)(1 - 0.4)}{100{,}000} = \$1.68$$

$$\sigma(EPS) = \frac{(1 - 0.4)}{100{,}000} (\$80{,}000) = \$0.48$$

For B:

$$E(EPS) = \frac{(\$280{,}000 - \$72{,}000)(1 - 0.4)}{60{,}000} = \$2.08$$

$$\sigma(EPS) = \frac{(1 - 0.4)}{60{,}000} (\$80{,}000) = \$0.80$$

For C:

$$E(EPS) = \frac{(\$280{,}000)(1-0.4) - \$75{,}000}{50{,}000} = \$1.86$$

$$\sigma(EPS) = \frac{(1-0.4)}{50{,}000}(\$80{,}000) = \$0.96$$

In effect the standard deviation of *EBIT* is allocated 40 percent to taxes and 60 percent to net income after interest and taxes. The 60 percent residual is spread over fewer common shares as the list of capital structures is calculated.

The efficiency conditions of Chapter 7 can be invoked in a more familiar form with these numerical results. C is dominated by B because C has a lower mean and a higher standard deviation, and therefore C could be eliminated from further consideration.

The analysis of variability of *EPS* could be further expanded if the entire probability distribution of *EBIT* were known. The probability of a particular value of *EBIT* is also the probability of the corresponding value of *EPS* for a capital structure, so the derivation of the entire probability distribution of *EPS* for a structure would be a matter of simple arithmetic. For each value of *EBIT* calculate the resulting *EPS*, and then transfer the probability number from the distribution of *EBIT* to that of *EPS*.

A Continuously Variable Example

Now suppose that the corporation's organizers are considering capital structures with a continuous range of debt instead of the three fixed examples considered before. The *E*(*EBIT*) and *σ*(*EBIT*) values are still \$280,000 and \$80,000, and the corporate tax rate remains at 40 percent. By consulting with investment bankers and loan brokers it has been determined that using various levels of debt in the range from \$5000,000 to \$1,000,000 will result in interest rates on that debt ranging from 6 percent to 11 percent. The specific estimates of the debt levels and interest rates are shown in the first two columns of Table 13.1.

TABLE 13.1
EPS Results for Continuous Example

(1) Debt	(2) Interest rate	(3) Total interest charges	(4) Number of common shares	(5) *E*(*EPS*)	(6) *σ*(*EPS*)
500,000	6%	30,000	75,000	2,000	0.640
600,000	7%	42,000	70,000	2.040	0.686
700,000	8%	56,000	65,000	2.068	0.738
800,000	9%	72,000	60,000	2.080	0.800
900,000	10%	90,000	55,000	2.073	0.873
1,000,000	11%	110,000	50,000	2.040	0.960

The interest rate on debt begins at a level of 6 percent and increases by 1 percent for each \$100,000 increase in debt. Accordingly the total interest charges shown in the third column of the table start at \$30,000 for \$500,000 debt, and increase to \$110,000 for \$1,000,000 debt.

As the debt used in the capital structure varies, so will the number of common shares. Assuming that common stock is sold at \$20 a share, the number of shares for the various debt levels is shown in column four.

Column five, $E(EPS)$, is computed using the procedures of the preceding section, as is the sixth column's entries, the $\sigma(EPS)$. For example, the $E(EPS)$ figure for \$500,000 of debt is

$$\frac{(\$280{,}000 - \$30{,}000)(1 - 0.4)}{75{,}000} = \$2{,}000$$

$\sigma(EPS)$ for \$500,000 is

$$\frac{(1 - 0.4)}{75{,}000}(\$80{,}000) = \$0.640$$

The effect of the varying debt levels can be seen from inspection of the numbers in column five of the table. Increasing debt increases the $E(EPS)$ level for a while, but after reaching \$800,000 debt the $E(EPS)$ level falls for further debt increases. Consider the move from \$700,000 debt to \$800,000: the reduction in common shares "saves" \$2.068 per share times 5,000 shares for a total of \$10,340; against this must be netted the after-tax increase in interest payments,

$$(\$72{,}000 - \$56{,}000)(1 - 0.4) = \$9{,}600$$

and because the net of

$$\$10{,}340 - \$9{,}600 = \$740$$

is positive, $E(EPS)$ increases for this debt increment. For the change from \$800,000 to \$900,000 the amount "saved" through the reduction of the number of common shares is

$$5{,}000(\$2.080) = \$10{,}400$$

the after-tax interest costs added are

$$(\$90{,}000 - \$72{,}000)(1 - 0.4) = \$10{,}800$$

and since the increased interest cost is greater than the savings in earnings by \$400 the $E(EPS)$ falls for this move.

In Table 13.1 the interest rates on debt shown in column 2 are average interest rates. It might be desirable to investigate the *marginal* interest rates more completely. When the debt is increased from

\$500,000 to \$600,000 the total interest charge goes from \$30,000 to \$42,000. Dividing the change in total interest charges by the change in debt, the marginal interest rate for this increment in debt can be derived:

$$\frac{\$42{,}000 - \$30{,}000}{\$600{,}000 - \$500{,}000} = 12\%$$

The marginal interest rate can be converted to an after-tax marginal interest rate by multiplying by the factor (1 – Tax Rate). For the example the corporate income tax rate is 40 percent, so the after-tax marginal interest rate for the increase from \$500,000 debt to \$600,000 debt is

$$12\%(1 - 0.4) = 7.2\%$$

Because the common stock is sold at a fixed price of \$20 a share in this example an expected earnings yield on common stock can be derived by dividing expected earnings per share, *E*(*EPS*), by the price of the common stock, \$20. Accordingly, the expected earnings yield at a debt level of \$500,000 is

$$\frac{\$2{,}000}{\$20} = 10\%$$

For the debt level of \$600,000 the expected earnings yield is

$$\frac{\$2{,}040}{\$20} = 10.2\%$$

In Table 13.2 the results of the computations of the before-tax marginal interest rate, the after-tax marginal interest rate, and the expected earnings yield for the example of Table 13.1 are summarized.

TABLE 13.2
Marginal Interest Rates and Yields for Continuous Example

Debt	Before-tax marginal interest rate	After-tax marginal interest rate	Expected earnings yield
500,000	-	-	10.000%
600,000	12%	7.2%	10.200%
700,000	14$	8.4%	10.340%
800,000	16%	9.6%	10.400%
900,000	18%	10.8%	10.365%
1,000,000	20%	12.0%	10.200%

E(*EPS*) increases as debt is expanded until the after-tax marginal interest rate exceeds the expected earnings yield on common stock. From Table 13.2 that would occur if debt were increased from \$800,000 to \$900,000. Therefore the highest *E*(*EPS*) is achieved with a debt level of \$800,000.

σ(*EPS*) increases as the debt level is increased because the after-tax total standard deviation, \$48,000, is spread over a smaller number of common shares.

Figure 13.8
E(*EPS*) and σ(*EPS*)
for Continuous Example

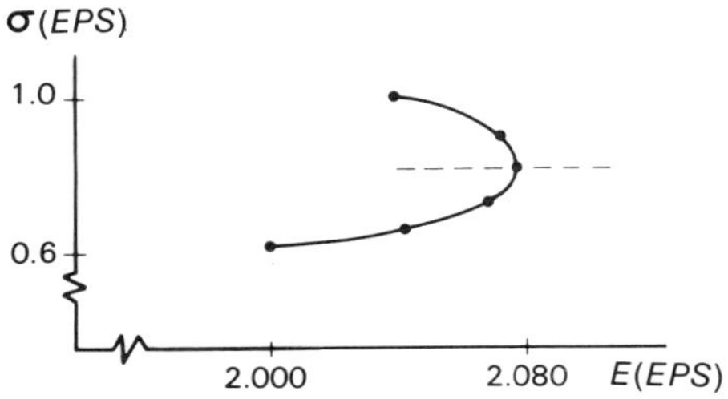

The results of this numerical example can be summarized graphically, as in Figure 13.8. In this diagram σ(*EPS*) is plotted against *E*(*EPS*) for the points included in Table 13.1. The combinations between those discrete values are derived by a free-hand curve connecting the six points.

In the curve of Figure 13.8 it can be seen again that σ(*EPS*) increases as the amount of debt is increased for all the values included in the numerical example. *E*(*EPS*) increases for a while, and then decreases. While the choice of the exact capital structure that will be optimal for the corporation's common stockholders cannot be made exactly without further knowledge of their return-risk preferences expressed in earnings per share, the inefficient region can be identified from the figure. The combinations above the dashed line are inefficient because the same *E*(*EPS*) can be obtained with a lower σ(*EPS*) by selecting a structure below the dashed line. The appropriate choice for the planners in the numerical example is some debt level below \$800,000.

Figure 13.9
Optimum Capital Structure
with Earnings Criterion

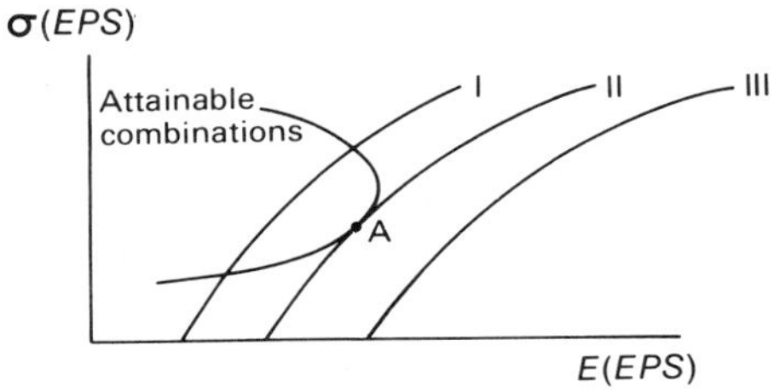

If the stockholders' return-risk preferences could be derived in some way, those preferences could be expressed by a set of indifference curves drawn in the *E*(*EPS*)–σ(*EPS*) plane. A set of three indifference curves are shown in Figure 13.9. As is usual the higher-numbered curves indicate higher levels of satisfaction. The highest obtainable indifference curve is at the point of tangency between the attainable capital structure and indifference curve II in the diagram, point A. This point represents the optimum capital structure when *EPS* is used as the criterion of selection.

Distributions of Income on Senior Securities

In studying the earnings per share of common stock for various capital structures under varying earnings levels, the interest payments on debt and the dividend payment on preferred stock were always treated as certain quantities not subject to statistical variation. This assumption of certainty is correct when the analysis is from the viewpoint of residual security-holders, the owners of the common stock, but must be modified when the analysis is from the viewpoint of the senior security-holder, the owner of the debt instrument or of the preferred stock.

The lender to a corporation cannot always be certain that the stated interest payments and principal repayments will be made in full on the scheduled date. The borrower may encounter financial difficulties, a cash shortage, and either delay the scheduled payments, or if the degree of the difficulty is severe enough, the amount of payment may be reduced. The lender may have to accept an extension or composition arrangement, or bankruptcy proceedings may legally result in delays or reduction in the payments. Accordingly the lender may anticipate varying degrees of financial risk in loan situations, and adjust the stated interest rate accordingly. Normally the larger the loan in proportion to the size or income of the borrower, the greater the degree of financial risk to the lender.

The financial risk to the purchaser of a preferred stock should be more obvious since the passing of a preferred dividend by the corporation does not result in default and subsequent bankruptcy actions by the security-holders. The payment of dividends is dependent on the corporation making an after-tax income, which may not happen. With a cumulative preferred stock the passed dividends are carried over to later periods, and the delay in receipt of some of the dividends would cause the holder's yield to be less than the stated yield.

These senior securities then may have a peculiar form of distribution of yields. The lender to a corporation on a nonmarketable loan at a stated interest rate of 8 percent will never receive a yield greater than 8 percent, but may receive less. A buyer of a corporate bond who holds the bond to maturity cannot receive a yield greater than the stated rate (equal to the coupon yield if he paid the par value for the bond), but he might receive less if the coupon payments or redemption payment are delayed or reduced. The buyer of a corporate bond could have an actual yield higher than the stated rate if (1) interest rates in the market fall, the price of the bond rises, and he sells the bond prior to maturity, or (2) if the bond is recalled by the corporation at a call price higher than the par value. Confining the analysis to financial risk considerations alone, though, results in a maximum possible yield on these debt securities.

If the distribution of yields to the security-holders is bounded at the upper end by the stated yield, the distribution may have the appearance of that one shown in Figure 13.10.

Figure 13.10
Distribution of Yield on Fixed-Interest Loan

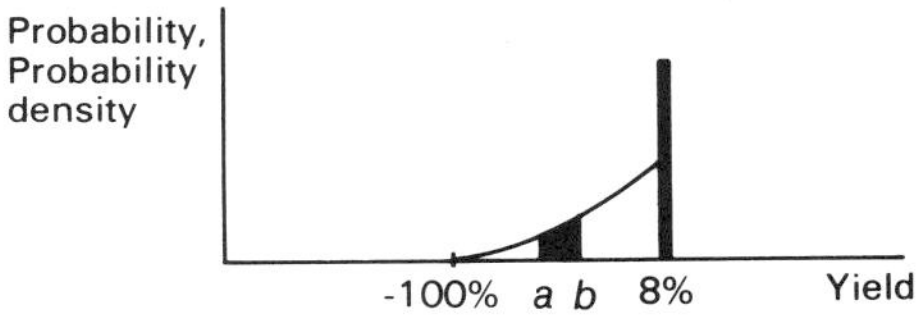

In Figure 13.10 the possible realized yields for a one-year loan at a stated interest rate of 8 percent are plotted. These yields range from a high of 8 percent that occurs if the interest and principal payments are made in full on schedule, to a low of −100 percent that occurs if the borrower defaults entirely, paying neither interest nor principal.

The vertical axis of Figure 13.10 measures the probability of the 8 percent yield, and the probability density of other possible yields. The probability of the stated yield of 8 percent is a nonzero number, such as 0.93, and is measured as the height of that vertical bar. Because the remainder of the distribution is continuous, a nonzero probability can only be derived for ranges of values on the horizontal axis, such as a yield between a and b, by integrating the probability density function over that range of values. The probability of a yield between a and b equals the shaded area under the probability density curve between those two limits in Figure 13.10.

The distribution of the yield on the fixed-income security shown in Figure 13.10 can be used to derive some characteristics about the parameters of the distribution of yields that can be applied to other senior securities.

First, the mean of the distribution is less than the stated yield by some amount. Although the stated yield is 8 percent the investor in the security may expect (in the statistical sense) to receive something less, say 7.8 percent.

The distribution of yields has a nonzero standard deviation because other outcomes besides 8 percent are possible. This standard deviation should be used in the investor's risk evaluation of the security.

The distribution in Figure 13.10 shows a negative skewness (the tail of the distribution is to the left). A negative skewness would probably be viewed unfavorably by the average investor because, as in this example, his possible gains are limited but he has some chance of large losses.

Figure 13.11
Distribution of Yield on a Marketable Fixed-Interest Security

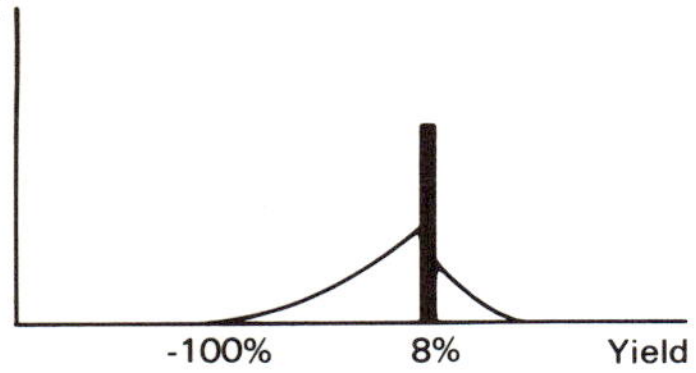

In Figure 13.11 is plotted a possible distribution of yields for a fixed-coupon (8 percent) security that is marketable, or callable at some premium over par value. The possibility of the investor selling this security at some price in excess of his purchase price is explicitly allowed for in this diagram by having a tail to the right in the distribution. For those outcomes to the right of the vertical bar, the stated yield, the investor realizes the higher yield through a capital gain on disposition of the security. Those outcomes to the left of the vertical bar include not only the cases where the issuer of the security defaults on some of the obligations, but also the cases where the investor suffers a capital loss on disposition of the security.

The distribution in Figure 13.11 would probably have a wider dispersion than that of Figure 13.10 because the addition of marketability to the security adds another type of risk to the security-holder. Not only does he have to consider the financial ability of the issuer, but now he has to take into account possible changes in market price due to fluctuations in the general level of interest rates in the economy, "interest-rate risk."

The Figure 13.11 distribution is still drawn with some degree of negative skewness because the probability of a realized yield less than the stated yield of 8 percent seems to be greater than that of a yield above 8 percent. Therefore the mean of the distribution would be slightly less than the stated yield. The standard deviation of yields is a positive number, an undesirable characteristic. The negative skewness is also probably undesirable to the investor.

Figure 13.12
Distribution of Yields on a Convertible Debenture

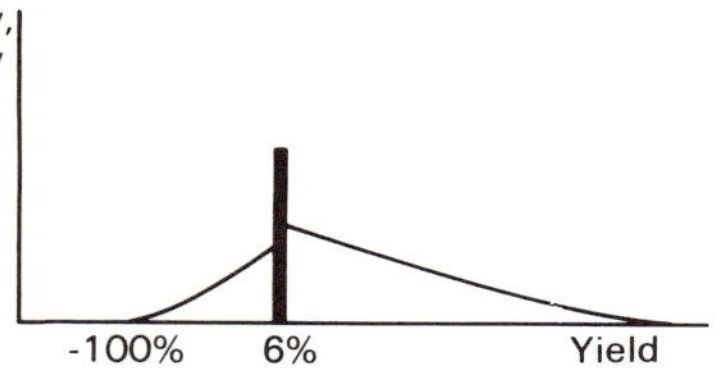

As a corporation modifies its capital structure by adding more debt or other senior securities, the perceived risk to those prospective lenders or security purchasers should increase. In terms of the diagrams in Figures 13.10 and 13.11 the probability of a yield less than the stated rate would increase. To compensate for the increased risk the lenders and investors will require a higher stated yield, the interest rate on loans and bonds or the dividend rate on preferred stock. By getting a higher stated yield the lenders and investors may increase their expected yields.

Distributions of Yields on Convertible Securities

Because convertible securities have such a different distribution of yields to the buyer, it is worthwhile to look at these security forms separately. When an investor buys a convertible debenture, for example, and plans to hold it to maturity or conversion time, whichever occurs first, the stated or coupon rate is only one of the possible yields he may achieve. A possible distribution of yields for a 6 percent coupon convertible debenture is shown in Figure 13.12.

A yield less than 6 percent would result if the corporation defaults on its interest or principal payments. The yield of 6 percent would be realized if the conversion privilege is never exercised, and the interest and principal payments are made on schedule. A yield greater than 6 percent can be achieved if it becomes worthwhile to convert into common stock having a greater value than the debenture's par value at some time before maturity.

If the buyer does not intend to hold the convertible until maturity or conversion, the outcomes below 6 percent would include those cases where the security is sold at a price less than par value. The outcomes above 6 percent would include the cases where the security is sold at a price greater than par value.

As drawn in Figure 13.12 it is possible for the expected yield on a convertible to be greater than the coupon yield. The distribution in Figure 13.12 is also positively skewed, in contrast to those of Figures 13.10 and 13.11 for nonconvertible senior securities. The chance of a large yield is the characteristic that distinguishes convertible issues from nonconvertible, and at least partially justifies the lower coupon interest rates required to market those issues successfully.

Summary

The choice of capital structure by the corporation's management determines the distribution of earnings per share on common stock. The choice of capital structures was developed first in terms of breakeven comparisons among fixed structures, and then in terms of a continuously variable capital structure with resulting expected earnings per share, $E(EPS)$, and standard deviation of earnings per share, $\sigma(EPS)$. The efficiency rules from Chapter 8 were invoked to screen out some capital structures from further consideration, but choice of an exact capital structure was still dependent on the common stockholders' return-risk preferences, expressed diagramatically in the form of indifference curves.

One of the factors in the capital structure models that affected the solution was the interest rate on debt. It is reasonable to assume that the interest rate on debt would increase as the debt proportion of the structure increases. While the corporation's managers may treat interest payments as a fixed quantity, investors are more likely to consider their yields on fixed-income securities as random variables. The stated or coupon yield may be the most likely value in the distribution, but it is probable that the expected yield would be less than the coupon yield because of the one-tailed nature of the distribution. When investigating convertible securities, however, the distribution of yields could be positively skewed, and the expected yield higher than the coupon yield.

The income or earnings criterion for capital structure design is not adequate for all situations. A more general optimization would be based on the wealth of common stockholders, determined by the market value of their common stock. The market value criterion is explored in the following chapter.

Note

[1] A lower dividend rate on preferred stock than the interest rate on bonds is used in this example because market yields tend to show this sort of perversity. Although the preferred stock would seem to be a riskier investment than bonds

because of the deferrability of dividend payments by the issuer, this seems to be outweighed by the preferential tax treatment of dividend income by a corporate holder. A corporation such as an insurance company holding preferred stock can exclude 85 percent of dividends received when computing taxable income, but interest receipts are fully taxable. Therefore even if the before-tax yield on preferred stocks is lower the after-tax yield may be sufficiently higher to compensate the corporate holder for the increased risk.

Chapter 13 Questions

1. When two capital structures are compared by an *EBIT-EPS* break-even chart, is it correct to make a decision based upon a single estimate of *EBIT* or should the whole range of possible *EBIT* values be considered?
2. Is *EPS* necessarily a linear function of *EBIT*? What happens when the corporate tax rate is not a constant, as when the $25,000 figure is reached and the marginal tax rate goes from 22 percent to 48 percent?
3. Is *EPS* the only criterion for capital structure decisions, or is the analysis of this chapter incomplete?
4. Does the tax-deductibility of interest payments imply that the government is subsidizing corporate bond issues?
5. How would a model based on the range and mode of *EBIT* (and *EPS*) differ from a model based on the standard deviation and mean? Is the range a less accurate measure of dispersion of outcomes than the standard deviation? What is the statistical relationship between the mode and the mean?
6. When calculating $\sigma(EPS)$ the standard deviation of interest payments or preferred dividend payments was assumed to be zero, implying that those payments are risk free (certain) from the aspect of the corporation that sold the securities. The holder of the bonds or preferred stock must view his returns as having some degree of risk, however. Is there any paradox in these two views?
7. Why should the average interest rate on debt increase as the proportion of debt in the capital structure increases?
8. Explain the relationship between the average interest rate and the marginal interest rate.
9. Why will $\sigma(EPS)$ always increase as the debt proportion of the capital structure increases?
10. Why does $E(EPS)$ sometimes increase and sometimes decrease as the debt proportion increases?
11. Summarize the circumstances where the holder of a bond might realize a return less than the stated yield. Do the same thing for returns greater than the stated yield.
12. In general would you expect the distribution of yields on a bond to be positively or negatively skewed? How about yields on a convertible?

Chapter 13 Problems

1. Corporation A has $5,000,000 of 8 percent bonds, 60,000 shares of $7 preferred stock, and 100,000 shares of common stock outstanding. The corporate income tax rate is 45 percent. At what level of *EBIT* will the *EPS* on common equal $1.00?

2. Corporation B has a choice of three capital structures:

1. 300,000 shares of common stock and $20,000,000 of 9 percent bonds.

2. 200,000 shares of common stock and 150,000 shares of $8 dividend preferred stock.

3. 500,000 shares of common stock. The corporate income tax rate is 50 percent.

a. For what range of *EBIT* values will structure 1 yield the highest *EPS* on common?

b. For what range of *EBIT* values will structure 2 yield the highest *EPS*?

c. For what range of *EBIT* values will structure 3 yield the highest *EPS*?

3. Corporation C has $2,000,000 of 7 percent bonds, $1,000,000 of 8 percent preferred stock, and 30,000 shares of common stock outstanding. The corporation's *EBIT* is a random variable with mean, $E(EBIT)$, of $700,000 and standard deviation, $\sigma(EBIT)$, of $200,000. The corporate income tax rate is 40 percent. Calculate:

a. $E(EPS)$.

b. $\sigma(EPS)$.

4. Corporation C's capital structure (described in problem 3) is to be used for a different distribution of *EBIT*. Instead of a known $E(EBIT)$ and $\sigma(EBIT)$ the entire probability distribution of *EBIT* is:

EBIT	Probability
300,000	0.1
400,000	0.3
500,000	0.4
900,000	0.2

Derive the probability distribution of *EPS* for Corporation C.

5. Corporation D must raise $3,000,000 of capital through a combination of bonds and stock. The common stock will be sold at $100 a share in all cases, but the interest rates on bonds will vary as the size of the bond issue. The investment banker's estimate of the interest rates for the variation size issues is:

Size of issue	Interest rate
400,000	6%
800,000	7%
1,200,000	8%
1,600,000	9%

The corporate income tax rate is 40 percent, $E(EBIT)$ is $300,000, and $\sigma(EBIT)$ is $100,000. For each of the four capital structures calculate $E(EPS)$ and $\sigma(EPS)$.

6. In problem 5 what are the marginal interest rates on debt?

Chapter 13 References

Baxter, Nevins D. "Leverage, Risk of Ruin and the Cost of Capital." *Journal of Finance*, September 1967.

Bierman, H., Jr. "Risk and Addition of Debt to the Capital Structure." *Journal of Financial and Quantitative Analysis*, December 1968.

Boness, A. James. "A Pedagogic Note on the Cost of Capital." *Journal of Finance*, March 1964.

Cragg, J. G., and Malkiel, B. G. "Consensus and Accuracy of Some Predictions of the Growth of Corporate Earnings." *Journal of Finance*, March 1968.

Gordon, Myron J. *The Investment, Financing and Valuation of the Corporation*. Homewood, Ill.: Irwin, 1962.

—— "Optimal Investment and Financing Policy." *Journal of Finance*, May 1963.

Murphy, J. E., Jr. "Effect of Leverage on Profitability, Growth, and Market Valuation of Common Stock." *Financial Analysts Journal*, July-August 1968.

Mumey, Glen A. *Theory of Financial Structure.* New York: Holt, Rinehart & Winston, 1969.

Porterfield, James T. S. *Investment Decisions and Capital Costs.* Englewood Cliffs, N. J.: Prentice-Hall, 1965.

Robichek, Alexander A., and Myers, Stewart C. *Optimal Financing Decisions*. Englewood Cliffs, N. J.: Prentice-Hall, 1965.

Schwartz, Eli. "Theory of the Capital Structure of the Firm." *Journal of Finance*, March 1959.

Solomon, Ezra. "Measuring a Company's Cost of Capital." *Journal of Business*, October 1955.

14

OPTIMUM CAPITAL STRUCTURE—MARKET VALUE CRITERION

In this chapter the capital structure of the corporation is studied from the aspect of market value per share of common stock. Variations in the capital structure, changing the debt-equity ratio, may cause a change in the total market value of the firm and therefore the market value per share of common stock.

To isolate the capital structure effect the assets of the corporation are held constant again. Those assets produce an annual revenue stream that is subject to some statistical variation, but with a known expected value and standard deviation.

Variations in the capital structure are accomplished by increasing the debt and reducing the number of common shares outstanding, or by decreasing the debt and increasing the number of common shares. Corporations in this chapter are limited to the two types of security, debt and common stock.

The debt is a type of marketable note that always sells at its par value in the numerical examples. The assumption of a fixed market value for debt is not unrealistic if the debt is defined to be one-year notes that are replaced each year with a new issue. The interest rates required on those notes are varied by purchasers on the basis of their assessments of the risk due to operations and capital structure of the issuing corporation.

The common stock analyzed is sold originally at a fixed price, but can fluctuate in market price later. It is possible, therefore, for a common stockholder to obtain a capital gain or suffer a capital loss as the per-share price varies.

Rather than present every example's results in terms of a price per share of common stock the summary will be in terms of the total value of the corporation's securities, the sum of the aggregate market value of debt and of common stock. For each example the original sales price of debt and equity is fixed at a total, and variations from that total occur in the total market value of common stock. Since the number of shares is fixed the variation must be in the price per share.

An example should help to clarify the points. Suppose a corporation needs \$200,000 original capital to acquire its assets. The corporation borrows \$60,000 through its debt issue, and sells 7,000 shares of common stock at \$20 a share. Now after the corporation acquires its assets and begins operations the securities are free to change in market value. Suppose the total market value of the corporation becomes \$220,000. The market value of the debt is still \$60,000 by assumption, and the market value of the common stock must therefore be

$$\$220{,}000 - \$60{,}000 = \$160{,}000$$

There are still 7,000 shares of common outstanding, so the market price per share is

$$\frac{\$160{,}000}{7{,}000} = \$22.86$$

The original subscribers to the common stock issue have received a capital gain of \$2.86 a share.

Now suppose a second corporation with a different capital structure is to be compared with the first. The second corporation also needs \$200,000 to acquire its assets, but sells \$100,000 of debt, and 5,000 shares of common at \$20 a share. After it begins operations the total market value of its securities becomes \$230,000. The market value of its debt is \$100,000, the issue price, and therefore the total market value of common is

$$\$230{,}000 - \$100{,}000 = \$130{,}000$$

Since there are 5,000 shares of common outstanding, the price per share of the second corporation is

$$\frac{\$130{,}000}{5{,}000} = \$26$$

The original subscribers to the common stock of the second corporation have received a capital gain of \$6 a share.

Now when the two corporations are compared to see which has the better capital structure, the analysis can be expressed in terms either of total market value of securities (total market value of the firm) or of the price per share of common stock. The second corporation has a better capital structure than the first corporation using either measure.

The results of capital structures can also be expressed in terms of market capitalization rates. A market capitalization rate is the expected yield to a purchaser of a security, and of course that yield varies (inversely) as the price paid for the security varies. If an investor pays \$26 for a share of common stock and anticipates an expected dividend annually of \$2.60, his yield is

$$\frac{\$2.60}{\$26} = 10\%$$

since the \$2.60 annual payment is a perpetuity. The market capitalization rate is usually expressed in terms of total values, so if the total market value of common stock is \$130,000 and the total expected dividends are \$13,000, the market capitalization rate is computed as

$$\frac{\$13{,}000}{\$130{,}000} = 10\%$$

There are three market capitalization rates shown for the corporations in the examples below, the debt rate, the equity rate, and an overall rate. The definitions of these rates are:

$$\text{Debt market capitalization rate} = \frac{\text{Total payments to debt-holders}}{\text{Total market value of debt}}$$

$$\text{Equity market capitalization rate} = \frac{\text{Total payments to common stockholders}}{\text{Total market value of common stock}}$$

$$\text{Overall market capitalization rate} = \frac{\text{Total payments to all security-holders}}{\text{Total market value of securities}}$$

If the second corporation above paid $9,000 interest on its debt and $13,000 dividends on common stock, the three capitalization rates for the market values assumed above would be:

$$\text{Debt market capitalization rate} = \frac{\$9{,}000}{\$100{,}000} = 9\%$$

$$\text{Equity market capitalization rate} = \frac{\$13{,}000}{\$130{,}000} = 10\%$$

$$\text{Overall market capitalization rate} = \frac{\$22{,}000}{\$230{,}000} = 9.56\%$$

In one stage of the model when corporation income taxes do not exist, the overall market capitalization rate can be interpreted as the corporation's cost of capital. At later stages, though, the total payments to security-holders are not equal to the *after-tax* payments of the corporation, so the cost of capital label cannot be used.

The model of the chapter is developed in three stages, with numerical examples being used to check for the existence of equilibrium at each stage. The first two stages correspond to two well-known models usually called after their authors, the "Modigliani-Miller models."[1] Briefly, in the first stage of this chapter's model, the "early Modigliani-Miller model," corporation and investor income taxes do not exist. In the second stage, the "later Modigliani-Miller model," corporation income taxes are introduced. In the final stage of the model, investor income taxes are considered. Although the implications of each stage's results for capital structure management will be discussed, application to actual capital structure decisions should be delayed until the third stage of the model where the list of assumptions used in the model comes closest to reality.

In each stage of the model a comparison will be made between two corporations identical in all respects except capital structure. The values of the two corporations' securities form a set of prices that can be checked for local equilibrium conditions. If the price of one corporation's common stock is too high relative to the other corporation's, there should be a tendency for investors to sell the high-priced stock and buy the lower-priced stock instead. This switching, or arbitrage, will cause a change in the relative prices of securities until those prices have moved into an equilibrium relationship. A set of equilibrium prices, therefore, is one in which there is no natural tendency toward change. The equilibrium prices to be explored here can be expressed as the market price of securities or as the market capitalization rate for the securities.

The Assumptions of the Model in Stage 1

Several assumptions must be made in the process of building the theoretical model. These assumptions fall into three categories: those regarding the behavior of investors, those regarding the corporations' actions, and those concerned with the tax environment of individuals and corporations.

There are four assumptions regarding investors:

1. Investors are free to buy and sell any securities at will.
2. Investors can borrow without restriction at the same terms as corporations.
3. Investors have perfect knowledge about the income characteristics of securities.
4. Transactions costs, the cost of buying and selling securities are zero.

These four assumptions will remain unchanged throughout the three stages of this chapter's model.

The assumptions about the actions of corporations are:

5. Corporations can be classified into "risk classes," depending on the characteristics of their income streams from assets.
6. Corporations pay all net earnings to security-holders.

The tax environment assumptions are:

7. There are no individual income taxes.
8. There are no corporation income taxes.

The assumptions about investor behavior define a perfectly competitive market situation for corporate securities. The ability of investors to buy and sell securities at will is at slight variance with real life since the investments of some economic units, such as banks, are restricted by government agencies. Investors may not be able to borrow at the same terms as corporations because of size economies passed on to borrowers by the lenders, and because of such nonprice restrictions as the margin regulations of the Federal Reserve Board. Investors will not always have exact knowledge about the income characteristics of the securities they evaluate. The perfect knowledge assumed here is about the statistical distribution of dividends on common stock, not an exact forecast of the amount of each dividend. The assumption of zero transactions costs is made for convenience rather than reality. It usually costs between 1 percent and 5 percent of the value of the transaction to buy or sell a common stock.

Corporations are not assumed to be homogeneous units, each engaged in the same business. Instead, the management of each corporation chooses the assets of the firm to meet varied goals. The classification of assumption 5 is performed by investors on the basis of their knowledge attained through the circumstances of assumption 3.

The assumption that corporations pay all net earnings to security-holders will be modified in stage 3 of the model. For now, each corporation first pays interest on debt from the period's earnings before interest and taxes (*EBIT*), and then distributes the residual as cash dividends to the holders of common stock. In stages 1 and 2 of the model there are no retained earnings, and therefore no expansion of the corporation is possible.

The assumptions that there are no income taxes, individual or corporate, are made in the early stages of the model to facilitate the derivation of equilibrium conditions. Accordingly, the early results of stages 1 and 2 are not to be applied directly to real-world analysis since serious distortions would result from the lack of consideration of the various provisions of the tax code. In stage 2 assumption 8 is modified, and in stage 3 assumption 7 is changed.

The Two-Corporation Example

To illustrate the model two example corporations, Babbitt Corp. and Hobbitt Corp., are used. Babbitt has no debt in its capital structure, only common stock. Hobbitt has sold \$75,000 of debt at an 8 percent annual interest rate, and the remainder of its capital structure is common stock. The debt is one-year debt, but is refinanced each time it is due. Therefore Hobbitt's annual interest charges, the only debt-servicing charges necessary, are \$6,000.

Each of the two corporations have invested in assets that produce an expected annual return, *E*(*EBIT*), of \$24,000, and a standard deviation, *σ*(*EBIT*), of \$15,000.

The first approximation to the value of Babbitt's common stock is \$200,000, which corresponds to a market capitalization rate of 12 percent. That is, the total value of \$200,000 is the result of capitalizing (finding the present value of) the expected annual return of \$24,000 when an interest rate of 12 percent is used:

$$\frac{\$24{,}000}{\$200{,}000} = 12\%$$

This equity market capitalization rate is the overall market capitalization rate for Babbitt since no other securities are outstanding.

The value of Hobbitt's common stock is \$150,000 if Hobbitt's equity market capitalization rate is assumed to be the same as Babbitt's, 12 percent. The expected annual dividend on Hobbitt's common stock is

$$\$24{,}000 - \$6{,}000 = \$18{,}000$$

and dividing this amount by 12 percent yields the total market value of common stock:

$$\frac{\$18{,}000}{12\%} = \$150{,}000$$

The market value of Hobbitt's debt is \$75,000 if the market capitalization for that debt is 8 percent, the coupon rate. Therefore the total market value of Hobbitt's securities, the market value of the firm, is

$$\$150{,}000 + \$75{,}000 = \$225{,}000$$

The overall market capitalization rate for Hobbitt (in this case the cost of capital) can be calculated by adding together the total payments to security-holders and dividing by the total value of outstanding securities:

$$\frac{\$18{,}000 + \$6{,}000}{\$150{,}000 + \$75{,}000} = \frac{\$24{,}000}{\$225{,}000} = 10\tfrac{2}{3}\%$$

In total security-holders have paid $225,000 to receive an expected income of $24,000 a year, so they receive a yield of 10 2/3 percent.

The discrepancy between the market evaluations of the two firms should begin to be apparent at this point. Babbitt's security-holders only had to pay $200,000 for the expected annual income stream of $24,000, while Hobbitt's security-holders paid $225,000 for the same income stream. Although Babbitt and Hobbitt have the same type of assets and size of assets, Babbitt is capitalized overall at 12 percent and Hobbitt at 10 2/3 percent. The set of market values, or the set of capitalization rates, used up to this point is not an equilbrium set.

Solution of Stage 1 by Arbitrage

The disequilibrium state can be shown through an investor's arbitrage operations. The set of values presented above would allow an investor to improve his income position by switching from one set of securities to another set. The switch is from the overvalued stock to the undervalued stock.

Suppose an investor initially holds $1,500 of Hobbitt stock. This stock represents the ownership of 1 percent of Hobbitt Corp. since the total market value of all Hobbitt stock outstanding is $150,000. The investor's interest can be expressed in terms of his share of the income stream from assets. One percent of $24,000 is $240, the share in the expected income stream from assets. One percent of the standard deviation, $\sigma(EBIT)$, is $150. One percent of the interest payment of $6,000 is $60, the fixed amount that must be deducted from the investor's $240 to yield $180 of expected dividends, 1 percent of the total expected dividend payment of $18,000. His 1 percent ownership can also be expressed in terms of the pro-rata share of Hobbitt's debt–his stock is encumbered with $750 of debt. Of course the debt is actually owed by the corporation, not by the investor, and with limited liability features of the corporate form of ownership he would not normally be required actually to pay this amount if the corporation is unable to pay it.

Suppose the investor now sells his stock in Hobbitt, realizing $1,500 in cash. He can use that $1,500 to buy stock in Babbitt, the unlevered firm, but he can also borrow additional funds to buy Babbitt stock if he desires. If he wants to have the same degree of risk after switching to Babbitt as he had when holding Hobbitt, he can borrow an amount so that his required interest is the same as his pro rata share of Hobbitt's required interest payment, \$60. Since it has been assumed that he can borrow at the same terms (rate) as a corporation, he would borrow an amount large enough so that the interest payment at 8 percent would equal \$60, or \$750. The size of this debt is the same as his former pro rata share of Hobbitt's debt.

Now the investor has the total of \$2,250 to purchase Babbitt stock, \$1,500 from his equity and \$750 from a debt issue. If he purchases \$2,250 of Babbitt common stock at the going market price he will receive an expected dividend of \$270. (12 percent of \$2,250 is \$270.) From the \$270 of dividends the \$60 interest payment must be deducted, leaving a residual expected income of \$210 after the investor completes the switch from Hobbitt to Babbitt common stock. His standard deviation of dividends is

$$\frac{2{,}250}{200{,}000}(15{,}000) = \$168.75$$

Now the question is whether the investor is clearly better off after the arbitrage than before. If his risk were measured only by the amount of the fixed interest payment[2] it would be the same after as before, \$60. But if risk is to be measured by standard deviation of dividends his risk has increased at the same time as his expected return as shown in Figure 14.1. In Figure 14.1 point *H* is the mean-standard deviation combination the investor had before the switch, and point *B* the combination after the switch.

Figure 14.1
First Arbitraging Results

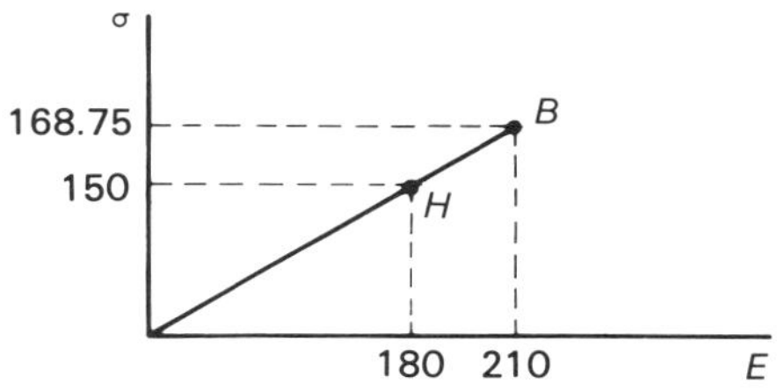

However, the investor does not have to invest the whole amount of \$2,250 in Babbitt stock. He can spend somewhat less on Babbitt stock and achieve the same combination of expected income and standard deviation of income as when he held Hobbitt stock.

If the investor spends \$2,000 on Babbitt stock his expected dividends will be \$240, from which is subtracted his interest payment of \$60 to yield an expected income of \$180. His standard deviation of income is

$$\frac{2{,}000}{200{,}000}(15{,}000) = \$150.$$

So he can achieve the same income characteristics from Babbitt stock as he had when he held Hobbitt stock, and have \$250 left over to spend on additional securities. (He actually is moving from point *B* back to point *H*, moving along the ray from the origin as he spends less.) Clearly the investor benefits from the switching operations.

If one investor can better his position by switching from Hobbit stock to Babbitt stock, so can other investors, since they all have perfect information and the ability to buy and sell stocks. The switching would tend to drive the price of Hobbitt stock down and the price of Babbitt up, changing the respective market capitalization rates of the two companies. The switching would presumably continue until there was no longer anything to be gained by investors, until the market price set moves into equilibrium.

The set of equilibrium prices in this stage of the model is where the total market values of the two corporations are the same. Since total payments to security-holders are the same, this equilibrium set can be expressed as the point where the overall market capitalization rates (the costs of capital) are equal.

Suppose that for some reason Babbitt's stock price does not change, and all the change occurs in Hobbitt's stock. If the total market value of Hobbitt's securities is to be \$200,000, the value of the common stock must go down to \$125,000 since the market value of Hobbitt's debt remains at \$75,000. At this value the market capitalization rate of Hobbitt's common stock is

$$\frac{\$18{,}000}{\$125{,}000} = 14.4\%$$

The overall market capitalization rate of Hobbitt is now 12 percent, the same as Babbitt's:

$$\frac{\$18{,}000 + \$6{,}000}{\$125{,}000 + \$75{,}000} = 12\%$$

The set of market values:

- \$200,000 for Babbitt common stock
- \$125,000 for Hobbitt common stock
- \$75,000 for Hobbitt debt

and the set of market capitalization rates:

- 12 percent for Babbitt common stock
- 12 percent overall for Babbitt
- 14.4 percent for Hobbitt common stock
- 8 percent for Hobbitt debt
- 12 percent overall for Hobbitt

are equilibrium values according to the assumptions of this stage of the model. The fact that the values are in equilibrium can be checked by tracing a switch by an investor to see if his position can be improved.

Suppose an investor with \$1,250 of Hobbitt common stock decides to sell that stock, borrow additional funds, and buy Babbitt common stock. Before the switch he owns 1 percent of the outstanding common of Hobbitt so his expected dividend is \$180, the residual when \$60 interest is deducted from \$240 income from assets, he has a standard deviation of income of (1,250/125,000)15,000 = \$150, and his pro-rata share of the debt of Hobbitt is \$750. He sells the Hobbitt stock for \$1,250, borrows an additional \$750 at 8 percent so his total interest payment is \$60, and buys \$2,000 of Babbitt common stock. His new expected dividend total is \$240 (12 percent of \$2,000), but his interest payments of \$60 must be deducted, leaving \$180 expected income. His new standard deviation of income is (2,000/200,000)15,000 = \$150. He has not changed his income position by the switch,[3] therefore the prices and capitalization rates are in equilibrium because there is no arbitrage possibility left for investors.

In the numerical example two corporations with the same assets wound up in equilibrium with the same total market value and the same overall market capitalization rate. When the two did not have the same total value and overall market capitalization rate, individual investors could improve their income positions by switching securities, forcing the values and rates into equilibrium.

The Significance of the Stage 1 Results

The two example capital structures can be characterized as "zero debt" and "37½ percent debt," but any other values between zero debt and 100 percent debt could have been chosen and the same total market values and overall market capitalization rates achieved in equilibrium. In this stage of the model, the total market value of the corporation is dependent only on the size and composition of assets, not on the capital structure.

Figure 14.2
Market Value as a Function of Capital Structure

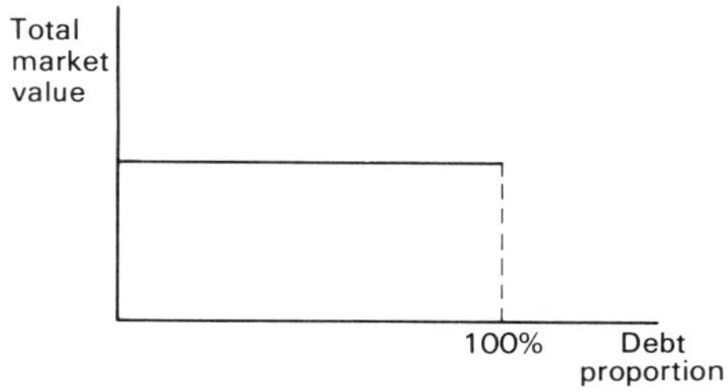

Accordingly, the results of this stage can be summarized graphically by plotting total market value of the firm against the debt proportion as in Figure 14.2.

The results of the model can also be expressed graphically by plotting the overall market capitalization rate (in this stage the overall cost of capital) against the debt proportion as in Figure 14.3.

Figure 14.3
Market Capitalization Rate as a Function of Capital Structure

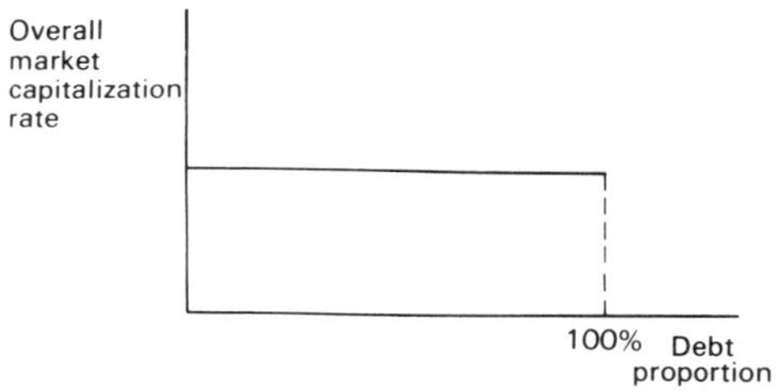

These results have significance for the managers of a corporation operating in the assumed environment. It is not possible by manipulating capital structure to alter the total market value of the firm or the overall cost of capital, and therefore capital structure is immaterial.

Of course the assumptions built into the model are not realistic enough to apply the results to actual business capital structure decisions.

Review of the Assumptions of Stage 1

It would be wise at this point to review the eight assumptions used in stage 1 of the model, the "early Modigliani-Miller model." The four assumptions about investors:

1. Investors are free to buy and sell any securities at will.
2. Investors can borrow without restriction at the same terms as corporations.
3. Investors have perfect knowledge about the income characteristics of securities.
4. Transactions costs, the cost of buying and selling securities, are zero.

serve to establish a perfect securities market for common stocks.

The first assumption simply establishes the lack of nonprice restrictions on holding securities so that some investors could be found who could switch from holding Hobbitt stock to holding Babbitt stock. The second assumption is crucial to the arbitrage process—the investor switching from the leveraged stock to the nonleveraged stock must be able to substitute "personal" leverage for "corporate" leverage at the same interest rate for the same proportion of debt. Assumption 3 is another normal assumption made to establish a perfect market so that investor uncertainty about the companies' activities will not inhibit their purchases. The fourth assumption makes the numerical examples simpler, although consideration of transactions costs would modify the arbitrage results so that the maximum variation between the firms' total market values would be limited to the sum of the purchase and the sales commissions.

The assumptions about the actions of corporations:

5. Corporations can be classified into "risk classes," depending on the characteristics of their income streams from assets.

6. Corporations pay all net earnings to security-holders.

were also used in stage 1 of the model. Assumption 5 is properly another part of the market definition. Only corporations of the same risk class (and same size) will necessarily have the same market value in equilibrium. Different market values and different overall market capitalization rates among risk classes are still possible. This model does not treat the risk structure of market capitalization rates.

The assumption that corporations pay out all the earnings to security-holders is necessary to make the model a static model rather than a dynamic model. If assumption 6 is changed (as it will be in stage 3 of the model) to allow retention of earnings, another set of capitalization problems is introduced—will retained earnings be considered the same as dividend receipts by stockholders? By holding to assumption 6 the interdependency of the corporation's asset acquisition (capital budgeting) decisions and the risk class designation is avoided. The corporation's operations remain unchanged through time.

The last two assumptions of this stage are:

7. There are no individual income taxes.

8. There are no corporation income taxes.

Assumption 7 means that the market capitalization rates, the equity rate, the debt rate, and the overall rate, are both before-tax yields and after-tax yields to the security-holder. The entire amounts received are spendable by the investor, and his selection of security types is not dependent on differential treatment of incomes by the tax authorities.

Because of assumption 8 the total payments to security-holders by a corporation are not altered by differences in capital structure. That is, the tax-deductibility of bond interest in the real world does not apply in the model because corporate income taxes are assumed away.

Stage 2 of the Model

To introduce a greater degree of reality to the model the eighth assumption must be modified to allow for corporate income taxes. Once this modification is made the model will have reached the second stage, which corresponds to the "later Modigliani-Miller" model.

Assumption 8 is discarded and in its place assumption 8a will be used:

8a. Corporation income taxes must be paid on net income after interest on debt.

The other seven assumptions remain unchanged.

The consequence of corporate income taxes with the tax-deductibility of interest payments is the alteration of total payments to security-holders as the capital structure is varied. As more debt is added interest payments rise, reducing taxable income and therefore corporate income taxes paid for any earnings from assets level. The government's tax collections vary so a portion of the $\sigma(EBIT)$ is "shifted" to the government.

The conclusions of the second stage of the model will be that the overall market capitalization rate decreases with leverage and the total market value of the corporation increases with leverage. A revision of the numerical example will be used to demonstrate these results.

The Revised Example

To illustrate the second stage suppose that Babbitt Corp. and Hobbitt Corp. each have assets that produce an $E(EBIT)$ of \$40,000 and $\sigma(EBIT)$ of \$20,000. Babbitt is financed entirely by common stock and Hobbitt has sold \$75,000 of debt at an interest rate of 8 percent. The corporate income tax rate is 40 percent.

The resulting expected payments of the two corporations are summarized in Table 14.1. Because the interest payments on debt are tax-deductible Hobbitt's expected total payments to security-holders are \$2,400 higher than Babbitt's.

TABLE 14.1
Payments to Security Holders

	Babbitt	Hobbitt
Expected earnings before interest and taxes	40,000	40,000
Interest	0	6,000
Earnings after interest	40,000	34,000
Corporate income taxes	16,000	13,600
Earnings after taxes	24,000	20,400
Dividends on common stock	24,000	20,400
Payments to debt-holders	0	6,000
Expected total payments to security-holders	24,000	26,400
Standard deviation of dividends	12,000	12,000

Suppose that the same overall market capitalization rate of 12 percent is used as the first approximation for each corporation. The total market value of Babbitt is then

$$\frac{\$24,000}{12\%} = \$200,000$$

Babbitt has no debt so the \$200,000 is the value of its common stock, and its equity market capitalization rate is 12 percent.

The total market value of Hobbitt is

$$\frac{\$26,400}{12\%} = \$220,000$$

Because Hobbitt's debt sells at its face value of \$75,000, the market value of Hobbitt common stock must be \$145,000. The expected annual dividend payment is \$20,400, so Hobbitt's equity market capitalization rate is

$$\frac{\$20,400}{\$145,000} = 14.0\%$$

Of course Hobbitt's debt market capitalization rate is 8 percent and the overall market capitalization rate is 12 percent.

To see if the two firms' overall market capitalization rates of 12 percent are equilibrium values, the opportunity for an investor to benefit from switching should be checked. Suppose that an investor starts out with 1 percent of Hobbitt's common stock. The market value of his stock is $1,450, and his expected dividend income is $204. His proportionate share of the corporation's interest payments is $60. His standard deviation of income is $120.

Now suppose he sells his Hobbitt stock for $1,450 and borrows $750 additional, paying 8 percent interest on the loan for a total annual interest charge of $60. He then buys $2,200 of Babbitt stock. The expected dividend on that stock is $264 (12 percent of $2,200). After subtracting his interest payment of $60 he is left with $204 expected income, exactly the same as he started with. His standard deviation of income is (2,200/200,000)12,000 = $132. His position is worse as a result of the switch, demonstrating that equal overall market capitalization rates for the two corporations are not equilibrium values.

In equilibrium the overall market capitalization rate for the levered corporation, Hobbitt, must be less than that of the unlevered corporation, Babbitt. A solution for the exact rates is possible only if the interest rate on debt is assumed fixed (at 8 percent) no matter what the borrower's debt-equity ratio.

If Hobbitt's overall capitalization rate is 12 percent, yielding a total market value for the corporation of $220,000, Babbitt's overall capitalization rate must be 12.63 percent to yield a total market value of $190,000.

To demonstrate that these are equilibrium values, consider an investor who starts out owning 1 percent of Hobbitt's common stock with a market value of $1,450, expected dividends of $204, and standard deviation of dividends of $120. The investor sells his Hobbitt stock, borrows $450 at an interest rate of 8 percent, and buys $1 900 of Babbitt stock. The $1,900 is also 1 percent of Babbitt so the investor gets an expected dividend of $240. After subtracting the $36 interest payment, his expected income is $204. The standard deviation is 1 percent of $12,000, $120. His arbitraging left his income combination unchanged, so the capitalization rates and market values are equilibrium quantities.

Figure 14.4
Market Capitalization Rate as a Function of Capital Structure

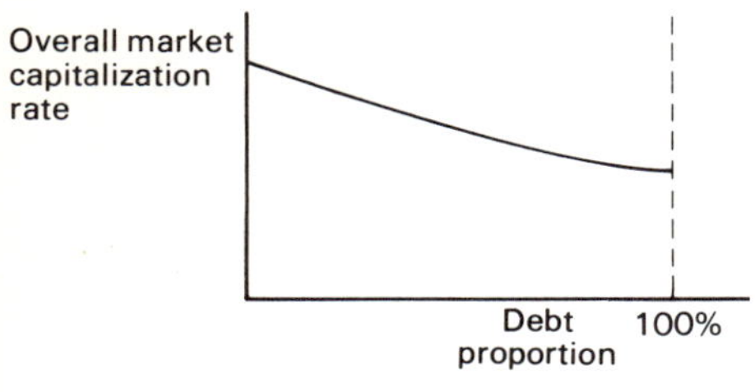

The exact numerical results in the equilibrium example are dependent on the interest rate on debt. Therefore the conclusion with respect to market capitalization rates of this stage are only that increasing leverage reduces the overall market capitalization rate, as shown in Figure 14.4.

In the numerical example the equilibrium total market value of Hobbitt was $220,000, and that of Babbitt was $190,000. In the example total market value increased with leverage.

The market value result should have been anticipated based on the total income payments to security-holders' characteristics. As leverage (debt) is increased, expected total payments increase because of the reduction in taxes. The standard deviation of payments to security-holders does not change with leverage. Therefore investors in the aggregate should be willing to pay more for the securities of the more leveraged corporation. Total market value should increase with leverage as shown in Figure 14.5.

The implication that can be drawn from Figure 14.5 is that the managers of a corporation should strive to attain as high a debt proportion as possible to maximize the total market value. Of course once again, the results of this stage of the model depend on the list of assumptions, some of which are not realistic. Therefore the application of the model to practical decision situations should be deferred until after further modifications are made.

Figure 14.5
Market Value as a Function of Capital Structure

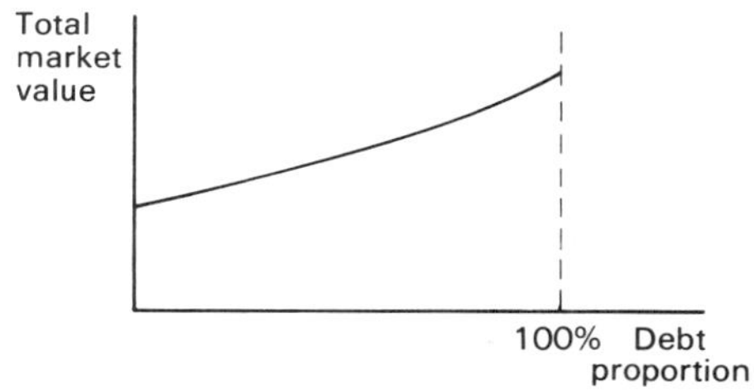

Further Modifications of the Model

The most obviously unrealistic assumption remaining in the model is number 7, that there are no income taxes for investors. In practice investor decisions are influenced by the differential treatment of various income sources under the tax code.

For example, if the investors in the model were corporations, the 85 percent exclusion rule for dividend income would make common stocks relatively more attractive than debt securities. Only \$15 out of each \$100 of dividend income would be subject to income taxes as opposed to \$100 out of each \$100 interest income. A corporate holder would therefore presumably be content with a much lower *before-tax* yield on stock than on debt securities.

Suppose that a corporate investor requires an after-tax yield of 5 percent on its security investments. If the corporation income tax rate is 40 percent, and the risk characteristics of the security payments are ignored, then the 5 percent after-tax yield could be achieved from debt securities with a before-tax yield of 8 1/3 percent:

$$(1 - 0.4)8\ 1/3\% = 5\%$$

or from equity securities with a before-tax yield of 5.32 percent:

$$[(1 - 0.4)(0.15)]\ 5.32\% = 5\%$$

Rather than assume incorporated investors, the modifications of the model will allow for income retention by the operating corporation, long-term capital gains for common stockholders, and the differential effective tax rate on that sort of income.

The Assumptions of Stage 3 of the Model

The first alteration made to the model is to change assumption 7 to allow for differential tax rates on ordinary (dividend and interest) income and long-term capital gains:

7a. Individuals are subject to ordinary income taxes on dividend and interest income, and to lower tax rates on long-term capital gains.

To provide for the realization of capital gains on common stock assumption 6 is changed to:

6. Corporations retain all net earnings after interest payments and corporate income taxes.

Rather than complicate the arithmetic by assuming a partial retention, a dividend pay-out ratio greater than zero, all the net income is retained and no dividends are paid on common stock.

To avoid the problem of the amount of capital gain resulting from the earnings retention in this stage, another assumption will be added specifying this relationship:

9. The price of a corporation's common stock increases by the amount of earnings retained.

An investor in the real world does not have to take capital gains when they occur, but can defer tax on the gain by simply holding on to his stocks. By deferral of the taxes the investor expects to earn additional amounts on the amount deferred if the stock continues to appreciate. If he sold the stock after the first gain, his amount invested for the later periods would be reduced by the amount of the taxes paid.

Suppose for example that an investor paid $100 for a stock January 1, 1972, and it increases in price to $110 by January 1, 1973. If he sells at that point realizing the $10 capital gain he might pay $3 in taxes, leaving $107 to be reinvested. If he can reinvest and earn 10 percent for the next year he would have a capital gain for the year 1973 of $10.70. Now suppose that instead of selling the stock on January 1, 1973, he continues to hold that stock and it appreciates by 10 percent during 1973. His capital gain for the year 1973 would be $11. Of course eventually he has to sell (or his heirs do) and pay a capital gain tax on the total appreciation over the years, but he has had the advantage of earning on a larger investment by the tax deferral.

To avoid the complications of this "lock-in-effect" of capital gains taxes in the model, another artificial assumption will be added at this stage:

10. All investors sell their common stocks each year (realize their capital gains) and pay long-term capital gains taxes on the amount of their gains.

The ten assumptions described above complete the necessary list for stage 3 of the model. Those assumptions are summarized in Table 14.2.

TABLE 14.2
Assumptions of the Third Stage

1. Investors are free to buy and sell any securities at will.
2. Investors can borrow without restriction at the same terms as corporations.
3. Investors have perfect knowledge about the income characteristics of securities.
4. Transactions costs, the cost of buying and selling securities, are zero.
5. Corporations can be classified into "risk classes," depending on the characteristics of their income streams from assets.

6a. Corporations retain all net earnings after interest payments and corporate income taxes.

7a. Individuals are subject to ordinary income taxes in dividend and interest income, and to lower tax rates on long-term capital gains.

8a. Corporation income taxes must be paid on net income after interest on debt.

9. The price of a corporation's common stock increases by the amount of earnings retained.
10. All investors sell their common stocks each year (realize their capital gains) and pay long-term capital gains taxes on the amount of their gains.

The Example in Stage 3

The two-corporation example is carried forward without change. Babbitt Corp. and Hobbitt Corp. each have an expected earnings from assets of $40,000, a standard deviation of earnings of $20,000, and are subject to 40 percent tax rates. Babbitt has no debt, and Hobbitt has $75,000 debt at an interest rate of 8 percent.

Babbitt's $24,000 expected net after taxes is distributed to stockholders in the form of a long-term capital gain under the assumptions of this stage. Hobbitt pays $6,000 interest to debt-holders, and distributes its $20,400 expected net to stockholders as a long-term capital gain.

The investors' personal income tax rate for ordinary income is assumed to be 70 percent from every investor, and the effective tax rate on long-term capital gains is 25 percent. Accordingly the holders of Babbitt common stock would receive an expected total income after personal taxes of $18,000:

$$(1 - 0.25)\ \$24{,}000 = \$18{,}000$$

The standard deviation of income after taxes is

$$(1 - 0.25)\ \$12{,}000 = \$9{,}000$$

(Again the government bears one-fourth of the standard deviation, $3,000.)

The holders of Hobbitt common would have expected receipts after personal taxes of

$$(1 - 0.25)\ \$20{,}400 = \$15{,}300$$

The standard deviation of after-tax receipts on common is

$$(1 - 0.25)\ \$12{,}000 = \$9{,}000$$

The holders of Hobbitt's debt receive as certain income after taxes

$$(1 - 0.7)\ \$6{,}000 = \$1{,}800$$

Because the interest payment is assumed to be certain the standard deviation for the debt-holders is zero.

Considered in total Hobbitt's security-holders receive an expected after-tax income of

$$\$15{,}300 + \$1{,}800 = \$17{,}100$$

The total deviation is $9,000.

The securities of Babbitt (all common stock) should be worth more than the securities of Hobbitt (debt and common stock) because the expected after-tax income is $18,000 campared to $17,100, and the standard deviations are the same, $9,000.

With the investors' tax rates used in the example, further increases in leverage beyond the level attained by Hobbitt will result in further reductions in the total market value of the firm. Increases in debt cause the after-personal-taxes payments to security-holders to fall. For example, suppose enough additional debt is added to increase interest payments by $100. Because that interest payment is tax-deductible, total payments to security-holders will increase by $40. That $40 net increase (before taxes of investors) is the residual of $100 increase in interest payments and a reduction of $60 in capital gain payments to stockholders. The interest payment is taxed to the debt-holder at a 70 percent rate, so the net after-personal-taxes increase of debt-holders is $30. Since the capital gain to the common stockholders is taxed at a 25 percent rate, the net after-personal-taxes decrease in receipts by those holders is $45. Netting the two changes together gives a reduction of $15 in total after-personal-taxes receipts by security-holders. Because those receipts fall with increases in debt at any level, and there is no change in standard deviation of after-tax receipts, the market value of the firm will look like that graphed in Figure 14.6

Figure 14.6
Total Market Value as a Function of Capital Structure

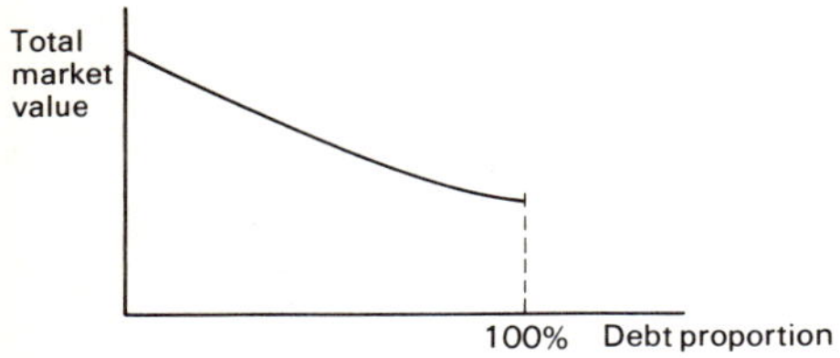

This result is dependent on the set of tax rates used in the example. A different set of tax rates could yield a market value that is constant as leverage increases, or a market value that rises as leverage increases.

To illustrate the effect of the choice of tax rates consider the original earnings from assets. If that income is to go to common stockholders, it is taxed first at the 40 percent corporate income tax rate, and then the residual is taxed at the investor's capital gain rate of 25 percent. Accordingly, out of $100 earnings from assets

$$\$100\,(1 - 0.4)(1 - 0.25) = \$45$$

gets to common stockholders after all levels of taxation are passed. Compare that to earnings that go to debt-holders—that amount is not taxed to the corporation, but is subject to a 70 percent personal income tax rate. So $100 of earnings from assets would result in

$$\$100\,(1 - 0.7) = \$30$$

receipts by debt-holders after all levels of taxation are passed.

If the personal income tax rate were changed to 55 percent and the other rates were unchanged, the net receipts of common and debt-holders would be the same, and if the personal income tax rate were less than 55 percent, the net interest payment would be greater than the net common payment. The numerical results of the example therefore should not be interpreted as meaning that zero leverage is always optimal, but that some optimal capital structure besides 100 percent debt may exist for a firm.

Practicality and Further Possible Modifications of the Model

The outcome of stage 3 of the model depends on the tax shelters built into those provisions of the code regarding capital gains taxation, just as the outcome of stage 2 depends on the tax-deductibility of interest payments by the corporation. At least three different special tax treatments for common stockholders could have been used to show the desirability of common stock over debt in the corporation's capital structure.

The preferential tax treatment (the 85 percent exclusion rule) given corporate recipients of dividends would make common stock relatively more attractive than debt to incorporated investors. For unincorporated investors the capital gain treatment actually used in the model required the corporation to retain earnings rather than pay dividends so that capital gains could occur. The earnings of the corporation were in effect distributed to common stockholders through the ninth assumption. Assumption 10 fixed the time at which the taxation of those gains occurred.

If assumption 10 were eliminated then the investor's taxes on capital gains would be deferred indefinitely, and common stock would become even more attractive to the corporation. In closely held corporations dominant investors may influence management's dividend and capital structure decisions, with the objective of deferring the investors' taxes on income indefinitely by retaining earnings and reinvesting profits within the corporate shell.

Assumption 9, "the price of a corporation's common stock increases by the amount of earnings retained," will be studied more in the next chapter. A corporation's retention of earnings does not automatically result in that amount of increase in the price of common stock. The corporation must use those retained earnings to buy profitable investments, and the additional earnings must be capitalized in the securities markets through an increase in the company's common stock price. As indicated in Chapter 12, there may not be a one-to-one correspondence between the amount of retained earnings and the market price increase.

Summary

When the market value per share of common stock is used as the objective to be maximized in capital structure design, the criterion could be stated as "maximize the total market value of the corporation." In the models used in this chapter all changes in market value came in the total value of common stock because the debt was short-term by definition.

To determine total market values for comparing corporations with differing capital structures, the concept of a set of equilibrium prices was defined and illustrated by an investor switching from one common stock to another. The arbitraging operations of a number of investors in the perfect securities markets insure that the computed equilibrium rates and prices would be reached.

The conclusions reached in the first stage of the model was that capital structure was immaterial to the market value of the corporation. That market value could be maximized in the second stage by increasing debt to 100 percent of the capital structure, but practical application was deferred until stage 3 where the assumptions used most closely approximated reality. In the third stage of the model the optimization results were found to depend on the tax rates assumed for the corporation, investors' ordinary income, and the rate on investors' long-term capital gains.

Notes

[1] Franco Modigliani and Merton H. Miller, "The Cost of Capital, Corporation Finance, and the Theory of Investment," *American Economic Review*, June 1958, and Modigliani and Miller, "Corporate Income Taxes and the Cost of Capital: A Correction," *American Economic Review*, June 1963.

[2] If risk is measured by the amount of possible capital loss the investor may not be better off. Before the switch his maximum possible loss was the value of his Hobbitt stock, $1,500, but after the switch he could possibly lose $2,250. This results from the lack of limited liability when personal leverage is used rather than corporate leverage. The argument can be countered by assuming that the investor utilizes a personal holding company for his investments, and the $750 is borrowed by his incorporated personal holding company.

[3] Again the possible loss is ignored.

Chapter 14 Questions

1. Is the purpose of an economic model such as used in this chapter to give a set of formulas which can be applied literally in a real life situation, or is it to indicate a direction that real life events will tend toward?
2. Could the "conglomerate boom" of the early 1960s be used as an example of the development of extremely leveraged capital structures based on the tax-deductibility of bond interest along the lines of the stage 2 model of the chapter?
3. What happened to cause the "conglomerate bust" of the late 1960s? Did it refute the capital structure theory of stage 2?
4. In acquiring operating corporations, frequently bonds of the acquirer are exchanged for common stock of the acquired corporation. Because of the tax-deductibility of the bond interest the result of the acquisition is that total payments to security holders increase by the amount of the reduced federal tax payments. Does this mean that the government subsidizes acquisitions?
5. How reasonable is the assumption that investors can borrow on the same terms as corporations? Does the size of loan have anything to do with the interest rate charged?
6. Where does a rule of thumb formula for capital structure such as "50 percent debt as a norm" fit into the theoretical analysis of this chapter? Is it possible that lending rates are established by people using such formulas, so that if a corporation tries to borrow excessively it will find sharply increasing interest charges quoted?
7. One way of expressing the market equilibrium conditions is to say that in equilibrium "two different prices cannot exist for the same object." Are the combinations an investor holds before and after his arbitraging switches the same object?
8. When is the overall market capitalization rate the corporation's cost of capital?
9. Summarize each stage of the model in terms of the total market value of the corporation and in terms of the overall market capitalization rate.
10. Is it more reasonable to assume that investors select on the basis of an after-personal-tax yield rather than on the basis of a before-tax yield?

11. Do retained earnings result in an equal increase in the market price of the common stock? If so, wouldn't this indicate that a corporation should never pay cash dividends?
12. Does the difference in ordinary income tax rates and the rate on long-term capital gains by stimulating earnings retention result in a growth bias to U.S. corporations?
13. What tax rates of investors can the corporation's management assume for planning a capital structure?
14. Where does the corporation's internal rate of return on investments enter into the capital structure analysis?
15. If the interest rate on debt increases with the proportion of debt, will any of the model results be changed?

Chapter 14 Problems

1. Stagnant Corp. has $12,000,000 of 8 percent bonds and 300,000 shares of common stock outstanding. Every year a dividend of $6 a share is expected on the common stock, and the market price of the stock is $90 a share. The bonds sell at par. Calculate:
   a. The market capitalization rate for debt.
   b. The market capitalization rate for equity.
   c. The overall market capitalization rate for the corporation.
2. To raise $3,000,000 Ibex Corp. sold 150,000 shares of common stock at an issue price of $20 a share. Gnu Corp. raised $3,000,000 by selling $1,000,000 of bonds at a 7 percent interest rate and 100,000 shares of common stock at $20 a share. Each corporation purchased assets that produce an expected annual earnings of $360,000. Neither corporation pays income taxes, and each corporation pays out all its earnings to its security holders.

   Currently Ibex common stock has a market price of $24 a share, Gnu's bonds sell at par, and Gnu's common stock sells for $28 a share.
   a. An investor holds 2,000 shares of Gnu stock. If he sells that stock, borrows enough to maintain the same debt-equity ratio, and buys Ibex common stock, how much will he increase his expected net income?
   b. Suppose the Ibex common stock price and the Gnu bond price are in equilibrium. What must Gnu common stock sell at for all the market values and capitalization rates to be in equilibrium?
3. Meme Corp. has no debt, and 400,000 shares of common stock outstanding. Chose Corp. has $1,500,000 debt at an 8 percent interest rate and 200,000 shares of common stock outstanding. Each corporation owns assets that produce $500,000 expected income each year with the same standard deviation, $300,000. Each corporation pays income tax at a 40 percent rate, and distributes all its income to security holders. Meme's common stock sells for $10 a share and Chose's for $11 a share.
   a. Which stock is overvalued?
   b. Suppose a person who owns 100 shares of Chose Corp. sells it, borrows, and buys Meme Corp. stock. How much will this switching

change his expected income? How much will his standard deviation of income change?

4. Hocus Corp. has $2,000,000 debt at 8 percent and 100,000 shares of common stock outstanding. The corporate income tax rate is 48 percent. Hocus pays out all its expected earnings on assets of $600,000, retaining nothing. The debt sells at par, and the common stock at $25 a share.

Pocus Investment Corp. has $40,000 to invest, and must select between Hocus debt and Hocus common stock. What will be Pocus' expected after-tax yield if it buys:

a. Hocus debt?

b. Hocus common stock?

5. (Refer to problem 4.) Suppose Hocus Corp. retains all its net income to invest in new assets, and the market price of its stock increases by the amount of retained earnings. An individual investor with personal income tax rates of 60 percent on ordinary income and 25 percent on long-term capital gains plans a one-year investment, either in Hocus debt or Hocus common stock. What will be his expected after-tax yield on the alternatives?

6. (Refer to problem 5.) Suppose a dollar of retained earnings only amounts to 80 cents of capital gains because Hocus cannot find profitable investments. Now what is the individual investor's expected after-tax yield on Hocus common stock?

Chapter 14 References

Archer, Stephen H., and D'Ambrosio, Charles A., eds. *The Theory of Business Finance*. New York: Macmillan, 1967.

Ben-Shahar, Haim. "The Capital Structure and the Cost of Capital: A Suggested Exposition." *Journal of Finance*, September 1968.

Lerner, Eugene M., and Carleton, Willard T. "Financing Decisions of the Firm." *Journal of Finance*, May 1966.

Lewellen, Wilbur G. *The Cost of Capital.* Belmont Cal.: Wadsworth, 1969.

Miller, Merton H., and Modigliani, Franco. "Dividend Policy, Growth and the Valuation of Shares." *Journal of Business*, October 1961.

Modigliani, Franco, and Miller, Merton H. "The Cost of Capital, Corporation Finance, and the Theory of Investment." *American Economic Review*, June 1958.

Modigliani, Franco, and Miller, Merton H. "Corporate Income Taxes and the Cost of Capital: A Correction." *American Economic Review*, June 1963.

Resek, R. W. "Multidimensional Risk and the Modigliani Miller Hypothesis." *Journal of Finance*, March 1970.

Robichek, Alexander A., and Myers, Stewart C. "Problems in the Theory of Optimal Capital Structure." *Journal of Financial and Quantitative Analysis*, June 1966.

Wippern, Ronald F. "Financial Structure and the Value of the Firm." *Journal of Finance*, December 1966.

15

CAPITAL STRUCTURE AND DIVIDEND POLICY

In the preceding chapters two approaches to determining the optimum capital structure of the firm were presented. In Chapter 13 the objective was to optimize with respect to the income characteristics of earnings per share on common stock. Chapter 14 was concerned with optimization of the total market value of the firm, which maximized the market value per share of common stock. In both cases the emphasis was on the capital structure mix between debt and equity.

In this chapter a further dimension to the capital structure problem will be explored, the dividend policy of the firm. The dividend size decision is part of the capital structure management since cash dividend payment is the alternative to earnings retention, one way to expand the total equity capital of the corporation. The decisions may be approached in a sequential fashion: first, do profitable investment opportunities exist; second, should expansion be financed through debt or equity; and third, should increases in equity come from new common stock issues or retention of earnings. Approached in this fashion the dividend payment by the corporation is a residual, the amount paid is what is left out of earnings after the retention is subtracted.

Dividend policy may be approached in a more positive fashion. The goal of a corporation's activities may be expressed in terms of a desired dividend level on common stock. The goal may be to meet a predetermined level at some point in the future, to maintain a level of dividends over all periods in the foreseeable future, or to maximize the growth rate of dividends starting from some base figure. The choice of goal will determine the corporation's asset acquisition policy as well as its choice of financial sources.

Besides some additional theoretical dividend models it will be necessary in this chapter to look at some pragmatic approaches to dividend policy used by corporation management. Besides general principles applicable to any corporation, the special problems of the small firm, the rapidly growing firm, and the mature firm will be indicated. Corporations do differ with respect to their investment opportunities as well as with respect to their access to capital markets.

Earnings Retention or New Common Stock Issues

A nonfinancial reason that may cause a corporation to choose retained earnings rather than new stock issues is the problem of voting control of the corporation. If new stock is issued and the existing controlling group of stockholders is unable or unwilling to purchase a proportionate share of the new issue, their voting share will be diluted and control over the corporation may be lost. To prevent this dilution the controlling group can simply require expansion of equity through earnings retention instead of new stock issues.

In comparing financially the two sources of new equity financing for the corporation, several important differences should be realized. If the choice is to be earnings retention the corporation will save the possibly very large flotation costs of a stock issue. The cost will vary with the size of the issue and the corporation, but will probably range from 5 percent to as much as 40 percent of the issue. Even if the rights-offering method is used to facilitate the sale the cost of the registration procedures, the bookkeeping costs and possible underwriters' fees may amount to a significant cost.

The purchasers of the new stock issue in a preemptive rights offering are not necessarily the stockholders who receive the rights to subscribe for the new stock. In the usual rights offering the rights are detachable, and can be sold if the stockholder does not care to exercise them. If the price of the common stock does not fall below the exercise price by the expiration date of the rights, the holder will exercise the rights rather than suffer the loss. The issuing corporation sells the new common stock to whoever exercises the rights.

If it were assumed that the purchasers of a new issue were the present stockholders of the corporation, the flow-through of dividends to stock purchase could be demonstrated. That is, the dividend receipt can be used by the stockholder to purchase new stock if he desires to. In the absence of investor income taxes the corporation should perhaps go ahead and pay out all earnings in cash dividends, and then let investors purchase newly issued common stock if they want the corporation to reinvest for them. This system would have the advantage of allowing stockholders free choice.

Unfortunately, though, stockholders are subject to income taxes on dividend receipts. Therefore, if the corporation reinvests for the stockholder by retaining earnings, a stage of taxation is saved.

The two savings of earnings retention, the sales costs of new stock issues and the avoidance of investors' income taxes on dividends, form powerful incentives for corporations to increase equity capital through retention rather than new issues. The amount of needed equity expansion in a period of time may exceed the available earnings, however.

The corporation's investment opportunities may be "lumpy," occurring in large blocks at points in time rather than at a smooth continuous rate. This characteristic causes difficulty in financing through retained earnings, since earnings available for retention during the time period may not be large enough. If the corporation's management still wants to avoid new stock issues and maintain a fixed capital structure, either earnings will have to be retained in advance of the new investment acquisition, or the corporation can borrow temporarily to buy the investment and repay the borrowings from funds saved by earnings retentions in later periods. In either case the corporation will diverge from the desired capital structure temporarily, returning to the desired structure eventually.

The choice between retained earnings and common stock issues is usually always resolved in favor of earnings retention. The real choice, then, is whether new equity in the form of retained earnings is better than dividend payment.

Dividend Income or Capital Gains

In the theoretical models presented in earlier chapters, it was implied and sometimes explicitly assumed that earnings retention would result in an automatic increase in the market value of the common stock. If the amounts of earnings retention and capital gains were the same, then the lower effective tax rate would mean that stockholders should prefer that the corporation retain earnings rather than pay cash dividends.

Even in a theoretical model the amount of capital gain depends on the after-tax yield the corporation can achieve on the earnings retained. Abstracting from an example used originally in Chapter 12, suppose that a corporation retains $1 per share to reinvest. That $1 of additional equity funds is combined with some debt capital and used to purchase an investment project. If the increase in earnings after taxes that results is 10 cents per share, then the corporation's yield on retained earnings is 10 percent. If the market capitalization rate expressed in terms of *earnings per share* is also 10 percent, the market price of the common stock will rise by $1 per share over what it would have been if the dividend had been paid. The two interest rates, the corporation's marginal yield on retained earnings and the market capitalization rate for the corporation's earnings, must be equal for an equality of the amount of earnings retention and the amount of capital gain.

The assumption that the corporation can earn 10 cents on the $1 of retained earnings ignores the capital structure problem of how much debt is combined with the equity, and therefore the required yield on the investment project selected by the corporation. If the corporation had an established capital structure of one-third debt, two-thirds equity, and desired to maintain that structure, then for every $1 added equity 50 cents of debt would be added. Assuming that the after-tax interest rate on the debt is 5 percent, the increase in interest charges for that 50 cents of debt is 2.5 cents. The $1.50 investment must return 12.5 cents after taxes to meet the 2.5 cents interest charge and the 10 cents increase in earnings per share. Therefore the corporation's yield on incremental investments must be

$$\frac{12.5¢}{\$1.50} = 8\tfrac{1}{3}\%$$

to allow the 10 percent yield on retained earnings.

The market capitalization rate for earnings is used here rather than a capitalization rate for dividends to keep the illustration simple. If the example corporation had a policy of 100 percent payout of earnings and temporarily modified that policy for one period to retain the $1 per share, then normal payout could be resumed the following period at a level 10 cents per share higher if the additional investments produced the scheduled earnings.

Using the 10 percent rate as a capitalization rate to be applied to dividends, the same capital gain results would be attained. If the dividend is reduced by $1 at time zero, and becomes 10 cents greater at time one and all successive periods, the present value of the 10 cent increase in dividends computed with an interest rate of 10 percent is $1, exactly offsetting the stockholders' loss of dividends.

In the simple dividend and growth models, the capitalization rates used have been applied indiscriminately to earnings whether those earnings were retained or paid in cash dividend form. So long as certainty of investment results and perfect market conditions exist, such an application may be appropriate, but the uncertainty of results should certainly be recognized in a more extensive model that will be used for the determination of a corporation's dividend policy.

The dividend-retained earnings decision can be analyzed better through a modification of the capital gain model specifically to recognize the risk elements in the sequence of events. Since the expected return of the corporation on retained earnings involves the acquisition of additional investment projects, that return should really be treated as a "risky" variable. Therefore retained earnings might be capitalized in the market with a higher interest rate than is applied to dividends.

Again suppose the corporation is considering making a one-time-only retention of $1 per share at time zero, and will resume payout of all earnings at time one. If the reinvestment of earnings is made, the expected yield on retained earnings is 10 percent, so the expected increase in dividend level beginning at time one is 10 cents per share. That increase in dividend level may be capitalized at a higher rate,[1] 12½ percent, than used before because of the risk feature. An annuity of 10 cents per period beginning one period in the future has a present value of

$$\frac{10¢}{12\frac{1}{2}\%} = 80¢$$

when the higher rate is used. Accordingly, the investors would be giving up $1, the present value of the passed dividend, to get an 80 cent increase in the present value of future dividends, an 80 cent capital gain. The stockholders would be rather unhappy with the actions of the corporation in this situation if their effective tax rates on dividend income and capital gains were the same. Only if the corporation could earn more than 12½ percent on retained earnings would the stockholders be better off in before-tax income from the retention.

The example could be modified still further to take account of the differential in taxation of income to the stockholders. If the capital gains tax rate is half that of the ordinary tax rate on dividends, for example, 80 cents of capital gains could amount to more after-tax income to the shareholder than $1 of dividend income. For an ordinary tax rate greater than 33 1/3 percent the capital gain of 80 cents would be better, and for an ordinary tax rate less than 33 1/3 percent the dividend of $1 would be better.

To utilize this model accurately to decide between dividend payment and earnings retention, the corporate planner must know at a minimum:

1. The incremental capital structure ratio of the corporation.
2. The after-corporate-tax interest rate on incremental debt.
3. The after-corporate-tax yield on incremental investments.
4. The market before-tax capitalization rate (risk-adjusted) for incremental earnings or dividends.
5. The stockholders' tax rates on dividend income and capital gains.

Formal Statement of the Dividend-Retained Earnings Decision Model

To generalize the model a symbolic notation should be defined for the five quantities listed above. The incremental capital structure ratio can be expressed as the fraction debt is of the total increase in capital, b. The after-corporate-tax interest rate on incremental debt is c, and the after-corporate-tax yield on incremental investments is r. The market before-tax capitalization rate for incremental earnings or dividends is k. Stockholders are taxed at the rate t for ordinary (dividend) income, and at the rate ½t for capital gains.

Using these symbols the stockholders' net after-tax income from $1 of cash dividends is

$$\$1\,(1 - t)$$

The stockholders' net after-tax income from $1 of retained earnings should be

$$\$1\;\frac{[\frac{1}{1-b}]r - c[\frac{b}{1-b}]}{k}\;(1 - \frac{1}{2}t)$$

The factor $1 [1/1 – b] is the amount of new investment made, and when it is multiplied by r the after-corporate-tax increase in profits before interest is derived. The quantity $1 [$b$/1 – b] is the amount of new debt added, and the multiplication by c yields the increase in after-corporate-tax interest payments. When the difference between the profits before interest and the interest payments is divided by the market capitalization rate, k, the amount of capital gain per share is the result. To complete the computation, the capital gain is reduced by the capital gains tax.

Suppose the corporation capital structure policy is such that any expansion in assets will be financed two-thirds by retained earnings and one-third (=b) by debt. That debt bears a 5 percent after-corporate-tax interest rate, c. The after-corporate-tax yield on incremental investments, r, is 10 percent. The market before-tax capitalization rate, k, is 12½ percent, and the stockholder ordinary income tax rate, t, is 30 percent. If $1 cash dividends are paid, the holder of a share of stock receives after taxes

$$\$1\,(1 - 30\%) = \$0.70$$

If the corporation retains the $1, the stockholder receives an after-tax capital gain of

$$\$1\;\frac{[\frac{1}{1-1/3}]\,10\% - 5\%[\frac{1/3}{1-1/3}]}{12\frac{1}{2}\%}\;(1 - \tfrac{1}{2}(30\%)) = \$0.85$$

For these assumed values the stockholders would be better off with earnings retention than with cash dividends.

The decision between dividends or earnings retention can therefore be based on a comparision of

$$(1 - t)$$

with

$$\frac{[\frac{1}{1-b}]r - c[\frac{b}{1-b}]}{k} \quad (1 - ½t)$$

The Cut-Off Rate for Capital Budgeting Criteria

To be worthwhile for the corporation to retain earnings and expand its assets this inequality must hold:

$$\frac{[\frac{1}{1-b}]r - c[\frac{b}{1-b}]}{k} \quad (1 - ½t) > (1 - t)$$

Each of the five constants is important in this inequality, but here attention is focused on r, the after-corporate-tax yield on new investments. The inequality can be manipulated to the form

$$r > \frac{1 - t}{1 - ½t} (1 - b)k + cb$$

This inequality must hold for the corporation to find it worthwhile to retain earnings and expand assets.

For the assumed values: $b = 1/3$; $c = 5\%$; $k = 12½\%$; and $t = 30\%$; the range of values for r can be derived from the inequality:

$$r > \frac{1 - 30\%}{1 - ½(30\%)} (1 - {}^1\!/_3)12½\% + 5\%({}^1\!/_3) > 8.53\%$$

Given all the assumed numbers the corporation must have investment projects that earn more than 8.53 percent before it is worthwhile to retain earnings and buy those investment projects.

So finally a cut-off rate has been defined for the selection of investment projects. That critical rate, r^*, is defined in terms of the variables of this chapter as

$$r^* = \frac{1 - t}{1 - ½t} (1 - b)k + cb$$

Dividend Policy in Practice

The dividend policy that corporations follow may differ from that indicated by the results of a theoretical model for many reasons that carry no implication of the irrationality of the executive decision-makers. The theoretical models are based upon a series of assumptions, sometimes not completely stated in the development of the model, and amounts of information that may not be attained in a real life decision situation.

For example, the capital gain model reviewed above is based on the assumptions of a perfect market, and in practice security markets are not perfect markets in the economic sense, investors do not have complete information about the corporation's investment opportunities and anticipated earnings per share, and the investment outcomes as well as the resulting market capitalization rates and prices should be considered as random variables rather than certain quantities. Accordingly a corporation may adopt a policy of paying cash dividends rather than retaining earnings, on the basis that the dividend is a certain receipt by the stockholder where the capital gain that might be sought is less certain, "the relative certainty reason."

The corporation's management may be hesitant to change an established dividend policy because of the "clientele effect." In this situation the corporation's past policy has attracted a body of stockholders that prefer the corporation's practices; if the corporation pays a high percentage of earnings as cash dividends the stockholders tend to be those investors who prefer dividends, or if it pays low dividends the stockholders tend to be those who prefer earnings retention with its implied high growth rate of the corporation. If the corporation's dividend policy were changed, those stockholders might be forced to switch to other corporations' common stocks. The widows and orphans who use dividend income for living expenses may not recognize or be able to take advantage of the possible capital gains when the corporation lowers its dividend rate. The lists maintained of eligible holdings by trusts and insurance companies by state regulatory commissions may require dividend payments, so the reduction or elimination of dividends may cause a group of stockholders to sell their stock. On the other hand, the investor that has been attracted by high earnings retention with its capital gains may be repelled if the corporation begins to pay high dividends because the investor's effective tax rate is increased by the move. Rather than force such switches the corporation's management may simply continue an existing dividend policy.

Stability of dividend payment over time is generally considered to be desirable. Boards of directors usually establish a regular quarterly dividend, whose size is based upon past earnings of the corporation and projected future averages. The quarterly dividend rate may be changed when the corporation has reached a new level of earnings that look as if it will be maintained. The earnings per share and dividend rates may therefore look like those shown in Figure 15.1.

Figure 15.1
Earnings Per Share and Dividend Rate in Stable Dividend Policy Situation

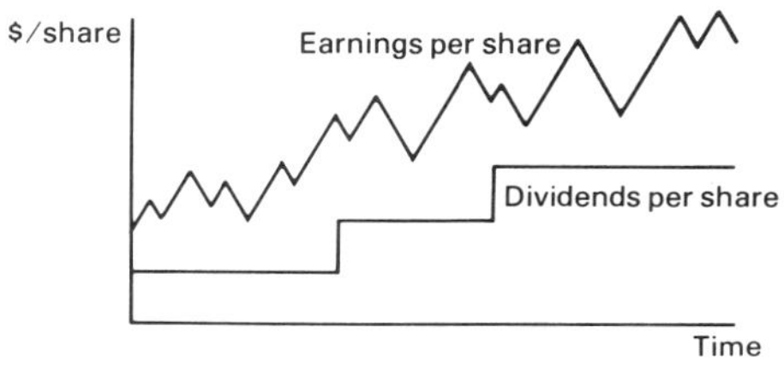

Stability is desirable because of the implied "information content" of the dividend level. The dividend is one means for the board of directors to communicate directly with stockholders regarding the board's opinion of the size and stability of future earnings per share. If the dividend is maintained during a period when earnings are down, the maintenance can be interpreted as signaling that the downturn is temporary. Otherwise if the dividend were reduced when earnings fell this reduction might be interpreted as an opinion that the fall is not temporary, and the result could be a considerable drop in the stock's market price. Under the stable dividend policy, an increase in the dividend level indicates a higher plateau of earnings has been reached that the board expects to be maintained in the future.

The stable dividend policy has some implications for the corporation's capital budget that should be mentioned at this point. If earnings are variable and dividends remain constant as shown in Figure 15.1, then retained earnings are a more highly variable residual quantity. When the capital budget of the corporation is based on the amount of retained earnings (under a constant capital structure), that budget varies considerably from period to period. The standard for investment project selection under a fixed budget appropriation, the capital rationing situation treated in Chapter 6, will therefore vary considerably over time. An investment project might be acceptable in a period of high earnings but unacceptable in a period of low earnings.

In practice, the corporation's management should probably not insist on a rigid capital structure, but increase the amount of borrowed capital when retained earnings are low, and decrease the borrowed proportion when retained earnings increase. This temporary change in the incremental capital structure would serve to smooth out the capital budget over time.

The stable dividend policy is modified by many corporations through the practice of declaring special year-end dividends in addition to regular quarterly dividends. If the earnings results for a year were good, the board declares a larger year-end special, or if the earnings were bad, the year-end is reduced. If the year-end dividend is paid regularly and changed in size frequently, the corporation no longer has a stable dividend policy but a variable dividend policy. The benefits, if any, of the stable dividend policy would be lost with this variable year-end dividend addition.

Special Problems of Small Firms

The analysis of dividend and capital structure policy has been presented in terms applicable to "most corporations." However, the general approach may be modified to allow for the special characteristics of specific corporations, and for those of specific classes of corporations.

The first special class of corporations to be discussed here is the small firm. This type of corporation is likely to be closely-held with little or no public market for its securities. The income criteria, such as presented in Chapter 13, should therefore be used in the capital structure design rather than the market value criteria of Chapter 14. The securities of this class of corporations would be salable only as a result of negotiations.

The small firm would normally find it difficult and expensive to sell bonds or preferred stock in a public issue. A private placement of those securities might be possible, but privately-placed bonds differ only slightly from loans. Accordingly the small firm must rely on negotiated loans for debt capital rather than securities.

The amount of debt capital available for the small firm is likely to be a lower proportion of the capital structure than a larger corporation's proportion, for several reasons having to do with lenders' willingness to lend. Small firms are less diversified than larger companies, so their variability of *EBIT* is likely to be greater. Having less relative bargaining power than a larger firm, it is possible that a smaller firm may have to accept less advantageous prices in sales contracts, resulting in lower profit margins. The small firm suffers from the lack of economies of scale in manufacturing and distribution of its product. In general the smaller firm may simply be less profitable relative to a dollar of sales or a dollar of assets.

As a result of the increased risk that may be perceived by lenders, the contract interest charged on loans may be higher, and the amount loaned lower than a larger company could obtain. Small corporations therefore can be expected to have a higher equity proportion in their capital structures.

Dividend payment is more likely to be restricted in loan agreements if the small corporation has been able to obtain large loans. The determination of dividend policy is not as difficult in the small closely held corporations, because the owners can communicate their desires directly to the board of directors if the principal owners are not in fact members of the board.

Special Problems of a Growth Corporation

By a growth corporation is meant a firm that has investment opportunities that are large in proportion to the corporation's present size. Usually these opportunities arise because the corporation is in an industry with rapidly changing or developing technology, such as medical electronics, computer peripheral equipment, and the like. Sometimes the growth opportunities are self-created, as in the conglomerate formation boom of the 1960s.

The basic capital structure characteristic of the growth corporation is that retained earnings, even if no dividends are paid, are inadequate to meet the expansion requirements of the corporation and keep a fixed equity proportion in the structure. Either the capital structure must become more highly leveraged with expansion, or additional equity must be raised through new security issues.

Frequently the growth corporation relies extensively on convertible securities for its rapid expansion. While a convertible security eventually results in the issue of additional common stock, the time of actual issue is deferred for quite a time. Assuming the lack of forced conversion through a call, the time of conversion is likely to be at the end of the security's term; for a 20-year convertible bond issue, at the end of 20 years. Convertible securities therefore do not result in dilution of control for present stockholders at the time of sale.

The convertible securities normally used are convertible subordinated debentures or convertible preferred stock. Because those securities' claims on income (and assets in the case of liquidation) are subordinated to other debt-holders, the corporation may be able to sell other bonds or take out other loans at a reasonable rate of interest. The other lenders to the corporation view at least moderate amounts of convertibles as a near-equity cushion, providing some margin of safety for their debt claims. Of course if extraordinarily large amounts of convertible debt are issued, the interest payments required may increase the possibility of the corporation's bankruptcy significantly, and the ordinary lenders to the corporation may be repelled by the possibility of the delay in payment or the reduction in payment that results from formal bankruptcy proceedings.

Because convertible securities give buyers a chance for a capital gain through the sharing of an appreciation in the common stock price, the coupon interest rate is normally significantly lower than the coupon rate on a nonconvertible issue. A corporation might only have to pay an 8 percent coupon rate on a convertible bond, but would have to pay 12 percent on a straight bond issue of the same size. The savings in cash payments during the issues life would be particularly significant for the growth corporation where extraordinarily high return is expected on cash spent on investment projects.

Although the earnings and control will be diluted eventually when convertible securities are used, the degrees of dilution are less than would occur if expansion were financed by the sale of common stock. The growth corporation could be expected to finance expansion as much as possible by earnings retention, paying little or no cash dividends, but that source of funds is not large enough.

Special Problems of a Large or Mature Corporation

The problem described in this section is just the opposite of the last—these corporations have minimal investment opportunities in proportion to their present sizes. The lack of investment opportunities may be due to government anti-trust regulations, to management inabilities, or special considerations such as the legal powers of operation specified in the corporate charter.

The federal government's anti-trust activities historically have been aimed at limiting the concentration of economic power in individual markets. As a result, when a firm obtains a high percentage of sales of a particular product, any further expansion could be limited by legal actions taken under the federal anti-trust statutes. In recent years a new doctrine of anti-trust actions has been evolving aimed at size rather than concentration in an individual market. So far under this new doctrine the only actions that have been taken were attempts to block mergers that would create extremely large corporations.[2] Normal expansion by a corporation in several markets has not been attacked yet.

After a corporation grows to some size and diversity of operations, the management structure that evolves may prove inadequate. Whether any real management limit should exist in theory is controversial, because such giant corporations as General Motors and American Telephone and Telegraph do not seem to have management limitations. (Some cynics suggest that the federal government does suffer from size, though.)

Because managment groups in the very large corporation tend to be self-perpetuating and to some extent divorced from precisely following stockholders' interests, a corporation's management may decide not to expand into another line of business even if the new line has the promise of being profitable. A steel company's management might have the viewpoint that they "know steel," but don't know how to sell mutual funds, for example. Therefore the steel company would not expand into mutual fund sales even though that expansion could be profitable. A counter to this management adequacy argument is what may be called the "Litton philosophy," after the corporation that pioneered in forming diversified conglomerates in the early 1960s. Under this philosophy "a manager is a manager everywhere," and the problems of running a mutual fund are similar enough to those of running a steel company that an adequate manager should be able to perform properly in either environment.

Corporations are limited in their activities to the powers prescribed in their charters. Particularly in mining and other natural resource production, a corporation might be formed to develop and produce a particular product, such as a mine. Once the ore is exhausted and the remains are sold, the corporation presumably is liquidated and terminates. For these corporations the dividend distribution is usually 100 percent or more of earnings, so the liquidation occurs over the life of the corporation. Obviously unless the objective of the corporation and its charter were changed, the corporation would have no need of raising additional capital.

The large or mature corporation would typically pay out a large proportion of earnings each period, perhaps retaining only enough to finance an expansion sufficient to maintain the market share of its products. The debt financing undertaken would be mainly that necessary for the refunding of maturing obligations.

Summary

Corporations usually find that it is preferable to expand equity capital through earnings retention rather than the sale of additional common stock. Earnings retention "saves" flotation costs and taxes for stockholders.

Dividend policy should therefore generally be approached from the aspect that the choice is between payment of cash dividends and expansion of the corporation's total capital. A comparison can be made between a stockholder's net after-tax income from cash dividends and his net after-tax income from the capital gain that results from earnings retention. While a serious analyst may find it desirable to modify the model presented in the chapter to achieve a better approximation of reality, the basic principles of comparison remain unchanged.

Dividend policy in practice may not be based on so formal a procedure because of the lack of sufficient information about the numerical values of the relevant variables. Dividends may be paid because the amount is certain income to the stockholder, while a capital gain from retained earnings is the result of several uncertain events. An established dividend policy may be continued unchanged because of the stockholder clientele built up from past payout policies. Because of the information content of dividends, a more stable dividend policy may be evolved than would be suggested by a theoretical model.

The chapter was concluded with a discussion of the special problems of small corporations, high growth corporations, and mature corporations. These types differ according to their access to the capital markets and their investment opportunities.

Notes

[1]The risk-adjusted discount rate method of adjustment is used rather than the certainty equivalent adjustment for simplicity of computation. Actually the same results would be achieved if the 10 cents were multiplied by the certainty equivalent adjustment factor of 0.8, and the result divided by the risk-free interest rate of 10 percent.

[2]Such as in the case of the International Telephone and Telegraph acquisition of Hartford Fire Insurance Co. in 1969.

Chapter 15 Questions

1. The decision model for earnings retention-dividends always results in either zero retention or 100 percent retention. How can it be adapted to handle something in between? Do all the available projects have the same yield, for example? Are investor tax rates a flat rate or are they graduated?
2. Could empirically determined price-earnings ratios be used to develop the "before-tax market capitalization rate for expected earnings?"
3. Describe the circumstances in which a corporation should sell new common stock.
4. Does the increase in certainty in cash dividends offset the tax advantages of earnings retention?
5. If a corporation adopts a policy of level quarterly dividends with a year-end extra, how large should the extra be in relation to the quarterly dividend?
6. If a widow bought a high dividend paying common stock for current income and then the corporation changed its dividend policy to a high retention rate, what can she do? Will she necessarily suffer a loss, or could she benefit from the corporation's change?
7. Do all small firms suffer from a lack of debt capital?
8. Why aren't the market value criteria applicable for the small corporation?
9. Compare two corporations issuing five-year warrants to obtain funds to buy investment projects. If the first corporation will get a 20 percent yield on its investments and the second corporation only a 10 percent yield, does that make the warrants automatically more attractive to the first corporation?
10. If a "growth corporation" has extraordinary investment opportunities, doesn't that mean its common stock will sell at a higher multiple of current earnings? Why do growth corporations avoid selling common stock to outsiders when the original owners will benefit anyway from the high proceeds of the stock sale being used to buy investments that all stockholders benefit from?
11. Is there any practical limit to the size of corporations?
12. If a corporation retains 50 percent of its earnings, does that imply that the corporation is not a "mature" corporation?

Chapter 15 Problems

1. Apollo Corp. is a closely held corporation operating in a high technology industry. Because of some important patents the corporation holds, there are always many investment projects available with after-tax yields of 20 percent or more. Due to past bank loan agreements

Apollo cannot borrow more than 50 percent of its equity total without being in default. Currently Apollo's debt is exactly at that limit.

The problem under consideration is what to do with the current year's earnings which total $500,000 on the 200,000 shares of common stock outstanding. One of the major stockholders (the owner of 20,000 shares) has suggested that the $500,000 be paid as a cash dividend, and that new equity funds be raised through a preemptive rights offering of common stock to existing shareholders. His major reason for suggesting those steps is to allow stockholders freedom of choice on the reinvestment of their profits.

The average personal income tax rate of stockholders is 40 percent, and the corporate income tax rate is 48 percent. In any expansion move Apollo will borrow the limit under its loan agreement, and the interest rate charged will be 9 percent.

The president of Apollo wants some figures to refute that major stockholder's argument for the cash dividend. Calculate next year's earnings of Apollo in total and for the shares held by the major stockholder under the two assumptions:

a. All current earnings are retained.

b. All current earnings are paid as dividends and all stockholders use their after-tax proceeds to buy new common stock of Apollo.

2. A corporation has investment projects available with a 9 percent after-tax internal rate of return, and the corporation pays 8 percent for borrowed funds. The optimum capital structure for the corporation is half debt, half equity (common stock). The tax rates are: corporate income 45 percent, personal ordinary income 30 percent, and personal long-term capital gains 15 percent. What is the minimum before-tax market capitalization rate for expected earnings to make it optimal for the corporation to pay dividends rather than retain earnings?

3. Suppose in problem 2 the before-tax market capitalization rate for expected earnings is 12 percent. What should be the corporation's cut-off rate or hurdle rate in capital budgeting selection of investment projects?

Chapter 15 References

Baumol, William J. "On Dividend Policy and Market Imperfection." *Journal of Business*, January 1963.

Brigham, Eugene F., and Gordon, Myron J. "Leverage, Dividend Policy, and the Cost of Capital." *Journal of Finance*, March 1968.

Brittain, J. A. *Corporate Dividend Policy*. Washington, D. C.: The Brookings Institution, 1966.

Dobrovolsky, S. P. "Economics of Corporate Internal and External Financing," *Journal of Finance*, March 1958.

Esslen, R. "How Do Dividends Affect Price-Earnings Ratios?" *Financial Executive*, February 1968.

Friend, Irwin, and Puckett, Marshall. "Dividends and Stock Prices." *American Economic Review*, September 1964.

Hakansson, Nils H. "On the Dividend Capitalization Model Under Uncertainty." *Journal of Financial and Quantitative Analysis*, March 1969.

Manne, A. S. "Optimal Dividend and Investment Policies for the Self-Financing Business Enterprise." *Management Science*, November 1968.

Plattner, R. H. "Fund Administration and Dividend Policy." *Quarterly Review of Economics and Business*, Summer 1969.

Turnovsky, S. J. "Allocation of Corporate Profits Between Dividends and Retained Earnings." *Review of Economics and Statistics*, November 1967.

Walter, James E. *Dividend Policy and Enterprise Valuation*, Belmont, Cal.: Wadsworth, 1967.

Table 1
Compound Interest

Period	1%	2%	3%	4%	5%	6%	7%	8%
1	1.01000	1.02000	1.03000	1.04000	1.05000	1.06000	1.07000	1.08000
2	1.02010	1.04040	1.06090	1.08160	1.10250	1.12360	1.14490	1.16640
3	1.03030	1.06121	1.09273	1.12486	1.15762	1.19102	1.22504	1.25971
4	1.04060	1.08243	1.12551	1.16986	1.21551	1.26248	1.31080	1.36049
5	1.05101	1.10408	1.15927	1.21665	1.27628	1.33823	1.40255	1.46933
6	1.06152	1.12616	1.19405	1.26532	1.34010	1.41852	1.50073	1.58687
7	1.07214	1.14869	1.22987	1.31593	1.40710	1.50363	1.60578	1.71382
8	1.08286	1.17166	1.26677	1.36857	1.47746	1.59385	1.71819	1.85093
9	1.09369	1.19509	1.30477	1.42331	1.55133	1.68948	1.83846	1.99900
10	1.10462	1.21899	1.34392	1.48024	1.62889	1.79085	1.96715	2.15892
11	1.11567	1.24337	1.38423	1.53945	1.71034	1.89830	2.10485	2.33164
12	1.12683	1.26824	1.42576	1.60103	1.79586	2.01220	2.25219	2.51817
13	1.13809	1.29361	1.46853	1.66507	1.88565	2.13293	2.40984	2.71962
14	1.14947	1.31948	1.51259	1.73168	1.97993	2.26090	2.57853	2.93719
15	1.16097	1.34587	1.55797	1.80094	2.07893	2.39656	2.75903	3.17217
16	1.17258	1.37279	1.60471	1.87298	2.18287	2.54035	2.95216	3.42594
17	1.18430	1.40024	1.65285	1.94790	2.29202	2.69277	3.15881	3.70002
18	1.19615	1.42825	1.70243	2.02582	2.40662	2.85434	3.37993	3.99602
19	1.20811	1.45681	1.75351	2.10685	2.52695	3.02560	3.61653	4.31570
20	1.22019	1.48595	1.80611	2.19112	2.65330	3.20714	3.86968	4.66096
21	1.23239	1.51567	1.86029	2.27877	2.78596	3.39956	4.14056	5.03383
22	1.24472	1.54598	1.91610	2.36992	2.92526	3.60354	4.43040	5.43654
23	1.25716	1.57690	1.97359	2.46472	3.07152	3.81975	4.74053	5.87146
24	1.26973	1.60844	2.03279	2.56330	3.22510	4.04893	5.07237	6.34118
25	1.28243	1.64061	2.09378	2.66584	3.38635	4.29187	5.42743	6.84847
26	1.29526	1.67342	2.15659	2.77247	3.55567	4.54938	5.80735	7.39635
27	1.30821	1.70689	2.22129	2.88337	3.73346	4.82235	6.21387	7.98806
28	1.32129	1.74102	2.28793	2.99870	3.92013	5.11169	6.64884	8.62710
29	1.33450	1.77584	2.35657	3.11865	4.11614	5.41839	7.11426	9.31727
30	1.34785	1.81136	2.42726	3.24340	4.32194	5.74349	7.61225	10.06265
31	1.36133	1.84759	2.50008	3.37313	4.53804	6.08810	8.14511	10.86766
32	1.37494	1.88454	2.57508	3.50806	4.76494	6.45339	8.71527	11.73708
33	1.38869	1.92223	2.65234	3.64838	5.00319	6.84059	9.32534	12.67604
34	1.40258	1.96068	2.73191	3.79432	5.25335	7.25102	9.97811	13.69013
35	1.41660	1.99989	2.81386	3.94609	5.51601	7.68609	10.67658	14.78534
36	1.43077	2.03989	2.89828	4.10393	5.79182	8.14725	11.42394	15.96816
37	1.44508	2.08069	2.98523	4.26809	6.08141	8.63609	12.22362	17.24562
38	1.45953	2.12230	3.07478	4.43881	6.38548	9.15425	13.07927	18.62526
39	1.47412	2.16474	3.16703	4.61637	6.70475	9.70351	13.99482	20.11529
40	1.48886	2.20804	3.26204	4.80102	7.03999	10.28572	14.97445	21.72451

TABLE 1 Cont.
Compound Interest

Period	9%	10%	11%	12%	13%	14%	15%	16%
1	1.09000	1.10000	1.11000	1.12000	1.13000	1.14000	1.15000	1.16000
2	1.18810	1.21000	1.23210	1.25440	1.27690	1.29960	1.32250	1.34560
3	1.29503	1.33100	1.36763	1.40493	1.44290	1.48154	1.52087	1.56090
4	1.41158	1.46410	1.51807	1.57352	1.63047	1.68896	1.74901	1.81064
5	1.53862	1.61051	1.68506	1.76234	1.84244	1.92541	2.01136	2.10034
6	1.67710	1.77156	1.87041	1.97382	2.08195	2.19497	2.31306	2.43640
7	1.82804	1.94872	2.07616	2.21068	2.35261	2.50227	2.66002	2.82622
8	1.99256	2.14359	2.30454	2.47596	2.65844	2.85259	3.05902	3.27841
9	2.17189	2.35795	2.55804	2.77308	3.00404	3.25195	3.51788	3.80296
10	2.36736	2.59374	2.83942	3.10585	3.39457	3.70722	4.04556	4.41143
11	2.58043	2.85312	3.15176	3.47855	3.83586	4.22623	4.65239	5.11726
12	2.81266	3.13843	3.49845	3.89597	4.33452	4.81790	5.35025	5.93602
13	3.06580	3.45227	3.88328	4.36349	4.89801	5.49241	6.15279	6.88579
14	3.34173	3.79750	4.31044	4.88711	5.53475	6.26135	7.07570	7.98751
15	3.64248	4.17725	4.78459	5.47356	6.25427	7.13794	8.13706	9.26552
16	3.97030	4.59497	5.31089	6.13039	7.06733	8.13725	9.35762	10.74800
17	4.32763	5.05447	5.89509	6.86604	7.98608	9.27646	10.76126	12.46768
18	4.71712	5.55991	6.54355	7.68996	9.02427	10.57517	12.37545	14.46251
19	5.14166	6.11591	7.26334	8.61275	10.19742	12.05569	14.23177	16.77651
20	5.60441	6.72750	8.06230	9.64628	11.52309	13.74349	16.36653	19.46075
21	6.10880	7.40024	8.94916	10.80384	13.02109	15.66757	18.82151	22.57447
22	6.65860	8.14027	9.93357	12.10030	14.71383	17.86103	21.64474	26.18638
23	7.25787	8.95430	11.02626	13.55233	16.62663	20.36158	24.89145	30.37620
24	7.91108	9.84972	12.23914	15.17861	18.78809	23.21220	28.62516	35.23639
25	8.62308	10.83470	13.58545	17.00004	21.23054	26.46191	32.91894	40.87421
26	9.39915	11.91817	15.07985	19.04005	23.99051	30.16657	37.85678	47.41409
27	10.24508	13.10998	16.73863	21.32485	27.10928	34.38989	43.53529	55.00034
28	11.16713	14.42098	18.57988	23.88383	30.63348	39.20448	50.06558	63.80039
29	12.17217	15.86308	20.62367	26.74989	34.61583	44.69311	57.57542	74.00845
30	13.26767	17.44939	22.89227	29.95988	39.11589	50.95014	66.21173	85.84980
31	14.46176	19.19432	25.41042	33.55506	44.20096	58.08316	76.14349	99.58577
32	15.76332	21.11375	38.30556	37.58167	49.94708	66.21480	87.56501	115.51949
33	17.18201	23.22513	21.20817	42.09147	56.44020	75.48487	100.69976	134.00260
34	18.72840	25.54764	34.75207	47.14244	63.77743	86.05275	115.80472	155.44301
35	20.41395	28.10240	38.57480	52.79953	72.06850	98.10014	133.17543	180.31389
36	22.25121	30.91264	42.81802	59.13547	81.43740	111.83415	153.15174	209.16411
37	24.25381	34.00391	47.52800	66.23172	92.02426	127.49093	176.12449	242.63036
38	26.43666	37.40430	52.75608	74.17953	103.98742	145.33966	202.54316	281.45121
39	28.81595	41.14473	58.55925	83.08106	117.50578	165.68721	232.92463	326.48339
40	31.40939	45.25920	65.00076	93.05079	132.78153	188.88342	267.86332	378.72072

TABLE 1 Cont.
Compound Interest

Period	17%	18%	19%	20%	21%	22%	23%	24%
1	1.17000	1.18000	1.19000	1.20000	1.21000	1.22000	1.23000	1.24000
2	1.36890	1.39240	1.41610	1.44000	1.46410	1.48840	1.51290	1.53760
3	1.60161	1.64303	1.68516	1.72800	1.77156	1.81585	1.86087	1.90662
4	1.87389	1.93878	2.00534	2.07360	2.14359	2.21533	2.28887	2.36421
5	2.19245	2.28776	2.38635	2.48832	2.59374	2.70271	2.81531	2.93162
6	2.56516	2.69955	2.83976	2.98598	3.13843	3.29730	3.46283	3.63521
7	3.00124	3.18547	3.37932	3.58318	3.79750	4.02271	4.25927	4.50767
8	3.51145	3.75886	4.02139	4.29982	4.59497	4.90771	5.23891	5.58950
9	4.10840	4.43545	4.78545	5.15978	5.55992	5.98740	6.44386	6.93099
10	4.80683	5.23383	5.69468	6.19174	6.72750	7.30463	7.92594	8.59442
11	5.62399	6.17592	6.77667	7.43008	8.14027	8.91165	9.74891	10.65708
12	6.58006	7.28759	8.06424	8.91610	9.84973	10.87221	11.99116	13.21478
13	7.69868	8.59935	9.59645	10.69932	11.91817	13.26410	14.74913	16.38633
14	9.00745	10.14724	11.41977	12.83918	14.42099	16.18220	18.14142	20.31905
15	10.53872	11.97374	13.58953	15.40702	17.44940	19.74228	22.31395	25.19562
16	12.33030	14.12901	16.17154	18.48842	21.11377	24.08558	27.44616	31.24256
17	14.42645	16.67223	19.24413	22.18611	25.54766	29.38441	33.75877	38.74078
18	16.87894	19.67324	22.90052	26.62333	30.91267	35.84898	41.52329	48.03856
19	19.74836	23.21442	27.25162	31.94799	37.40433	43.73575	51.07364	59.56782
20	23.10558	27.39301	32.42942	38.33759	45.25924	53.35761	62.82058	73.86409
21	27.03353	32.32375	38.59101	46.00511	54.76368	65.09629	77.26931	91.59147
22	31.62923	38.14202	45.92330	55.20613	66.26405	79.41747	95.04125	113.57342
23	37.00620	45.00759	54.64873	66.24736	80.17950	96.88931	116.90073	140.83103
24	43.29725	53.10895	65.03199	79.49683	97.01719	118.20495	143.78790	174.63047
25	50.65778	62.66856	77.38807	95.39619	117.39080	144.21004	176.85911	216.54177
26	59.26960	73.94889	92.09180	114.47543	142.04287	175.93624	217.53669	268.51179
27	69.34543	87.25969	109.58924	137.37052	171.87187	214.64221	267.57013	332.95461
28	81.13415	102.96643	130.41120	164.84462	207.96495	261.86349	329.11124	412.86369
29	94.92695	121.50038	155.18933	197.81354	251.63759	319.47345	404.80682	511.95096
30	111.06453	143.37045	184.67530	237.37624	304.48148	389.75760	497.91237	634.81916
31	129.94549	169.17712	219.76361	284.85149	368.42258	475.50426	612.43219	787.17573
32	152.03622	199.62899	261.51869	341.82178	445.79132	580.11518	753.29157	976.09787
33	177.88237	235.56220	311.20724	410.18614	539.40748	707.74050	926.54860	1210.36131
34	208.12237	277.96339	370.33662	492.22336	652.68304	863.44339	1139.65474	1500.84796
35	243.50316	327.99678	440.70058	590.66802	789.74647	1053.40091	1401.77529	1861.05140
36	284.89869	387.03618	524.43368	708.80162	955.59321	1285.14907	1724.18355	2307.70364
37	333.33145	456.70268	624.07608	850.56194	1156.26776	1567.88183	2120.74569	2861.55239
38	389.99779	538.90913	742.65054	1020.67431	1399.08397	1912.81578	2608.51712	3548.32483
39	456.29739	635.91275	883.75414	1224.80917	1692.89157	2333.63519	3208.47595	4399.92261
40	533.86793	750.37701	1051.66742	1469.77098	2048.39876	2847.03487	3946.42529	5455.90381

TABLE 1 Cont.
Compound Interest

Period	25%	26%	27%	28%	29%	30%	31%	32%
1	1.25000	1.26000	1.27000	1.28000	1.29000	1.30000	1.31000	1.32000
2	1.56250	1.58760	1.61290	1.63840	1.66410	1.69000	1.71610	1.74240
3	1.95313	2.00038	2.04838	2.09715	2.14669	2.19700	2.24809	2.29997
4	2.44141	2.52047	2.60145	2.68435	2.76923	2.85610	2.94500	3.03596
5	3.05176	3.17580	3.30384	3.43597	3.57230	3.71293	3.85795	4.00746
6	3.81470	4.00150	4.19587	4.39805	4.60827	4.82681	5.05391	5.28985
7	4.76837	5.04189	5.32876	5.62950	5.94467	6.27485	6.62062	6.98261
8	5.96046	6.35279	6.76752	7.20576	7.66863	8.15730	8.67302	9.21704
9	7.45058	8.00451	8.59475	9.22337	9.89253	10.60450	11.36165	12.16649
10	9.31323	10.08569	10.91534	11.80591	12.76136	13.78584	14.88376	16.05977
11	11.64153	12.70796	13.86248	15.11157	16.46215	17.92160	19.49773	21.19889
12	14.55192	16.01203	17.60535	19.34281	21.23618	23.29807	25.54202	27.98254
13	18.18989	20.17516	22.35879	24.75879	27.39467	30.28750	33.46005	36.93695
14	22.73737	25.42070	28.39566	31.69126	35.33912	39.37374	43.83266	48.75678
15	28.42171	32.03009	36.06249	40.56481	45.58747	51.18586	57.42079	64.35895
16	35.52714	40.35791	45.79936	51.92295	58.80783	66.54162	75.22123	84.95381
17	44.40892	50.85097	58.16519	66.46137	75.86210	86.50411	98.53981	112.13903
18	55.51115	64.07222	73.86979	85.07056	97.86211	112.45533	129.08714	148.02352
19	69.38894	80.73099	93.81463	108.89031	126.24211	146.19193	169.10415	195.39104
20	86.73617	101.72105	119.14458	139.37960	162.85232	190.04950	221.52642	257.91617
21	108.42022	128.16852	151.31361	178.40588	210.07949	247.06434	290.19960	340.44935
22	135.52527	161.49234	192.16829	228.35952	271.00253	321.18363	380.16146	449.39314
23	169.40659	203.48034	244.05372	292.30018	349.59325	417.53870	498.01149	593.19894
24	211.75824	256.38523	309.94822	374.14422	450.97528	542.80029	652.39502	783.02259
25	264.69780	323.04539	393.63423	478.90459	581.75810	705.64035	854.63745	1033.58982
26	330.87225	407.03719	499.91547	612.99786	750.46792	917.33243	1119.57500	1364.33855
27	413.59031	512.86685	634.89264	784.63724	968.10359	1192.53211	1466.64319	1800.92687
28	516.98788	646.21223	806.31364	1004.33565	1248.85360	1550.29169	1921.30250	2377.22346
29	646.23485	814.22740	1024.01830	1285.54960	1611.02109	2015.37912	2516.90616	3137.93495
30	807.79357	1025.92652	1300.50322	1645.50345	2078.21715	2619.99276	3297.14693	4142.07412
31	1009.74196	1292.66740	1651.63907	2106.24437	2680.90004	3405.99046	4319.26229	5467.53780
32	1262.17745	1628.76091	2097.58159	2695.99274	3458.36095	4427.78744	5658.23335	7217.14986
33	1577.72181	2052.23873	2663.92857	3450.87063	4461.28549	5756.12346	7412.28536	9526.63776
34	1972.15226	2585.82079	3383.18924	4417.11431	5755.05811	7482.96023	9710.09340	12575.16178
35	2465.19033	3258.13417	4296.65027	5653.90618	7424.02475	9727.84794	12720.22180	16599.21346
36	3081.48791	4105.24902	5456.74576	7236.99975	9576.99164	12646.20185	16663.48983	21910.96165
37	3851.85989	5172.61372	6930.06701	9263.35948	12354.31885	16440.06181	21829.17072	28922.46922
38	4814.82486	6517.49324	8801.18497	11857.09987	15937.07085	21372.07957	28596.21239	38177.65916
39	6018.53108	8212.04142	11177.50475	15177.08749	20558.82079	27783.70242	37461.03660	50394.50982
40	7523.16385	10347.17212	14195.43081	19426.67155	26520.87803	36118.81182	49073.95580	66520.75260

TABLE 1 Cont.
Compound Interest

Period	33%	34%	35%	36%	37%	38%	39%	40%
1	1.33000	1.34000	1.35000	1.36000	1.37000	1.38000	1.39000	1.40000
2	1.76890	1.79560	1.82250	1.84960	1.87690	1.90440	1.93210	1.96000
3	2.35264	2.40610	2.46037	2.51546	2.57135	2.62807	2.68562	2.74400
4	3.12901	3.22418	3.32151	3.42102	3.52275	3.62674	3.73301	3.84160
5	4.16158	4.32040	4.48403	4.65259	4.82617	5.00490	5.18888	5.37824
6	5.53490	5.78934	6.05344	6.32752	6.61185	6.90676	7.21255	7.52954
7	7.36142	7.75771	8.17215	8.60542	9.05824	9.53133	10.02544	10.54135
8	9.79069	10.39533	11.03240	11.70338	12.40979	13.15324	13.93537	14.75789
9	13.02161	13.92974	14.89374	15.91659	17.00141	18.15147	19.37016	20.66104
10	17.31874	18.66586	20.10655	21.64656	23.29193	25.04903	26.92452	28.92546
11	23.03393	25.01225	27.14384	29.43932	31.90994	34.56766	37.42508	40.49564
12	30.63512	33.51641	36.64419	40.03748	43.71662	47.70337	52.02086	56.69390
13	40.74471	44.91199	49.46965	54.45097	59.89177	65.83064	72.30900	79.37146
14	54.19047	60.18206	66.78403	74.05332	82.05172	90.84629	100.50951	111.12004
15	72.07332	80.64396	90.15843	100.71251	112.41085	125.36788	139.70821	155.56806
16	95.85752	108.06290	121.71388	136.96901	154.00286	173.00767	194.19441	217.79527
17	127.49049	144.80429	164.31374	186.27784	210.98391	238.75058	269.93023	304.91338
18	169.56235	194.03774	221.82354	253.33786	289.04795	329.47581	375.20302	426.87872
19	225.51793	260.01057	299.46177	344.53947	395.99568	454.67661	521.53219	597.63020
20	299.93884	348.41416	404.27337	468.57367	542.51406	627.45372	724.92974	836.68227
21	398.91865	466.87497	545.76904	637.26017	743.24423	865.88613	1007.65233	1171.35516
22	530.56180	625.61244	736.78819	866.67380	1018.24455	1194.92285	1400.63672	1639.89719
23	705.64719	838.32066	994.66403	1178.67632	1394.99498	1648.99353	1946.88502	2295.85603
24	938.51075	1123.34966	1342.79640	1602.99975	1911.14305	2275.61107	2706.17015	3214.19839
25	1248.21928	1505.28851	1812.77509	2180.07958	2618.26587	3140.34326	3761.57647	4499.87766
26	1660.13163	2017.08656	2447.24631	2964.90813	3587.02410	4333.67369	5228.59123	6299.82862
27	2207.97504	2702.89594	3303.78243	4032.27493	4914.22282	5980.46967	7267.74174	8819.75992
28	2936.60676	3621.88049	4460.10616	5483.89372	6732.48499	8253.04812	10102.16091	12347.66368
29	3905.68694	4853.31976	6021.14315	7458.09521	9223.50406	11389.20636	14042.00353	17286.72886
30	5194.56357	6503.44836	8128.54304	10143.00915	12636.20006	15717.10473	19518.38470	24201.41999
31	6908.76946	8714.62063	10973.53282	13794.49198	17311.59339	21689.60445	27130.55445	33881.98741
32	9188.66327	11677.59141	14814.26891	18760.50847	23716.88200	29931.65404	37711.47030	47434.78157
33	12220.92200	15647.97219	19999.26250	25514.29067	32492.12703	41305.68243	52418.94318	66408.69306
34	16253.82605	20968.28232	26999.00365	34699.43415	44514.21225	57001.84155	72862.33027	92972.16870
35	21617.58838	28097.49776	36448.65397	47191.22887	60984.46835	78662.54107	***** *****	***** *****
36	28751.39218	37650.64626	49205.68155	64180.06913	83548.71829	***** *****	***** *****	***** *****
37	38239.35112	50451.86500	66427.66834	87284.89111	***** *****	***** *****	***** *****	***** *****
38	50858.33635	67605.49778	89677.34988	***** *****	***** *****	***** *****	***** *****	***** *****
39	67641.58650	90591.36526	***** *****	***** *****	***** *****	***** *****	***** *****	***** *****
40	89963.30891	***** *****	***** *****	***** *****	***** *****	***** *****	***** *****	***** *****

TABLE 2
Present Value of $1

Period	1%	2%	3%	4%	5%	6%	7%	8%
1	0.99010	0.98039	0.97087	0.96154	0.95238	0.94340	0.93458	0.92593
2	0.98030	0.96117	0.94260	0.92456	0.90703	0.89000	0.87344	0.85734
3	0.97059	0.94232	0.91514	0.88900	0.86384	0.83962	0.81630	0.79383
4	0.96098	0.92385	0.88849	0.85480	0.82270	0.79209	0.76290	0.73503
5	0.95147	0.90573	0.86261	0.82193	0.78353	0.74726	0.71299	0.68058
6	0.94205	0.88797	0.83748	0.79031	0.74622	0.70496	0.66634	0.63017
7	0.93272	0.87056	0.81309	0.75992	0.71068	0.66506	0.62275	0.58349
8	0.92348	0.85349	0.78941	0.73069	0.67684	0.62741	0.58201	0.54027
9	0.91434	0.83676	0.76642	0.70259	0.64461	0.59190	0.54393	0.50025
10	0.90529	0.82035	0.74409	0.67556	0.61391	0.55839	0.50835	0.46319
11	0.89632	0.80426	0.72242	0.64958	0.58468	0.52679	0.47509	0.42888
12	0.88745	0.78849	0.70138	0.62460	0.55684	0.49697	0.44401	0.39711
13	0.87866	0.77303	0.68095	0.60057	0.53032	0.46884	0.41496	0.36770
14	0.86996	0.75788	0.66112	0.57748	0.50507	0.44230	0.38782	0.34046
15	9.86135	0.74301	0.64186	0.55526	0.48102	0.41727	0.36245	0.31524
16	0.85282	0.72845	0.62317	0.53391	0.45811	0.39365	0.33873	0.29189
17	0.84438	0.71416	0.60502	0.51337	0.43630	0.37136	0.31657	0.27027
18	0.83602	0.70016	0.58739	0.49363	0.41552	0.35034	0.29586	0.25025
19	0.82774	0.68643	0.57029	0.47464	0.39573	0.33051	0.27651	0.23171
20	0.81954	0.67297	0.55368	0.45639	0.37689	0.31180	0.25842	0.21455
21	0.81143	0.65978	0.53755	0.43883	0.35894	0.29416	0.24151	0.19866
22	0.80340	0.64684	0.52189	0.42196	0.34185	0.27751	0.22571	0.18394
23	0.79544	0.63416	0.50669	0.40573	0.32557	0.26180	0.21095	0.17032
24	0.78757	0.62172	0.49193	0.39012	0.31007	0.24698	0.19715	0.15770
25	0.77977	0.60953	0.47761	0.37512	0.29530	0.23300	0.18425	0.14602
26	0.77205	0.59758	0.46369	0.36069	0.28124	0.21981	0.17220	0.13520
27	0.76440	0.58586	0.45019	0.34682	0.26785	0.20737	0.16093	0.12519
28	0.75684	0.57437	0.43708	0.33348	0.25509	0.19563	0.15040	0.11591
29	0.74934	0.56311	0.42435	0.32065	0.24295	0.18456	0.14056	0.10733
30	0.74192	0.55207	0.41199	0.30832	0.23138	0.17411	0.13137	0.09938
31	0.73458	0.54125	0.39999	0.29646	0.22036	0.16425	0.12277	0.09202
32	0.72730	0.53063	0.38834	0.28506	0.20987	0.15496	0.11474	0.08520
33	0.72010	0.52023	0.37703	0.27409	0.19987	0.14619	0.10723	0.07889
34	0.71297	0.51003	0.36604	0.26355	0.19035	0.13791	0.10022	0.07305
35	0.70591	0.50003	0.35538	0.25342	0.18129	0.13011	0.09366	0.06763
36	0.69893	0.49022	0.34503	0.24367	0.17266	0.12274	0.08754	0.06262
37	0.69200	0.48061	0.33498	0.23430	0.16444	0.11579	0.08181	0.05799
38	0.68515	0.47119	0.32523	0.22529	0.15661	0.10924	0.07646	0.05369
39	0.67837	0.46195	0.31575	0.21662	0.14915	0.10306	0.07146	0.04971
40	0.67165	0.45289	0.30656	0.20829	0.14205	0.09722	0.06678	0.04603

TABLE 2 Cont.
Present Value of $1

Period	9%	10%	11%	12%	13%	14%	15%	16%
1	0.91743	0.90909	0.90090	0.89286	0.88496	0.87719	0.86957	0.86207
2	0.84168	0.82645	0.81162	0.79719	0.78315	0.76947	0.74614	0.74316
3	0.77218	0.75131	0.73119	0.71178	0.69305	0.67497	0.65752	0.64066
4	0.70843	0.68301	0.65873	0.63552	0.61332	0.59208	0.57175	0.55229
5	0.64993	0.62092	0.59345	0.56743	0.54276	0.51937	0.49718	0.47611
6	0.59627	0.56447	0.53464	0.50663	0.48032	0.45559	0.43233	0.41044
7	0.54703	0.51316	0.48166	0.45235	0.42506	0.39964	0.37594	0.35383
8	0.50187	0.46651	0.43393	0.40388	0.37616	0.35056	0.32690	0.30503
9	0.46043	0.42410	0.39092	0.36061	0.33288	0.30751	0.28426	0.26295
10	0.42241	0.38554	0.35218	0.32197	0.29459	0.26974	0.24718	0.22668
11	0.38753	0.35049	0.31728	0.28748	0.26070	0.23662	0.21494	0.19542
12	0.35553	0.31863	0.28584	0.25668	0.23071	0.20756	0.18691	0.16846
13	0.32618	0.28966	0.25751	0.22917	0.20416	0.18207	0.16253	0.14523
14	0.29925	0.26333	0.23199	0.20462	0.18068	0.15971	0.14133	0.12520
15	0.27454	0.23939	0.20900	0.18270	0.15989	0.14010	0.12289	0.10793
16	0.25187	0.21763	0.18829	0.16312	0.14150	0.12289	0.10686	0.09304
17	0.23107	0.19784	0.16963	0.14564	0.12522	0.10780	0.09293	0.08021
18	0.21199	0.17986	0.15282	0.13004	0.11081	0.09456	0.08081	0.06914
19	0.19449	0.16351	0.13768	0.11611	0.09806	0.08295	0.07027	0.05961
20	0.17843	0.14864	0.12403	0.10367	0.08678	0.07276	0.06110	0.05139
21	0.16370	0.13513	0.11174	0.09256	0.07680	0.06383	0.05313	0.04430
22	0.15018	0.12285	0.10067	0.08264	0.06796	0.05599	0.04620	0.03819
23	0.13778	0.11168	0.09069	0.07379	0.06014	0.04911	0.04017	0.03292
24	0.12641	0.10153	0.08171	0.06588	0.05323	0.04308	0.03493	0.02838
25	0.11597	0.09230	0.07361	0.05882	0.04710	0.03779	0.03038	0.02447
26	0.10639	0.08391	0.06631	0.05252	0.04168	0.03315	0.02642	0.02109
27	0.09761	0.07628	0.05974	0.04689	0.03689	0.02908	0.02297	0.01818
28	0.08955	0.06934	0.05382	0.04187	0.03264	0.02551	0.01997	0.01567
29	0.08215	0.06304	0.04849	0.03738	0.02889	0.02237	0.01737	0.01351
30	0.07537	0.05731	0.04368	0.03338	0.02557	0.01963	0.01510	0.01165
31	0.06915	0.05210	0.03935	0.02980	0.02262	0.01722	0.01313	0.01004
32	0.06344	0.04736	0.03545	0.02661	0.02002	0.01510	0.01142	0.00866
33	0.05820	0.04306	0.03194	0.02376	0.01772	0.01325	0.00993	0.00746
34	0.05339	0.03914	0.02878	0.02121	0.01568	0.01162	0.00864	0.00643
35	0.04899	0.03558	0.02592	0.01894	0.01388	0.01019	0.00751	0.00555
36	0.04494	0.03235	0.02335	0.01691	0.01228	0.00894	0.00653	0.00478
37	0.04123	0.02941	0.02104	0.01510	0.01087	0.00784	0.00568	0.00412
38	0.03783	0.02673	0.01896	0.01348	0.00962	0.00688	0.00494	0.00355
39	0.03470	0.02430	0.01708	0.01204	0.00851	0.00604	0.00429	0.00306
40	0.03184	0.02209	0.01538	0.01075	0.00753	0.00529	0.00373	0.00264

TABLE 2 Cont.
Present Value of $1

Period	17%	18%	19%	20%	21%	22%	23%	24%
1	0.85470	0.84746	0.84034	0.83333	0.82645	0.81967	0.81301	0.80645
2	0.73051	0.71818	0.70616	0.69444	0.68301	0.67186	0.66098	0.65036
3	0.62437	0.60863	0.59342	0.57870	0.56447	0.55071	0.53738	0.52449
4	0.53365	0.51579	0.49867	0.48225	0.46651	0.45140	0.43690	0.42297
5	0.45611	0.43711	0.41905	0.40188	0.38554	0.37000	0.35520	0.34111
6	0.38984	0.37043	0.35214	0.33490	0.31863	0.30328	0.28878	0.27509
7	0.33320	0.31393	0.29592	0.27908	0.26333	0.24859	0.23478	0.22184
8	0.28478	0.26604	0.24867	0.23257	0.21763	0.20376	0.19088	0.17891
9	0.24340	0.22546	0.20897	0.19381	0.17986	0.16702	0.15519	0.14428
10	0.20804	0.19106	0.17560	0.16151	0.14864	0.13690	0.12617	0.11635
11	0.17781	0.16192	0.14757	0.13459	0.12285	0.11221	0.10258	0.09383
12	0.15197	0.13722	0.12400	0.11216	0.10153	0.09198	0.08339	0.07567
13	0.12989	0.11629	0.10421	0.09346	0.08391	0.07539	0.06780	0.06103
14	0.11102	0.09855	0.08757	0.07789	0.06934	0.06180	0.05512	0.04921
15	0.09489	0.08352	0.07359	0.06491	0.05731	0.05065	0.04482	0.03969
16	0.08110	0.07078	0.06184	0.05409	0.04736	0.04152	0.03643	0.03201
17	0.06932	0.05998	0.05196	0.04507	0.03914	0.03403	0.02962	0.02581
18	0.05925	0.05083	0.04367	0.03756	0.03235	0.02789	0.02408	0.02082
19	0.05064	0.04308	0.03670	0.03130	0.02673	0.02286	0.01958	0.01679
20	0.04328	0.03651	0.03084	0.02608	0.02209	0.01874	0.01592	0.01354
21	0.03699	0.03094	0.02591	0.02174	0.01826	0.01536	0.01294	0.01092
22	0.03162	0.02622	0.02178	0.01811	0.01509	0.01259	0.01052	0.00880
23	0.02702	0.02222	0.01830	0.01509	0.01247	0.01032	0.00855	0.00710
24	0.02310	0.01883	0.01538	0.01258	0.01031	0.00846	0.00695	0.00573
25	0.01974	0.01596	0.01292	0.01048	0.00852	0.00693	0.00565	0.00462
26	0.01687	0.01352	0.01086	0.00874	0.00704	0.00568	0.00460	0.00372
27	0.01442	0.01146	0.00912	0.00728	0.00582	0.00466	0.00374	0.00300
28	0.01233	0.00971	0.00767	0.00607	0.00481	0.00382	0.00304	0.00242
29	0.01053	0.00823	0.00644	0.00506	0.00397	0.00313	0.00247	0.00195
30	0.00900	0.00697	0.00541	0.00421	0.00328	0.00257	0.00201	0.00158
31	0.00770	0.00591	0.00455	0.00351	0.00271	0.00210	0.00163	0.00127
32	0.00658	0.00501	0.00382	0.00293	0.00224	0.00172	0.00133	0.00102
33	0.00562	0.00425	0.00321	0.00244	0.00185	0.00141	0.00108	0.00083
34	0.00480	0.00360	0.00270	0.00203	0.00153	0.00116	0.00088	0.00067
35	0.00411	0.00305	0.00227	0.00169	0.00127	0.00095	0.00071	0.00054
36	0.00351	0.00258	0.00191	0.00141	0.00105	0.00078	0.00058	0.00043
37	0.00300	0.00219	0.00160	0.00118	0.00086	0.00064	0.00047	0.00035
38	0.00256	0.00186	0.00135	0.00098	0.00071	0.00052	0.00038	0.00028
39	0.00219	0.00157	0.00113	0.00082	0.00059	0.00043	0.00031	0.00023
40	0.00187	0.00133	0.00095	0.00068	0.00049	0.00035	0.00025	0.00018

TABLE 2
Present Value of $1

Period	25%	26%	27%	28%	29%	30%	31%	32%
1	0.80000	0.79365	0.78740	0.78125	0.77519	0.76923	0.76336	0.75758
2	0.64000	0.62988	0.62000	0.61035	0.60093	0.59172	0.58272	0.57392
3	0.51200	0.49991	0.48819	0.47684	0.46583	0.45517	0.44482	0.43479
4	0.40960	0.39675	0.38440	0.37253	0.36111	0.35013	0.33956	0.32939
5	0.32768	0.31488	0.30268	0.29104	0.27993	0.26933	0.25921	0.24953
6	0.26214	0.24991	0.23833	0.22737	0.21700	0.20718	0.19787	0.18904
7	0.20972	0.19834	0.18766	0.17764	0.16822	0.15937	0.15104	0.14321
8	0.16777	0.15741	0.14776	0.13878	0.13040	0.12259	0.11530	0.10849
9	0.13422	0.12493	0.11635	0.10842	0.10109	0.09430	0.08802	0.08219
10	0.10737	0.09915	0.09161	0.08470	0.07836	0.07254	0.06719	0.06227
11	0.08590	0.07869	0.07214	0.06617	0.06075	0.05580	0.05129	0.04717
12	0.06872	0.06245	0.05680	0.05170	0.04709	0.04292	0.03915	0.03574
13	0.05498	0.04957	0.04473	0.04039	0.03650	0.03302	0.02989	0.02707
14	0.04398	0.03934	0.03522	0.03155	0.02830	0.02540	0.02281	0.02051
15	0.03518	0.03122	0.02773	0.02465	0.02194	0.01954	0.01742	0.01554
16	0.02815	0.02478	0.02183	0.01926	0.01700	0.01503	0.01329	0.01177
17	0.02252	0.01967	0.01719	0.01505	0.01318	0.01156	0.01015	0.00892
18	0.01801	0.01561	0.01354	0.01175	0.01022	0.00889	0.00775	0.00676
19	0.01441	0.01239	0.01066	0.00918	0.00792	0.00684	0.00591	0.00512
20	0.01153	0.00983	0.00839	0.00717	0.00614	0.00526	0.00451	0.00388
21	0.00922	0.00780	0.00661	0.00561	0.00476	0.00405	0.00345	0.00294
22	0.00738	0.00619	0.00520	0.00438	0.00369	0.00311	0.00263	0.00223
23	0.00590	0.00491	0.00410	0.00342	0.00286	0.00239	0.00201	0.00169
24	0.00472	0.00390	0.00323	0.00267	0.00222	0.00184	0.00153	0.00128
25	0.00378	0.00310	0.00254	0.00209	0.00172	0.00142	0.00117	0.00097
26	0.00302	0.00246	0.00200	0.00163	0.00133	0.00109	0.00089	0.00073
27	0.00242	0.00195	0.00158	0.00127	0.00103	0.00084	0.00068	0.00056
28	0.00193	0.00155	0.00124	0.00100	0.00080	0.00065	0.00052	0.00042
29	0.00155	0.00123	0.00098	0.00078	0.00062	0.00050	0.00040	0.00032
30	0.00124	0.00097	0.00077	0.00061	0.00048	0.00038	0.00030	0.00024
31	0.00099	0.00077	0.00061	0.00047	0.00037	0.00029	0.00023	0.00018
32	0.00079	0.00061	0.00048	0.00037	0.00029	0.00023	0.00018	0.00014
33	0.00063	0.00049	0.00038	0.00029	0.00022	0.00017	0.00013	0.00010
34	0.00051	0.00039	0.00030	0.00023	0.00017	0.00013	0.00010	0.00008
35	0.00041	0.00031	0.00023	0.00018	0.00013	0.00010	0.00008	0.00006
36	0.00032	0.00024	0.00018	0.00014	0.00010	0.00008	0.00006	0.00005
37	0.00026	0.00019	0.00014	0.00011	0.00008	0.00006	0.00005	0.00003
38	0.00021	0.00015	0.00011	0.00008	0.00006	0.00005	0.00003	0.00003
39	0.00017	0.00012	0.00009	0.00007	0.00005	0.00004	0.00003	0.00002
40	0.00013	0.00010	0.00007	0.00005	0.00004	0.00003	0.00002	0.00002

TABLE 2 Cont.
Present Value of $1

Period	33%	34%	35%	36%	37%	38%	39%	40%
1	0.75188	0.74627	0.74074	0.73529	0.72993	0.72464	0.71942	0.71429
2	0.56532	0.55692	0.54870	0.54066	0.53279	0.52510	0.51757	0.51020
3	0.42505	0.41561	0.40644	0.39754	0.38890	0.38051	0.37235	0.36443
4	0.31959	0.31016	0.30107	0.29231	0.28387	0.27573	0.26788	0.26031
5	0.24029	0.23146	0.22301	0.21493	0.20720	0.19980	0.19272	0.18593
6	0.18067	0.17273	0.16520	0.15804	0.15124	0.14479	0.13865	0.13281
7	0.13584	0.12890	0.12237	0.11621	0.11040	0.10492	0.09975	0.09486
8	0.10214	0.09620	0.09064	0.08545	0.08058	0.07603	0.07176	0.06776
9	0.07680	0.07179	0.06714	0.06283	0.05882	0.05509	0.05163	0.04840
10	0.05774	0.05357	0.04974	0.04620	0.04293	0.03992	0.03714	0.03457
11	0.04341	0.03998	0.03684	0.03397	0.03134	0.02893	0.02672	0.02469
12	0.03264	0.02984	0.02729	0.02498	0.02287	0.02096	0.01922	0.01764
13	0.02454	0.02227	0.02021	0.01837	0.01670	0.01519	0.01383	0.01260
14	0.01845	0.01662	0.01497	0.01350	0.01219	0.01101	0.00995	0.00900
15	0.01387	0.01240	0.01109	0.00993	0.00890	0.00798	0.00716	0.00643
16	0.01043	0.00925	0.00822	0.00730	0.00649	0.00578	0.00515	0.00459
17	0.00784	0.00691	0.00609	0.00537	0.00474	0.00419	0.00370	0.00328
18	0.00590	0.00515	0.00451	0.00395	0.00346	0.00304	0.00267	0.00234
19	0.00443	0.00385	0.00334	0.00290	0.00253	0.00220	0.00192	0.00167
20	0.00333	0.00287	0.00247	0.00213	0.00184	0.00159	0.00138	0.00120
21	0.00251	0.00214	0.00183	0.00157	0.00135	0.00115	0.00099	0.00085
22	0.00188	0.00160	0.00136	0.00115	0.00098	0.00084	0.00071	0.00061
23	0.00142	0.00119	0.00101	0.00085	0.00072	0.00061	0.00051	0.00044
24	0.00107	0.00089	0.00074	0.00062	0.00052	0.00044	0.00037	0.00031
25	0.00080	0.00066	0.00055	0.00046	0.00038	0.00032	0.00027	0.00022
26	0.00060	0.00050	0.00041	0.00034	0.00028	0.00023	0.00019	0.00016
27	0.00045	0.00037	0.00030	0.00025	0.00020	0.00017	0.00014	0.00011
28	0.00034	0.00028	0.00022	0.00018	0.00015	0.00012	0.00010	0.00008
29	0.00026	0.00021	0.00017	0.00013	0.00011	0.00009	0.00007	0.00006
30	0.00019	0.00015	0.00012	0.00010	0.00008	0.00006	0.00005	0.00004
31	0.00014	0.00011	0.00009	0.00007	0.00006	0.00005	0.00004	0.00003
32	0.00011	0.00009	0.00007	0.00005	0.00004	0.00003	0.00003	0.00002
33	0.00008	0.00006	0.00005	0.00004	0.00003	0.00002	0.00002	0.00002
34	0.00006	0.00005	0.00004	0.00003	0.00002	0.00002	0.00001	0.00001
35	0.00005	0.00004	0.00003	0.00002	0.00002	0.00001	0.00001	0.00001
36	0.00003	0.00003	0.00002	0.00002	0.00001	0.00001	0.00001	0.00001
37	0.00003	0.00002	0.00002	0.00001	0.00001	0.00001	0.00001	0.00000
38	0.00002	0.00001	0.00001	0.00001	0.00001	0.00000	0.00000	0.00000
39	0.00001	0.00001	0.00001	0.00001	0.00000	0.00000	0.00000	0.00000
40	0.00001	0.00001	0.00001	0.00000	0.00000	0.00000	0.00000	0.00000

TABLE 3
Present Value of an Annuity of $1 (End of Period)

Period	1%	2%	3%	4%	5%	6%	7%	8%
1	0.99010	0.98039	0.97087	0.96154	0.95238	0.94340	0.93458	0.92593
2	1.97040	1.94156	1.91347	1.88609	1.85941	1.83339	1.80802	1.78326
3	2.94099	2.88388	2.82861	2.77509	2.72325	2.67301	2.62432	2.57710
4	3.90197	3.80773	3.71710	3.62990	3.54595	3.46511	3.38721	3.31213
5	4.85343	4.71346	4.57971	4.45182	4.32948	4.21236	4.10020	3.99271
6	5.79548	5.60143	5.41719	5.24214	5.07569	4.91732	4.76654	4.62288
7	6.72819	6.47199	6.23028	6.00205	5.78637	5.58238	5.38929	5.20637
8	7.65168	7.32548	7.01969	6.73274	6.46321	6.20979	5.79130	5.74664
9	8.56602	8.16224	7.78611	7.43533	7.10782	6.80169	6.51523	6.24689
10	9.47130	8.98259	8.53020	8.11090	7.72174	7.36009	7.02358	6.71008
11	10.36763	9.78685	9.25262	8.76048	8.30641	7.88687	7.49867	7.13896
12	11.25508	10.57534	9.95400	9.38507	8.86325	8.38384	7.94269	7.53608
13	12.13374	11.34837	10.63496	9.98565	9.39357	8.85268	8.35765	7.90378
14	13.00370	12.10625	11.29607	10.56312	9.89864	9.29498	8.74547	8.24424
15	13.86505	12.84926	11.93794	11.11839	10.37966	9.71225	9.10791	8.55948
16	14.71787	13.57771	12.56110	11.65230	10.83777	10.10590	9.44665	8.85137
17	15.56225	14.29187	13.16612	12.16567	11.27407	10.47726	9.76322	9.12164
18	16.39827	14.99203	13.75351	12.65930	11.68959	10.82760	10.05909	9.37189
19	17.22601	15.67846	14.32380	13.13394	12.08532	11.15812	10.33560	9.60360
20	18.04555	16.35143	14.87748	13.59033	12.46221	11.46992	10.59401	9.81815
21	18.85698	17.01121	15.41502	14.02916	12.82115	11.76408	10.83553	10.01680
22	19.66038	17.65805	15.93692	14.45112	13.16300	12.04158	11.06124	10.20075
23	20.45582	18.29220	16.44361	14.85684	13.48857	12.30338	11.27219	10.37106
24	21.24339	18.91393	16.93554	15.24696	13.79864	12.55036	11.46933	10.52876
25	22.02316	19.52346	17.41315	15.62208	14.09394	12.78336	11.65358	10.67478
26	22.79520	20.12104	17.87684	15.98277	14.37519	13.00317	11.82578	10.80998
27	23.55961	20.70690	18.32703	16.32959	14.64303	13.21053	11.98671	10.93517
28	24.31644	21.28127	18.76411	16.66306	14.89813	13.40616	12.13711	11.05108
29	25.06579	21.84438	19.18846	16.98371	15.14107	13.59072	12.27767	11.15841
30	25.80771	22.39646	19.60044	17.29203	15.37245	13.76483	12.40904	11.25779
31	26.54229	22.93770	20.00043	17.58849	15.59281	13.92909	12.53182	11.34980
32	27.26959	23.46833	20.38877	17.87355	15.80268	14.08404	12.64656	11.43500
33	27.98969	23.98856	20.76579	18.14765	16.00255	14.23023	12.75379	11.51389
34	28.70267	24.49859	21.13184	18.41120	16.19290	14.36814	12.85401	11.58694
35	29.40858	24.99862	21.48722	18.66461	16.37419	14.49825	12.94767	11.65457
36	30.10751	25.48884	21.83225	18.90828	16.54685	14.62099	13.03521	11.71719
37	30.79951	25.96945	22.16724	19.14258	16.71129	14.73678	13.11702	11.77518
38	31.48466	26.44064	22.49246	19.36786	16.86789	14.84602	13.19347	11.82887
39	32.16303	26.90259	22.80822	19.58449	17.01704	14.94907	13.26493	11.87858
40	32.83469	27.35548	23.11477	19.79277	17.15909	15.04630	13.33171	11.92462

TABLE 3 Cont.
Present Value of an Annuity of $1 (End of Period)

Period	9%	10%	11%	12%	13%	14%	15%	16%
1	0.91743	0.90909	0.90090	0.89286	0.88496	0.87719	0.86957	0.86207
2	1.75911	1.73554	1.71252	1.69005	1.66810	1.64666	1.62571	1.60523
3	2.53129	2.48685	2.44371	2.40183	2.36115	2.32163	2.28323	2.24589
4	3.23972	3.16987	3.10245	3.03735	2.97447	2.91371	2.85498	2.79818
5	3.88965	3.79079	3.69590	3.60478	3.51723	3.43308	3.35216	3.27429
6	4.48592	4.35526	4.23054	4.11141	3.99755	3.88867	3.78448	3.68474
7	5.03295	4.86842	4.71220	4.56376	4.42261	4.28831	4.16042	4.03857
8	5.53482	5.33493	5.14612	4.96764	4.79877	4.63886	4.48732	4.34359
9	5.99525	5.75902	5.53705	5.32825	5.13166	4.94637	4.77158	4.60654
10	6.41766	6.14457	5.88923	5.65022	5.42624	5.21612	5.01877	4.83323
11	6.80519	6.49506	6.20652	5.93770	5.68694	5.45273	5.23371	5.02865
12	7.16073	6.81369	6.49236	6.19438	5.91765	5.66029	5.42062	5.19711
13	7.48690	7.10336	6.74987	6.42355	6.12181	5.84236	5.58315	5.34233
14	7.78615	7.36669	6.98187	6.62817	6.30249	6.00207	5.72448	5.46753
15	8.06069	7.60608	7.19087	6.81087	6.46238	6.14217	5.84737	5.57546
16	8.31256	7.82371	7.37916	6.97399	6.60388	6.26506	5.95424	5.66850
17	8.54363	8.02156	7.54880	7.11963	6.72909	6.37286	6.04716	5.74870
18	8.75563	8.20141	7.70162	7.24967	6.83991	6.46742	6.12797	5.81785
19	8.95012	8.36492	7.83930	7.36578	6.93797	6.55037	6.19823	5.87746
20	9.12855	8.51357	7.96333	7.46945	7.02475	6.62313	6.25933	5.92884
21	9.29225	8.64870	8.07507	7.56201	7.10155	6.68696	6.31246	5.97314
22	9.44243	8.77154	8.17574	7.64465	7.16951	6.74294	6.35866	6.01133
23	9.58021	8.88322	8.26643	7.71844	7.22966	6.79206	6.39884	6.04425
24	9.70661	8.98475	8.34814	7.78432	7.28288	6.83514	6.43377	6.07263
25	9.82258	9.07704	8.42175	7.84314	7.32999	6.87293	6.46415	6.09709
26	9.92897	9.16095	8.48806	7.89566	7.37167	6.90608	6.49057	6.11818
27	10.02658	9.23723	8.54780	7.94256	7.40856	6.93516	6.51354	6.13637
28	10.11613	9.30657	8.60162	7.98443	7.44120	6.96066	6.53351	6.15204
29	10.19829	9.36961	8.65011	8.02181	7.47009	6.98304	6.55088	6.16555
30	10.27366	9.42692	8.69380	8.05519	7.49565	7.00266	6.56598	6.17720
31	10.34280	9.47902	8.73315	8.08499	7.51828	7.01988	6.57911	6.18724
32	10.40624	9.52638	8.76860	8.11160	7.53830	7.03498	6.59053	6.19590
33	10.46444	9.56944	8.80054	8.13536	7.55602	7.04823	6.60046	6.20336
34	10.51784	9.60858	8.82932	8.15657	7.57170	7.05985	6.60910	6.20979
35	10.56682	9.64416	8.85524	8.17551	7.58557	7.07005	6.61661	6.21534
36	10.61177	9.67651	8.87860	8.19242	7.59785	7.07899	6.62314	6.22012
37	10.65300	9.70592	8.89964	8.20752	7.60872	7.08683	6.62882	6.22424
38	10.69082	9.73265	8.91859	8.22100	7.61833	7.09371	6.63375	6.22779
39	10.72553	9.75696	8.93567	8.23303	7.62684	7.09975	6.63805	6.23086
40	10.75736	9.77905	8.95105	8.24378	7.63438	7.10504	6.64178	6.23350

TABLE 3 Cont.
Present Value of an Annuity of $1 (End of Period)

Period	17%	18%	19%	20%	21%	22%	23%	24%
1	0.85470	0.84746	0.84034	0.83333	0.82645	0.81967	0.81301	0.80645
2	1.58521	1.56564	1.54650	1.52778	1.50946	1.49153	1.47399	1.45682
3	2.20959	2.17427	2.13992	2.10648	2.07393	2.04224	2.01137	1.98130
4	2.74324	2.69006	2.63859	2.58873	2.54044	2.49364	2.44827	2.40428
5	3.19935	3.12717	3.05763	2.99061	2.92598	2.86364	2.80347	2.74538
6	3.58919	3.49760	3.40978	3.32551	3.24462	3.16692	3.09225	3.02047
7	3.92238	3.81153	3.70570	3.60459	3.50795	3.41551	3.32704	3.24232
8	4.20716	4.07757	3.95437	3.83716	3.72558	3.61927	3.51792	3.42122
9	4.45057	4.30302	4.16333	4.03097	3.90543	3.78629	3.67310	3.56550
10	4.65860	4.49409	4.33893	4.19247	4.05408	3.92318	3.79927	3.68186
11	4.83641	4.65601	4.48650	4.32706	4.17692	4.03540	3.90185	3.77569
12	4.98839	4.79323	4.61050	4.43922	4.27845	4.12738	3.98524	3.85136
13	5.11828	4.90951	4.71471	4.53268	4.36236	4.20277	4.05304	4.91239
14	5.22930	5.00806	4.80228	4.61057	4.43170	4.26456	4.10816	3.96161
15	5.32419	5.09158	4.87586	4.67547	4.48901	4.31522	4.15298	4.00129
16	5.40529	5.16236	4.93770	4.72956	4.53637	4.35673	4.18941	4.03330
17	5.47461	5.22234	4.98966	4.77463	4.57551	4.39077	4.21904	4.05912
18	5.53385	5.27317	5.03333	4.81220	4.60786	4.41866	4.24312	4.07993
19	5.58449	5.31624	5.07003	4.84350	4.63460	4.44153	4.26270	4.09672
20	5.62777	5.35275	5.10086	4.86958	4.65669	4.46027	4.27862	4.11026
21	5.66476	5.38368	5.12677	4.89132	4.67495	4.47563	4.29156	4.12118
22	5.69638	5.40990	5.14855	4.90943	4.69004	4.48822	4.30208	4.12998
23	5.72340	5.43212	5.16685	4.92453	4.70251	4.49854	4.31063	4.13708
24	5.74649	5.45095	5.18223	4.93710	4.71282	4.50700	4.31759	4.14281
25	5.76623	5.46691	5.19515	4.94759	4.72134	4.51394	4.32324	4.14743
26	5.78311	5.48043	5.20601	4.95632	4.72838	4.51962	4.32784	4.15115
27	5.79753	5.49189	5.21513	4.96360	4.73420	4.52428	4.33158	4.15415
28	5.80985	5.50160	5.22280	4.96967	4.73901	4.52810	4.33462	4.15658
29	5.82039	5.50983	5.22924	4.97472	4.74298	4.53123	4.33709	4.15853
30	5.82939	5.51681	5.23466	4.97894	4.74627	4.53379	4.33909	4.16010
31	5.83709	5.52272	5.23921	4.98245	4.74898	4.53590	4.34073	4.16137
32	5.84366	5.52773	5.24303	4.98537	4.75122	4.53762	4.34206	4.16240
33	5.84929	5.53197	5.24625	4.98781	4.75308	4.53903	4.34313	4.16323
34	5.85409	5.53557	5.24895	4.98984	4.75461	4.54019	4.34401	4.16389
35	5.85820	5.53862	5.25122	4.99154	4.75588	4.54114	4.34473	4.16443
36	5.86171	5.54120	5.25312	4.99295	4.75692	4.54192	4.34531	4.16486
37	5.86471	5.54339	5.25472	4.99412	4.75779	4.54256	4.34578	4.16521
38	5.86727	5.54525	5.25607	4.99510	4.75850	4.54308	4.34616	4.16549
39	5.86946	5.54682	5.25720	4.99592	4.75909	4.54351	4.34647	4.16572
40	5.87134	5.54815	5.25815	4.99660	4.75958	4.54386	4.34673	4.16590

TABLE 3 Cont.
Present Value of an Annuity of $1 (End of Period)

Period	25%	26%	27%	28%	29%	30%	31%	32%
1	0.80000	0.79365	0.78740	0.78125	0.77519	0.76923	0.76336	0.75758
2	1.44000	1.42353	1.40740	1.39160	1.37612	1.36095	1.34608	1.33150
3	1.95200	1.92344	1.89559	1.86844	1.84195	1.81611	1.79090	1.76629
4	2.36160	2.32019	2.27999	2.24097	2.20306	2.16624	2.13046	2.09567
5	2.68928	2.63507	2.58267	2.53201	2.48300	2.43557	2.38966	2.34521
6	2.95142	2.88498	2.82100	2.75938	2.70000	2.64275	2.58753	2.53425
7	3.16114	3.08332	3.00866	2.93702	2.86821	2.80211	2.73857	2.67746
8	3.32891	3.24073	3.15643	3.07579	2.99862	2.92470	2.85387	2.78595
9	3.46313	3.36566	3.27278	3.18421	3.09970	3.01900	2.94189	2.86815
10	3.57050	3.46481	3.36439	3.26892	3.17806	3.09154	3.00907	2.93041
11	3.65640	3.54350	3.43653	3.33509	3.23881	3.14734	3.06036	2.97759
12	3.72512	3.60595	3.49333	3.38679	3.28590	3.19026	3.09951	3.01332
13	3.78010	3.65552	3.53806	3.42718	3.32240	3.22328	3.12940	3.04040
14	3.82408	3.69485	3.57327	3.45873	3.35070	3.24868	3.15221	3.06091
15	3.85926	3.72607	3.60100	3.48339	3.37264	3.26821	3.16963	3.07644
16	3.88741	3.75085	3.62284	3.50265	3.38964	3.28324	3.18292	3.08822
17	3.90993	3.77052	3.64003	3.51769	3.40282	3.29480	3.19307	3.09713
18	3.92794	3.78613	3.65357	3.52945	3.41304	3.30369	3.20082	3.10389
19	3.94235	3.79851	3.66423	3.53863	3.42096	3.31053	3.20673	3.10901
20	3.95388	3.80834	3.67262	3.54581	3.42710	3.31579	3.21125	3.11288
21	3.96311	3.81615	3.67923	3.55141	3.43186	3.31984	3.21469	3.11582
22	3.97049	3.82234	3.68443	3.55579	3.43555	3.32296	3.21732	3.11805
23	3.97639	3.82725	3.68853	3.55921	3.43841	3.32535	3.21933	3.11973
24	3.98111	3.83115	3.69175	3.56188	3.44063	3.32719	3.22086	3.12101
25	3.98489	3.83425	3.69429	3.56397	3.44235	3.32861	3.22203	3.12198
26	3.98791	3.83670	3.69630	3.56560	3.44368	3.32970	3.22293	3.12271
27	3.99033	3.83865	3.69787	3.56688	3.44471	3.33054	3.22361	3.12326
28	3.99226	3.84020	3.69911	3.56787	3.44552	3.33118	3.22413	3.12369
29	3.99381	3.84143	3.70009	3.56865	3.44614	3.33168	3.22453	3.12400
30	3.99505	3.84241	3.70086	3.56926	3.44662	3.33206	3.22483	3.12425
31	3.99604	3.84318	3.70146	3.56973	3.44699	3.33236	3.22506	3.12443
32	3.99683	3.84379	3.70194	3.57010	3.44728	3.33258	3.22524	3.12457
33	3.99746	3.84428	3.70231	3.57039	3.44750	3.33275	3.22537	3.12467
34	3.99797	3.84467	3.70261	3.57062	3.44768	3.33289	3.22547	3.12475
35	3.99838	3.84497	3.70284	3.57080	3.44781	3.33299	3.22555	3.12481
36	3.99870	3.84522	3.70303	3.57094	3.44792	3.33307	3.22561	3.12486
37	3.99896	3.84541	3.70317	3.57104	3.44800	3.33313	3.22566	3.12489
38	3.99917	3.84556	3.70328	3.57113	3.44806	3.33318	3.22569	3.12492
39	3.99934	3.84569	3.70337	3.57119	3.44811	3.33321	3.22572	3.12494
40	3.99947	3.84578	3.70344	3.57125	3.44815	3.33324	3.22574	3.12495

TABLE 3 Cont.
Present Value of an Annuity of $1 (End of Period)

Period	33%	34%	35%	36%	37%	38%	39%	40%
1	0.75188	0.74627	0.74074	0.73529	0.72993	0.72464	0.71942	0.71429
2	1.31720	1.30319	1.28944	1.27595	1.26272	1.24974	1.23700	1.22449
3	1.74226	1.71880	1.69588	1.67349	1.65162	1.63024	1.60935	1.58892
4	2.06185	2.02895	1.99695	1.96580	1.93549	1.90597	1.87723	1.84923
5	2.30214	2.26041	2.21996	2.18074	2.14269	2.10578	2.06995	2.03516
6	2.48281	2.43314	2.38516	2.33878	2.29394	2.25056	2.20860	2.16797
7	2.61866	2.56205	2.50752	2.45498	2.40433	2.35548	2.30834	2.26284
8	2.72079	2.65824	2.59817	2.54043	2.48492	2.43151	2.38010	2.33060
9	2.79759	2.73003	2.66531	2.60326	2.54373	2.48660	2.43173	2.37900
10	2.85533	2.78361	2.71504	2.64945	2.58667	2.52652	2.46887	2.41357
11	2.89874	2.82359	2.75188	2.68342	2.61801	2.55545	2.49559	2.43827
12	2.93139	2.85342	2.77917	2.70840	2.64088	2.57641	2.51481	2.45590
13	2.95593	2.87569	2.79939	2.72676	2.65758	2.59160	2.52864	2.46850
14	2.97438	2.89231	2.81436	2.74027	2.66976	2.60261	2.53859	2.47750
15	2.98826	2.90471	2.82545	2.75020	2.67866	2.61059	2.54575	2.48393
16	2.99869	2.91396	2.83367	2.75750	2.68515	2.61637	2.55090	2.48852
17	3.00653	2.92087	2.83975	2.76287	2.68989	2.62056	2.55460	2.49180
18	3.01243	2.92602	2.84426	2.76681	2.69335	2.62359	2.55727	2.49414
19	3.01687	2.92986	2.84760	2.76972	2.69588	2.62579	2.55919	2.49582
20	3.02020	2.93274	2.85008	2.77185	2.69772	2.62738	2.56057	2.49701
21	3.02271	2.93488	2.85191	2.77342	2.69907	2.62854	2.56156	2.49787
22	3.02459	2.93648	2.85327	2.77457	2.70005	2.62938	2.56227	2.49848
23	3.02601	2.93767	2.85427	2.77542	2.70077	2.62998	2.56279	2.49891
24	3.02707	2.93856	2.85502	2.77605	2.70129	2.63042	2.56316	2.49922
25	3.02788	2.93922	2.85557	2.77650	2.70167	2.63074	2.56342	2.49944
26	3.02848	2.93972	2.85598	2.77684	2.70195	2.63097	2.56361	2.49960
27	3.02893	2.94009	2.85628	2.77709	2.70215	2.63114	2.56375	2.49972
28	3.02927	2.94036	2.85650	2.77727	2.70230	2.63126	2.56385	2.49980
29	3.02953	2.94057	2.85667	2.77741	2.70241	2.63135	2.56392	2.49986
30	3.02972	2.94072	2.85679	2.77750	2.70249	2.63141	2.56397	2.49990
31	3.02986	2.94084	2.85688	2.77758	2.70255	2.63146	2.56401	2.49993
32	3.02997	2.94092	2.85695	2.77763	2.70259	2.63149	2.56403	2.49995
33	3.03006	2.94099	2.85700	2.77767	2.70262	2.63152	2.56405	2.49996
34	3.03012	2.94104	2.85704	2.77770	2.70264	2.63153	2.56407	2.49997
35	3.03016	2.94107	2.85706	2.77772	2.70266	2.63155	2.56408	2.49998
36	3.03020	2.94110	2.85709	2.77773	2.70267	2.63155	2.56408	2.49999
37	3.03022	2.94112	2.85710	2.77775	2.70268	2.63156	2.56409	2.49999
38	3.03024	2.94113	2.85711	2.77775	2.70269	2.63157	2.56409	2.49999
39	3.03026	2.94114	2.85712	2.77776	2.70269	2.63157	2.56410	2.50000
40	3.03027	2.94115	2.85713	2.77777	2.70269	2.63157	2.56410	2.50000

INDEX